A SMALL SAMPLING FROM 4,000 OF THE WORLD'S BEST QUOTATIONS IN *THE NEW INTERNATIONAL DICTIONARY OF QUOTATIONS*

"Man thinks. God laughs."   —Jewish proverb

"This nation cannot afford to be materially rich and spiritually poor."   —John F. Kennedy

"The use of language is all we have to pit against death and silence."   —Joyce Carol Oates

"I know only two tunes: one is 'Yankee Doodle,' and the other isn't."   —Ulysses S. Grant

"Judicial decrees may not change the heart, but they can restrain the heartless."
—Martin Luther King, Jr.

"In politics, if you want anything said, ask a man; if you want anything done, ask a woman."
—Margaret Thatcher

"I used to be Snow White, but I drifted."
—Mae West

"Love all, trust a few."   —Shakespeare

MARGARET MINER AND HUGH RAWSON have collaborated as editors of *The Dictionary of Quotations From the Bible* and *The Dictionary of Quotations From Shakespeare*, and have written, contributed to, or edited a number of other books. They live in Roxbury, Connecticut.

THE NEW INTERNATIONAL DICTIONARY OF QUOTATIONS

SECOND EDITION

Selected and Annotated by
Margaret Miner
and
Hugh Rawson

A SIGNET BOOK

SIGNET
Published by the Penguin Group
Penguin Books USA Inc., 375 Hudson Street,
New York, New York 10014, U.S.A.
Penguin Books Ltd, 27 Wrights Lane,
London W8 5TZ, England
Penguin Books Australia Ltd, Ringwood,
Victoria, Australia
Penguin Books Canada Ltd, 10 Alcorn Avenue,
Toronto, Ontario, Canada M4V 3B2
Penguin Books (N.Z.) Ltd, 182–190 Wairau Road,
Auckland 10, New Zealand

Penguin Books Ltd, Registered Offices:
Harmondsworth, Middlesex, England

Published by Signet, an imprint of Dutton Signet, a division of Penguin Books
USA Inc. Previously published in a Dutton edition

First Signet Printing (Second Edition), June, 1994
10 9 8 7 6 5 4 3 2

For
Nathaniel and Catherine

ACKNOWLEDGMENTS

We thank our excellent copy editors, Henry Price and Ronny Johnson. Our friends Bob Nadder, Ken Silverman, Pat Barrett, and Bob Creamer helped in verifying quotes and sources. For aid in tracking citations, we thank Lee Seidler, John Peterson, Krishna Winston at Wesleyan University, Margrit Gillespie at The Taft School, Martin Gardner, Egon Schwarz at Washington University in St. Louis (who found the citation for a fine but little-known Rilke quotation), and Jack Zipes at the University of Minnesota. In verifying quotations, David Gergen, Clayton Rawson, Helen Stark at *The New Yorker*, and Victor K. McElheny were especially kind. At the Hodge Memorial Library in Roxbury, Tim Beard, Susie Juram, and Betty Synnestvedt graciously coped with numerous questions.

Finally, we thank Arnold Dolin for suggesting that we undertake this project.

INTRODUCTION

The aim of *The New International Dictionary of Quotations* is to distill the most memorable words of the past with a view to the concerns of the present. The most memorable words are not necessarily the "best" words in a literary sense. Rather, they are the words that best encapsule the ideas, hopes, fears, loves, hates, that have been common to men and women throughout history. Thus, this dictionary is international in scope and it covers all periods, from ancient times to the present. Its bias, however, is toward the tried and the true—the familiar quotations that are on, or almost on, the tip of everyone's tongue, but whose exact wording, authorship, or source may have been forgotten.

To this end, *The New International Dictionary of Quotations* includes ample selections from the Bible, Shakespeare, Aesop, Burke, Carlyle, Churchill, Disraeli, Emerson, Euripides, Johnson, Pope, Shaw, Tennyson, and the works of other famous writers whose words have shaped the thoughts of everyone who has lived after them. At the same time, the dictionary also includes the observations of such luminaries as P. T. Barnum, Samuel Beckett, Leo Durocher, W. C. Fields, Arthur Miller, Satchel Paige, Dorothy Parker, and Mae West, who in their own highly quotable ways have contributed to the residual wisdom of the human race.

In sum, this dictionary of quotations differs from others that have been compiled by including in it relatively more quotes from well-known writers; relatively more prose compared to poetry; relatively more quotes from doers—politicians, entertainers, generals, athletes, and so on—as opposed to strictly literary figures; relatively more American material; and relatively more quotes from women, minority leaders, scientists, and others who have addressed topics of special importance to our times. Meanwhile, an attempt has been made to weed out platitudes and other trite expressions that do not bear repetition; nursery rhymes; lyrics from popular songs whose currency depends largely on knowing the accompanying music; quotations that are so closely linked to particular historic occasions that they are rarely used in other contexts; and contemporary quotes and catch phrases that have not yet been ratified by the test of time. Some exceptions have been allowed to these rules, and any readers who feel that their own favorite quotations have been unfairly excluded for whatever reason are invited to submit them to the editors, in care of the publisher, and they will be considered for inclusion when this dictionary is revised.

Although not an encyclopedic work (several excellent examples of which already exist, including *Bartlett's Familiar Quotations*, 16th edition, 1992; *The Oxford Dictionary of Quotations*, 3rd edition, 1979; *The International Thesaurus of Quotations*, Rhoda Thomas Tripp, 1970; and H. L. Mencken's *A New Dictionary of Quotations on Historical Principles*, 1942), *The New International Dictionary of Quotations* should be a useful addition to most bookshelves. It brings together in compact, easily accessible form the basic stock of quotations that will satisfy most needs of most contemporary users of English. It should be of especial value to students and others seeking to track down references to quotations they have read; to writers and speakers who wish to enhance their own words by drawing upon the best of the rhetoric of the past; and, finally, to all lovers of language, who will relish the riches here.

The New International Dictionary of Quotations is arranged to give readers at least two chances to find the quotes they want—through the main text, which is organized by subject, and through the author index. In the main text, subjects are listed alphabetically, with the principal topics printed in boldface capital letters along the left-hand margin of the page. Thus:

ACCOMPLISHMENT

ACTION

ACTORS & ACTING

and so on, through to

YESTERDAY

YOUTH

ZEAL

Most subject categories also include references to related topics. These are printed in small cap letters along the right-hand margin of the text. For example:

ACCOMPLISHMENT   See also DOING; GREATNESS;
                                    SUCCESS & FAME; WORK
                                    & WORKERS

Within the subject categories, quotations are arranged alphabetically by author, frequently beginning with that wise and prolific writer, ANONYMOUS. In cases of well-known works by unknown authors, or by groups of authors, such as The Bible, The Book of Common Prayer, and the Talmud, the titles are treated as though they are authors' names and quotations from them are alphabetized accordingly.

All foreign quotations have been translated into English. Those from The Bible are from the Authorized, or King James, Version unless noted specifically otherwise. Quotations are given in a foreign language as well as in English in instances where they are encountered frequently in their original form.

Following each quotation is the name of the author and the title of its source. In addition, many quotes are followed by notes from the editors. [These are printed in brackets, like this sentence.] The notes provide additional information on a variety of topics; earlier examples of a particular turn of phrase; use of similar expressions by later writers; the circumstances in which something was first said or written; the way a particular quote has been commonly mistranslated, misquoted, or "improved," and so on. The notes often cite additional sources for attributions and refer the reader to other subject categories.

Where the name of the author is known, the user of this dictionary may find the sought-for quotation even more quickly by consulting the index beginning on page 413. Here, names of authors (and titles of some works) are listed alphabetically in the same way as in the subject categories, along with key words, phrases, and page numbers for each of their quotations. Birth and death dates of authors also are given in the index.

Whether approaching the text via the subject categories or the author index, the user of this dictionary is likely to make many happy discoveries, including the fact that it is possible to drive home any point one wishes to make through the artful use of quotation. As Winston Churchill noted, "It is a good thing for an uneducated man to read books of quotations" ("Roving Commission" in *My Early Life*). Or as Ralph Waldo Emerson wrote in his *Journal* (1849): "I hate quotations. Tell me what you know." The same authority may even support both sides of the question: "Next to the originator of a good sentence is the first quoter of it" (Emerson, *Quotation and Originality*, 1876).

NOTE FOR
THE SECOND EDITION

No sooner had the first edition of *The New International Dictionary of Quotations* gone to press than we began to find additions and improvements that we wanted to make—a fate that befalls all creators of reference works. So we thank our publisher for giving us this opportunity to bring out a larger, more detailed version of the book.

This second edition includes more than four hundred new quotes, as well as many dozens of new categories and new explanatory notes.

Our teenage son irreverently asked, "If you covered the great quotations the first time, why do you need to add more?" Hours of watching television news has convinced him that almost nothing memorable has been said in the past five years.

Some of the additional quotes here are recent discoveries or rediscoveries. For example, newly found papers of Abraham Lincoln include the following from notes for a lecture in 1850: "If in your judgment you cannot be an honest lawyer, resolve to be honest without being a lawyer. Choose some other profession." (See LAWYERS.)

Increased attention to the works of women writers has yielded wonderful insights, ranging, in our new quotes, from Juliana of Norwich's definition of God, beginning, "He is to us all-thing that is good and comfortable to our help" (see GOD), to Joyce Carol Oates' observation in accepting a 1969 National Book Award: "The use of language is all we have to pit against death and silence." (See LANGUAGE & WORDS.)

Sometimes a contemporary event revives an old quote. Thus, before the Gulf War, President George Bush used a saying favored by George Washington from the works of the classic military analyst Vegetius: "He . . . who desires peace should prepare for war. He who aspires to victory should spare no pains to form his soldiers. And he who hopes for success should fight on principle, not chance." (See WAR.)

The current rage for physical fitness has given fresh poignancy to Shakespeare's observation, "There be some sports are painful." (See SPORTS.)

Also included in the new edition are a number of exquisite sayings we simply overlooked the first time around, for example Dr. Thomas Arnold's, "Flowers are my music." (See NATURE: GARDENS, FLOWERS & TREES.)

Many of the additional explanatory notes reflect detective work done by numerous scholars and educated amateurs in the past few years. Thus, we are now able to offer more information on whether Vince Lombardi said, "Winning isn't everything, it's the only thing." (See WINNING & LOSING, VICTORY & DEFEAT.) Similarly, at MONEY we have a more complete note in this edition on what Hemingway did or did not say about F. Scott Fitzgerald's observation that the rich are different from the rest of us.

While we are cautious in adding contemporary remarks to a selective collection of great quotes, we have added a few that seem likely to stand the test of time, from the amusing "Round up the usual suspects" in the movie *Casablanca* (see CRIME); to the wise "All politics is local," a saying popularized by Tip O'Neill; and the pithy "voodoo economics" (see ECONOMICS), which unfortunately has proved to be an apt description not only of supply-side "Reaganomics" but of an array of economic theories.

Finally, we would like to credit several sources that proved especially useful in preparing this edition: *Respectfully Quoted*, published by the Library of Congress, 1989; *The Great Quotations*, edited by George Seldes, 1960; *The Quotable Woman*, 2 vols., 1985; *The Quotable Lawyer*, edited by David Shrager and Elizabeth Frost, 1986; and *The Oxford Dictionary of Modern Quotations*, 1991.

A

ACCOMPLISHMENT   See also DOING; GREATNESS; SUCCESS & FAME; WORK & WORKERS

Better is the end of a thing than the beginning thereof.
—BIBLE, *Ecclesiastes* 7:8

I have fought a good fight, I have finished my course, I have kept the faith.   —BIBLE, *II Timothy* 4:7

Death closes all: but something ere the end,
Some work of noble note, may yet be done,
Not unbecoming men that strove with gods.
—ALFRED, LORD TENNYSON, *Ulysses*

ACTION   See also BOLDNESS & INITIATIVE; DOING

We become just by performing just actions, temperate by performing temperate actions, brave by performing brave actions.
—ARISTOTLE, *Nicomachean Ethics*

Action is eloquence.   —SHAKESPEARE, *Coriolanus*, III, ii

ACTORS & ACTING   See ARTS: DRAMA & ACTING

ADVERSITY   See TROUBLE

ADVERTISING   See also PUBLICITY &
                                    PUBLIC RELATIONS

They all laughed when I sat down at the piano, but
oh!, when I began to play . . .
—JOHN CAPLES, legendary advertisement for
mail-order piano lessons, 1925

You can tell the ideals of a nation by its advertise-
ments.   —NORMAN DOUGLAS, *South Wind*

We grew up founding our dreams on the infinite
promise of American advertising.
—ZELDA FITZGERALD, *Save Me the Waltz*

The trade of advertising is now so near perfection
that it is not easy to propose any improvement.
—SAMUEL JOHNSON, in the *Idler* papers, 1758

Ads push the principle of noise all the way to the
plateau of persuasion. They are quite in accord with
the procedures of brainwashing.
—MARSHALL MCLUHAN, *Understanding Media*

Half the money I spend on advertising is wasted, and
the trouble is, I don't know which half.
—JOHN WANAMAKER, quoted in David Ogilvy,
Confessions of an Advertising Man

ADVICE

There is nothing we receive with so much reluctance
as advice.
—JOSEPH ADDISON, *The Spectator*, Oct. 12, 1712

Good but rarely came from good advice.
—LORD BYRON, *Don Juan*

Advice is seldom welcome; and those who want it
the most always like it the least.
—EARL OF CHESTERFIELD,
letter to his son, Jan. 29, 1748

When we ask advice, we are usually looking for an accomplice.   —MARQUIS DE LAGRANGE, *Pensées*

One gives nothing so freely as advice.
                        —LA ROCHEFOUCAULD, *Maxims*

People ask you for criticism, but they only want praise.
    —W. SOMERSET MAUGHAM, *Of Human Bondage*

AESTHETICS   See ARTS: AESTHETICS

AFRICA   See NATIONS

AFTERNOON   See NATURE: TIMES OF DAY

AFRICAN AMERICANS   See RACES & PEOPLES

AGE & AGING   See also MIDDLE AGE &
                                MID-LIFE CRISIS;
                          OLD THINGS, OLD FRIENDS

Old men are always young enough to learn, with profit.   —AESCHYLUS, *Agamemnon*

To me, old age is always fifteen years older than I am.   —BERNARD BARUCH, news reports on his
            85th birthday, Aug. 20, 1955

When everything else physical and mental seems to diminish, the appreciation of beauty is on the increase.
        —BERNARD BERENSON, *Sunset and Twilight*

With the ancient is wisdom; and in length of days understanding.   —BIBLE, *Job* 12:12

Grow old along with me!
The best is yet to be,
The last of life, for which the first was made.
            —ROBERT BROWNING, *Rabbi Ben Ezra*

So, we'll go no more a roving
So late into the night,
Though the heart be still as loving,
And the moon be still as bright.
    —LORD BYRON, *So, We'll Go No More a Roving*

"You are old, Father William," the young man said,
"And your hair has become very white;
And yet you incessantly stand on your head—
Do you think, at your age, it is right?"
—LEWIS CARROLL,
Alice's Adventures in Wonderland
[This is a parody of Robert Southey's pious *The Old Man's Comforts and How He Gained Them*, which also begins, "You are old, Father William . . ." The young man then asks why William is so hale. The answer:
In the days of my youth, I remembered my God,
And he hath not forgotten my age.]

One keeps on forgetting old age up to the very brink of the grave. —COLETTE, *My Mother and Illness*

When a man fell into his anecdotage it was a sign for him to retire from the world.
—BENJAMIN DISRAELI, *Lothair*

I grow old . . . I grow old . . .
I shall wear the bottoms of my trousers rolled.
—T. S. ELIOT,
The Love Song of J. Alfred Prufrock

One aged man—one man—can't fill a house.
—ROBERT FROST, *An Old Man's Winter Night*

To be seventy years young is sometimes far more cheerful and hopeful than to be forty years old.
—OLIVER WENDELL HOLMES, SR.,
letter to Julia Ward Howe
on her 70th birthday

The riders in a race do not stop short when they reach the goal. There is a little finishing canter.
—OLIVER WENDELL HOLMES, JR.,
radio address on his 90th birthday, 1931

Oh, to be seventy again! [At age 92, upon seeing a pretty, young woman]
—OLIVER WENDELL HOLMES, JR., attributed
[Also attributed to Georges Clemenceau.]

My only fear is that I may live too long. This would be a subject of dread to me.
> —THOMAS JEFFERSON,
> letter to Philip Mazzei, March 1801

Where are the songs of spring? Ay, where are they? Think not of them, thou hast thy music too . . .
> —JOHN KEATS, *To Autumn*

All, all are gone, the old familiar faces.
> —CHARLES LAMB, *The Old Familiar Faces*

La vieillesse est l'enfer des femmes.
Old age is woman's hell.
> —NINON DE LENCLOS, attributed

dance mehitabel dance
caper and shake a leg
what little blood is left will fizz like wine in a keg.
> —DON MARQUIS, *archy and mehitabel*

Old age has its pleasures, which, though different, are not less than the pleasures of youth.
> —W. SOMERSET MAUGHAM, *The Summing Up*

Being seventy is not a sin.
> —GOLDA MEIR, quoted by David Reed,
> *Reader's Digest*, July 1971

The older I grow, the more I distrust the familiar doctrine that age brings wisdom.
> —H. L. MENCKEN, *Prejudices: Third Series*

How old would you be if you didn't know how old you was?   —SATCHEL PAIGE, attributed

Old age has a great sense of calm and freedom. When the passions have relaxed their hold, you have escaped not from one master but from many.
> —PLATO, *The Republic*

Darling, I am growing old,
Silver threads among the gold.
> —EBEN EUGENE REXFORD,
> *Silver Threads among the Gold*

For you and I are past our dancing days.
—SHAKESPEARE, *Romeo and Juliet,* I, v

Nobody loves life like him who is growing old.
—SOPHOCLES, *Acrisius*

Being over seventy is like being engaged in a war. All our friends are going or gone and we survive amongst the dead and dying as on a battlefield.
—MURIEL SPARK, *Memento Mori*

There are so few who can grow old with a good grace.
—RICHARD STEELE, *The Spectator,* no. 263, 1711

Every man desires to live long, but no man would be old.   —JONATHAN SWIFT,
Thoughts on Various Subjects

Old age is the most unexpected of all the things that can happen to a man.
—LEON TROTSKY, *Diary in Exile*

The tragedy of old age is not that one is old, but that one is young.
—OSCAR WILDE, *The Picture of Dorian Gray*

AGES   See FUTURE, THE; GENERATIONS;
MODERN TIMES; PAST, THE;
PRESENT, THE; TURBULENT TIMES

ALCOHOL & DRINKING   See also FOOD, WINE, &
EATING; SIN, VICE, & NAUGHTINESS

In vino veritas.
With wine comes truth.   —ANONYMOUS (Proverb)
[Can be traced to Greek sources, including Alcaeus and Plato; the closest Latin source is Pliny.]

Let's get out of these wet clothes and into a dry martini.   —ROBERT BENCHLEY, quoted by
Howard Teichmann, *George S. Kaufman*
[Benchley made this quip his own, although it was probably not original with him. Mae West used the line in *Every Day's a Holiday,* 1937: "You ought to get out of those wet clothes and into a dry martini." In the 1942 movie *The Major and the Minor,* writers Billy Wilder

and Charles Brackett gave Benchley the line, "Why don't you slip out of those wet clothes and into a dry martini?" Alexander Woollcott has also been credited with the suggestion.]

Drink no longer water, but use a little wine for thy stomach's sake and thine often infirmities.
—BIBLE, *I Timothy* 5:23

I have taken more good from alcohol than alcohol has taken from me.
—WINSTON CHURCHILL,
quoted by Quentin Reynolds,
By Quentin Reynolds

Malt does more than Milton can
To justify God's ways to man.
—A. E. HOUSMAN, *A Shropshire Lad*
[The reference is to Milton's stated purpose in writing *Paradise Lost*; see Milton at PRAYERS.]

Tell me what brand Grant drinks so I can send some to all my generals.—ABRAHAM LINCOLN,
to congressional delegation, 1863
[Lincoln told Chaplain John Eaton that he had made this answer while meeting with congressmen who had urged Grant's dismissal on grounds that he was a drunk.]

Better sleep with a sober cannibal than a drunken Christian.   —HERMAN MELVILLE, *Moby-Dick*

Candy
Is dandy
But liquor
Is quicker.   —OGDEN NASH,
Reflections on Ice-Breaking

Three highballs, and I think I'm St. Francis of Assisi.
—DOROTHY PARKER, *Just a Little One*
[See also Parker at SIN, VICE, & NAUGHTINESS.]

Water is best.   —PINDAR, *Olympian Odes*

MACDUFF: What three things does drink especially provoke?

PORTER: Marry, sir, nose-painting, sleep, and urine. Lechery, sir, it provokes and unprovokes; it provokes the desire, but it takes away the performance.
—SHAKESPEARE, *Macbeth,* II, iii
["Nose-painting" revers to the drunkard's characteristically red nose.]

It's a long time between drinks.
—ROBERT LOUIS STEVENSON, *The Wrong Box*
[Quoting a governor of North Carolina, probably John M. Morehead.]

Father, dear father, come home with me now;
The clock in the steeple strikes one;
You promised, dear father, that you would come home
As soon as your day's work was done.
—HENRY CLAY WORK, *Father,*
Dear Father, Come Home with Me Now

Though in silence, with blighted affection, I pine,
Yet the lips that touch liquor must never touch mine!
—GEORGE W. YOUNG,
The Lips That Touch Liquor

ALIENATION   See also DANGEROUS PEOPLE

I have been a stranger in a strange land.
—BIBLE, *Exodus* 2:22
[The same phrase was used by Sophocles in *Oedipus at Colonus.*]

I, a stranger and afraid
In a world I never made.
—A. E. HOUSMAN, *Last Poems*

I would prefer not to.
—HERMAN MELVILLE, *Bartleby the Scrivener*
[The phrase with which Bartleby repeatedly rejects—everything.]

AMBITION   See also BOLDNESS & INITIATIVE;
ELITE; GREATNESS; PRIDE & VANITY

Aut Caesar, aut nihil.
Either Caesar or nothing.
                              —CESARE BORGIA, motto

Ah, but a man's reach should exceed his grasp,
Or what's a heaven for?
                    —ROBERT BROWNING, *Andrea del Sarto*

Hitch your wagon to a star.
                    —RALPH WALDO EMERSON, *Civilization*

First say to yourself what you would be; and then do
what you have to do.   —EPICTETUS, *Discourses*

All or nothing.   —HENRIK IBSEN, *Brand*

I would sooner fail than not be among the greatest.
                    —JOHN KEATS, letter to
                    J. A. Hessey, Oct. 9, 1818

Ambition . . .
The glorious fault of angels and of gods.
            —ALEXANDER POPE, *Elegy to the Memory
            of an Unfortunate Lady*

The ripest peach is highest on the tree.
      —JAMES WHITCOMB RILEY, *The Ripest Peach*

Ambition, old as mankind, the immemorial weakness
of the strong.
  —VITA SACKVILLE-WEST, *No Signposts in the Sea*

Ambition should be made of sterner stuff.
            —SHAKESPEARE, *Julius Caesar*, III, ii

AMERICA & AMERICANS   See also AMERICAN
            HISTORY: MEMORABLE MOMENTS

Westward the course of empire takes its way;
The four first acts already past,
A fifth shall close the drama with the day:
Time's noblest offspring is the last.
            —GEORGE BERKELEY, *On the Prospect of
            Planting Arts and Learning in America*

[Bishop Berkeley's verse, written in 1752, was echoed a century later by Arthur Hugh Clough in *Say Not the Struggle Nought Availeth*, 1862: "In front the sun climbs slow, how slowly, / But westward, look, the land is bright." See also John Soule's "Go west, young man," in the section AMERICAN HISTORY: MEMORABLE MOMENTS.]

The chief business of the American people is business.   —CALVIN COOLIDGE, speech, Jan. 17, 1925
[See also Charles F. Wilson on General Motors and the U.S., at BUSINESS.]

America is a country of young men.
                —RALPH WALDO EMERSON, *Old Age*

There are no second acts in American lives.
      —F. SCOTT FITZGERALD, *The Last Tycoon*, Notes

The American system of rugged individualism.
            —HERBERT HOOVER, speech, Oct. 22, 1928

If there is any fixed star in our constitutional constellation, it is that no official, high or petty, can prescribe what shall be orthodox in politics, nationalism, religion, or other matters of opinion or force citizens to confess by word or act their faith therein.
      —ROBERT H. JACKSON, Supreme Court ruling in
      West Virginia Department of Education v.
      Barnette, 1943
[The Court misspelled the name of the plaintiff, Walter Barnett.]

The spirit of this country is totally adverse to a large military force.   —THOMAS JEFFERSON,
                letter to Chandler Price, 1807

Indeed, I tremble for my country when I reflect that God is just.   —THOMAS JEFFERSON,
                Notes on the State of Virginia

I am willing to love all mankind, *except an American*.
            —SAMUEL JOHNSON, James Boswell,
            Life of Johnson, April 15, 1778

The essential American soul is hard, isolate, stoic, a killer.   —D. H. LAWRENCE,
"Cooper's Leatherstocking Novels,"
in *Studies in Classic American Literature*

This country, with its institutions, belongs to the people who inhabit it. Whenever they shall grow weary of the existing government, they can exercise their constitutional right of amending it, or their revolutionary right to dismember or overthrow it.
—ABRAHAM LINCOLN,
First Inaugural Address, 1861

Thou, too, sail on O Ship of State!
Sail on, O Union, strong and great!
Humanity with all its fears,
With all the hopes of future years,
Is hanging breathless on thy fate!
—HENRY WADSWORTH LONGFELLOW,
The Building of the Ship

We need Hawaii just as much and a good deal more than we did California. It is manifest destiny.
—WILLIAM MCKINLEY, remark to his
presidential aide George Cortelyou, 1898
[See also John L. O'Sullivan below.]

The men the American people admire most extravagantly are the most daring liars; the men they detest most violently are those who try to tell the truth.
—H. L. MENCKEN, quoted in Alistair Cooke,
ed., *The Vintage Mencken*

No man ever went broke underestimating the intelligence of the American voter.
—H. L. MENCKEN, attributed
[One of many variants of Mencken's remark, in "Notes on Journalism," *Chicago Tribune*, Sept. 26, 1926: "No one . . . has ever lost money by underestimating the intelligence of the great masses of the plain people."]

Of nothing [in the U.S.] are you allowed to get the real odor or savor. Everything is sterilized and wrapped in cellophane.   —HENRY MILLER,
The Air-Conditioned Nightmare,
title essay

Don't sell America short.
—J. P. MORGAN, popularized version
of one of his favorite sayings
[Morgan's aphorism ran on the lines of "Don't be a bear on America." He was referring to a stock-market bear, who would bet on a stock price to drop, as opposed to a bull, who would expect a rise in price. This saying may have originated with J. P. Morgan's father, Junius Spenser Morgan.]

If when the chips are down the United States acts like a pitiful helpless giant, the forces of totalitarianism and anarchy will threaten free nations and free institutions throughout the world.
—RICHARD M. NIXON, speech, April 30, 1970

Our manifest destiny is to overspread the continent allotted by Providence for the free development of our yearly multiplying millions.
—JOHN L. O'SULLIVAN, *United States Magazine*,
July–Aug., 1845

In America, public opinion is the leader.
—FRANCES PERKINS, *People at Work*

You cannot conquer America.
—WILLIAM PITT, EARL OF CHATHAM, speech,
Nov. 18, 1777

All races and religions: that's America to me.
—EARL ROBINSON,
quoted in *The New York Times*,
obituary, July 23, 1991
[Robinson was the author of the music for "Joe Hill," the words coming from Alfred Hayes's poem about labor organizer Joe Hill, executed in 1915.]

We must be the great arsenal of democracy.
—FRANKLIN D. ROOSEVELT,
radio speech, Dec. 29, 1940

There can be no fifty-fifty Americanism in this country. There is room here for only hundred percent Americanism.
   —THEODORE ROOSEVELT, speech, July 19, 1918

Americans are suckers for good news.
   —ADLAI STEVENSON, speech, June 8, 1958

I know of no country, indeed, where the love of money has taken a stronger hold on the affections of men.   —ALEXIS DE TOCQUEVILLE,
   Democracy in America

America is a land of wonders, in which everything is in constant motion and every change seems an improvement. . . . No natural boundary seems to be set to the efforts of man; and in his eyes, what is not yet done is only what he has not yet attempted to do.   —*Ibid.*

The next Augustan age will dawn on the other side of the Atlantic.
   —HORACE WALPOLE, letter to Horace Mann, Nov. 24, 1774

The Constitution does not provide for first and second class citizens.   —WENDELL WILLKIE,
   An American Programme

For we must consider that we shall be as a city upon a hill. The eyes of all people are upon us.
   —JOHN WINTHROP, speech founding the Massachusetts Bay Colony, 1630
[The allusion is to the Sermon on the Mount, *Matthew* 5:14: "Ye are the light of the world. A city that is set on an hill cannot be hid."]

America is God's crucible, the great melting pot.
   —ISRAEL ZANGWILL, *The Melting Pot*
[The image was not original to Zangwill. Michel Guillaume Jean de Crèvecoeur reported in *Letters from an American Farmer* (1782) that "Here individuals of all nations are melted into a new race of men."]

AMERICAN HISTORY: See also AMERICA &
MEMORABLE MOMENTS   AMERICANS; MILITARY
                                                        BATTLES; PATRIOTISM

What a glorious morning for America!
—SAMUEL ADAMS, upon hearing the sound of
guns at Lexington, 1775, a traditional attribution

Declare the United States the winner and begin de-
escalation.   —SEN. GEORGE AIKEN advice to,
Lyndon Johnson on Vietnam, 1966

Remember the Maine!   —ANONYMOUS
[Slogan popularized in Hearst and Pulitzer newspapers,
1898, leading to the invasion of Cuba in the Spanish-
American War.]

Let us not be deceived—we are today in the midst
of a cold war.   —BERNARD BARUCH,
speech, April 16, 1947
[For Winston Churchill's "Iron Curtain" speech, see
COMMUNISM.]

Bury my heart at Wounded Knee.
—STEPHEN VINCENT BENÉT, *American Names*
[The last important battle in the Indian Wars was a
massacre of two hundred Sioux warriors and women
and children at Wounded Knee Creek in South Dakota,
Dec. 29, 1890.]

You shall not press down upon the brow of labor this
crown of thorns. You shall not crucify mankind upon
a cross of gold.
—WILLIAM JENNINGS BRYAN, speech,
Democratic National Convention, 1896
[Bryan's impassioned speech so impressed delegates at
the convention that it won him the presidential nomination although he was only age 36. Bryan supported
the populist Free Silver movement, which essentially
called for more available, more inflationary money, in
opposition especially to Eastern financiers, who supported a tight, gold-based currency. Bryan had developed the "cross of gold" metaphor some years earlier.
Bartlett's cites a similar passage from an 1894 speech in
Congress.]

Well, I think we ought to let him hang there. Let him twist slowly, slowly in the wind.
> —JOHN EHRLICHMAN,
> speaking to John Dean about
> F.B.I. head Patrick Gray, March 6, 1973

In the councils of government, we must guard against the acquisition of unwarranted influence, whether sought or unsought, by the military–industrial complex. The potential for the disastrous rise of misplaced power exists and will persist.
> —DWIGHT D. EISENHOWER,
> presidential farewell speech, Jan. 17, 1961
[See also Eisenhower at MILITARY, THE.]

Here once the embattled farmers stood,
And fired the shot heard round the world.
> —RALPH WALDO EMERSON, *Hymn Sung at the Completion of the Battle Monument, Concord*

Damn the torpedoes! Captain Drayton, go ahead. Jouett, full speed!
> —DAVID FARRAGUT,
> Battle of Mobile Bay, Aug. 5, 1864
[Usually shortened to "Damn the torpedoes! Full speed ahead." The Confederate torpedoes, incidentally, were actually water mines.]

Praise the Lord and pass the ammunition.
> —HOWELL M. FORGY,
> chaplain on the cruiser *New Orleans*,
> during the attack on Pearl Harbor,
> December 7, 1941

We must, indeed, all hang together or, most assuredly, we shall all hang separately.
> —BENJAMIN FRANKLIN, at the signing of the Declaration of Independence, July 4, 1776
[A late attribution, ca. 1840.]

I would remind you that extremism in the defense of liberty is no vice. And let me remind you also that moderation in the pursuit of justice is no virtue!
> —BARRY GOLDWATER, presidential nomination acceptance speech, 1964

I propose to fight it out on this line if it takes all summer.   —ULYSSES S. GRANT, dispatch
to Washington, May 11, 1864

I only regret that I have but one life to lose for my country.   —NATHAN HALE, before being
hanged as a spy, Sept. 22, 1776
[The thought comes from Joseph Addison's play *Cato* (1713): "What a pity is it / That we can die but once to serve our country."]

As for me, give me liberty or give me death!
            —PATRICK HENRY, speech, March 23, 1775

We hold these truths to be self-evident; that all men are created equal; that they are endowed by their creator with certain unalienable rights; that among these are life, liberty, and the pursuit of happiness.
—THOMAS JEFFERSON, Declaration of Independence
[Jefferson originally wrote "We hold these truths to be sacred and undeniable." Benjamin Franklin substituted "self-evident."]

Peace, commerce, and honest friendship with all nations—entangling alliances with none.
—THOMAS JEFFERSON, *First Inaugural Address*, 1801

I have not yet begun to fight.
    —JOHN PAUL JONES, on the *Bonhomme Richard*,
    Sept. 23, 1779

Ich bin ein Berliner.
            —JOHN F. KENNEDY, speech, June 26, 1963

Don't give up the ship.
                —JAMES LAWRENCE, June 1, 1813
[Commander Lawrence issued this order as his frigate, the *Chesapeake*, was being boarded by British sailors from H.M.S. *Shannon*. Reportedly, he said, "Tell the men to fire faster! Don't give up the ship!" He died of his wounds on June 4, continuing to call it out in his last hours. The captain of the *Shannon*, too, was mortally wounded in the battle. Some credit the famous order to Oliver Hazard Perry, who signaled this by flag during the Battle of Lake Erie, Sept. 10, 1813.]

Give me your tired, your poor,
Your huddled masses yearning to breathe free.
　　—EMMA LAZARUS, *The New Colossus:*
　　　Inscription for the Statue of Liberty

First in war, first in peace, first in the hearts of his countrymen.
　　—HENRY LEE, memorial address to Congress after
　　　the death of George Washington, 1799

A house divided against itself cannot stand. I believe this government cannot endure permanently half slave and half free.
　　　—ABRAHAM LINCOLN, speech, June 16, 1858
[For the Biblical allusion, see CONFLICT.]

Fourscore and seven years ago our fathers brought forth on this continent, a new nation conceived in Liberty, and dedicated to the proposition that all men are created equal.
　　　—ABRAHAM LINCOLN, Address at Gettysburg,
　　　　Nov. 19, 1863
[See also GOVERNMENT.]

With malice toward none, with charity for all, with firmness in the right, as God gives us to see the right, let us strive on to finish the work we are in, to bind up the nation's wounds.
　　　　—ABRAHAM LINCOLN,
　　　　　Second Inaugural Address, 1865

I shall return.
　　　—GEN. DOUGLAS MACARTHUR,
　　　　after leaving the Philippines, March 1942

Old soldiers never die; they just fade away. And like the old soldier in that ballad, I now close my military career and just fade away, an old soldier who tried to do his duty as God gave him the sight to see that duty.
　　　—GEN. DOUGLAS MACARTHUR,
　　　　speech to Congress
　　　　after having been relieved of duty
　　　　by President Truman, April 19, 1951

Nuts!   —GEN. ANTHONY MCAULIFFE,
                in refusing to surrender at Bastogne
                in the Battle of the Bulge, Dec. 22, 1944
[This is the reply publicized, evidently a euphemism for
a stronger term.]

All quiet along the Potomac.
                    —GEN. GEORGE B. MCCLELLAN,
                        in dispatches to Washington, 1861

You won't have Nixon to kick around anymore, because, gentlemen, this is my last press conference.
    —RICHARD M. NIXON, after losing the California
        gubernatorial race, 1962

I'm not a crook.
                    —RICHARD M. NIXON,
                        press conference, Nov. 11, 1973

These are the times that try men's souls. The summer
soldier and the sunshine patriot will, in this crisis, shrink
from the service of their country.
                    —THOMAS PAINE, *The American Crisis*

We have met the enemy, and they are ours.
        —OLIVER PERRY, dispatch, Battle of Lake Erie,
            Sept. 10, 1813
[For Walt Kelly's version, see HUMANS & HUMAN
NATURE.]

Don't fire until you see the whites of their eyes.
                —ISRAEL PUTNAM, Battle of Bunker Hill,
                    June 17, 1775
[Also attributed to William Prescott, but we accept the
word of militiaman Israel Potter, cited in Richard
Wheeler's *The Voices of 1776*.]

I pledge you, I pledge myself, to a new deal for the
American people.
    —FRANKLIN D. ROOSEVELT,
        presidential nomination acceptance speech, 1932

The only thing we have to fear is fear itself.
                    —FRANKLIN D. ROOSEVELT,
                        First Inaugural Address, 1933
[Cf. Wellington's similar comment, under FEAR.]

To some generations much is given. Of others much is expected. This generation of Americans has a rendezvous with destiny.
   —FRANKLIN D. ROOSEVELT, second presidential nomination acceptance speech, 1936

Yesterday, December 7, 1941—a date which will live in infamy—the United States of America was suddenly and deliberately attacked by naval and air forces of the Empire of Japan.
   —FRANKLIN D. ROOSEVELT, speech to Congress

A man who is good enough to shed his blood for his country is good enough to be given a square deal afterward.
   —THEODORE ROOSEVELT, speech, July 4, 1903

Hold out; relief is coming.
   —WILLIAM TECUMSEH SHERMAN, signal to Gen. John Murray Corse, Allatoona Pass, 1864
[Usually quoted as "Hold the fort! for I am coming," which is the way it was rendered in an 1874 gospel song by Philip Paul Bliss.]

I will not accept if nominated, and will not serve if elected.
   —WILLIAM TECUMSEH SHERMAN, telegram to Republican National Convention, 1884

Go west, young man, go west.
   —JOHN B. L. SOULE, editorial, *Terre Haute Express*, 1851
[The saying was popularized by Horace Greeley, who reprinted Soule's editorial in *The Herald Tribune*. In an editorial of his own, Greeley expanded Soule's advice to read: "Go west, young man, and grow up with the country."]

Lafayette, we are here.
   —CHARLES E. STANTON, at the grave of the Marquis de Lafayette, Paris, July 4, 1917
[Probably the best-remembered statement by an American in World War I. It is often attributed to Gen. John Pershing rather than Col. Stanton, with evidence for both attributions from people who were there.]

I'm going to fight hard. I'm going to give them hell.
                              —HARRY S TRUMAN, to Alben Barkley,
                                   Sept. 27, 1948

In the field of public education, the doctrine of "separate but equal" has no place. Separate educational facilities are inherently unequal.
                              —EARL WARREN,
                                   Brown v. *Board of Education of Topeka*
[The 1954 unanimous ruling was supplemented by a unanimous implementation ruling the following year, when the Court ordered desegregation of schools to proceed "with all deliberate speed."]

It is our true policy to steer clear of permanent alliances with any portion of the foreign world.
                              —GEORGE WASHINGTON, *Farewell Address*,
                                   published Sept. 19, 1796

The world must be made safe for democracy.
                              —WOODROW WILSON, speech, April 2, 1917,
                                   asking Congress for a declaration of war

AMERICAN INDIANS   See RACES & PEOPLES

ANGER   See also HATE; VIOLENCE & FORCE

Whosoever shall say, Thou fool, shall be in danger of hell fire.   —BIBLE, *Matthew* 5:22

Be ye angry and sin not: let not the sun go down upon your wrath.   —BIBLE, *Ephesians* 4:26

Envy and wrath shorten the life.
                              —BIBLE, *Ecclesiasticus* 30:24

Speak when you are angry and you will make the best speech you will ever regret.
                              —AMBROSE BIERCE, *The Devil's Dictionary*

I was angry with my friend:
I told my wrath, my wrath did end.
I was angry with my foe:
I told it not, my wrath did grow.
> —WILLIAM BLAKE, *A Poison Tree*

The tigers of wrath are wiser than the horses of instruction.
> —WILLIAM BLAKE,
> *The Marriage of Heaven and Hell*

Anger makes dull men witty, but it keeps them poor.
> —ELIZABETH I, quoted in Francis Bacon,
> *Apophthegms*

Anger is a brief madness.   —HORACE, *Epistles*

When angry, count four; when very angry, swear.
> —MARK TWAIN, "Pudd'nhead Wilson's Calendar,"
> in *Pudd'nhead Wilson*

Anger supplies arms.   —VIRGIL, *Aeneid*

ANIMALS   See NATURE: ANIMALS

ANNUNCIATION   See JESUS CHRIST

ANSWERS   See QUESTIONS & ANSWERS

APPEARANCES   See also BEAUTY; FASHION &
CLOTHES; STYLE

Appearances are often deceiving.
> —AESOP, *The Wolf in Sheep's Clothing*

To establish oneself in the world, one has to do all one can to appear established.
> —LA ROCHEFOUCAULD, *Maxims*

The Lord prefers common-looking people. That is the reason he makes so many of them.
> —ABRAHAM LINCOLN, Dec. 23, 1863
[Quoted by John Hay, *Letters of John Hay and Extracts from His Diary*, C. L. Hay, ed., 1908, reprint 1969. Lincoln recalled this comment from a dream in which Lincoln was in a crowd, and someone, recognizing him, had said, "He is a very common-looking man." The president responded with the above remark.]

Men should not care too much for good looks; neglect is becoming. —OVID, *Ars amatoria*

All that glisters is not gold.
—SHAKESPEARE, *The Merchant of Venice*, II, vii
[Shakespeare observed that this was a popular proverb.]

It is only shallow people who do not judge by appearances. The true mystery of the world is the visible, not the invisible.
—OSCAR WILDE, *The Picture of Dorian Gray*

APPEASEMENT VS.   See also OBEDIENCE;
RESISTANCE   PACIFISM; PEACE; RESIGNATION;
REVOLUTION; SURVIVAL

Better Red than dead.
—ANONYMOUS, slogan of British ban-the-bomb
movement, comments by Bertrand Russell
[Equally well known was the response, "Better dead than Red," which William Safire in his *Political Dictionary* notes was also the title of a book by an Englishman, Stanley Reynolds.]

I believe it is peace for our time.
—NEVILLE CHAMBERLAIN, speech, Sept. 30, 1938,
after the Munich Conference

The name of peace is sweet and the thing itself is good, but between peace and slavery there is the greatest difference. —CICERO, *Philippics*

'Tis better to have fought and lost,
Than never to have fought at all.
—ARTHUR HUGH CLOUGH, *Peschiera*

It is better to die on your feet than live on your knees!
They shall not pass!
—DOLORES IBARRURI ("LA PASIONARIA"),
radio broadcast, 1936
[The last phrase—*"no pasarán"*—became the rallying cry of the Republicans in the Spanish Civil War. See also Nivelle's order under MILITARY BATTLES.]

If once you have paid him the Dane-geld
You never get rid of the Dane.
      —RUDYARD KIPLING, *Dane-geld*

Better that we should die fighting than be outraged
and dishonored. . . . Better to die than to live in slavery.
   —EMMELINE PANKHURST, speech in Petrograd,
  Aug. 1917

There is a price which is too great to pay for peace,
and that price can be put in one word. One cannot pay
the price of self-respect.
    —WOODROW WILSON, speech, Feb. 1, 1916

APRIL   See NATURE: SEASONS

ARCHITECTURE   See ARTS: ARCHITECTURE

ARMIES   See MILITARY, THE;
         MILITARY BATTLES; WAR

ARTS   See also LANGUAGE; STYLE

Ars longa, vita brevis.
Art is long, life is short.   —ANONYMOUS
[This has been the most common rendering of the concept expressed by Hippocrates—see under LIFE—and
others. Longfellow put it thus: "Art is long, and Time
is fleeting," *A Psalm of Life*.]

The object of art is to give life shape.
      —JEAN ANOUILH, *The Rehearsal*

Il faut épater le bourgeois.
One must shock the bourgeois.
      —CHARLES BAUDELAIRE, attributed

In everything that can be called art there is a quality
of redemption.   —RAYMOND CHANDLER,
        The Simple Art of Murder

An artist will betray himself by some sort of sincerity.
 —G. K. CHESTERTON, "The Dagger with Wings,"
  in *The Incredulity of Father Brown*

Art is a jealous mistress.
> —RALPH WALDO EMERSON, *Wealth*

Art without life is a poor affair.
> —HENRY JAMES, *The Art of Fiction*

Is not a patron, my Lord, one who looks with un-
concern on a man struggling for life in the water, and,
when he has reached ground, encumbers him with help?
> —SAMUEL JOHNSON, letter to Lord Chesterfield,
> Feb. 7, 1755

Whenever I hear the word "culture," . . . I release
the safety catch on my Browning!
> —HANNS JOHST, *Schlageter*
[Usually attributed to Hermann Goering thus: "When
I hear anyone talk of culture, I reach for my revolver."]

Welcome O Life! I go to encounter for the millionth
time the reality of experience and to forge in the smithy
of my soul the uncreated conscience of my race.
> —JAMES JOYCE,
> *A Portrait of the Artist as a Young Man*

This nation cannot afford to be materially rich and
spiritually poor.
> —JOHN F. KENNEDY,
> State of the Union address, 1963
[Inscription on the Kennedy Center for the Performing
Arts in Washington, D.C.]

Music is the universal language of mankind—poetry
their universal pastime and delight.
> —HENRY WADSWORTH LONGFELLOW, *Outre-Mer*

Great artists have no country.
> ALFRED DE MUSSET, *Lorenzaccio*

There seem to be two causes of the deterioration of
the arts . . . wealth . . . and poverty; . . . the one is
the parent of luxury and indolence, and the other of
meanness and viciousness, and both of discontent.
> —PLATO, *The Republic*

Only through art can we emerge from ourselves and know what another person sees.
—MARCEL PROUST, *Maxims*

All art is but imitation of nature.
—SENECA, *Epistles*

O! for a Muse of fire, that would ascend
The brightest heaven of invention!
—SHAKESPEARE, *Henry V*, Prologue

The true artist will let his wife starve, his children go barefoot, his mother drudge for his living at seventy, sooner than work at anything but his art.
—GEORGE BERNARD SHAW, *Man and Superman*

Art is a microscope which the artist fixes on the secrets of his soul, and shows to people these secrets which are common to all.
—LEO TOLSTOY, *Diaries*, May 17, 1896

Mrs. Ballinger is one of the ladies who pursue Culture in bands, as though it were dangerous to meet it alone.
—EDITH WHARTON, *Xingu*

All art is quite useless.   —OSCAR WILDE,
The Picture of Dorian Gray

ARTS: AESTHETICS   See also ARTS:
STYLE IN WRITING
& EXPRESSION; BEAUTY;
SIMPLICITY; STYLE

Tragedy is an imitation of an action that is serious, complete, and of a certain magnitude, effecting through pity and fear the proper purgation [*katharsis*] of these emotions.   —ARISTOTLE, *Poetics*

That willing suspension of disbelief for the moment, which constitutes poetic faith.
—SAMUEL TAYLOR COLERIDGE,
Biographia Literaria

The only way of expressing emotion in the form of art is by finding an "objective correlative"; in other words, a set of objects, a situation, a chain of events which shall be the formula of that *particular* emotion.
—T. S. ELIOT, *Hamlet*

Less is more.
—LUDWIG MIES VAN DER ROHE, motto
[Borrowed from Robert Browning—see Browning at SIMPLICITY. For an opposing view, see Mstislav Rostropovich at EXCESS, note to Mae West quote.]

A falseness in all our impressions of external things, which I would generally characterize as the "pathetic fallacy."   —JOHN RUSKIN, *Modern Painters*

ARTS: ARCHITECTURE

Form ever follows function.
—LOUIS HENRI SULLIVAN,
   "The Tall Office Building Artistically Considered,"
   in *Lippincott's Magazine*, March 1896
["Form follows function" was the motto of the Bauhaus.]

Architecture is inhabited sculpture.
—BRANCUSI, quoted by Igor Stravinsky and
   Robert Craft, *Themes and Episodes*

Une maison est une machine à habiter.
A house is a machine for living in.
—LE CORBUSIER, *Vers une architecture*

I call architecture frozen music.
—GOETHE, letter to Eckermann, Feb. 4, 1829
[Goethe made the phrase famous; Friedrich von Schelling, however, used the "frozen music" metaphor earlier, in *Philosophie der Kunst*, 1809.]

One might regard architecture as history arrested in stone.   —A. L. ROWSE, *The Use of History*

When we build, let us think that we build forever.
> —JOHN RUSKIN,
> *The Seven Lamps of Architecture*

The most beautiful house in the world is the one that you build for yourself.
> —WITOLD RYBCZYSNKI,
> *The Most Beautiful House in the World*

Si monumentum requiris circumspice.
If you seek a monument, look around.
> —CHRISTOPHER WREN, inscription in
> St. Paul's Cathedral, London,
> written by his son

ARTS: See also INSULTS &
CRITICISM & CRITICS   PUT-DOWNS

Pleasure is by no means an infallible guide, but it is the least fallible.
> —W. H. AUDEN, *The Dyer's Hand*

Reviewers are usually people who would have been poets, historians, biographers, if they could; they have tried their talents at one or the other, and have failed; therefore they turn critics.
> —SAMUEL TAYLOR COLERIDGE,
> *Lectures on Shakespeare and Milton*

[Reviewing] is no easy matter. To begin with, you must be sure that writing is your vocation, next you must be convinced that reviewing is not writing, hence the conclusion that your vocation is not reviewing. Well, once you feel that, you can start.
> —CYRIL CONNOLLY, journal, quoted in
> *The New Yorker*, Sept. 3, 1984

A man is a critic when he cannot be an artist, in the same way that a man becomes an informer when he cannot be a soldier.
> —GUSTAVE FLAUBERT,
> letter to Louise Colet, Oct. 1846

A good critic is one who describes his adventures among masterpieces.   —ANATOLE FRANCE,
La Vie littéraire

You *may* abuse a tragedy, though you cannot write one. You may scold a carpenter who has made you a bad table, though you cannot make a table. It is not your trade to make tables.
—SAMUEL JOHNSON, quoted in James Boswell,
Life of Johnson, May 24, 1763

I would rather be attacked than unnoticed. For the worst thing you can do to an author is to be silent as to his works.
—SAMUEL JOHNSON, quoted in James Boswell,
Life of Johnson, March 26, 1779

Our American professors like their literature clear and cold and pure and very dead.
—SINCLAIR LEWIS,
Nobel Prize acceptance speech, 1930

I cried all the way to the bank [response to negative reviews].
—LIBERACE, *Liberace: An Autobiography*

Nor in the critic let the man be lost.
—ALEXANDER POPE, *An Essay on Criticism*

Interpretation is the revenge of the intellect upon art.
—SUSAN SONTAG,
Against Interpretation, title essay

ARTS: DRAMA & ACTING

Never meddle with play actors, for they're a favored race.   —CERVANTES, *Don Quixote*
[The more common view was expressed by the eighteenth-century English satirist Charles Churchill: "The strolling tribe; a despicable race," *Apology*.]

If a gun is hanging on the wall in the first act, it must fire in the last.
　　—ANTON CHEKHOV, advice to a novice
　　　playwright, quoted in John Gassner and
　　　Edward Quinn, eds., *The Reader's Encyclopedia of World Drama*

Satire is what closes on Saturday night.
　　　　　—GEORGE S. KAUFMAN, attributed,
　　　　　　Howard Teichmann, *George S. Kaufman*
[See also Lady Mary Wortley Montague on satire at ARTS: WRITING and James Thurber at HUMOR.]

Drama is action, sir, action and not confounded philosophy.　—LUIGI PIRANDELLO,
　　　　　Six Characters in Search of an Author

The play's the thing
Wherein I'll catch the conscience of the king.
　　　　　—SHAKESPEARE, *Hamlet*, II, ii

Speak the speech, I pray you, as I pronounced it to you, trippingly on the tongue.　　—*Ibid.*, III, ii

Suit the action to the word, the word to the action, with this special observance, that you o'erstep not the modesty of nature.　　　　　—*Ibid.*

Hold as 'twere the mirror up to nature.　　—*Ibid.*

Exit, pursued by a bear.
　　　　　—SHAKESPEARE, *The Winter's Tale*,
　　　　　stage direction, III, iii

ARTS: MUSIC & DANCE

Music, the greatest good that mortals know,
And all of heaven we have here below.
　　—JOSEPH ADDISON, *A Song for St. Cecilia's Day*

The flute is not an instrument that has a good moral effect; it is too exciting.   —ARISTOTLE, *Politics*

Whether angels play only Bach in praising God, I am not sure. I am sure, however, that *en famille* they play Mozart.
> —KARL BARTH, quoted in *The New York Times*, obituary, Dec. 11, 1968

A symphony is no joke.
> —JOHANNES BRAHMS, cited by Donal Henahan, *The New York Times*, March 17, 1985

The heart of the melody can never be put down on paper.   —PABLO CASALS, *Conversations*

Where there's music, there can be no evil.
> —CERVANTES, *Don Quixote*

Opera . . . is one of the strangest inventions of Western man.
It could not have been foreseen by any logical process.   —SIR KENNETH CLARK, *Civilization*
[Re how operas end, see ENDINGS.]

Music has charms to soothe a savage breast,
To soften rocks, or bend a knotted oak.
> —WILLIAM CONGREVE, *The Mourning Bride*

Extraordinary how potent cheap music is.
> —NOËL COWARD, *Private Lives*

What passion cannot music raise and quell?
> —JOHN DRYDEN, *A Song for St. Cecilia's Day*

Dance is the loftiest, the most moving, the most beautiful of the arts, because it is no mere translation or abstraction from life; it is life itself.
> —HAVELOCK ELLIS, *The Dance of Life*

One becomes . . . an athlete of God.
> —MARTHA GRAHAM, May 15, 1945
[More at GRACE.]

Dancing is just discovery, discovery, discovery.
—MARTHA GRAHAM, interview
The New York Times, March 31, 1985

Dance is the hidden language of the soul.   —*Ibid.*

I know only two tunes: one is "Yankee Doodle," and
the other isn't.   —ULYSSES S. GRANT, attributed

If the king loves music, there is little wrong in the
land.   —MENCIUS, *Discourses*

All art constantly aspires towards the condition of
music.   —WALTER PATER, *Giorgione*, in
Studies in the History of the Renaissance

If music be the food of love, play on.
—SHAKESPEARE, *Twelfth Night*, I, i

I am never merry when I hear sweet music.
—SHAKESPEARE, *The Merchant of Venice*, V, i

Hell is full of musical amateurs.
—GEORGE BERNARD SHAW, *Man and Superman*

My soul is an enchanted boat,
Which, like a sleeping swan, doth float
Upon the silver waves of thy sweet singing.
—PERCY BYSSHE SHELLEY, *Prometheus Unbound*

Our sweetest songs are those that tell of saddest
thoughts.   —PERCY BYSSHE SHELLEY,
To a Skylark

If, as is nearly always the case, music appears to
express something, this is only an illusion and not a
reality.   —IGOR STRAVINSKY, *An Autobiography*

He was a fiddler, and consequently a rogue.
—JONATHAN SWIFT, letter to Stella, July 25, 1711
[In the Middle Ages, acrobats, jugglers, actors, and
fiddlers wandered from town to town, and acquired a
raffish reputation that to a degree has endured to our
time.]

Lady, if you got to ask, you ain't got it [on being asked to explain rhythm].
—THOMAS "FATS" WALLER,
quoted in Eddie Condon and Thomas Sugrue,
We Called It Music

[Sign over a piano] Please do not shoot the pianist. He is doing his best.   —OSCAR WILDE, "Leadville,"
in *Impressions of America*

ARTS: PAINTING

One is never tired of painting, because you have to set down, not what you knew already, but what you have just discovered. There is a continual creation out of nothing going on.
—WILLIAM HAZLITT, *The Pleasure of Painting*

All art worthy of the name is religious. Be it a creation of lines and colors, if it is not religious, it does not exist. If it is not religious, it is only a matter of documentary art, anecdotal art, which is no longer art.
—HENRI MATISSE, quoted in
Pierre Schneider, *Matisse*

With color one obtains an energy that seems to stem from witchcraft.
—HENRI MATISSE, quoted by Michael Brenson,
The New York Times, May 26, 1985

I try to apply colors like words that shape poems, like notes that shape music.
—JOAN MIRÓ, quoted in John Gruen, *Close-Up*

The painter who draws by practice and judgment of the eye without the use of reason is like the mirror which reproduces within itself all the objects which are set opposite to it without knowledge of the same.
—LEONARDO DA VINCI, *Notebooks*

A picture is a model of reality.
—LUDWIG WITTGENSTEIN,
Tractatus logico-philosophicus

ARTS: POETRY & POETS

All poets are mad.
> —ROBERT BURTON,
> *The Anatomy of Melancholy*

Poetry does not necessarily have to be beautiful to stick in the depths of our memory.
> —COLETTE, "Under the Blue Lantern,"
> in *Earthly Paradise*

For that fine madness still he did retain
Which rightly should possess a poet's brain.
> —MICHAEL DRAYTON,
> *To Henry Reynolds, of Poets and Poesy*

[Drayton is speaking of Christopher Marlowe.]

Genuine poetry can communicate before it is understood.
> —T. S. ELIOT, *Dante*

The figure a poem makes. It begins in delight and ends in wisdom. The figure is the same as for love.
> —ROBERT FROST, *Figure a Poem Makes*

I'd as soon write free verse as play tennis with the net down.
> —ROBERT FROST, quoted in Edward Lathem,
> *Interviews with Robert Frost*

The only thing that can save the world is the reclaiming of the awareness of the world. That's what poetry does.
> —ALLEN GINSBERG, quoted in Helen Weaver,
> review of Ginsberg's *Collected Poems*,
> in *The Litchfield County Times*, May 31, 1985

If there's no money in poetry, neither is there poetry in money.
> —ROBERT GRAVES, speech, Dec. 6, 1963

The poetical language of an age should be the current language heightened.
> —GERARD MANLEY HOPKINS, letter to
> Robert Bridges, Aug. 14, 1879

To be a mediocre poet, neither gods, nor men, nor booksellers have allowed.
—HORACE, *Art of Poetry*

To a poet nothing can be useless.
SAMUEL JOHNSON, *Rasselas*

Poetry should surprise by a fine excess and not by singularity—it should strike the reader as a wording of his own highest thoughts, and appear almost a remembrance.
—JOHN KEATS, letter to John Taylor, Feb. 27, 1818

If poetry comes not as naturally as the leaves to a tree, it had better not come at all.   —*Ibid.*

When power narrows the areas of man's concern, poetry reminds him of the richness and diversity of his existence. When power corrupts, poetry cleanses.
—JOHN F. KENNEDY, speech, Oct. 26, 1963

Publishing a volume of poetry is like dropping a rose petal down the Grand Canyon and waiting for the echo.
—DON MARQUIS, *The Sun Dial*

The subject of it [his book of poems] is war, and the pity of war.
The poetry is in the pity.
All a poet can do is warn.
—WILFRED OWEN, *Poems*, preface

Chameleons feed on light and air:
Poets' food is love and fame.
—PERCY BYSSHE SHELLEY, *An Exhortation*

Poetry is the record of the best and happiest moments of the happiest and best minds.
—PERCY BYSSHE SHELLEY, *A Defense of Poetry*

Poets tell many lies.   —SOLON, fragment
[For another less than flattering view of poets see the note at Swift in the category NATURE: ANIMALS.]

The poet is the priest of the invisible.
                    —WALLACE STEVENS, *Adagia*

To have great poets, there must be great audiences,
too.   —WALT WHITMAN,
                    "Ventures on an Old Theme,"
                    in *Notes Left Over*

Poetry is the spontaneous overflow of powerful feelings: it takes its origin from emotion recollected in
tranquillity.
          —WILLIAM WORDSWORTH, *Lyrical Ballads*,
          Preface to 2nd edition.

We poets in our youth begin in gladness;
But thereof come in the end despondency and madness.   —WILLIAM WORDSWORTH,
                    Resolution and Independence

ARTS: STYLE IN WRITING   See also LANGUAGE &
& EXPRESSION   WORDS; SIMPLICITY; STYLE

The greatest thing in style is to have a command of
metaphor.   —ARISTOTLE, *Poetics*

A good style must, first of all, be clear. It must . . .
be appropriate.   —ARISTOTLE, *Rhetoric*

A good style must have an air of novelty, at the same
time concealing its art.   —*Ibid.*

This is the sort of English up with which I will not
put.   —WINSTON CHURCHILL, attributed
[Comment in margin of a document—it refers to a
proofreader's excessive nicety in avoiding placing a
preposition at the end of a sentence, quoted by Sir
Ernest Gowers, *Plain Words*.]

Read over your compositions, and wherever you
meet with a passage which you think is particularly fine,
strike it out.
     —SAMUEL JOHNSON, quoting a college tutor,
       in James Boswell, *Life of Johnson*, April 30, 1773

For a man to write well, there are required three necessaries: to read the best authors, observe the best speakers, and much exercise of his own style.
—BEN JONSON, *Discoveries*

Whatever is clearly expressed is well wrote.
—LADY MARY WORTLEY MONTAGU, letter to James Steuart, July 19, 1759

Verbal felicity is the fruit of art and diligence and refusing to be false.
—MARIANNE MOORE, quoted by Louise Bogan, *College English*, Feb. 1953

I have made this letter longer than usual, because I lack the time to make it short.
—PASCAL, *Lettres provinciales*

True wit is nature to advantage dressed,
What oft was thought, but ne'er so well expressed.
—ALEXANDER POPE, *Essay on Criticism*

Brevity is the soul of wit.
—SHAKESPEARE, *Hamlet*, II, ii

Vigorous writing is concise.
—WILLIAM STRUNK, *Elements of Style*

Proper words in proper places make the true definition of style.
—JONATHAN SWIFT, letter to a young clergyman, Jan. 9, 1720

The difference between the almost right word and the right word is really a large matter—'tis the difference between the lightning bug and the lightning.
—MARK TWAIN, *The Art of Authorship*

As to the Adjective: when in doubt, strike it out.
—MARK TWAIN, "Pudd'nhead Wilson's Calendar," in *Pudd'nhead Wilson*

Take eloquence and wring its neck.
—PAUL VERLAINE, "L'art poétique," in *Jadis et Naguère*

Style is the dress of thought.
>—SAMUEL WESLEY, *An Epistle
>to a Friend Concerning Poetry*

[Later, in 1746, the Earl of Chesterfield wrote to his son, "Style is the dress of thoughts." See also Johnson at LANGUAGE.]

ARTS: THEATER   See ARTS: DRAMA & ACTING

ARTS: WRITING   See also ARTS: POETRY & POETS;
ARTS: STYLE IN WRITING & EXPRESSION;
BOOKS & READING; LANGUAGE & WORDS; STORIES

Of making many books, there is no end.
>—BIBLE, *Ecclesiastes* 12:12

[Also translated as, "Writing books involves endless hard work," The Jerusalem Bible, 1966.]

Writing is nothing more than a guided dream.
>—JORGE LUIS BORGES,
>*Dr. Brodie's Report*, Preface

A well-written life is almost as rare as a well-spent one.   —THOMAS CARLYLE, *Richter*

A good novel tells us the truth about its hero; but a bad novel tells us the truth about its author.
>—G. K. CHESTERTON, *Heretics*

A work that aspires, however humbly, to the condition of art should carry its justification in every line.
>—JOSEPH CONRAD,
>*Nigger of the Narcissus*, Preface

Be kind and considerate with your criticism. . . . It's just as hard to write a bad book as it is to write a good book.
>—MALCOLM COWLEY, quoted by Ken Kesey,
>*The New York Times*, Dec. 31, 1989

All writing comes by the grace of God.
>—RALPH WALDO EMERSON, *Experience*

If a writer has to rob his mother, he will not hesitate; the "Ode on a Grecian Urn" is worth any number of old ladies.   —WILLIAM FAULKNER, quoted in
>*The Paris Review Interviews*, 1959

It is with noble sentiments that bad literature gets written.   —ANDRÉ GIDE, *Journal*, Sept. 2, 1940

Often you must turn your stylus to erase, if you hope to write anything worth a second reading.
>—HORACE, *Satires*

A man may write at any time, if he will set himself doggedly to it.
>—SAMUEL JOHNSON, quoted in James Boswell,
>*Life of Johnson*, March 1750

No man but a blockhead ever wrote, except for money.   —*Ibid.*, April 5, 1776

Lexicographer, n. A writer of dictionaries, a harmless drudge.   —SAMUEL JOHNSON, *Dictionary*

An inveterate and incurable itch for writing besets many and grows old with their sick hearts.
>—JUVENAL, *Satires*

He writes nothing whose writings are not read.
>—MARTIAL, *Epigrams*

If you steal from one author it's plagiarism; if you steal from many it's research.
>—WILSON MIZNER, quoted in
>John Burke, *Rogue's Progress*

Satire should, like a polished razor keen,
Wound with a touch that's scarcely felt or seen.
>—LADY MARY WORTLEY MONTAGU,
>*To the Imitator of the First Satire of Horace*

[See also George S. Kaufman on satire at ARTS: DRAMA & ACTING.]

If there's a book you really want to read but it hasn't been written yet, then you must write it.

—TONI MORRISON

[This has been attributed to Ms. Morrison in *The New York Times* and elsewhere; she does not remember precisely the occasion on which she said it—just that it was in a speech.]

True ease in writing comes from art, not chance.
—ALEXANDER POPE, *An Essay on Criticism*

Our passions shape our books, repose writes them in the intervals.
—MARCEL PROUST, *Remembrance of Things Past: The Past Recaptured*

An honest tale speeds best being plainly told.
—SHAKESPEARE, *Richard III*, IV, iv

Keep away from books and from men who get their ideas from books, and your own books will always be fresh.
—GEORGE BERNARD SHAW, *Bernard Shaw's Letters to Siegfried Trebitsch*

Of all those arts in which the wise excel,
Nature's chief masterpiece is writing well.
—JOHN SHEFFIELD, *Essay on Poetry*

There's nothing to writing. All you do is sit down at a typewriter and open a vein.
—WALTER ("RED") SMITH, in *Reader's Digest*, July 1982

A great writer is, so to speak, a second government in his country. And for that reason no regime has ever loved great writers, only minor ones.
—ALEXANDER SOLZHENITSYN, *The First Circle*

Writing, when properly managed (as you may be sure I think mine is), is but a different name for conversation.
—LAURENCE STERNE, *Tristram Shandy*

Writing may be either the record of a deed or a deed. It is nobler when it is a deed.
—HENRY DAVID THOREAU, *Journal*, Jan. 7, 1844

Three hours a day will produce as much as a man ought to write.
—ANTHONY TROLLOPE, *An Autobiography*

There is no way of writing well and also of writing easily.   —ANTHONY TROLLOPE, *Barchester Towers*

Being a great writer is not the same as writing great.
—JOHN UPDIKE, *The New Yorker*, May 20, 1985

ASTRONOMY   See SCIENCE: PHYSICS
                                         & COSMOLOGY

ATHEISM   See also GOD; FAITH;
                                         RELIGION; SKEPTICISM

The fool hath said in his heart, There is no God.
—BIBLE, *Psalms* 14:1 & 53:1

I am an atheist still, thank God.
—LUIS BUÑUEL, quoted in
Ado Kyrou, *Luis Buñuel*

There are no atheists in the foxholes.
—WILLIAM THOMAS CUMMINGS, field sermon,
Bataan, 1942

In spite of all the yearnings of men, no one can produce a single fact or reason to support the belief in God and in personal immortality.
—CLARENCE DARROW, *Sign* magazine, May 1938

I believe that when I die I shall rot, and nothing of my ego will survive. . . . But I should scorn to shiver with terror at the thought of annihilation. Happiness is nonetheless true happiness because it must come to an

end, nor do thought and love lose their value because
they are not everlasting.
—BERTRAND RUSSELL, *What I Believe*

My atheism . . . is true piety towards the universe
and denies only gods fashioned by men in their own
image, to be servants of their human interests.
—GEORGE SANTAYANA, *On My Friendly Critics*

An atheist is a man who has no invisible means of
support.   —FULTON J. SHEEN,
Look magazine, Dec. 14, 1955

AUTOMOBILES   See TECHNOLOGY

AUTUMN   See NATURE: SEASONS

B

BABIES	See CHILDREN & CHILDHOOD
BAD TIMES	See TROUBLE; TURBULENT TIMES
BANKS	See BUSINESS
BATTLES	See MILITARY BATTLES
BEAUTY	See also APPEARANCES; ART: AESTHETICS; CHARM; GRACE; WOMEN, BEAUTIFUL & HOMELY

Beauty is the gift of God.
　　　　—ARISTOTLE, quoted in Diogenes Laërtius,
　　　　　Lives of Eminent Philosophers

What do I care if you are good?
Be beautiful! and be sad!
　　　—CHARLES BAUDELAIRE,
　　　　　"Madrigal triste," in *Nouvelles Fleurs du mal*

For beauty being the best of all we know
Sums up the unsearchable and secret aims
Of nature.　　　　　　　—ROBERT BRIDGES,
　　　　　　　　　　　　The Growth of Love

Think of all the beauty still left around you and be
happy.　　　—ANNE FRANK, *Diary of a Young Girl*

Beauty is in the eye of the beholder.
　　　　—MARGARET HUNGERFORD, *Molly Bawn*
[David Hume, in *Of Tragedy*, put it: "Beauty in things
exists in the mind which contemplates them."]

A thing of beauty is a joy for ever:
Its loveliness increases; it will never
Pass into nothingness.
> —JOHN KEATS, *Endymion*

"Beauty is truth, truth beauty,"—that is all
Ye know on earth, and all ye need to know.
> —JOHN KEATS, *Ode on a Grecian Urn*

I'm tired of all this business about beauty being only skin-deep. That's deep enough. What do you want— an adorable pancreas?
> —JEAN KERR, "Mirror, Mirror on the Wall," in *The Snake Has All the Lines*

Beauty is everlasting
And dust is for a time.
> —MARIANNE MOORE, *In Distrust of Merits*

Remember that the most beautiful things in the world are the most useless: peacocks and lilies, for instance.
> —JOHN RUSKIN, *The Stones of Venice*

It is amazing how complete is the delusion that beauty is goodness. —LEO TOLSTOY, *The Kreutzer Sonata*

The superior gratification derived from the use and contemplation of costly and supposedly beautiful products is, commonly, in great measure, a gratification of our sense of costliness masquerading under the name of beauty. —THORSTEIN VEBLEN, *The Theory of the Leisure Class*

The beauty of the world which is soon to perish, has two edges, one of laughter, one of anguish, cutting the heart asunder.
> —VIRGINIA WOOLF, *A Room of One's Own*

BEGINNINGS See also FATE

A good beginning makes a good ending.
> —ANONYMOUS (ENGLISH PROVERB)

A hard beginning maketh a good ending.
                    —JOHN HEYWOOD, *Proverbs*

Who has begun has half done. Have the courage to be wise. Begin!   —HORACE, *Epistles*
[Former New York City mayor Ed Koch kept this motto on his desk, with a different, freer translation: "Begin, be bold, and venture to be wise." The Latin reads: *Dimindium facti qui coepit habet. Sapere aude. Incipe!*]

A journey of a thousand miles must begin with a single step.   —LAO-TZU, *Tao Te Ching*

Things are always at their best in their beginning.
                    —PASCAL, *Lettres provinciales*

The beginning is the most important part of the work.
                    —PLATO, *The Republic*

BELIEF   See FAITH; RELIGION

BETRAYAL

This night, before the cock crow, thou shalt deny me thrice.   —BIBLE, *Matthew* 26:34

Judas, betrayest thou the Son of man with a kiss?
                    —BIBLE, *Luke* 23:48

Et tu, Brute!
                    —SHAKESPEARE, *Julius Caesar*, III, i

This was the most unkindest cut of all.
                    —*Ibid.*, III, ii

Each man kills the thing he loves.
        —OSCAR WILDE, *The Ballad of Reading Gaol*
[For more, see CRIME.]

BIBLE   See RELIGION

BIRDS   See NATURE: ANIMALS

BLACKS   See RACES & PEOPLES

BOASTING

Big boast, small roast.
                    —ANONYMOUS (ENGLISH PROVERB)
[An early equivalent of "Where's the beef?"]

It ain't braggin' if you kin do it.
                    —DIZZY DEAN, attributed

BOATING   See SEAS & SHIPS, SAILING & BOATING

BODY, HUMAN   See also HEALTH;
                                ILLNESS & REMEDIES

The Spirit indeed is willing, but the flesh is weak.
                    —BIBLE, *Matthew* 26:41
[See also TEMPTATION.]

Your body is the temple of the Holy Ghost, which is
in you, which ye have of God, and ye are not your own.
                    —BIBLE, *I Corinthians* 6:19

Alas, after a certain age, every man is responsible
for his own face.   —ALBERT CAMUS, *The Fall*

The strongest, surest way to the soul is through the
flesh.   —MABEL DODGE, *Lorenzo in Taos*

Love's mysteries in souls do grow,
But yet the body is his book.
                    —JOHN DONNE, *The Ecstasy*

I see no objection to stoutness, in moderation.
                    —W. S. GILBERT, *Iolanthe*

The body says what words cannot.
                    —MARTHA GRAHAM, interview,
                    The New York Times, March 31, 1985

I'm fat, but I'm thin inside. Has it ever struck you that there's a thin man inside every fat man?
—GEORGE ORWELL, *Coming Up for Air*
[It may have been said first by Cyril Connolly: "Imprisoned in every fat man is a thin one wildly signaling to be let out," published in his book of aphorisms, *The Unquiet Grave*.]

From a man's face, I can read his character; if I can see him walk, I know his thoughts.
—PETRONIUS, *Satyricon*

O! that this too too solid flesh would melt,
Thaw and resolve itself into a dew.
—SHAKESPEARE, *Hamlet*, I, ii

I have more flesh than another man, and therefore more frailty.
—SHAKESPEARE, *Henry IV, Part I*, III, iii

If anything is sacred the human body is sacred.
—WALT WHITMAN, *I Sing the Body Electric*

BOLDNESS & INITIATIVE   See also ACTION;
AMBITION; COURAGE; DECISION,
MOMENT OF; GREATNESS;
OPPORTUNITY; REVOLUTION;
SELF-CONFIDENCE; SELF-RELIANCE

Ask, and it shall be given you; seek, and ye shall find; knock, and it shall be opened unto you.
—BIBLE, *Matthew* 7:7

Faint heart never won fair lady.
—CERVANTES, *Don Quixote*
[Identified as "an old saying."]

He who seizes the right moment,
Is the right man.   —GOETHE, *Faust*

The first blow is half the battle.
—OLIVER GOLDSMITH, *She Stoops to Conquer*

He either fears his fate too much,
Or his deserts are small,

That puts it not unto the touch
To win or lose it all.
    —JAMES GRAHAM (MARQUIS OF MONTROSE),
        My Dear and Only Love
[Sent in a message from Field-Marshal Montgomery
to U.S. troops sailing toward Normandy on June 5,
1944. They landed the next morning, D-Day.]

Cruelties should be committed all at once.
    —MACHIAVELLI, *The Prince*

Take calculated risks. That is quite different from
being rash.   —GEN. GEORGE S. PATTON,
        letter to his son, June 6, 1944

If it were done when 'tis done, then 'twere well
It were done quickly.
    —SHAKESPEARE, *Macbeth*, I, vii

Fortune sides with him who dares.
    —VIRGIL, *Aeneid*

BOOKS & READING   See also ARTS: POETRY &
        POETS; ARTS: WRITING;
        CENSORSHIP; STORIES

Big book, big bore.
    —CALLIMACHUS, *On Himself*
[Traditionally rendered: "Great book, great evil," but
evil seems the wrong word, considering that the author
headed the library at Alexandria. This translation is by
Peter Jay.]

Reading all the good books is like a conversation with
the finest men of past centuries.
    —RENÉ DESCARTES, *Discourse on Method*

Books are for nothing but to inspire.
    —RALPH WALDO EMERSON,
        The American Scholar

Read in order to live.
    —GUSTAVE FLAUBERT, letter to
        Mlle. de Chantpie, June 1857

All good books are alike in that they are truer than if they really happened and after you are finished reading one you will feel that it all happened to you, and afterwards it all belongs to you.
—ERNEST HEMINGWAY, *An Old Newsman Writes*

I cannot live without books.
—THOMAS JEFFERSON, letter to John Adams, June 10, 1815

Literature is my utopia.   —HELEN KELLER, *The Story of My Life*

We shouldn't teach great books; we should teach a love of reading.
—B. F. SKINNER, quoted in Richard I. Evans, *B. F. Skinner: The Man and His Ideas*

People say that life is the thing, but I prefer reading.
—LOGAN PEARSALL SMITH, *Afterthoughts*

Literature . . . becomes the living memory of a nation.
—ALEXANDER SOLZHENITSYN, Nobel Prize acceptance speech, 1972

Reading is to the mind what exercise is to the body.
—RICHARD STEELE, *The Tatler*, no. 147

Books are good enough in their own way, but they are a mighty bloodless substitute for life.
—ROBERT LOUIS STEVENSON, "An Apology for Idlers," in *Virginibus Puerisque*

Books are the treasured wealth of the world and the fit inheritance of generations and nations.
—HENRY DAVID THOREAU, *Walden*

How many a man has dated a new era in his life from the reading of a book.   —*Ibid.*

A good book is the best of friends, the same today and forever.
—MARTIN E. TUPPER, *Of Reading*, in *Proverbial Philosophy*

"Classic." A book which people praise and don't read.
  —MARK TWAIN, "Pudd'nhead Wilson's
    New Calendar," in *Following the Equator*, 1897

There is no such thing as a moral or an immoral book. Books are well written, or badly written.
  —OSCAR WILDE, *The Picture of Dorian Gray*

BOSTON   See CITIES

BRAGGING   See BOASTING

BRAVERY   See COURAGE

BROTHERHOOD   See EQUALITY; HUMANS & HUMAN
                            NATURE; RACES & PEOPLES

BUSINESS   See also AMERICA & AMERICANS;
                         CAPITALISM; ECONOMICS;
                         MONEY; WORK & WORKERS

Buying and selling is essentially antisocial.
  —EDWARD BELLAMY, *Looking Backward*

What is robbing a bank compared with founding a bank?
  —BERTOLT BRECHT, *The Threepenny Opera*

It is better to lose opportunity than capital.
  —SUSAN M. BYRNE,
      on "Wall St. Week in Review,"
      Feb. 15, 1985

Few people do business well who do nothing else.
  —EARL OF CHESTERFIELD, letter to his son,
      Aug. 7, 1749

They [corporations] cannot commit treason, nor be outlawed, nor excommunicate, for they have no souls.
>   —EDWARD COKE, *Sutton's Hospital Case*

No nation was ever ruined by trade.
>   —BENJAMIN FRANKLIN, *Thoughts on Commercial Subjects*

I just want to say one word to you. Just one word. Are you listening? *Plastics*.
>   —BUCK HENRY and CALDER WILLINGHAM, *The Graduate*
[Based on Charles Webb's novel.]

When a person with experience meets a person with money, the person with experience will get the money. And the person with the money will get some experience.
>   —LEONARD LAUDER, on the early years of the Estée Lauder company, speech, Woman's Economic Development Corporation, Feb. 1985

Trade is a social act.
>   —JOHN STUART MILL, *On Liberty*

The customer is always right.
>   —H. GORDON SELFRIDGE, slogan of his store in London

Corporations have neither bodies to be punished, nor souls to be condemned, they therefore do as they like.
>   —EDWARD, FIRST BARON THURLOW, attributed by Poynder, *Literary Extracts*

No one on his deathbed ever said, "I wish I had spent more time on my business."
>   —PAUL E. TSONGAS, quoting a letter from a friend
[The thought was expressed in a variety of forms in the 1980s. Sen. Tsongas's friend wrote after the senator had decided not to finish his 1979–85 term as junior senator from Massachusetts. Anna Quindlen called this "the quote of the decade" in her column in *The New York Times*, Jan. 14, 1987.]

The public be damned! I'm working for my stock-holders.
——WILLIAM HENRY VANDERBILT, news reports,
Oct. 2, 1882

For years I thought what was good for our country was good for General Motors and vice versa. The difference did not exist.
——CHARLES E. WILSON, testimony,
Senate Armed Services Committee,
Jan. 15, 1953

[Often misquoted as, "What is good for General Motors is good for the country." Mr. Wilson, chairman of General Motors, made the remark in hearings on his nomination to be Secretary of Defense. Wilson's comment is a qualified version of Calvin Coolidge's blunt judgment that the business of America is business; see under AMERICA & AMERICANS.]

There was a time when corporations played a minor part in our business affairs, but now they play the chief part, and most men are the servants of corporations.
——WOODROW WILSON, *The New Freedom*

C

CANADA   See NATIONS

CAPITALISM   See also BUSINESS; COMMUNISM;
                              ECONOMICS; MONEY; SOCIALISM;
                                          WORK & WORKERS

A market is a place set apart for men to deceive and
get the better of one another.
  —ANACHARSIS, quoted in Diogenes Laërtius,
      Lives of Eminent Philosophers

Laissez faire.
Let business go forward. No interference.
  —MARQUIS D' ARGENSON, *Mémoires*, 1736, Vol. 5
[The phrase is difficult to translate and has complicated
origins: *The Concise Oxford Dictionary of Quotations*
notes that in 1751, when Jean Baptiste Colbert, France's
minister of finance, asked a group of commerce deputies
what he could do to help business, one of them replied,
"Laissez-nous faire," which may be translated: "Let us
get on with it." In 1758, in a speech, the economist
Vincent de Gournay urged, *"Laissez faire, laissez passer,"* calling for free passage of goods and people; the
phrase was a favorite with him. François Quesnay also
used *"laissez passer . . . laissez faire"* with reference to
buyers, sellers, and sound commerce.]

Capital has its rights, which are as worthy of protection as any other rights.
  —ABRAHAM LINCOLN,
      first annual message to Congress, Dec. 3, 1861.

[But see also his comments on labor under WORK & WORKERS.]

The forces of a capitalist society, if left unchecked, tend to make the rich richer and the poor poorer.
—JAWAHARLAL NEHRU, *Credo*

La propriété c'est le vol.
Property is theft. —PIERRE-JOSEPH PROUDHON,
Qu'est-ce que la propriété?

The revolution eats its own. Capitalism recreates itself. —MORDECAI RICHLER, *Cocksure*

Property is organized robbery.
—GEORGE BERNARD SHAW,
Major Barbara, Preface

Every individual . . . intends only his own gain, and he is in this, as in many other cases, led by an invisible hand to promote an end which was no part of his intention. By pursuing his own interest he frequently promotes that of the society more effectively than when he really intends to promote it. I have never known much good done by those who affected to trade for the public good. —ADAM SMITH, *Wealth of Nations*

It is not from the benevolence of the butcher, the brewer, or the baker that we expect our dinner, but from their regard to their own self-interest.
—*Ibid.*

Conspicuous consumption of valuable goods is a means of reputability to the gentleman of leisure.
—THORSTEIN VEBLEN, *The Theory of the Leisure Class*

The trouble with the profit system has always been that it was highly unprofitable to most people.
—E. B. WHITE, *One Man's Meat*

CARDS   See GAMES

CARS   See TECHNOLOGY

CATS   See NATURE: ANIMALS

CAUTION   See PRUDENCE & PRACTICAL WISDOM

CENSORSHIP   See also FREE SPEECH; PRESS, THE

Every suppressed or expunged word reverberates through the earth from side to side.
　　　　　　—RALPH WALDO EMERSON, *Compensation*

Wherever they burn books, they will also, in the end, burn people.   —HEINRICH HEINE, *Almansor*

As good almost kill a man as kill a good book: who kills a man kills a reasonable creature, God's image; but he who destroys a good book kills reason itself.
　　　　　　—JOHN MILTON, *Areopagitica*

Scenes of passion should not be introduced when not essential to the plot. In general, passion should be so treated that these scenes do not stimulate the lower and baser element.
　　　　　　—THE MOTION PICTURE PRODUCERS AND
　　　　　　DISTRIBUTORS OF AMERICA, INC.,
　　　　　　Code for the Industry, 1931

Sex perversion or any inference of it is forbidden. White slavery shall not be treated. Miscegenation is forbidden. . . . Scenes of actual childbirth, in fact or in silhouette, are never to be represented.   —*Ibid.*

Assassination is the extreme form of censorship.
　　　　　　—GEORGE BERNARD SHAW,
　　　　　　The Rejected Statement

We write frankly and freely but then we "modify" before we print.
　　　　　　—MARK TWAIN, *Life on the Mississippi*
[Self-censorship—a hot contemporary issue, an old problem.]

CEYLON See NATIONS

CHANGE See also NEW THINGS;
PROGRESS; VARIETY

Nature's mighty law is change.
—ROBERT BURNS, *Let Not Women E'er Complain*

Change is inevitable in a progressive society. Change
is constant.
—BENJAMIN DISRAELI, speech, Oct. 20, 1867

Unless one says goodbye to what one loves, and unless one travels to completely new territories, one can
expect merely a long wearing away of oneself and an
eventual extinction.
—JEAN DUBUFFET,
quoted in *The New York Times*,
obituary, May 15, 1985

For the times they are a-changin'.
—BOB DYLAN,
The Times They Are a-Changin'

You can't step twice into the same river.
—HERACLITUS, *On the Universe*

Everything flows, nothing stays still.
—HERACLITUS, quoted in Plato, *Cratylus*

Nothing is permanent but change.
—HERACLITUS, quoted in Diogenes Laërtius,
Lives of Eminent Philosophers

Plus ça change, plus c'est la même chose.
The more things change, the more they remain the
same. —ALPHONSE KARR, *Les Guêpes*

The wind of change is blowing through this Conti-
nent.
—HAROLD MACMILLAN, speech, Cape Town,
Feb. 3, 1960
[More of this is given at NATIONS.]

The basic fact of today is the tremendous pace of change in human life.
>   —JAWAHARLAL NEHRU, *Credo*

The old order changeth, yielding place to new,
And God fulfills Himself in many ways,
Lest one good custom should corrupt the world.
>   —ALFRED, LORD TENNYSON, *Morte D'Arthur*
[Later added to *Idylls of the King*.]

CHARITY   See CHARITY: PHILANTHROPY;
>   LOVE & CHARITY: BIBLICAL REFERENCES

CHARITY: PHILANTHROPY

All that is not given is lost.
>   —ANONYMOUS (INDIAN PROVERB),
>   associated with Calcutta

The living need charity more than the dead.
>   —GEORGE ARNOLD, *The Jolly Old Pedagogue*

Cast thy bread upon the waters.
>   —BIBLE, *Ecclesiastes* 11:1

Take heed that ye do not your alms before men, to be seen of them: otherwise you have no reward of your Father which is in heaven.

Therefore when thou doest thine alms, do not sound a trumpet before thee, as the hypocrites do in the synagogues and in the streets, that they may have glory of men. Verily, I say unto you, They have their reward.

But when thou doest alms, let not thy left hand know what thy right hand doeth.
>   —BIBLE, *Matthew* 6:1–3

Jesus said unto him, If thou wilt be perfect, go and sell that thou hast, and give to the poor, and thou shalt have treasure in heaven.   —BIBLE, *Matthew* 19:21

I was an hungred, and ye gave me meat: I was thirsty, and ye gave me drink: I was a stranger, and ye took me in:

Naked, and ye clothed me: I was sick, and ye visited me: I was in prison, and ye came unto me.
——*Ibid.*, 25:35, 36

It is more blessed to give than to receive.
——BIBLE, *Acts* 20:35

God loveth a cheerful giver.
——BIBLE, *II Corinthians* 9:7

He is rich who hath enough to be charitable.
——SIR THOMAS BROWNE, *Religio medici*

Philanthropy is commendable, but it must not cause the philanthropist to overlook the circumstances of economic injustice which make philanthropy necessary.
——MARTIN LUTHER KING, JR.,
Strength of Love

He gives twice who gives promptly.
——PUBLILIUS SYRUS, *Moral Sayings*
[Also, Cervantes in *Don Quixote:* "He that gives quickly gives twice."]

CHARM   See also BEAUTY; GRACE

It's a sort of bloom on a woman. If you have it, you don't need to have anything else; and if you don't have it, it doesn't much matter what else you have.
——J. M. BARRIE, *What Every Woman Knows*

Charm is a way of getting the answer yes without ever having asked a clear question.
——ALBERT CAMUS, *The Fall*

All charming people have something to conceal, usually their total dependence on the appreciation of others.   ——CYRIL CONNOLLY, *Enemies of Promise*

He had that nameless charm, with a strong magnetism, which can only be called "It."
——ELINOR GLYN, *It*
[The movie made from Glyn's 1927 novel starred Clara Bow, the "it" girl. The term probably had been around for a while. "It" appears in Kipling's *Traffic and Dis-*

coveries, published in 1904: "'Tisn't beauty, so to speak, nor good talk, necessarily. It's just It. Some women'll stay in a man's memory if they once walk down a street."]

All charming people, I fancy, are spoiled. It is the secret of their attraction.
　　　　　—OSCAR WILDE, *The Portrait of Mr. W. H.*

CHICAGO   See CITIES

CHILDREN & CHILDHOOD   See also INNOCENCE; FAMILY; PARENTS & PARENTHOOD

Out of the mouth of babes and sucklings hast thou ordained strength.　　　　　—BIBLE, *Psalms* 8:2

A little child shall lead them.
　　　　　　　　　　—BIBLE, *Isaiah* 11:6
[The entire verse is given under PEACE.]

But whoso shall offend one of these little ones which believe in me, it were better for him that a millstone were hanged about his neck, and that he were drowned in the depth of the sea.　　　—BIBLE, *Matthew* 18:6

Suffer the little children to come unto me, and forbid them not: for of such is the kingdom of God.
　　　　　　　　　　—BIBLE, *Mark* 10:14

When I was a child, I spake as a child, I understood as a child, I thought as a child: but when I became a man, I put away childish things.
　　　　　　　　　　—BIBLE, *I Corinthians* 9:11

Every baby born into the world is a finer one than the last.　　—CHARLES DICKENS, *Nicholas Nickleby*

There is always one moment in childhood when the door opens and lets the future in.
　　　　　　　　　　—GRAHAM GREENE,
　　　　　　　　　　　The Power and the Glory

Between the dark and the daylight,
When the night is beginning to lower,

Comes a pause in the day's occupations,
That is known as the Children's Hour.
>   —HENRY WADSWORTH LONGFELLOW,
>   *The Children's Hour*

There was a little girl
Who had a little curl
Right in the middle of her forehead;
And when she was good
She was very, very good,
But when she was bad she was horrid.
>   —HENRY WADSWORTH LONGFELLOW,
>   *There Was a Little Girl*

Childhood is the kingdom where no one dies.
>   —EDNA ST. VINCENT MILLAY, title of poem in
>   *Wine from these Grapes*

Children's games are hardly games. Children are never more serious than when they play.
>   —MONTAIGNE, *Essays*

Of all the animals, the boy is the most unmanageable.
>   —PLATO, *Theaetetus*

But soon a milder age will follow. An age of truer wisdom.
Then the careful state will spare her children.
>   —J. C. F. VON SCHILLER,
>   *Don Carlos*

A child should always say what's true
And speak when he is spoken to,
And behave mannerly at table:
At least as far as he is able.
>   —ROBERT LOUIS STEVENSON,
>   *A Child's Garden of Verses*

A baby is an inestimable blessing and bother.
>   —MARK TWAIN, letter to Annie Webster,
>   Sept. 1, 1876

Our birth is but a sleep and a forgetting:
The soul that rises with us, our life's Star,
Hath had elsewhere its setting,

And cometh from afar:
Not in entire forgetfulness,
And not in utter nakedness,
But trailing clouds of glory do we come
From God, who is our home:
Heaven lies about us in our infancy!
—WILLIAM WORDSWORTH,
Intimations of Immortality

The child is father of the man.
—WILLIAM WORDSWORTH,
My Heart Leaps Up

CHINA   See NATIONS; ORIENT, THE

CHRIST   See CHRISTMAS; JESUS

CHRISTMAS   See also JESUS

And she brought forth her first-born son, and
wrapped him in swaddling clothes, and laid him in a
manger; because there was no room for them in the
inn.   —BIBLE, *Luke* 2:7

Glory to God in the highest, and on earth peace,
good will toward men.   —*Ibid.*, 2:14

"Bah," said Scrooge. "Humbug!
—CHARLES DICKENS,
A Christmas Carol

"God bless us every one!" said Tiny Tim, the last of
all.   —*Ibid.*

A cold coming we had of it,
Just the worst time of the year.
—T. S. ELIOT,
Journey of the Magi

It was the winter wild
While the Heaven-born child
All meanly wrapt in the rude manger lies.
—JOHN MILTON,
On the Morning of Christ's Nativity

'Twas the night before Christmas, when all through
  the house
Not a creature was stirring, not even a mouse;
The stockings were hung by the chimney with care,
In hopes that St. Nicholas soon would be there.
The children were nestled all snug in their beds,
While visions of sugar-plums danced in their heads.
    —CLEMENT C. MOORE,
     The Night Before Christmas

Now, *Dasher!* now, *Dancer!* now, *Prancer* and *Vixen!*
On, *Comet!* on, *Cupid!* on, *Donner* and *Blitzen!*
       —*Ibid.*

He had a broad face and a little round belly,
That shook when he laughed, like a bowlful of
  jelly.   —*Ibid.*

But I heard him exclaim, ere he drove out of sight,
"Happy Christmas to all and to all a good night!"
       —*Ibid.*

Heap on more wood! the wind is chill,
But let it whistle as it will,
We'll keep our Christmas merry still.
    —SIR WALTER SCOTT,
     Marmion

The time draws near the birth of Christ;
The moon is hid; the night is still;
The Christmas bells from hill to hill
Answer each other in the mist
   —ALFRED, LORD TENNYSON, *In Memoriam*

CHURCH   See RELIGION

CITIES

 Ten measures of beauty came into the world; Jerusalem received nine measures, and the rest of the world
one.   —ANONYMOUS (HEBREW PROVERB)

See Naples and die.   —ANONYMOUS (ITALIAN
                                          PROVERB)

Omnis civitas corpus est.
Every city is a living body.
                    —ST. AUGUSTINE, *City of God*
[Plutarch expressed a similar idea: "A city, like a living
thing, is a united and continuous whole," *Morals*.]

And this is good old Boston,
The home of the bean and the cod,
Where the Lowells talk to the Cabots
And the Cabots talk only to God.
                    —JOHN COLLINS BOSSIDY, toast at
                        Holy Cross alumni dinner, 1910

Everyone soon or late comes round by Rome.
        —ROBERT BROWNING, *The Ring and the Book*

Match me such a marvel save in Eastern clime,
A rose-red city "half as old as time."
                    —JOHN WILLIAM BURGON, *Petra*

Carthago delenda est.
Carthage must be destroyed.
                    —CATO, in speeches after the
                        Second Punic War

Chicago is the product of modern capitalism, and,
like other great commercial centers, is unfit for human
habitation.   —EUGENE DEBS 1908,
                    quoted in Kevin Tierney, *Darrow*
[Hostility to cities is a constant theme in American politics; see also the Jefferson and *New York Daily News*
quotes below.]

The first requisite to happiness is to be born in a
famous city.   —EURIPIDES, *On Alcibiades*

On the whole I'd rather be in Philadelphia.
                    —W. C. FIELDS, epitaph
[See also Fields in INSULTS & PUT-DOWNS.]

If you are lucky enough to have lived in Paris as a young man, then wherever you go for the rest of your life, it stays with you, for Paris is a moveable feast.
—ERNEST HEMINGWAY,
A Moveable Feast, epigraph
[For another appreciation of Paris, see Henry IV at EXPEDIENCY.]

It couldn't have happened anywhere but in little old New York. —O. HENRY, *A Little Local Color*

O sweep of stars over Harlem streets,
O little breath of oblivion that is night.
A city building to a mother's song,
A city dreaming to a lullaby.
—LANGSTON HUGHES,
"Stars," in *From My People*

When we get piled upon one another in large cities, as in Europe, we shall become as corrupt as Europe.
—THOMAS JEFFERSON,
letter to James Madison, 1787

By seeing London, I have seen as much of life as the world can show.
—SAMUEL JOHNSON, quoted by James Boswell, *Tour to the Hebrides*

Washington is a city of southern efficiency and northern charm. —JOHN F. KENNEDY, quoted in
Arthur M. Schlesinger, Jr.,
A Thousand Days

[Re New York:] There is no greenery. It is enough to make a stone sad.
—NIKITA KHRUSHCHEV, cited by Bruce Weber, *The New York Times*, June 21, 1992

Ford to City: Drop Dead.
—New York DAILY NEWS
headline, Oct. 30, 1975
[President Gerald Ford had just pledged to veto any bill that would provide bailout funds for the nearly bankrupt New York City. Columnist Jimmy Breslin re-

calls that the two reporters who came up with this line were William Brink and Michael O'Neill.]

Today's city is the most vulnerable social structure ever conceived by man.   —MARTIN OPPENHEIMER,
Urban Guerilla

[Re Pittsburgh:] Hell with the lid taken off.
—JAMES PARTON,
article in *Atlantic Monthly*, 1868

Any ordinary city is in fact two cities, one the city of the poor and the other the city of the rich, each at war with the other.   —PLATO, *The Republic*

Cities are the abyss of the human species.
—JEAN JACQUES ROUSSEAU, *Émile*

Hog butcher for the world,
Tool maker, stacker of wheat,
Player with railroads and the nation's freight handler;
Stormy, husky, brawling,
City of the big shoulders.   —CARL SANDBURG,
Chicago

What is the city but the people?
—SHAKESPEARE,
Coriolanus, III, i

Hell is a city much like London—
A populous and smoky city.
—PERCY BYSSHE SHELLEY, *Peter Bell the Third*

The City is of night; perchance of death,
But certainly of night.
—JAMES THOMSON, *The City of Dreadful Night*

CIVIL SERVANTS   See GOVERNMENT

CIVILIZATION   See also MODERN TIMES; PROGRESS

The three great elements of modern civilization, Gunpowder, Printing, and the Protestant Religion.
—THOMAS CARLYLE,
The State of German Literature

Civilized men arrive in the Pacific, armed with alcohol, syphilis, trousers, and the Bible.
—HAVELOCK ELLIS, *The Dance of Life*

We think our civilization near its meridian, but we are yet only at the cock-crowing and the morning star.
—RALPH WALDO EMERSON, *Politics*

The resources of civilization are not yet exhausted.
—W. E. GLADSTONE, speech, May 7, 1877

What men call civilization
always results in deserts.   —DON MARQUIS,
archy and mehitabel

Our civilization depends largely on paper.
—PLINY, *Natural History*

Civilization is the progress toward a society of privacy.   —AYN RAND, *The Fountainhead*

You can't say civilization don't advance . . . in every war they kill you in a new way.
—WILL ROGERS, *The Autobiography of Will Rogers*

Civilization advances by extending the number of important operations which we can perform without thinking about them.   —ALFRED NORTH WHITEHEAD,
An Introduction to Mathematics

CLEANLINESS

[Re not doing housework:] After the first four years, the dirt doesn't get any worse.
—QUENTIN CRISP, *The Naked Civil Servant*

Cleanliness is indeed next to godliness.
—JOHN WESLEY, sermon 93

CLERGY	See GOD; RELIGION
CLOTHES	See FASHION & CLOTHES
COLOR	See ARTS: PAINTING
COMEDY	See HUMOR
COMMUNICATION	See CONVERSATION; LANGUAGE & WORDS; MEDIA; TALK
COMMUNISM	See also CAPITALISM; ECONOMICS; REVOLUTION; SOCIALISM

That which is common to the greatest number has the least care bestowed upon it.
—ARISTOTLE, *Politics*

From Stettin in the Baltic to Trieste in the Adriatic, an iron curtain has descended across the Continent.
—WINSTON CHURCHILL, speech, March 5, 1946
[Churchill made the phrase famous. *Bartlett's*, however, notes several earlier uses, including one by Queen Elizabeth of Belgium in 1914, referring to Germany. *The Penguin Dictionary of Quotations* cites an article by St. Vincent Troubridge in 1945, stating, "There is an iron curtain across Europe." William Safire, in his dictionary of political terms, points out that the phrase has a theatrical origin, an iron curtain having been used in theaters since the 18th century to retard fires. He believes the metaphor was used in the political sense as early as 1819, and notes that Goebbels, in 1945, employed it with specific reference to Russia.]

What is a communist? One who hath yearnings
For equal division of unequal earnings.
—EBENEZER ELLIOTT, *Epigram*

[Communism] has never come to power in a country that was not disrupted by war or internal corruption or both.   —JOHN F. KENNEDY, speech, July 3, 1963

We Communists are like seeds and the people are the soil. Wherever we go, we must unite with the people, take root and blossom among them.
—Mao Zedung, *Quotations from Chairman Mao Zedung*, 1966

A specter is haunting Europe—the specter of Communism.
—Karl Marx, *Manifesto of the Communist Party*

From each according to his abilities, and to each according to his needs. —Karl Marx, *Critique of the Gotha Program*

Its [Communism's] unfortunate association with violence encourages a certain evil tendency in human beings. —Jawaharlal Nehru, *Credo*

The economy of Communism is an economy which grows in an atmosphere of misery and want.
—Eleanor Roosevelt, *My Day*, syndicated column, Feb. 12, 1947

Communism is the corruption of a dream of justice.
—Adlai Stevenson, speech, Urbana, Ill., 1951

COMPARISONS

Comparisons are odious.
—John Fortescue, *De Laudibus Legum Angliae* [*Bartlett's* gives this as the earliest use, noting that the phrase was common in the 14th century; and it appears often thereafter. Shakespeare wrote "Comparisons are *odorous*"—italics added—*Much Ado About Nothing*, III, v.]

COMPASSION & PITY   See also FORGIVENESS & MERCY

One cannot weep for the entire world. It is beyond human strength. One must choose.
—Jean Anouilh, *Cecile*

To him that is afflicted pity should be showed from his friend.   —BIBLE, *Job* 6:14

Human it is to have compassion on the unhappy.
         —BOCCACCIO, opening line of the *Decameron*

More helpful than all wisdom is one draught of simple human pity that will not forsake us.
                              —GEORGE ELIOT,
                              The Mill on the Floss

The poetry is in the pity.   —WILFRED OWEN,
                              Poems, Preface
[More at ARTS: POETRY.]

No beast so fierce but knows some touch of pity.
              —SHAKESPEARE, *Richard III*, I, ii

Pity is the virtue of the law.
                              —SHAKESPEARE,
                              Timon of Athens, III, v
[The meaning is that pity, or mercy, is the best characteristic of law.]

CONFIDENCE   See BOLDNESS & INITIATIVE;
                              SELF-CONFIDENCE

CONFLICT   See also TROUBLE; TURBULENT TIMES;
                              UNITY & LOYALTY; WAR

Every kingdom divided against itself is brought to desolation; and every city or house divided against itself, shall not stand.   —BIBLE, *Matthew* 12:25
[*Mark* 3:25 reads: "If a house be divided against itself, that house cannot stand." For Lincoln's use of the thought, see under AMERICAN HISTORY: MEMORABLE MOMENTS.]

When one prefers one's own children to the children of others, war is near.   —MAHABHARATA

CONSCIENCE   See also ETHICS & MORALITY

Conscience is the perfect interpreter of life.
              —KARL BARTH, *The Word of God and the Word of Man*

I cannot and will not cut my conscience to suit this year's fashions.
—LILLIAN HELLMAN, letter to the chairman of the House Committee on Un-American Activities, May 19, 1952

Conscience is the inner voice that warns us somebody may be looking.   —H. L. MENCKEN, *A Mencken Chrestomathy*, 1949

CONSISTENCY

Consistency requires you to be as ignorant today as you were a year ago.   —BERNARD BERENSON, *Notebook*, 1892

A foolish consistency is the hobgoblin of little minds, adored by little statesmen and philosophers and divines.
—RALPH WALDO EMERSON, *Self-Reliance*

Do I contradict myself?
Very well then I contradict myself,
(I am large, I contain multitudes.)
—WALT WHITMAN, "Song of Myself," in *Leaves of Grass*

CONVERSATION   See also TALK

"The time has come," the Walrus said,
"To talk of many things:
Of shoes—and ships—and sealing wax—
Of cabbages—and kings—
And why the sea is boiling hot—
And whether pigs have wings."
—LEWIS CARROLL, *Through the Looking-Glass*

In the room the women come and go
Talking of Michelangelo.
—T. S. ELIOT, *The Love Song of J. Alfred Prufrock*

If you can't say anything good about someone, sit right here by me.
> —ALICE ROOSEVELT LONGWORTH, saying, quoted in *The New York Times*, obituary

We do not talk—we bludgeon one another with facts and theories gleaned from cursory readings of newspapers, magazines, and digests.
> —HENRY MILLER, "The Shadows," in *The Air-Conditioned Nightmare*

The more the pleasures of the body fade away, the greater to me is the pleasure and charm of conversation.
> —PLATO, *The Republic*

Teas,
Where small talk dies in agonies.
> —PERCY BYSSHE SHELLEY, *Peter Bell the Third*

I cannot hold with those who wish to put down the insignificant chatter of the world.
> —ANTHONY TROLLOPE, *Framley Parsonage*

COUNTRY, ONE'S OWN   See PATRIOTISM

COUNTRY, THE   See also NATURE

Nothing ages a woman like living in the country.
> —COLETTE, *On Tour*

It is my belief, Watson, founded upon my experience, that the lowest and vilest alleys in London do not present a more dreadful record of sin than does the smiling and beautiful countryside.
> —A. CONAN DOYLE, *Adventure of the Copper Beeches*

When I am in the country I wish to vegetate like the country.
> —WILLIAM HAZLITT, *On Going a Journey*

I have no relish for the country; it is a kind of healthy grave.
> —SYDNEY SMITH, letter to Miss G. Harcourt, 1838

Anybody can be good in the country.
—OSCAR WILDE, *The Picture of Dorian Gray*

COURAGE   See also BOLDNESS & INITIATIVE;
                     FEAR; HEROES

Often the test of courage is not to die but to live.
—VITTORIO ALFIERI, *Oreste*

Until the day of his death, no man can be sure of his
courage.   —JEAN ANOUILH, *Becket*

Courage is almost a contradiction in terms. It means
a strong desire to live taking the form of a readiness to
die.   —G. K. CHESTERTON, *Orthodoxy*

Tender-handed stroke a nettle,
And it stings you for your pains;
Grasp it like a man of mettle,
And it soft as silk remains.
—AARON HILL, *Verses Written on a
Window in Scotland*

One man with courage makes a majority.
—ANDREW JACKSON, saying
[For a majority consisting of one man with God, see
under Knox at GOD. See also Coolidge at LAW.]

Cowards die many times before their deaths;
The valiant never taste of death but once.
—SHAKESPEARE, *Julius Caesar*, II, ii

But screw your courage to the sticking place
And we'll not fail.
—SHAKESPEARE, *Macbeth*, I, vii

Courage is resistance to fear, mastery of fear—not
absence of fear. —MARK TWAIN,
"Pudd'nhead Wilson's Calendar,"
in *Pudd'nhead Wilson*

CRAFTINESS   See also DISHONESTY & LIES

To make a living, craftiness is better than learnedness.   —PIERRE-AUGUSTIN DE BEAUMARCHAIS,
The Marriage of Figaro

Let not thy left hand know what thy right hand doeth.
—BIBLE, *Matthew* 6:3
[For the context, see CHARITY: PHILANTHROPY.]

Make to yourselves friends of the mammon of unrighteousness.   —BIBLE, *Luke* 16:9

Open not thine heart to every man, lest he requite thee with a shrewd turn.

—BIBLE, *Ecclesiasticus* 8:19

Never fight fair with a stranger, boy. You'll never get out of the jungle that way.

—ARTHUR MILLER, *Death of a Salesman*

The fox knows many tricks, but the hedgehog's trick is the best of all.   —PIGRES, attributed by Zenobius
[A different version of this, attributed to Archilochus, is given under WISDOM.]

I know a trick worth two of that.
—SHAKESPEARE, *Henry IV, Part I*, II, i

Friends, Romans, countrymen, lend me your ears;
I come to bury Caesar, not to praise him.
—SHAKESPEARE, *Julius Caesar*, III, ii

CREATION, DIVINE   See also NATURE; SCIENCES:
PHYSICS & COSMOLOGY;
UNIVERSE

All things bright and beautiful
All creatures great and small,
All things wise and wonderful,
The Lord God made them all.
—CECIL FRANCES ALEXANDER, hymn,
All Things Bright and Beautiful

In the beginning God created the heaven and the earth.

And the earth was without form, and void; and darkness was upon the face of the deep. And the spirit of God moved upon the face of the waters.

And God said, Let there be light: and there was light.   —BIBLE, *Genesis* 1:1–4

We made from water every living thing. —KORAN

Nothing can be created out of nothing.
                                —Lucretius,
                                De rerum natura

CRIME   See also DANGEROUS PEOPLE; EVIDENCE;
                                EVIL; GUILT; PUNISHMENT;
                                VIOLENCE & FORCE

Murder will out.   —ANONYMOUS (PROVERB)
[The idea has been expressed by many writers, including Chaucer, John Webster, Shakespeare, and Emerson— see their quotes below.]

Le mauvais goût mène au crime.
Poor taste leads to crime.
        —ANONYMOUS (FRENCH PROVERB), quoted by
        A. Conan Doyle in *The Sign of Four*

And the Lord set a mark upon Cain.
                                —BIBLE, *Genesis* 4:15

These, having not the law, are a law unto themselves.
                                —BIBLE, *Romans* 2:14

The soul of a murderer is blind.
                                —ALBERT CAMUS, *The Plague*

Murder will out, certain, it will not fail.
                        —CHAUCER, "The Prioress's Tale,"
                        in *The Canterbury Tales*
[One of many expressions of this proverbial concept; see the first entry in this section.]

If once a man indulges himself in murder, very soon he comes to think little of robbing; and from robbing he comes next to drinking and Sabbath-breaking, and from that to incivility and procrastination.

> —THOMAS DE QUINCEY,
> *Murder Considered as One
> of the Fine Arts*

It's a wicked world, and when a clever man turns his brains to crime, it is the worst of all.

> —A. CONAN DOYLE,
> *Adventure of the Speckled Band*

Any man might do a girl in
Any man has to, needs to wants to
Once in a lifetime, do a girl in.

> —T. S. ELIOT, *Sweeney Agonistes*

[Dickens, in *Our Mutual Friend*, similarly commented on the universality of homicidal feelings: "If a murder, anybody might have done it. Burglary or pocket-picking wanted 'prenticeship. Not so murder. We were all of us up to that."]

Character is always known. Thefts never enrich; alms never impoverish; murder will speak out of stone walls.

> —RALPH WALDO EMERSON, commencement
> address, Harvard Divinity School, 1838

[The concept that even stones will testify against atrocities appears in the Bible in *Habakkuk* 2:11, "The stone shall cry out of the wall"; and in *Luke* 19:40. Shakespeare used the image twice in *Macbeth*: "The very stones prate of my whereabout," II, i; and "Blood will have blood./ Stones have been known to move and trees to speak," III, iv.]

Round up the usual suspects.

> —JULIUS EPSTEIN, PHILIP EPSTEIN,
> and HOWARD KOCH, *Casablanca*

Cherchez la femme.
Find the woman.   —JOSEPH FOUCHÉ, attributed

[Also used by Alexandre Dumas in *The Mohicans of Paris*, one of the first collections of detective stories: "There is a woman in every case; as soon as they bring me a report, I say, 'Look for the woman.' " Fouché, by the way, was Napoleon's feared minister of justice.]

I've got a little list—I've got a little list.
Of society offenders who might well be underground,
And who never would be missed—who never would
be missed.   —W. S. GILBERT, *The Mikado*

The policeman's lot is not a happy one.
        —W. S. GILBERT, *Pirates of Penzance*

It was beautiful and simple, as all truly great swindles
are.   —O. HENRY, "The Octopus Marooned," in
        The Gentle Grafter

Crime, like virtue, has its degrees.
        —RACINE, *Phèdre*

Successful and fortunate crime is called virtue.
        —SENECA, *Hercules Furens*

Murder most foul, as in the best it is,
But this most foul, strange, and unnatural.
        —SHAKESPEARE *Hamlet*, I, v

Murder, though it have no tongue, will speak.
        —SHAKESPEARE, *Hamlet*, II, ii
[Similarly, Shakespeare wrote, "Truth will come to
light; murder cannot be hid long," *The Merchant of
Venice* II, ii; and in *Richard III*, a murderer concludes,
"This will out," I, iv. See also the quotes from Emerson,
above, and John Webster, below.]

Yet who would have thought the old man to have
had so much blood in him?   —SHAKESPEARE,
        Macbeth, V, i

The robbed that smiles steals something from the
thief.   —SHAKESPEARE, *Othello*, I, iii

He who bears the brand of Cain shall rule the earth.
        —GEORGE BERNARD SHAW, *Back to Methuselah*

People of the same trade seldom meet together, even
for merriment and diversion, but the conversation ends
in a conspiracy against the public, or in some contrivance to raise prices.   —ADAM SMITH,
        Wealth of Nations

Why do you rob banks?
Because that's where the money is.
                    —WILLIE SUTTON, attributed
[A famous line, but Mr. Sutton, a notorious bank robber, disclaimed it, crediting a reporter with making it up.]

The rich rob the poor and the poor rob one another.
                    —SOJOURNER TRUTH, saying

Other sins only speak; murder shrieks out.
                    —JOHN WEBSTER, *The Duchess of Malfi*

Yet each man kills the thing he loves
. . . . The coward does it with a kiss,
The brave man with a sword.
                    —OSCAR WILDE, *The Ballad of Reading Gaol*

CRISIS   See MIDDLE AGE & MID-LIFE
                          CRISIS; RUIN; TROUBLE;
                          TURBULENT TIMES

CRITICISM   See ADVICE;
                    ARTS: CRITICISM & CRITICS

CULTURE   See ARTS entries;
                    CIVILIZATION; EDUCATION

CUSTOM   See also HABIT; MANNERS

Custom reconciles us to everything.
    —EDMUND BURKE, *On the Sublime and Beautiful*

Custom, then, is the great guide of human life.
                    —DAVID HUME, *An Enquiry Concerning
                    Human Understanding*

Custom is king over all.   —PINDAR, fragment

It is a custom
More honored in the breach than the observance.
                    —SHAKESPEARE, *Hamlet*, I, iv
[The custom was the Danish habit of draining a goblet
of wine with each toast.]

D

DANCE   See ARTS: MUSIC DANCE

DANGER   See also DANGEROUS PEOPLE; EVIL;
                                            RUIN; TROUBLE;
                                            TURBULENT TIMES

Dangers by being despised grow great.
> —EDMUND BURKE, speech on the Petition
> of the Unitarians, 1792

'Twas brillig, and the slithy toves
Did gyre and gimble in the wabe;
All mimsy were the borogoves,
And the mome raths outgrabe.
Beware the Jabberwock, my son!
The jaws that bite, the claws that catch!
Beware the Jubjub bird, and shun
The frumious Bandersnatch!
> —LEWIS CARROLL, "Jabber-
> wocky," in *Through the
> Looking-Glass*

Nothing in life is so exhilarating as to be shot at
without result.
> —WINSTON CHURCHILL,
>   *The Story of the Malakand Field Force*

[Often misquoted as: ". . . shot at and missed." U.S.
President Ronald Reagan, in 1981, after being wounded
in an assassination attempt, offered a close variant on
Churchill's observation: "There is no more exhilarating
feeling than being shot at without result."]

To vanquish without danger is to triumph without glory.
—PIERRE CORNEILLE, *Le Cid*

Wisdom consists in being able to distinguish among dangers and make a choice of the least harmful.
—MACHIAVELLI, *The Prince*

Beware the ides of March.
—SHAKESPEARE, *Julius Caesar*, I, ii

A snake lurks in the grass.   —VIRGIL, *Eclogues*

DANGEROUS PEOPLE   See also DANGER;
EVIL; POWER

He stood a stranger in this breathing world,
An erring spirit from another hurled;
A thing of dark imaginings.

—LORD BYRON, *Lara*

People who make no noise are dangerous.
—LA FONTAINE, *Fables*

Yond Cassius has a lean and hungry look;
He thinks too much: such men are dangerous.
—SHAKESPEARE, *Julius Caesar*, I, ii

DAY   See NATURE: TIMES OF DAY

DEATH   See also EPITAPHS; IMMORTALITY; LAST
JUDGMENT & THE
HEREAFTER; SUICIDE

O death, where is thy sting? O grave, where is thy victory?   —BIBLE, *I Corinthians* 15:55

And I looked, and behold a pale horse: and his name that sat on him was Death.   —BIBLE, *Revelation* 6:8

Because I could not stop for Death—
He kindly stopped for me—
The Carriage held but just Ourselves—
And Immortality.

—EMILY DICKINSON, poem no. 712

Death be not proud, though some have called thee
Mighty and dreadful, for, thou art not so,
For, those, whom thou think'st thou dost overthrow,
Die not, poor death, nor yet can'st thou kill me.
—JOHN DONNE, *Death Be Not Proud*

Death is nothing to us, since when we are, death has
not come, and when death has come, we are not.
—EPICURUS, quoted in Diogenes Laërtius,
Lives of Eminent Philosophers

It hath often been said that it is not death but dying
that is terrible.   —HENRY FIELDING, *Amelia*

Let us cross over the river and rest under the shade
of the trees.   —THOMAS "STONEWALL" JACKSON,
dying words, May 10, 1863
[He had been shot inadvertently by his own men.]

Depend upon it, Sir, when a man knows he is to be
hanged in a fortnight, it concentrates his mind won-
derfully.
—SAMUEL JOHNSON, quoted in James
Boswell, *Life of Johnson*, Sept. 19, 1777

The only religious way to think of death is as part
and parcel of life.
—THOMAS MANN, *The Magic Mountain*

Whom the Gods love dies young.
—MENANDER, *The Double Deceiver*
[Expressed by many other writers, including Words-
worth, see below.]

It costs me never a stab nor squirm
To tread by chance upon a worm.
"Aha, my little dear," I say,
"Your clan will pay me back one day."
—DOROTHY PARKER,
Thoughts for a Sunshiny Morning

He hath joined the great majority.
—PETRONIUS, *Satyricon*

Dying
Is an art, like everything else.
—SYLVIA PLATH, *Lady
Lazarus*

*Je vais quérir un grand peut-être. . . . Tirez le rideau,
la farce est jouée,*
I am going to seek a great perhaps. . . . Pull down
the curtain, the farce is ended.
—RABELAIS, by tradition, his last words
[Note similar last words in Leoncavallo, *I Pagliacci*, "*La
commedia è finita*"—"The comedy is ended."]

So little done, so much to do.
—CECIL RHODES, dying words, 1902

When I am dead, my dearest,
Sing no sad songs for me.
—CHRISTINA G. ROSSETTI, *Song*

Death is an evil; the gods have so judged; had it been
good, they would die.   —SAPPHO, fragment

There is no death. Only a change of worlds.
—SEATTLE, quoted in Joseph Epes Brown,
*The Spiritual Legacy of the
American Indian*

I have a rendezvous with Death
At some disputed barricade.
—ALAN SEEGER, *I Have a Rendezvous with Death*

All that live must die,
Passing through nature to eternity.
—SHAKESPEARE, *Hamlet*, I, ii

Alas! poor Yorick. I knew him, Horatio.
—*Ibid.*, V, i

A man can die but once. We owe God a death.
—SHAKESPEARE, *Henry IV, Part II*, III, ii

Men must endure
Their going hence even as their coming hither.
—SHAKESPEARE, *King Lear*, V, ii

Nothing in his life
Became him like the leaving it.
—SHAKESPEARE, *Macbeth*, I, iv

How oft when men are at the point of death
Have they been merry!
—SHAKESPEARE, *Romeo and Juliet*, V, iii

He that dies pays all debts.
—SHAKESPEARE, *The Tempest*, III, ii

Death is the veil which those who live call life:
They sleep, and it is lifted.
—PERCY BYSSHE SHELLEY, *Prometheus Unbound*

A single death is a tragedy, a million deaths is a
statistic.   —JOSEPH STALIN, attributed
[George Seldes in *The Great Quotations* is the only
collector we know to offer even a secondary citation for
this—Anne Fremantle, *The New York Times Book Review*, Sept. 28, 1958.]

Home is the sailor, home from the sea,
And the hunter home from the hill.
—ROBERT LOUIS STEVENSON, *Requiem*
[More at EPITAPHS.]

Sunset and evening star,
And one clear call for me!
And may there be no moaning of the bar,
When I put out to sea.
—ALFRED, LORD TENNYSON, *Crossing the Bar*

He seems so near and yet so far.
—ALFRED, LORD TENNYSON, *In Memoriam*

And a day less or more
At sea or shore,
We die—does it matter when?
—ALFRED, LORD TENNYSON, *The Revenge*

Man comes and tills the field and lies beneath,
And after many a summer dies the swan.
—ALFRED, LORD TENNYSON, *Tithonus*

Do not go gentle into that good night,
Old age should burn and rave at close of day;
Rage, rage against the dying of the light.
—DYLAN THOMAS,
Do Not Go Gentle into That Good Night

Death is not an event in life; we do not experience
death.   —LUDWIG WITTGENSTEIN,
Tractatus logico-philosophicus
[Diderot, in *Le Neveu de Rameau*, said it thus: "The
dead do not hear the bells tolling."]

The good die first,
And they whose hearts are dry as summer dust
Burn to the socket.   —WILLIAM WORDSWORTH,
The Excursion

DECEPTION   See CRAFTINESS; DISHONESTY & LIES

DECISION, MOMENT OF

The die is cast.
—JULIUS CAESAR, quoted in Plutarch, *Lives*

There is a tide in the affairs of men.
—SHAKESPEARE,
Julius Caesar, IV, iii

[More at OPPORTUNITY.]

DEEDS   See ACTION; DOING

DEFEAT   See WINNING & LOSING,
VICTORY & DEFEAT

DELAY   See PROCRASTINATION

DEMOCRACY   See also AMERICA & AMERICANS;
AMERICAN HISTORY: MEMORABLE
MOMENTS; EQUALITY; FREEDOM;
PEOPLE, THE; RIGHTS

Democracy is the worst form of government except
all those other forms that have been tried from time to
time.   —WINSTON CHURCHILL, speech,
House of Commons, Nov. 1947

The ballot is stronger than the bullet.
—ABRAHAM LINCOLN, speech, May 19, 1856

Under democracy, one party always devotes its chief
efforts to trying to prove that the other is unfit to rule
—and both commonly succeed and are right.
—H. L. MENCKEN, *Minority Report:
Mencken's Notebooks*

The blind lead the blind. It's the democratic way.
—HENRY MILLER,
"With Edgard Varèse in the Gobi Desert,"
in *The Air-Conditioned Nightmare*

Democracy and socialism are means to an end, not
the end itself.   —JAWAHARLAL NEHRU, *Credo*

Democracy . . . is a charming form of government,
full of variety and disorder. It dispenses a sort of equality to equals and unequals alike.
—PLATO, *The Republic*

Democracy passes into despotism.   —*Ibid.*

Democracy substitutes election by the incompetent
many for appointment by the corrupt few.
—GEORGE BERNARD SHAW, *Man and Superman*

DEPRESSION   See DESPAIR, DEPRESSION, MISERY

DEPRESSION, ECONOMIC   See ECONOMICS

DESPAIR, DEPRESSION, MISERY   See also
SORROW, SADNESS,
& SUFFERING; SUICIDE;
TROUBLE

My days are swifter than a weaver's shuttle, and are
spent without hope.   —BIBLE, *Job* 5:7

My God, my God, why hast thou forsaken me?
—BIBLE, *Psalms* 22:1; *Matthew* 27:46;
Mark 15:34

Vanity of vanities, saith the preacher, vanity of vanities: all is vanity.   —BIBLE, *Ecclesiastes* 1:2

I write of melancholy, by being busy to avoid mel-
ancholy.
—ROBERT BURTON, *The Anatomy of Melancholy*
[Moods that we would probably associate with "depres-
sion" were in the past commonly called "melancholy."
Burton's more general cure for melancholy is given at
WORK.]

In the real dark night of the soul it is always three
o'clock in the morning.
—F. SCOTT FITZGERALD,
"The Hours," in *The Crack-Up*
[The allusion is to St. John of the Cross; see under
MYSTICISM.]

Here lies one whose name was writ in water.
—JOHN KEATS, epitaph for himself

La chair est triste, hélas! et j'ai lu tous les livres.
The flesh is sad, alas, and I've read all the books.
—STÉPHANE MALLARMÉ, *Brise marine*

O! what a rogue and peasant slave am I.
—SHAKESPEARE, *Hamlet*, II, ii

Tomorrow, and tomorrow, and tomorrow,
Creeps in this petty pace from day to day,
To the last syllable of recorded time.
—SHAKESPEARE, *Macbeth*, V, v

I was much further out than you thought
And not waving but drowning.
—STEVIE SMITH, *Not Waving but Drowning*

DESPOTS   See TYRANNY & TOTALITARIANISM

DESTINY   See FATE

DETECTIVES & DETECTION   See CRIME

DETAILS & OTHER SMALL THINGS

The devil is in the details.
—ANONYMOUS (GERMAN PROVERB)
[This is an old saying, and may not be German in its
ultimate origin. It is popular among diplomats negoti-
ating international treaties. A major variant is "God is
in the details," used by Mies van der Rohe with reference to architecture, but probably also coming from
a much earlier source.]

He that contemneth small things shall fall by little
and little.   —BIBLE, *Ecclesiasticus* 19:1

Little drops of water,
Little grains of sand,
Make the mighty ocean
And the pleasant land:

So the little minutes,
Humble though they be,
Make the mighty ages
Of eternity.

. . .
Little deeds of kindness,
Little words of love,
Help to make earth happy
Like the heaven above.
　　　　　　　—JULIA CARNEY, *Little Things*

Little things affect little minds.
　　　　　　　—BENJAMIN DISRAELI, *Sybil*

I neglect God and his Angels for the noise of a fly,
for the rattling of a coach, for the whining of a door.
　　　—JOHN DONNE, sermon, Dec. 12, 1626

It has long been an axiom of mine that the little
things are infinitely the most important.
　　　　—A. CONAN DOYLE, *A Case of Identity*

Large streams from little fountains flow,
Tall oaks from little acorns grow.
　　　　—DAVID EVERETT,
　　　　　Lines written for a school declamation
[Drawn from proverbial comment on acorns and oaks.]

A little neglect may breed great mischief . . . for the
want of a nail the shoe was lost; for the want of a shoe
the horse was lost; and for the want of a horse the rider
was lost.
　　—BENJAMIN FRANKLIN, *Poor Richard's Almanac*

Men who love wisdom should acquaint themselves
with a great many particulars.
　　　　　　　—HERACLITUS, fragment

Small is beautiful.
　　　　　　　—E. F. SCHUMACHER, book title

Our life is frittered away by detail. . . . Simplify,
simplify.　　　　—HENRY DAVID THOREAU, *Walden*

DEVIL

How art thou fallen from heaven, O Lucifer, son of
the morning!

　　　　　　　—BIBLE, *Isaiah* 14:12

An apology for the Devil: It must be remembered that we have only heard one side of the case. God has written all the books.
> —SAMUEL BUTLER, "Higgledy-Piggledy,"
> in *Notebooks*

Wherever God erects a house of prayer,
The Devil always builds a chapel there,
And 'twill be found upon examination,
The latter has the largest congregation.
> —DANIEL DEFOE, *The True-Born Englishman*

The prince of darkness is a gentleman.
> —SHAKESPEARE, *King Lear*, III, iv

[Also, Percy Bysshe Shelley, "Sometimes / The Devil is a gentleman," *Peter Bell the Third*.]

DICTATORS   See TYRANNY & TOTALITARIANISM

DIPLOMACY   See also NEGOTIATION

Diplomacy is to do and say
The nastiest thing in the nicest way.
> —ISAAC GOLDBERG,
> *The Reflex*

An ambassador is an honest man sent to lie abroad for the good of his country.
> —SIR HENRY WOTTON, *Reliquiae Wottonianae*

All diplomacy is a continuation of war by other means.   —ZHOU EN-LAI, quoted by Edgar Snow, *Saturday Evening Post*, March 27, 1954
[The unstated reference is to von Clausewitz's famous observation on war and diplomacy; see under WAR.]

DISCOVERY   See SCIENCE: DISCOVERY

DISHONESTY & LIES   See also CRAFTINESS;
                                      CRIME; HYPOCRISY

Unless a man feels he has a good enough memory,
he should never venture to lie.

—MONTAIGNE, *Essays*

A lie is an abomination unto the Lord and an ever-
present help in time of need.

—JOHN A. TYLER MORGAN,
comment in the U.S. Senate
[Sen. Morgan of Alabama was an ardent supporter of
a Nicaraguan (not Panamanian) canal; he is quoted in
David McCullough's *The Path Between the Seas*. More
recently, Adlai Stevenson made essentially the same
remark in a speech in Springfield, Ill., Jan 1951.]

White lies always introduce others of a darker com-
plexion.

—WILLIAM PALEY, *The Principles of Moral
and Political Philosophy*

O, what a tangled web we weave,
When first we practise to deceive!

—SIR WALTER SCOTT,
Marmion

Don't lie if you don't have to.

—LEO SZILARD, *Science*,
no. 176, 1972

DOCTORS & THE PRACTICE   See also ILLNESS
OF MEDICINE   & REMEDIES; SCIENCE:
                      PSYCHOLOGY & PSYCHOANALYSIS

Physician, heal thyself.   —BIBLE, *Luke* 4:23
[Identified as a proverb.]

Honour a physician with the honour due unto him
for the uses which you may have of him: for the Lord
hath created him.   —BIBLE, *Ecclesiasticus* 38:1

The most high hath created medicines out of the earth, and a wise man will not abhor them.
—*Ibid.*, 38:4

Every physician almost hath his favorite disease
—HENRY FIELDING, *Tom Jones*

God heals and the doctor takes the fees.
—BENJAMIN FRANKLIN, *Poor Richard's Almanac*

Wherever the art of medicine is loved, there also is love of humanity.   —HIPPOCRATES, *Aphorisms*

The life so short, the craft so long to learn.
—*Ibid.*
[One of the several translations of this saying. See also the first quote at ARTS.]

I often say a great doctor kills more people than a great general.   —G. W. LEIBNIZ, attributed

I hate doctors! They'll do anything—anything to keep you coming to them. They'll sell their souls! What's worse, they'll sell yours, and you never know it till one day you find yourself in hell.
—EUGENE O'NEILL,
Long Day's Journey into Night

Physicians acquire their knowledge from our dangers, making experiments at the cost of our lives.
—PLINY, *Natural History*

Who shall decide when doctors disagree?
—ALEXANDER POPE, *Of the Use of Riches*

Cured yesterday of my disease,
I died last night of the physician.
—MATTHEW PRIOR, *The Remedy Worse
Than the Disease*

DOGS   See NATURE: ANIMALS

DOING   See also ACCOMPLISHMENT; ACTION;
                          EFFORT; PERSEVERANCE & ENDURANCE;
                          VIRTUE; WORK & WORKERS

Whatsoever thy hand findeth to do, do it with thy
might; for there is no work, nor device, nor knowledge,
nor wisdom, in the grave, whither thou goest.
                          —BIBLE, *Ecclesiastes* 9:10

It is better to light one candle than to curse the
darkness.   —CHRISTOPHER SOCIETY, motto
[At VIRTUE, see Adlai Stevenson for his use of this idea
with reference to Eleanor Roosevelt.]

I leave this rule for others when I'm dead,
Be always sure you're right—then go ahead.
    —DAVID CROCKETT, his motto from
        the War of 1812, cited in
        Narrative of the Life of David Crockett, 1834

Our deeds determine us, as much as we determine
our deeds.   —GEORGE ELIOT, *Adam Bede*

Let's meet and either do or die.
                    —JOHN FLETCHER, *The Island Princess*

Do noble things, do not dream them all day long.
                    —CHARLES KINGSLEY, *A Farewell*
[More of this at VIRTUE.]

Watch what we do, not what we say.
                    —JOHN MITCHELL, remark, July 1969
[This is the usual rendering; in *Respectfully Quoted*,
published by the Library of Congress, the line is: "You
will be better advised to watch what we do instead of
what we say." The attorney general was referring to
the Nixon administration's approach to civil rights.]

Men are all alike in their promises. It is only in their deeds that they differ. —MOLIÈRE, *The Miser*

Saying is one thing and doing is another.
　　　　　　　　　　　—MONTAIGNE, *Essays*

Our nature lies in movement; complete rest is death.
　　　　　　　　　　　—PASCAL, *Pensées*

No one knows what he can do till he tries.
　　　　　　　—PUBLILIUS SYRUS, *Moral Sayings*

One must learn by doing the thing; though you think you know it, you have no certainty until you try.
　　　　　　　　　　　—SOPHOCLES, *Trachiniae*
[See also the entry at EDUCATION under Anonymous (Proverb).]

DOUBT　　　　　　　　　　　See SKEPTICISM

DRAMA　　　　　　　See ARTS: DRAMA & ACTING

DREAMERS & DREAMS　　　　　See AMBITION; SCIENCE: PSYCHOLOGY & PSYCHOANALYSIS; SLEEP & DREAMS; VISION & VISIONARIES

DRINKING　　　　　　See ALCOHOL & DRINKING; FOOD, WINE, & EATING

E

EARTH — See CREATION, DIVINE; ENVIRONMENT; NATURE; SCIENCE

EAST, THE — See ORIENT, THE

EATING — See FOOD, WINE, & EATING

ECONOMICS — See also BUSINESS; CAPITALISM; COMMUNISM; MONEY; SOCIALISM; TAXES

There's no such thing as a free lunch.
— ANONYMOUS

[The saying goes back to the 19th century, when bars offered "free" sandwiches and snacks to attract customers—but of course you had to buy a drink to get the food. In 1934, New York Mayor Fiorello La Guardia gave us the Italian version—*E finite la cuccagna!* (quoted in Robert A. Caro, *The Power Brokers*). The phrase was taken up by political conservatives, and is most often associated with economist Milton Friedman. In the form "TANSTAAFL" (There ain't no such thing as a free lunch) the saying was used in one of Robert Heinlein's bestsellers, *The Moon Is a Harsh Mistress*.]

Recession is when your neighbor loses his job; depression is when you lose yours. — ANONYMOUS

[Sometimes attributed to Harry S Truman.]

Voodoo economics.
— GEORGE BUSH, speech, April 1980

[In the Republican presidential primary in Pennsylvania, contender George Bush used this neat phrase to describe the "supply-side" economic theory espoused by his opponent, Ronald Reagan. According to this theory, a tax cut would increase government revenues by stimulating the economy. After Bush became Reagan's running mate, he remarked, "God, I wish I hadn't said that."]

What we might call, by way of eminence, the Dismal Science.
>—THOMAS CARLYLE, *On the Negro Question*

Political institutions are a superstructure resting on an economic foundation.
>—V. I. LENIN, *The Three Sources and Three Constituent Parts of Marxism*

We have heard it said that five percent is the natural interest of money.
>—THOMAS BABINGTON MACAULAY, *Southey's Colloquies on Society*

He is well paid that is well satisfied.
>—SHAKESPEARE, *The Merchant of Venice*, IV, i

The truth is we are all caught in a great economic system which is heartless. —WOODROW WILSON, *The New Freedom*

EDUCATION & LEARNING   See also SCIENCE

They know enough who know how to learn.
>—HENRY BROOKS ADAMS, *The Education of Henry Adams*

A teacher affects eternity; he can never tell where his influence stops. —HENRY BROOKS ADAMS, *Ibid.*

Learn by doing.   —ANONYMOUS (PROVERB)
[An ancient proverb, in modern times associated with the educational views of John Dewey. In the *Nicomachean Ethics*, Aristotle wrote, "For the things we have to learn before we can do them, we learn by doing them." See also Sophocles at DOING.]

Education is the best provision for old age.
>—ARISTOTLE, quoted in Diogenes Laërtius, *Lives of Eminent Philosophers*

Knowledge itself is power.   —FRANCIS BACON,
                                    Of Heresies

My people are destroyed for lack of knowledge.
                                    —BIBLE, *Hosea* 4:6

If you think education is expensive, try ignorance.
                                    —DEREK BOK, attributed
[The saying was widely used in the 1980s and appeared
on bumper stickers. It is not clear whether it was original
with Mr. Bok, then president of Harvard University.]

A Master of Art
Is not worth a Fart.
                            —ANDREW BOORDE, *The Jests of Scoggin*

What I want is Facts. Teach these boys and girls
nothing but Facts. Facts alone are wanted in life. Plant
nothing else, and root out everything else.
                                    —CHARLES DICKENS, *Hard Times*

The foundation of every state is the education of its
youth.
                            —DIOGENES ("THE CYNIC"), quoted in
                                Diogenes Laërtius, *Lives of
                                Eminent Philosophers*

Only the educated are free.
                                    —EPICTETUS, *Discourses*

Education, c'est délivrance.
Education is freedom.   —ANDRÉ GIDE, *Journal*

I find no other pleasure than learning.
                                    —INIGO JONES,
                                    Notebooks, Rome, 1614

I find that the three major administrative problems
on campus are sex for the students, athletics for the
alumni, and parking for the faculty.
                            —CLARK KERR, speech at the University of
                                Washington, reported in *Time*, Nov. 17, 1958
[Mr. Kerr had recently taken the helm at the University
of California.]

If by being overstudious, we impair our health and spoil our good humor, let us give it up.
—MONTAIGNE, *Essays*

The direction in which education starts a man will determine his future life. —PLATO, *The Republic*

A little learning is a dangerous thing.
—ALEXANDER POPE, *An Essay on Criticism*

'Tis education forms the common mind,
Just as the twig is bent, the tree's inclined.
—ALEXANDER POPE, *Moral Essays*, Epistle I

In an examination those who do not wish to know ask questions of those who cannot tell.
—SIR WALTER A. RALEIGH,
Some Thoughts on Examinations

You can't expect a boy to be depraved until he has been to a good school. —SAKI, *A Baker's Dozen*

The vanity of teaching often tempteth a man to forget he is a blockhead. —GEORGE SAVILE, *Maxims*

Then the whining schoolboy, with his satchel
And shining morning face, creeping like a snail
Unwillingly to school.
—SHAKESPEARE, *As You Like It*, II, vii
[From the "seven ages of man" speech. William Blake also sympathized with reluctant young scholars: "But to go to school in a summer morn, / Oh, it drives all joy away! / Under a cruel eye outworn, / The little ones spend the day— / In sighing and dismay," *The Schoolboy*.]

There is . . . nothing on earth intended for innocent people so horrible as a school.
—GEORGE BERNARD SHAW,
Parents and Children

He who can, does. He who cannot, teaches.
—GEORGE BERNARD SHAW, *Man and Superman*

Education is what survives when what has been learnt has been forgotten.
—B. F. SKINNER, *Education in 1984*

I was moving among two groups . . . who had almost ceased to communicate at all, who in intellectual, moral, and psychological climate had so little in common that . . . one might have crossed the ocean.
—C. P. SNOW, *The Two Cultures and the Scientific Revolution*

[C. P. Snow in his famous 1959 "two cultures" Rede Lecture highlighted the differences and absence of understanding between those in the world of science and those in the world of arts and humanities. He described being among people who complained of "the illiteracy of scientists." But when he asked those present if they could describe the second law of thermodynamics, "The response was cold: it was also negative."]

Education has for its object the formation of character.   —HERBERT SPENCER, *Social Statics*

Education . . . has produced a vast population able to read but unable to distinguish what is worth reading.
—G. M. TREVELYAN, *English Social History*

Training is everything. The peach was once a bitter almond; cauliflower is nothing but a cabbage with a college education.
—MARK TWAIN, "Pudd'nhead Wilson's Calendar," in *Pudd'nhead Wilson*

Soap and education are not as sudden as a massacre, but they are more deadly in the long run.
—MARK TWAIN, "The Facts Concerning the Recent Resignation," in *Sketches New and Old*

The founding fathers in their wisdom decided that children were an unnatural strain on parents. So they provided jails called schools, equipped with torture called education.   —JOHN UPDIKE, *The Centaur*

Separate educational facilities are inherently un-
equal.   —EARL WARREN, *Brown* v. *Board of*
Education of Topeka
[More at AMERICAN HISTORY: MEMORABLE MOMENTS.]

Human history becomes more and more a race between education and catastrophe.
               —H. G. WELLS, *The Outline of History*

EFFORT   See also ACTION; DOING;
                  PERSEVERANCE & ENDURANCE;
                              WORK & WORKERS

It takes all the running you can do to keep in the
same place.
         —LEWIS CARROLL, *Through the Looking-Glass*

Much effort, much prosperity.
               —EURIPIDES, *The Suppliant Women*

Striving to do better, oft we mar what's well.
               —SHAKESPEARE, *King Lear*, I, iv

There are no gains without pains.
         —ADLAI STEVENSON, presidential nomination
            acceptance speech, 1952

ELITE   See also GENIUS; GREATNESS;
                  HIGH POSITION: RULERS & LEADERS

For many are called, but few are chosen.
               —BIBLE, *Matthew* 22:14

What is aristocracy? A corporation of the best, of the
bravest.   —THOMAS CARLYLE, *Chartism*
[The similar phrase, "the best and the brightest," used
as a book title by David Halberstam in 1969, comes
from an 1811 hymn by Bishop Reginald Heber:
    Brightest and best of the sons of the morning,
    Dawn on our darkness, and lend us thine aid!]

The minority is always right.
               —HENRIK IBSEN, *An Enemy of the People*

I don't want to belong to any club that would accept me as a member.   —GROUCHO MARX, attributed

We few, we happy few, we band of brothers.
                    —SHAKESPEARE, *Henry V*, IV, iii

The difficult we do immediately. The impossible takes a little longer.
                    —U. S. ARMY CORPS OF ENGINEERS, slogan

To consider oneself different from ordinary men is wrong, but it is right to hope that one will not remain like ordinary men.
                    —YOSHIDA SHOIN, *Yoshida Shoin Zenshu*

EMOTIONS   See also ANGER; DESPAIR, DEPRESSION,
                    MISERY; ENTHUSIASM, ENERGY, ZEAL;
                    GUILT; HAPPINESS; HATE; HEART;
                    LOVE; SORROW, SADNESS, & SUFFERING

It is not a good time out in the world for emotions, anymore.   —RAINER WERNER FASSBINDER,
                    The Marriage of Maria Braun

Sturm und drang.
Storm and stress.   —FRIEDRICH MAXIMILIAN VON
                    KLINGER, title of play, 1776
[Usually associated with the writings of Goethe.]

I have something more to do than feel.
                    —CHARLES LAMB, letter to Coleridge, 1796
[A great line but a strange context: the letter was written just after the death of Lamb's mother. Lamb also wrote to Southey in 1815, "Anything awful makes me laugh. I misbehaved once at a funeral."]

You are not wood, you are not stones, but men.
                    —SHAKESPEARE, *Julius Caesar*, III, ii

ENDINGS   See also ACCOMPLISHMENT; BEGINNINGS

The opera ain't over till the fat lady sings.
                    —ANONYMOUS
[This was popularized in the late 1970s by Coach Dick Motta of the Chicago Bulls. In a column in *The New*

York Times Magazine, Feb. 15, 1987, William Safire traces it to a remark by the sportswriter Dan Cook in 1975, but it is probably a folk adage. *Southern Words and Sayings*, edited by Fabia R. Smith and Charles R. Smith, includes this version: "Church ain't out until the fat lady sings."]

ENDS & MEANS　　　　See also ETHICS & MORALITY; EXPEDIENCY; SELF-INTEREST

Whoever wills the end, wills also . . . the means.
　　　—IMMANUEL KANT, *Groundwork of the Metaphysic of Morals*

The end must justify the means.
　　　—MATTHEW PRIOR, *Hans Carvel*

To do a great right do a little wrong.
　　　—SHAKESPEARE, *The Merchant of Venice*, IV, i
[Bassanio pleading that the pound-of-flesh contract be broken.]

The end excuses any evil.　　　—SOPHOCLES, *Electra*
[Ends and means were specifically coupled by St. Jerome, who referred to "The line often adopted by strong men . . . of justifying the means by the end," letter 48. See also the Theodore Roosevelt quote at EVIL.]

ENDURANCE　　　　See PERSEVERANCE & ENDURANCE; SURVIVAL

ENEMIES

Love your enemies.　　　—BIBLE, *Matthew* 5:44

You shall judge of a man by his foes as well as by friends.　　　—JOSEPH CONRAD, *Lord Jim*

The art of leadership . . . consists in consolidating the attention of the people against a single adversary and taking care that nothing will split up that attention.
　　　—ADOLF HITLER, *Mein Kampf*

He makes no friend who never made a foe.
> —ALFRED, LORD TENNYSON, "Lancelot and
> Elaine" in *Idylls of the King*

A man cannot be too careful in the choice of his enemies.
> —OSCAR WILDE, *The Picture of Dorian Gray*

ENERGY   See ENTHUSIASM, ENERGY, ZEAL

ENGLAND   See also CITIES; NATIONS

If I should die, think only this of me:
That there's some corner of a foreign field
That is forever England
> —RUPERT BROOKE, *The Soldier*

Oh, to be in England now that April's there.
> —ROBERT BROWNING, *Home Thoughts,
> from Abroad*

I have nothing to offer but blood, toil, tears, and sweat.
> —WINSTON CHURCHILL, speech, May 13, 1940

We shall go on to the end . . . we shall defend our island, whatever the cost may be, we shall fight on the beaches, we shall fight on the landing grounds, we shall fight in the fields and in the streets, we shall fight in the hills; we shall never surrender.
> —WINSTON CHURCHILL, speech, June 4, 1940

[See also Churchill on victory at WINNING & LOSING, VICTORY & DEFEAT.]

This was their finest hour.
> —WINSTON CHURCHILL, speech, June 18, 1940

Never in the field of human conflict was so much owed by so many to so few.
> —WINSTON CHURCHILL, speech, Aug. 20, 1940

[He was speaking of the Royal Air Force.]

England is the paradise of women, the purgatory of men, and the hell of horses.
> —JOHN FLORIO, *Second Frutes*

[See also NATIONS, the Burton quote.]

The stately homes of England!
How beautiful they stand.
—FELICIA HEMANS, *The Homes of England*
[For a different perspective, see Virginia Woolf below.]

England is a nation of shopkeepers.
—NAPOLEON BONAPARTE, attributed,
B. E. O'Meara, *Napoleon at St. Helena*
[This is the usual attribution, but the phrase had been around for a while; *Bartlett's* quotes a tract by Josiah Tucker dated 1763.]

There'll always be an England.
—ROSS PARKER & HUGH CHARLES, poem title

Once more unto the breach, dear friends, once more,
Or close the wall up with our English dead!
—SHAKESPEARE, *Henry V*, III, i

The game's afoot.
Follow your spirit, and upon this charge
Cry "God for Harry, England, and Saint George!"
—*Ibid.*

This England never did, nor never shall,
Lie at the proud foot of a conqueror.
—SHAKESPEARE, *King John*, V, vii

This royal throne of kings, this sceptered isle,
—SHAKESPEARE, *Richard II*, II, i

This happy breed of men, this little world
This precious stone set in the silver sea.   —*Ibid.*

This blessed plot, this earth, this realm, this England.   —*Ibid.*

An Englishman thinks he is moral when he is only uncomfortable.
—GEORGE BERNARD SHAW, *Man and Superman*

The English take their pleasures sadly after the fashion of their country.   —DUC DE SULLY, *Memoirs*

Those comfortably padded lunatic asylums which are known, euphemistically, as the stately homes of England.
    —VIRGINIA WOOLF, "Lady Dorothy Nevill," in *The Common Reader*

ENTHUSIASM, ENERGY, ZEAL

My zeal hath consumed me.   —BIBLE, *Psalms* 50:2

Energy is eternal delight.
    —WILLIAM BLAKE, *The Marriage of Heaven and Hell*

The greatest dangers to liberty lurk in insidious encroachment by men of zeal, well-meaning but without understanding.
    —LOUIS D. BRANDEIS, *Olmstead* v. *the United States*

Only passions, great passions, can elevate the soul to great things.
    —DENIS DIDEROT, *Discours sur la poésie dramatique*

Nothing great was ever achieved without enthusiasm.
    —RALPH WALDO EMERSON, *Circles*
[See also Hegel, below.]

Zeal is fit only for wise men, but is found mostly in fools.   —THOMAS FULLER, *Gnomologia*

Nothing great in the world has been accomplished without passion.   —HEGEL, *Philosophy of History*

Fanaticism consists in redoubling your efforts when you have forgotten your aim.
    —GEORGE SANTAYANA, *The Life of Reason*

Pas trop de zèle.
Not too much enthusiasm.
>—CHARLES-MAURICE DE TALLEYRAND,
>attributed by several writers, including
>C. A. Saint-Beuve, *Portrait des Femmes*

ENVIRONMENT See also FUTURE; NATURE;
POPULATION

We are the children of our landscape.
>—LAWRENCE DURRELL, *Justine*

I am a passenger on the spaceship Earth.
>—R. BUCKMINSTER FULLER, *Operating Manual
>for Spaceship Earth*

What would the world be once bereft
Of wet and wildness? Let them be left,
O let them be left, wildness and wet;
Long live the weeds and the wilderness yet.
>GERARD MANLEY HOPKINS, *Inversnaid*

The earth is given as common stock for man to labor
and live on. —THOMAS JEFFERSON, letter to James
Madison, 1785

The supreme reality of our time is . . . the vulnera-
bility of our planet. —JOHN F. KENNEDY, speech,
June 28, 1963

Conservation is a state of harmony between men and
land. —ALDO LEOPOLD, *A Sand County Almanac*

Pity the Meek, for they shall inherit the earth.
>—DON MARQUIS, quoted in Frederick B. Wilcox,
>*A Little Book of Aphorisms*

The nation that destroys its soil destroys itself.
>—FRANKLIN D. ROOSEVELT, letter to
>state governors, Feb. 26, 1937

We have forgotten how to be good guests, how to
walk lightly on the earth as its other creatures do.
>—STOCKHOLM CONFERENCE,
>*Only One Earth*, 1972

In wildness is the preservation of the world.
                                    —HENRY DAVID THOREAU,
                                    Walking

We must make our garden grow.   —VOLTAIRE,
                                    Candide
[The conclusion of Part One of *Candide*. Used by British Prime Minister John Major at the 1992 international conference in Brazil on the environment with reference to saving the planet. A more literal translation is, "We must cultivate our garden." Sometimes "garden" is pluralized.]

EPITAPHS   See also DEATH

Sit tibi terra levis.
May the earth lie light upon thee.   —ANONYMOUS
[This common Roman epitaph was often abbreviated S.T.T.L.]

Epitaph, n. An inscription on a tomb showing that virtues acquired by death have a retroactive effect.
                                    —AMBROSE BIERCE, *The Devil's Dictionary*

Born 1711. Died 1776. Leaving it to posterity to add the rest.   —DAVID HUME, written by himself, 1775

In lapidary inscriptions a man is not upon oath.
                                    —SAMUEL JOHNSON, quoted in James Boswell,
                                    Life of Johnson, April 18, 1775

Here lies one whose name was writ in water.
                                    —JOHN KEATS,
                                    epitaph for himself

This be the verse you grave for me:
Here he lies where he longed to be;
Home is the sailor, home from the sea,
And the hunter home from the hill.
                                    —ROBERT LOUIS STEVENSON,
                                    Requiem, in *Underwoods*

Warm summer sun, shine kindly here;
Warm southern wind, blow softly here;
Green sod above, lie light, lie light—
Good night, dear heart, good night, good night.
                    —MARK TWAIN, epitaph for an adopted
                        daughter, ca. 1885

EQUALITY

When Adam delved and Eve span,
Who was then a gentleman?
                    —JOHN BALL, sermon at Blackheath in
                        Wat Tyler's Rebellion, 1381
[From an earlier poem—by Richard Rolle, according
to *The Penguin Dictionary of Quotations*.]

Have we not all one father? hath not one God created
us?   —BIBLE, *Malachi* 2:10

A man's a man for a'that!   —ROBERT BURNS,
                                    poem title

There is no king who has not had a slave among his
ancestors, and no slave who has not had a king among
his.   —HELEN KELLER, *The Story of My Life*

The boundaries of democracy have to be widened so
as to include economic equality also. This is the great
revolution through which we are all passing.
                    —JAWAHARLAL NEHRU,
                        Glimpses of World History

All animals are equal, but some animals are more
equal than others.   —GEORGE ORWELL,
                            Animal Farm

ERAS   See FUTURE, THE; GENERATIONS;
         MODERN TIMES; PAST, THE; PRESENT, THE;
                            TURBULENT TIMES

ERROR   See FAILINGS; MISTAKES

ESCAPE   See also TRAVEL

> Oh that I had wings like a dove! for then I would fly
> away, and be at rest.   —BIBLE, *Psalms* 55:6

> listen: there's a hell
> of a good universe next door: let's go.
> —E. E. CUMMINGS, *Times One*

> O! for a horse with wings!
> —SHAKESPEARE, *Cymbeline*, III, iii

> Let us rise up and part; she will not know.
> Let us go seaward as the great winds go,
> Full of blown sand and foam.
> —ALGERNON CHARLES SWINBURNE,
> *A Leave-taking*

> I will arise and go now, and go to Innisfree,
> And a small cabin build there, of clay and wattles
> made:
> Nine bean-rows will I have there, a hive for the
> honeybee,
> And live alone in the bee-loud glade.
> —WILLIAM BUTLER YEATS,
> *The Lake Isle of Innisfree*

ESTHETICS   See ARTS: AESTHETICS

ETHICS & MORALITY   See also CONSCIENCE;
                                   ENDS & MEANS; EVIL;
                                   PHILOSOPHY; VIRTUE

> It is easier to fight for one's principles than to live up
> to them.
> —ALFRED ADLER, quoted in P. Bottome,
> *Alfred Adler*

> No morality can be founded on authority, even if the
> authority were divine.   —A. J. AYER, *Essay on
> Humanism*

Expedients are for the hour, but principles are for the ages. —HENRY WARD BEECHER, *Proverbs from Plymouth Pulpit*

The greatest happiness of the greatest number is the foundation of morals and legislation.
—JEREMY BENTHAM,
The Commonplace Book

No actions are bad in themselves—even murder can be justified.
—DIETRICH BONHOEFFER, *No Rusty Swords*

The world has achieved brilliance without conscience. Ours is a world of nuclear giants and ethical infants.
—GEN. OMAR BRADLEY, speech,
Armistice Day, 1948

It doesn't matter what you do, as long as you don't do it in public and frighten the horses.
—MRS. PATRICK CAMPBELL, traditional attribution

"Do the duty which lies nearest thee," which thou knowest to be a duty! Thy second duty will already have become clearer.
—THOMAS CARLYLE, *Sartor Resartus*

The number of people in possession of any criteria for discriminating between good and evil is very small.
—T. S. ELIOT, Virginia lectures, 1933

Rise above principle and do what's right.
—WALTER HELLER,
speech to Congress, May 7, 1985

I know only that what is moral is what you feel good after and what is immoral is what you feel bad after.
—ERNEST HEMINGWAY, *Death in the Afternoon*

If he does really think that there is no distinction between virtue and vice, why, Sir, when he leaves our houses, let us count our spoons.
—SAMUEL JOHNSON, quoted in James Boswell, *Life of Johnson*, July 14, 1763
[The quote refers to James Macpherson, the Scotsman who wrote *The Poems of Ossian* and tried to pass it off as a translation of ancient Gaelic poetry. For another occasion on which to count spoons, see Emerson under SELF-RIGHTEOUSNESS.]

Morality is not properly the doctrine of how we may make ourselves happy, but how we may make ourselves worthy of happiness.
—IMMANUEL KANT, *Critique of Practical Reason*

Act only on that maxim which you can at the same time wish that it should become a universal law [definition of the categorical imperative].
—IMMANUEL KANT, *Groundwork of the Metaphysic of Morals*

Morality is the herd instinct in the individual.
—FRIEDRICH NIETZSCHE, *Die fröhliche Wissenschaft*

My country is the world, and my religion is to do good. —THOMAS PAINE, *The Rights of Man*

As soon as one is unhappy, one becomes moral.
—MARCEL PROUST, *Remembrance of Things Past: Within a Budding Grove*

Ethical metaphysics is fundamentally an attempt, however disguised, to give legislative force to our own wishes.
—BERTRAND RUSSELL, "On Scientific Method in Philosophy," in *Mysticism and Logic*.

No one can be perfectly free till all are free; no one can be perfectly moral till all are moral; no one can be perfectly happy till all are happy.
—HERBERT SPENCER, *Social Statics*

One impulse from a vernal wood
May teach you more of man,
Of moral evil and of good,
Than all the sages can.
　　　—WILLIAM WORDSWORTH, *The Tables Turned*

EVENING　　　　　　　　See NATURE: TIMES OF DAY

EVIDENCE　　　　　　　　See also CRIME; GUILT

You should not decide until you have heard what both have to say.　　　—ARISTOPHANES, *The Wasps*

Hear the other side.
　　　　　　　—ST. AUGUSTINE, *De Duabus Animabus*

By their fruits you shall know them.
　　　　　　　—BIBLE, *Matthew* 7:20

Out of thine own mouth will I judge thee.
　　　　　　　—BIBLE, *Luke* 19:22

"Is there any point to which you would wish to draw my attention?"
"To the curious incident of the dog in the night-time."
"The dog did nothing in the night-time."
"That was the curious incident," remarked Sherlock Holmes.　　　—A. CONAN DOYLE, *Silver Blaze*

If it walks like a duck, and quacks like a duck, then it just may be a duck.
　　　　　　　—WALTER REUTHER, attributed by William Safire, *Safire's Political Dictionary*

The most savage controversies are about those matters as to which there is no good evidence either way.
　　　—BERTRAND RUSSELL, "An Outline of Intellectual Rubbish," in *Unpopular Essays*

Things seen are mightier than things heard.
　　　—ALFRED, LORD TENNYSON, *Enoch Arden*
[The notion can be traced as far back as Herodotus: "We are less convinced by what we hear than by what we see."]

Some circumstantial evidence is very strong, as when you find a trout in the milk.
—HENRY DAVID THOREAU,
Journal, Nov. 11, 1850

EVIL   See also CRIME; DANGEROUS PEOPLE;
ENDS & MEANS; HELL; SIN, VICE, &
NAUGHTINESS; TEMPTATION; TROUBLE;
VIOLENCE & FORCE

Evil is unspectacular and always human
And shares our bed and eats at our own table.
—W. H. AUDEN, *Herman Melville*

I had rather be a doorkeeper in the house of my God, than to dwell in the tents of wickedness.
—BIBLE, *Psalms* 84:10

For wide is the gate, and broad is the way, that leadeth to destruction.   —BIBLE, *Matthew* 7:13

Men loved darkness rather than light, because their deeds were evil.   —BIBLE, *John* 3:19

For the wages of sin is death.
—BIBLE, *Romans* 6:23

Be not overcome of evil, but overcome evil of good.
—BIBLE, *Romans* 12:21

He that toucheth pitch shall be defiled therewith.
—BIBLE, *Ecclesiasticus* 13:1

The only thing necessary for the triumph of evil is for good men to do nothing.
—EDMUND BURKE, traditional attribution
but no known source
[For a similar concept in Burke, see UNITY & LOYALTY.]

The evil that is in the world almost always comes of ignorance, and good intentions may do as much harm as malevolence if they lack understanding.
—ALBERT CAMUS, *The Plague*

Pity the criminal all you like, but don't call evil good.
—FEODOR DOSTOEVSKI, *Crime and Punishment*

There is a capacity of virtue in us, and there is a capacity of vice to make your blood creep.
—RALPH WALDO EMERSON, *Journals*

Sin is whatever obscures the soul.
—ANDRÉ GIDE, *La Symphonie pastorale*

Wickedness is always easier than virtue; for it takes the short cut to everything.
—SAMUEL JOHNSON, quoted by James Boswell, *Tour to the Hebrides*, Sept. 17, 1773

No one becomes depraved all at once.
—JUVENAL, *Satires*

He who accepts evil without protesting against it is really cooperating with it.
—MARTIN LUTHER KING, JR., *Stride Toward Freedom*

Surely God wrongs not men, but themselves men wrong.
—KORAN

Destruction never comes with weapon in hand. It comes on tiptoe, seeing good in bad and bad in good.
—MAHABHARATA

A man does not sin by commission only, but often by omission.   —MARCUS AURELIUS, *Meditations*

So farewell hope, and with hope farewell fear,
Farewell remorse: all good to me is lost;
Evil be thou my good.
—JOHN MILTON, *Paradise Lost*

Whoever fights monsters should see to it that in the process he does not become a monster. And when you look long into an abyss, the abyss also looks into you.
—FRIEDRICH NIETZSCHE, *Beyond Good and Evil*

All human evil comes from this: a man's being unable
to sit still in a room.   —PASCAL, *Pensées*

No man is justified in doing evil on the ground of
expediency.   —THEODORE ROOSEVELT, *The
Strenuous Life,* title essay

The evil that men do lives after them,
The good is oft interred with their bones.
                         —SHAKESPEARE, *Julius Caesar*, III, ii

If one good deed in all my life I did,
I do repent it from my very soul.
                         —SHAKESPEARE, *Titus Andronicus*, V, iii

All spirits are enslaved that serve things evil.
    —PERCY BYSSHE SHELLEY, *Prometheus Unbound*

Between two evils, I always like to take the one I've
never tried before.   —MAE WEST, *Klondike Annie*

EVOLUTION   See SCIENCE: BIOLOGY

EXCELLENCE   See AMBITION; ELITE; GRACE;
                                                     GREATNESS

EXCESS   See also HEDONISM

Drinking when we are not thirsty and making love at
any time, madame: that is all there is to distinguish us
from the other animals.
                         —PIERRE-AUGUSTIN DE BEAUMARCHAIS,
                         The Marriage of Figaro

The road of excess leads to the palace of wisdom.
                         —WILLIAM BLAKE, *The Marriage of
                         Heaven and Hell*

Those who have great passions find themselves all
their lives both happy and unhappy at being cured of
them.   —LA ROCHEFOUCAULD, *Maxims*

Excess on occasion is exhilarating. It prevents moderation from acquiring the deadening effect of habit.
> —W. SOMERSET MAUGHAM, *The Summing Up*

My candle burns at both ends;
It will not last the night;
But ah, my foes, and oh my friends—
It gives a lovely light!
> —EDNA ST. VINCENT MILLAY,
> "First Fig," in *A Few Figs from Thistles*

Can one desire too much of a good thing?
> —SHAKESPEARE, *As You Like It*, IV, i

These violent delights have violent ends.
> —SHAKESPEARE, *Romeo and Juliet*, II, vi

Nothing to excess.
> —SOLON, quoted in Diogenes Laërtius,
> *Lives of Eminent Philosophers*

Too much of a good thing can be wonderful.
> —MAE WEST, quoted in Joseph Weintraub, ed.,
> *The Wit and Wisdom of Mae West*

[Or as cellist Mstislav Rostropovich puts it, "More is more," quoted in the Kennedy Center Honors Performance, Dec. 30, 1992.]

Nothing succeeds like excess.
> —OSCAR WILDE,
> *A Woman of No Importance*

[See Dumas at SUCCESS.]

Never . . . murder a man who is committing suicide.
> —WOODROW WILSON, letter to
> Bernard Baruch, 1916

EXCUSES

Qui s'excuse, s'accuse.
Who excuses himself, accuses himself.
> —ANONYMOUS (PROVERB)

It's not how you win or lose, it's how you place the
blame.   —ANONYMOUS
[Baseball slugger Ralph Kiner quoted this saying
while broadcasting a Mets game. It's a variation, of
course, of the commonplace, "It's not how you win
or lose, it's how you play the game," formalized by
Grantland Rice; see WINNING & LOSING; VICTORY &
DEFEAT.]

Never complain, never explain.
                              —HENRY FORD II
[*The New York Times* obituary credited Ford with
making this remark after being arrested for drunk
driving. It is the title of Victor Lasky's biography of
Ford.]

Several excuses are always less convincing than one.
                              —ALDOUS HUXLEY,
                                Point Counter Point

[On being observed by his wife kissing a chorus girl]
I wasn't kissing her, I was whispering into her mouth.
                              —CHICO MARX, attributed

And oftentimes excusing of a fault
Doth make the fault the worse by the excuse.
                              —SHAKESPEARE, *King John*, IV, ii

I am a man
More sinned against than sinning.
                              —SHAKESPEARE, *King Lear*, III, ii

Two wrongs don't make a right, but they make a
good excuse.
                              —THOMAS SZASZ,
                                "Social Relations," in *The Second Sin*

EXERCISE   See PHYSICAL FITNESS; SPORTS

EXPEDIENCY   See also ENDS & MEANS;
                                              SELF-INTEREST

In practice, such trifles as contradictions in principle
are easily set aside; the faculty of ignoring them makes
the practical man.
                              —HENRY BROOKS ADAMS,
                                    The Education of Henry Adams
[But see Theodore Roosevelt at EVIL.]

And this is the law I will maintain,
Until my dying day, Sir,
That whatsoever king shall reign,
I'll still be the Vicar of Bray, Sir.

                                            —ANONYMOUS
[This verse from a song attributed to an anonymous
British dragoon serving under George I celebrates the
legendary Vicar of Bray. The song refers to an expedient vicar who served under Charles II and George I.
But the legend is older and more likely is based on the
career of Simon Aleyn, who was sufficiently flexible in
religion to hold on to his office from ca. 1540–1588,
through the alternating changes in England's state creed
in the reigns of Henry VIII, Edward VI, Mary I, and
Elizabeth I. See also Henry IV, below.]

We do what we must, and call it by the best names.
            —RALPH WALDO EMERSON, "Considerations
                By the Way," in *The Conduct of Life*

Paris is well worth a mass.

                              —HENRY IV, attributed
[A survivor in a period of religious wars, Henry of Na-
varre became Henry IV of France. Tradition holds that
he made this remark in 1593, when, abjuring Protes-
tantism for the second time in his career, he effected
reconciliation with the Catholic forces in control of
Paris. He was welcomed into Paris in 1594, ruling until
1610. A skilled and popular king, he wanted every peasant family to have a chicken in the pot for Sunday
dinner; see FOOD, WINE, & EATING.]

Policy sits above conscience.
                              —SHAKESPEARE, *Timon of Athens*, III, ii

In every sort of danger, there are various ways of winning through, if one is ready to do and say anything whatever.   —SOCRATES, quoted in Plato, *Apology*

Custom adapts itself to expediency.
                                    —TACITUS, *Annals*

EXPERIENCE   See also DOING; LIFE

All experience is an arch to build up.
                        —HENRY BROOKS ADAMS,
                            The Education of Henry Adams

A man should have the fine point of his soul taken off to become fit for this world.
                        —JOHN KEATS, letter to J. H. Reynolds,
                            Nov. 22, 1817

No man's knowledge here can go beyond his experience.   —JOHN LOCKE, *Essay Concerning
                            Human Understanding*

The journey not the arrival matters.
                                    —MONTAIGNE, *Essays*

Experience is the name everyone gives to their mistakes.   —OSCAR WILDE,
                            Lady Windermere's Fan

EXPERTS   See also DOCTORS & THE PRACTICE
                        OF MEDICINE; LAWYERS

Professionals built the *Titanic*—amateurs the ark.
                —ANONYMOUS, cited by Frank S. Pepper,
                    Handbook of 20th Century Quotes, source:
                    BBC radio, The News Quiz, Oct. 27, 1979

An expert is one who knows more and more about less and less.
                —NICHOLAS MURRAY BUTLER, attributed,
                    commencement speech, Columbia University

An expert is someone who knows some of the worst mistakes that can be made in his subject and how to avoid them.

—WERNER HEISENBERG, *Physics and Beyond*

EXPLORATION   See SCIENCE: DISCOVERY; TRAVEL

F

FACE   See BODY, HUMAN

FACTS

In this life we want nothing but facts, sir; nothing but facts.   —CHARLES DICKENS, *Hard Times*
[For more of Gradgrind's philosophy, see under EDUCATION.]

A little fact is worth a whole limbo of dreams.
      —RALPH WALDO EMERSON, *The Superlative*

Her taste exact
For faultless fact
Amounts to a disease.
      —W. S. GILBERT, *The Mikado*

The smallest fact is a window through which the infinite may be seen.
      —ALDOUS HUXLEY, cited in Richard
        Norton Smith, *Thomas E. Dewey*

The vocation of mankind is to create facts.
      —EMMANUEL MOUNIER, said in May 1933
[William Pfaff, in a *New Yorker* article on André Malraux, July 9, 1990, credited M. Mounier, a French Catholic writer and editor, with this shrewd remark.]

Learn, compare, collect the facts!
      —IVAN PETROVICH PAVLOV, *Bequest to the
        Academic Youth of Soviet Russia*

The facts are to blame my friend. We are all imprisoned by facts.
> —LUIGI PIRANDELLO, *The Rules of the Game*

Mere fact will never stop an Englishman.
> —GEORGE BERNARD SHAW,
> speech, Oct. 28, 1930

Let us not underrate the value of a fact; it will one day flower into a truth.
> —HENRY DAVID THOREAU, *Excursions*

You Could Look It Up.
> —JAMES THURBER, story title

[The phrase was a favorite expression of baseball manager Casey Stengel, but in a letter to *The New York Times*, Dennis Flanagan pointed out that the phrase probably originated with Thurber's 1941 story in the *Saturday Evening Post* about a manager who sends a midget up to bat. In 1951, Bill Veeck, owner of the St. Louis Browns, actually tried this maneuver.]

Get your facts first, and then you can distort them as much as you please.
> —MARK TWAIN, quoted in Rudyard Kipling,
> *From Sea to Sea*

FAILINGS   See also MISTAKES

No rose without a thorn.
> —ANONYMOUS (FRENCH PROVERB)

Thou art weighed in the balances, and art found wanting.
> —BIBLE, *Daniel* 5:27

She had
A heart—how shall I say?—too soon made glad,
Too easily impressed.
> —ROBERT BROWNING, *My Last Duchess*

Sometimes even excellent Homer nods.
> —HORACE, *Art of Poetry*

Ignorance, pure ignorance.
> —SAMUEL JOHNSON, explaining why in his *Dictionary* he had defined *pastern* as the knee of a horse, quoted in James Boswell, *Life of Johnson*, 1762

All men are liable to error; and most men are, in many points, by passion or interest, under temptation to it.
> —JOHN LOCKE, *Essay Concerning Human Understanding*

He's liked, but he's not well liked.
> —ARTHUR MILLER, *Death of a Salesman*

He wants the natural touch.
> —SHAKESPEARE, *Macbeth*, IV, ii

But men are men, the best sometimes forget.
> —SHAKESPEARE, *Othello*, II, iii

FAILURE   See HAVES & HAVE-NOTS; RUIN; WINNING & LOSING, VICTORY & DEFEAT

FAIRNESS   See EVIDENCE; JUSTICE

FAITH   See also ATHEISM; GOD; RELIGION; SKEPTICISM

Unless you believe, you shall not understand.
> —BIBLE, *Isaiah* 7:9 (Septuagint Version)

[A favorite saying of St. Augustine, who formulated it in several ways, including: "Understanding is the reward of faith" and "We believe in order to know," *In Joannis evangelium tractatus*. St. Anselm put it: *Credo ut intelligam*," "I believe in order that I may understand," *Proslogion*.]

O thou of little faith, wherefore didst thou doubt?
> —BIBLE, *Matthew* 14:31

For by grace are ye saved through faith; and that not of yourselves; it is the gift of God.
> —BIBLE, *Ephesians* 2:8

Faith without works is dead.
—BIBLE, *James* 2:20

You can do very little with faith, but you can do nothing without it.
—SAMUEL BUTLER, *Rebelliousness*, in *Notebooks*

"Well, now that we *have* seen each other," said the Unicorn, "if you believe in me, I'll believe in you. Is that a bargain?"
—LEWIS CARROLL, *Through the Looking-Glass*

Faith in a holy cause is to a considerable extent a substitute for the lost faith in ourselves.
—ERIC HOFFER, *The True Believer*

The constant assertion of belief is an indication of fear.
—KRISHNAMURTI, *The Second Penguin Krishnamurti Reader*

Faith may be defined briefly as an illogical belief in the occurrence of the improbable.
—H. L. MENCKEN, *Prejudices*

Faith has need of the whole truth.
—PIERRE TEILHARD DE CHARDIN, *The Appearance of Man*

Certum est quia impossibile.
It is certain because it is impossible.
—TERTULLIAN, *De Carne Cristi*
[Traditionally given as: *Credo quia impossibile,* "I believe because it is impossible."]

To believe in God is to yearn for His existence, and furthermore, it is to act as if He did exist.
—MIGUEL DE UNAMUNO, *The Tragic Sense of Life*

FALL   See NATURE: SEASONS

FAME   See SUCCESS & FAME

FAMILIARITY   See INTIMACY & FAMILIARITY

FAMILY   See also CHILDREN & CHILDHOOD;
                    HOME; MARRIAGE;
                    PARENTS & PARENTHOOD

He that hath a wife and children hath given hostages to fortune; for they are impediments to great enterprises.   —FRANCIS BACON, *Of Marriage*

It is a melancholy truth that even great men have their poor relations.
                    —CHARLES DICKENS, *Bleak House*

Accidents will occur in the best regulated families.
                    —CHARLES DICKENS, *David Copperfield*

Good families are generally worse than any others.
                    —ANTHONY HOPE, *The Prisoner of Zenda*

Home life ceases to be free and beautiful as soon as it is founded on borrowing and debt.
                    —HENRIK IBSEN, *A Doll's House*

One would be in less danger
From the wiles of the stranger
If one's own kin and kith
Were more fun to be with.
                    —OGDEN NASH, *Family Court*

Crabbèd age and youth cannot live together;
Youth is full of pleasance, age is full of care.
                    —SHAKESPEARE, *Passionate Pilgrim*

Happy families are all alike; every unhappy family is unhappy in its own way.
                    —LEO TOLSTOY, *Anna Karenina*

Birds in their little nest agree;
And 'tis a shameful sight,
When children of one family
Fall out, and chide, and fight.
                    —ISAAC WATTS, *Love Between Brothers
                    and Sisters*

FANATICISM   See ENTHUSIASM, ENERGY, ZEAL

FAREWELLS

All farewells should be sudden.
—LORD BYRON, *Sardanapalus*

Parting is all we know of heaven,
And all we need of hell.
—EMILY DICKINSON, poem no. 1732

Good night, good night! Parting is such sweet sorrow
That I shall say good night till it be morrow.
—SHAKESPEARE,
Romeo and Juliet, II, ii
[Shakespeare wrote several "good nights," cheerful and
grievous, including: "Good night, ladies, good night.
Sweet ladies, good night, good night," *Hamlet*, IV, v;
and also from *Hamlet*, Horatio's farewell to his dying
friend, "Good night, sweet Prince," V, ii.]

Forever, and forever, farewell, Cassius!
If we do meet again, why we shall smile;
If not, why then this parting was well made.
—SHAKESPEARE, *Julius Caesar*, V, i

FASHION & CLOTHES   See also APPEARANCES

A little of what you call frippery is very necessary
towards looking like the rest of the world.
—ABIGAIL ADAMS, letter to John Adams,
May 1, 1780

It is not only fine feathers that make fine birds.
—AESOP, *The Jay and the Peacock*

Clothes make the man.
—ANONYMOUS (LATIN PROVERB)

The fashion of this world passeth away.
—BIBLE, *I Corinthians* 7:31

Clothes never shut up.
—SUSAN BROWNMILLER, *Femininity*

The sense of being well-dressed gives a feeling of inward tranquillity which religion is powerless to bestow. —RALPH WALDO EMERSON, *Social Aims*
[He was reporting a comment by Miss C. F. Forbes.]

Good clothes open all doors.
—THOMAS FULLER, *Gnomologia*

A sweet disorder in the dress
Kindles in clothes a wantonness.
—ROBERT HERRICK, *Delight in Disorder*

A good exterior is a silent recommendation.
—PUBLILIUS SYRUS, *Moral Sayings*

The apparel oft proclaims the man.
—SHAKESPEARE, *Hamlet*, I, iii

Beware of all enterprises that require new clothes.
—HENRY DAVID THOREAU, *Walden*

All dressed up, with nowhere to go.
—WILLIAM ALLEN WHITE, attributed
[He was referring to the Progressive Party after Theodore Roosevelt left the presidential campaign.]

FATE   See also LUCK; RESPONSIBILITY;
                                       SELF-RELIANCE

I want to seize fate by the throat.
—LUDWIG VAN BEETHOVEN, letter to
Dr. Franz Wegeler, Nov. 16, 1801

In my beginning is my end.
—T. S. ELIOT, *East Coker*

A man's character is his fate.
—HERACLITUS, quoted by Diogenes Laërtius,
Lives of Eminent Philosophers

I claim not to have controlled events, but confess plainly that events have controlled me.
—ABRAHAM LINCOLN, letter to A. G. Hodges,
April 4, 1864

O! I am Fortune's fool.
                    —SHAKESPEARE, *Romeo and Juliet*, III, i

For man is man and master of his fate.
            —ALFRED, LORD TENNYSON, "Lancelot and
            Elaine," in *Idylls of the King*

Man may his fate foresee, but not prevent. . . .
'Tis better to be fortunate than wise.
                    —JOHN WEBSTER, *The White Devil*

FATHERS   See PARENTS & PARENTHOOD

FATNESS   See BODY, HUMAN

FEAR   See also COURAGE

A fool without fear is sometimes wiser than an angel
with fear.   —NANCY ASTOR, *My Two Countries*

Fear has many eyes and can see things underground.
                    —CERVANTES, *Don Quixote*

The thing I fear most is fear.
                —MONTAIGNE, *Essays: To the Reader*
[See also Wellington, below; for Franklin D. Roose-
velt's version, see AMERICAN HISTORY: MEMORABLE
MOMENTS.]

Fear is the main source of superstition, and one of
the main sources of cruelty. To conquer fear is the
beginning of wisdom.
                —BERTRAND RUSSELL, *An Outline of
                Intellectual Rubbish*

If we let things terrify us, life will not be worth living.
                        —SENECA, *Epistles*

The only thing I am afraid of is fear.
                —DUKE OF WELLINGTON, quoted in Philip
                Henry, Earl of Stanhope, *Notes of
                Conversations with . . . Wellington*
[In addition to Montaigne, quoted above, and Franklin
D. Roosevelt, cited at AMERICAN HISTORY: MEMO-

RABLE MOMENTS, Francis Bacon, Henry David Thoreau, and others made similar comments. Thoreau put it: "Nothing is so much to be feared as fear," *Journal*, Sept. 7, 1851]

FEMINISM   See WOMEN; WOMEN & MEN

FIGHTING BACK   See APPEASEMENT VS. RESISTANCE; STRENGTH

FITNESS   See PHYSICAL FITNESS

FLATTERY

Every woman is infallibly to be gained by every sort of flattery, and every man by one sort or other.
    —EARL OF CHESTERFIELD, letter to his son, March 16, 1752

Imitation is the sincerest of flattery.
    —CHARLES CALEB COLTON, *The Lacon*

But when I tell him he hates flatterers,
He says he does, being then most flattered.
    —SHAKESPEARE, *Julius Caesar*, II, i

None are more taken in by flattery than the proud who wish to be first and are not.   —SPINOZA, *Ethics*

'Tis an old maxim in the schools,
That flattery's the food of fools;
Yet now and then your men of wit
Will condescend to take a bit.
    —JONATHAN SWIFT, *Cadenus and Vanessa*

FLESH   See BODY, HUMAN

FLOWERS   See NATURE: GARDENS, FLOWERS, & TREES

FOOD, WINE, & EATING   See also ALCOHOL &
DRINKING

A man hath no better thing under the sun than to
eat, and to drink, and to be merry.
—BIBLE, *Ecclesiastes* 8:15

A feast is made for laughter, and wine maketh merry.
—*Ibid.*, 10:19
[The passage is cited at greater length at MONEY.]

Bring hither the fatted calf and kill it; and let us eat,
and be merry.   —BIBLE, *Luke* 15:23

The destiny of countries depends on the way they
feed themselves.
—ANTHELME BRILLAT-SAVARIN, *Physiologie
du goût*

Tell me what you eat, and I will tell you what you
are.   —*Ibid.*

Since Eve ate apples, much depends on dinner.
—LORD BYRON, *Don Juan*

Hunger is the best sauce in the world.
—CERVANTES, *Don Quixote*

Life is too short to stuff a mushroom.
—SHIRLEY CONRAN, *Superwoman*, epigraph

It's a very odd thing—
As odd as can be—
That whatever Miss T. eats
Turns into Miss T.
—WALTER DE LA MARE, *Miss T.*

Gluttony is an emotional escape, a sign something is
eating us.
—PETER DE VRIES, *Comfort Me with Apples*

Der Mensch ist, was er isst.
Man is what he eats.
—LUDWIG FEUERBACH, *Lehre der
Nahrungsmittel: für das volk*

Eat to live, and not live to eat.
  —BENJAMIN FRANKLIN, *Poor Richard's Almanac*

More die in the United States of too much food than
of too little.   —JOHN KENNETH GALBRAITH,
                                        The Affluent Society

I want there to be no peasant in my kingdom so poor
that he cannot have a chicken in his pot every Sunday.
                                        —HENRY IV, attributed
[The modern political slogan "A chicken in every pot"
was not, according to William Safire in *Safire's Political
Dictionary*, uttered by Herbert Hoover. Rather it was
the title of a Republican campaign flyer of 1928.]

He was a bold man who first swallowed an oyster.
              —JAMES I, attributed by Thomas Fuller,
                      Jonathan Swift, and others

Oats, n. A grain, which in England is generally given
to horses, but in Scotland supports the people.
                          —SAMUEL JOHNSON, *Dictionary*
[Lord Elibank responded, "Very true, and where will
you find such horses, and such men?"]

Some people have a foolish way of not minding, or
pretending not to mind, what they eat. For my part, I
mind my belly very studiously, and very carefully; for
I look upon it, that he who does not mind his belly will
hardly mind anything else.
          —SAMUEL JOHNSON, quoted in James Boswell,
                  Life of Johnson, Aug. 5, 1763

Qu'ils mangent de la brioche.
Let them eat cake.
                      —MARIE ANTOINETTE, traditional but
                              wrong attribution
[The remark, perhaps apocryphal, was attributed to
others much earlier.]

By and by
God caught his eye.
                  —DAVID McCORD, *Epitaphs: The Waiter*

Lunch kills half of Paris, supper the other half.
> —MONTESQUIEU, *Variétés*

A good cook is like a sorceress who dispenses happiness. —ELSA SCHIAPARELLI, *Shocking Life*

He hath eaten me out of house and home.
> —SHAKESPEARE, *Henry IV, Part II*, II, i

I am a great eater of beef and I believe that does harm to my wit.
> —SHAKESPEARE, *Twelfth Night*, I, iii

Digestion is the great secret of life.
> —REV. SYDNEY SMITH, letter to
> Arthur Kinglake, Sept. 30, 1837

In eating, a third of the stomach should be filled with food, a third with drink, and the rest left empty.
> —TALMUD

It's a naïve domestic burgundy, without any breeding, but I think you'll be amused by its presumption.
> —JAMES THURBER, *Men, Women & Dogs*,
> cartoon caption

It's broccoli dear.
I say it's spinach, and I say the hell with it.
> —E. B. WHITE, caption for a Carl Rose cartoon,
> *The New Yorker*, Dec. 8, 1928

One cannot think well, love well, sleep well, if one has not dined well.
> —VIRGINIA WOOLF, *A Room of One's Own*

FOOLS & STUPIDITY

Never give a sucker an even break.
> —ANONYMOUS

[Popularized by Prohibition-era nightclub owner Texas Guinan about 1925, according to H. L. Mencken. Possibly originated by Edward F. Albee, co-owner of the Keith-Albee circuit of vaudeville theaters. Others credit W. C. Fields, who ad-libbed the line in the 1923 play *Poppy*, and used it as a movie title in 1941.]

There's a sucker born every minute.
—P. T. BARNUM, attributed

A fool uttereth all his mind.
—BIBLE, *Proverbs* 29:11

For ye suffer fools gladly, seeing ye yourselves are
wise.   —BIBLE, *II Corinthians* 11:19

We are the hollow men
We are the stuffed men
Leaning together
Headpiece filled with straw. Alas!
—T. S. ELIOT, *The Hollow Men*

Nothing is more humiliating than to see idiots succeed
in enterprises we have failed in.
—FLAUBERT, *Sentimental Education*

There are some who speak one moment before they
think.   —LA BRUYÈRE, *Les Caractères*

Small things amuse small minds.
—DORIS LESSING, "A Woman on a Roof," in
A Man and Two Women

For fools rush in where angels fear to tread.
—ALEXANDER POPE, *An Essay on Criticism*

They never taste who always drink:
They always talk who never think.
—MATTHEW PRIOR, *Upon this
Passage in the Scaligeriana*

Against stupidity, the gods themselves struggle in
vain.
—J. C. F. VON SCHILLER, *The Maid of Orleans*

Lord, what fools these mortals be!
—SHAKESPEARE, *A Midsummer Night's Dream*
[Seneca said the same thing, though in Latin, in his
Epistles: "Tanta stultitia mortalium est."]

Let us be thankful for the fools. But for them the rest of us could not succeed.
—MARK TWAIN, "Pudd'nhead Wilson's New Calendar," in *Following the Equator*

There is no sin except stupidity.
—OSCAR WILDE, *The Critic as Artist*

FORCE See VIOLENCE & FORCE

FORGIVENESS & MERCY See also COMPASSION & PITY; TOLERANCE & UNDERSTANDING

Blessed are the merciful: for they shall obtain mercy.
—BIBLE, *Matthew* 5:7
[For other verses from the Sermon on the Mount, see VIRTUE.]

Forgive, and ye shall be forgiven.
—BIBLE, *Luke* 6:37
[More of this verse is cited under TOLERANCE & UNDERSTANDING.]

Rejoice with me; for I have found my sheep which was lost. . . . joy shall be in heaven over one that repenteth, more than over ninety and nine just persons, which need no repentance. —BIBLE, *Luke* 15:6,7

Father forgive them; for they know not what they do. —*Ibid.*, 23:34

Forgive but never forget.
—JOHN F. KENNEDY, saying attributed by Theodore Sorenson in *Kennedy*

To err is human, to forgive, divine.
—ALEXANDER POPE, *An Essay on Criticism*

The quality of mercy is not strained.
It droppeth as the gentle rain from heaven.
—SHAKESPEARE, *Merchant of Venice*, IV, i

Sweet mercy is nobility's true badge.
　　　　　—SHAKESPEARE, *Titus Andronicus*, I, i

It is by forgiving that one is forgiven.
　　　　　—MOTHER TERESA, *For the Brotherhood of Man*

Love truth, but pardon error.
　　　　　—VOLTAIRE, *Sept discours en vers sur l'homme*

FORM　　　　　　　　See ARTS: AESTHETICS

FORTUNE　　　　　　See FATE; HAPPINESS; LUCK

FRANCE　　　　　　　See CITIES; NATIONS

FREEDOM　　See also APPEASEMENT VS. RESISTANCE;
　　　　　　　　DEMOCRACY; FREE SPEECH; RIGHTS

The condition upon which God has given liberty to man is eternal vigilance.
　　　　　—JOHN PHILPOT CURRAN, speech, July 10, 1790
[Curran, an Irish orator and magistrate, inspired the American abolitionist Wendell Phillips, who said, "Eternal vigilance is the price of liberty" in a speech entitled "Public Opinion," given at the Massachusetts Anti-Slavery Society, Jan. 28, 1852.]

You can only protect your liberties in this world by protecting the other man's freedom. You can only be free if I am free.
　　　　　—CLARENCE DARROW, *People* v. *Lloyd*, 1920

I only ask to be free. The butterflies are free.
　　　　　—CHARLES DICKENS, *Bleak House*

There can be no real freedom without the freedom to fail.　　　—ERIC HOFFER, *The Ordeal of Change*

What stands if freedom fall?
　　　　　—RUDYARD KIPLING, *For All We Have and Are*

Those who deny freedom to others deserve it not for themselves.　　　—ABRAHAM LINCOLN, letter to
H. L. Pierce *et al.*, April 6, 1859

Like bone to the human body, and the axle to the wheel, and the song to a bird, and air to the wing, thus is liberty the essence of life. Whatever is done without it is imperfect.
　　　　　—JOSE MARTÍ, quoted by William Pfaff,
The New Yorker, May 27, 1985

License they mean when they cry liberty.
　　　　　　—JOHN MILTON, *On the Same*
["The Same" refers to his sonnet *On the Detraction . . .*]

A nation may lose its liberties in a day, and not miss them for a century.　　　—MONTESQUIEU, *De l'esprit
des lois*

Liberty is the right to do everything which the laws allow.　　　　　　　　　　　—*Ibid.*

Those men and women are fortunate who are born at a time when a great struggle for human freedom is in progress.　　—EMMELINE PANKHURST, *My Own Story*

O liberty, o liberty, what crimes are committed in your name.
　—MADAME ROLAND, being taken to the guillotine,
attributed in Lamartine, *Histoire des Girondins*

We look forward to a world founded upon four essential freedoms [freedom of speech, freedom of worship, freedom from want, freedom from fear].
　—FRANKLIN D. ROOSEVELT, speech, Jan. 6, 1941

Man is condemned to be free.
—JEAN-PAUL SARTRE, *Existentialism Is a Humanism*

Carelessness about our security is dangerous; carelessness about our freedom is also dangerous.
　　　　　—ADLAI STEVENSON, speech, Oct. 7, 1952

The secret of happiness is freedom, and the secret of freedom, courage.   —THUCYDIDES, funeral speech for Pericles

I had reasoned this out in my mind: There was two things I had a right to, liberty and death. If I could not have one, I would have the other, for no man should take me alive.
            —HARRIET TUBMAN, quoted in Marcy Galen, *Lost Women: Harriet Tubman* . . .

Caged birds accept each other but flight is what they long for.   —TENNESSEE WILLIAMS, *Camino Real*

FREE SPEECH   See also CENSORSHIP; FREEDOM; PRESS, THE

Some people's idea of [free speech] is that they are free to say what they like, but if anyone says anything back, that is an outrage.
            —WINSTON CHURCHILL, speech, Oct. 13, 1943

In a free state there must be free speech.
            —DOMITIAN, attributed

Let reason be opposed to reason, and argument to argument, and every good government will be safe.   ·
            —THOMAS ERSKINE, *In Defense of Thomas Paine*

The most stringent protection of free speech would not protect a man from falsely shouting fire in a theater and causing a panic.
            —OLIVER WENDELL HOLMES, JR., *Schenck* v. *U.S.*, 1919

When men have realized that time has upset many fighting faiths, they may come to believe . . . that the ultimate good desired is reached by the free trade in ideas—that the best test of truth is the power of the thought to get itself accepted in the competition of the market. . . . That at any rate is the theory of our Constitution.   —OLIVER WENDELL HOLMES, JR., *Abrams* v. *the U.S.*, dissent, 1919

I disapprove of what you say, but I will defend to the death your right to say it.　　—VOLTAIRE, attributed [The source for the attribution is E. Beatrice Hall's *The Friends of Voltaire*. But the author later said that the statement was meant as a paraphrase, not an exact quote. *Bartlett's* credits Norbert Guterman's *A Book of French Quotations* with finding the closest verifiable quotation, in a letter from Voltaire to M. le Riche, Feb. 6, 1770: "I detest what you write, but I would give my life to make it possible for you to continue to write."]

FRIENDS & FRIENDSHIP　　See also OLD THINGS, OLD FRIENDS

Friends are born, not made.
　　　　—HENRY BROOKS ADAMS,
　　　　　The Education of Henry Adams

One friend in a life is much, two are many, three are hardly possible.　　　　　—*Ibid.*

Greater love hath no man than this, that a man lay down his life for his friends.　　—BIBLE, *John* 15:13

Forsake not an old friend; for the new is not comparable to him; a new friend is as new wine.
　　　　　—BIBLE, *Ecclesiasticus* 9:10

My true friends have always given me that supreme proof of devotion, a spontaneous aversion for the man I loved.　　　　　—COLETTE, *Break of Day*

Have no friends not equal to yourself.
　　　　　—CONFUCIUS, *Analects*

A friend may well be reckoned the masterpiece of nature.　　—RALPH WALDO EMERSON, *Friendship*

A friend is a person with whom I may be sincere. Before him, I may think aloud.　　　　　—*Ibid.*

If I had to choose between betraying my country and betraying my friend, I hope I should have the guts to betray my country.
　　　　—E. M. FORSTER, "What I Believe," in
　　　　　Two Cheers for Democracy

Friendship needs no words—it is solitude delivered from the anguish of loneliness.
—DAG HAMMARSKJÖLD, *Markings*

If a man does not make new acquaintances as he advances through life, he will soon find himself left alone.
—SAMUEL JOHNSON, quoted in James Boswell, *Life of Johnson*, April 1755

A true friend is the most precious of all possessions and the one we take the least thought about acquiring.
—LA ROCHEFOUCAULD, *Maxims*

The zeal of friends it is that knocks me down, and not the hate of enemies.   —J. C. F. VON SCHILLER, *Wallensteins Tod*
[See also the remark by the Duc de Villars, below.]

Those friends thou hast, and their adoption tried, Grapple them to thy soul with hoops of steel.
—SHAKESPEARE, *Hamlet*, I, iii

To me, fair friend, you never can be old.
—SHAKESPEARE, sonnet 104

The holy passion of friendship is so sweet and steady and loyal and enduring in nature that it will last through a whole lifetime, if not asked to lend money.
—MARK TWAIN, "Pudd'nhead Wilson's Calendar," in *Pudd'nhead Wilson*

May God defend me from my friends; I can defend myself from my enemies.   —DUC DE VILLARS, attributed
[Sometimes attributed to Voltaire.]

It is not often that someone comes along who is a true friend and a good writer.
—E. B. WHITE, *Charlotte's Web*

FUTURE, THE   See also ENVIRONMENT, THE;
                          POPULATION; PROGRESS

The future struggles against being mastered.
                —ANONYMOUS (LATIN PROVERB)

The future ain't what it used to be.
                —LAWRENCE PETER "YOGI" BERRA,
                    attributed

You cannot fight against the future. Time is on our
side.   —WILLIAM GLADSTONE, speech on the
                    Reform Bill, 1866

I hold that man is in the right who is most closely in
league with the future.
                    —HENRIK IBSEN, letter to
                        Georg Brandes, Jan. 3, 1882

I like the dreams of the future better than the history
of the past.   —THOMAS JEFFERSON, letter to
                        John Adams, 1816

You ain't heard nothin' yet, folks.
                    —AL JOLSON, *The Jazz Singer*

In the long run . . . we are all dead.
    —JOHN MAYNARD KEYNES, attributed, in Claude
    Cockburn, *Aspects of English History*

I'll think of it all tomorrow at Tara. . . . After all,
tomorrow is another day.
                        —MARGARET MITCHELL,
                            Gone with the Wind

If you want a picture of the future, imagine a boot
stamping on a human face—forever.
                        —GEORGE ORWELL, *1984*

There's a gude time coming.
                        —SIR WALTER SCOTT,
                            Rob Roy

I have seen the future and it works.
—LINCOLN STEFFENS, saying,
after visiting Russia in 1919

Time and space—time to be alone, space to move about—these may well be the greatest scarcities of tomorrow.
—EDWIN WAY TEALE, *Autumn Across America*

G

GAMES   See also SPORTS; WINNING & LOSING,
                                            VICTORY & DEFEAT

To play billiards is a sign of misspent youth.
                                            —ANONYMOUS
[Often attributed to Herbert Spencer, because he recorded this remark in a letter. It had been said to him
by a Mr. Charles Roupell, but it's not clear if it was
original.]

There are two great pleasures in gambling: winning
and losing.   —ANONYMOUS (FRENCH PROVERB)

Life's too short for chess.   —HENRY J. BYRON,
                                            Our Boys

Poets do not go mad, but chess players do.
                            —G. K. CHESTERTON, *Orthodoxy*

When in doubt, win the trick.
                            —EDMOND HOYLE, *Hoyle's Games*,
                                            rule 12 for whist

I am sorry I have not learnt to play at cards. It is
very useful in life: it generates kindness and consoli-
dates society.
            —SAMUEL JOHNSON, quoted by James Boswell,
                            Tour to the Hebrides, Nov. 21, 1773

Cards are war in disguise of a sport.
>—CHARLES LAMB, *Mrs. Battle's Opinions on Whist*

The roulette table pays nobody except him who keeps it. Nevertheless, a passion for gaming is common, though a passion for keeping roulette wheels is unknown.
>—GEORGE BERNARD SHAW, *Man and Superman*, "Maxims for Revolutionists"

GARDENS   See NATURE: GARDENS, FLOWERS, & TREES

GENERATIONS   See also LIFE

One generation passeth away, and another generation cometh: but the earth abideth forever.
The sun also ariseth.   —BIBLE, *Ecclesiastes* 1:4–5

Let us now praise famous men, and our fathers that begat us.   —*Ibid.*, 44:1

The gods
Visit the sins of the fathers upon the children.
>—EURIPIDES, *Phrixus*

[Similar lines are found in *Exodus*, *The Merchant of Venice*, and elsewhere.]

As is the generations of leaves, so is that of humanity.
The wind scatters the leaves on the ground, but the live timber
Burgeons with leaves again in the season of spring returning.
So one generation of men will grow while another
Dies.   —HOMER, *Iliad*

The generations of living things pass in a short time, and like runners hand on the torch of life.
>—LUCRETIUS, *De rerum natura*

Each generation wastes a little more
of the future with greed and lust for riches.
>—DON MARQUIS, *archy and mehitabel*

What has posterity ever done for me?
                    —GROUCHO MARX, attributed

Every generation revolts against its fathers and makes
friends with its grandfathers.   —LEWIS MUMFORD,
                    The Brown Decades

Every moment dies a man,
Every moment one is born.
    —ALFRED, LORD TENNYSON, *The Vision of Sin*
[Charles Babbage, inventor of the analytical engine,
similar to a modern computer, put matters this way in
a letter to Tennyson: "Every moment dies a man. Every
moment one and one sixteenth is born."]

GENEROSITY   See CHARITY: PHILANTHROPY;
                    HOSPITALITY

GENIUS   See also GREATNESS; MIND,
                    THOUGHT, & UNDERSTANDING;
                    VISION & VISIONARIES

A genius is a man who has *two* great ideas.
                    —JACOB BRONOWSKI, *The Ascent of Man*

Genius . . . means transcendent capacity of taking
trouble.   —THOMAS CARLYLE,
                    Life of Frederick the Great

Genius is one per cent inspiration and ninety-nine
per cent perspiration.   —THOMAS ALVA EDISON,
                    Life

Towering genius disdains a beaten path. It seeks re-
gions hitherto unexplored.   —ABRAHAM LINCOLN,
                    speech, Jan. 27, 1838

Genius is an African who dreams up snow.
                    —VLADIMIR NABOKOV, *The Gift*

There is no great genius without some touch of
madness.   —SENECA, *On Tranquillity of the Mind*

Everybody is born with genius, but most people only keep it a few minutes.
> —EDGARD VARÈSE, quoted by Martha Graham, interview, *The New York Times*, March 31, 1985

GERMANY   See NATIONS

GETTING AWAY FROM IT ALL   See ESCAPE; TRAVEL

GIVING   See CHARITY: PHILANTHROPY

GLORY   See SUCCESS & FAME; WAR

GOD   See also CREATION, DIVINE; FAITH; JESUS; PRAYERS; PROVIDENCE, DIVINE; RELIGION

God is not dead but alive and well and working on a much less ambitious project.   —ANONYMOUS (Graffito)
[This has been widely quoted, but it may be apocryphal. Some sources trace it to London; *The Penguin Dictionary of Modern Quotations* says that it was noted in the *Guardian*, Nov. 27, 1975.]

I am all that has been, and that is, and that shall remain, and no one unworthy has ever unraveled, loosened, or even touched the surface of my woven veil.
> —ANONYMOUS, carving on an ancient statue of Pallas Athena, cited in Plutarch's *Lives*

God is that, the greater than which cannot be conceived.   —ST. ANSELM, *Proslogion*

And God said unto Moses, I AM THAT I AM.
> —BIBLE, *Exodus* 3:14

The Lord is my shepherd; I shall not want.
—BIBLE, *Psalms* 23:1
[The entire psalm is given at PROVIDENCE, DIVINE.]

God is our refuge and strength, a very present help in trouble. —*Ibid.*, 46:1

Thy word is lamp unto my feet, and a light unto my path. —*Ibid.*, 119:105

His mercy endureth forever. —*Ibid.*, 136:1

With God all things are possible.
—BIBLE, *Matthew* 19:26

Thou shalt love the Lord thy God with all thy heart, and with all thy soul, and with all thy mind.
—*Ibid.*, 22:37

I am the resurrection, and the life.
—BIBLE, *John* 11:25

In my Father's house are many mansions.
—*Ibid.*, 14:2

I am the way, the truth, and the life: no man cometh unto the Father, but by me. —*Ibid.*, 14:6

God is no respecter of persons.
—BIBLE, *Acts* 10:34

All things work together for good to them that love God. —BIBLE, *Romans* 8:28

If God be for us, who can be against us?
—*Ibid.*, 8:31

He that loveth not knoweth not God, for God is love.
—BIBLE, *I John* 4:8

I am the Alpha and the Omega, the beginning and the end, the first and the last.
—BIBLE, *Revelation* 22:13

God is under repair. —CÉLINE, epigraph, *The School for Corpses*

Do not take liberties with the gods, or weary them.
——CONFUCIUS, *The Book of Rites*

It is the final proof of God's omnipotence that he need not exist in order to save us.
——PETER DE VRIES, *The Mackerel Plaza*

Raffiniert ist der Herr Gott, aber boshaft ist er nicht.
God is subtle, but he is not malicious.
——ALBERT EINSTEIN, inscription in Fine Hall, Princeton University
[Alan L. Mackay, in *The Harvest of a Quiet Eye*, gives Einstein's own translation as "God is slick, but he ain't mean." For Einstein's dictum on God playing dice, see under SCIENCE: PHYSICS & COSMOLOGY.]

God is a circle whose center is everywhere and whose circumference is nowhere. ——EMPEDOCLES, fragment

At bottom God is nothing more than an exalted father.   ——FREUD, *Totem and Taboo*

God, to me, it seems is a verb.
——R. BUCKMINSTER FULLER, *No More Secondhand God*

Toward what should we aim if not toward God?
——ANDRÉ GIDE, *Thésée*

God lies ahead. . . . He depends on us. It is through us that God is achieved. ——ANDRÉ GIDE, *Journals*

God will forgive me, it is his business.
——HEINRICH HEINE, last words, attributed in many sources, including the Goncourt *Journals*

The world is charged with the grandeur of God.
——GERARD MANLEY HOPKINS, *God's Grandeur*

An honest God's the noblest work of man.
——ROBERT G. INGERSOLL, *The Gods*
[Also in Samuel Butler, *Notebooks*.]

My dear child, you must believe in God despite what
the clergy tell you.
    —BENJAMIN JOWETT, quoted by Margot Asquith,
    Autobiography

He is to us all-thing that is good and comfortable for
our help. He is our clothing, for love; He enwraps us
and envelops us, embraces and encloses us for tender
love, that He may never leave us.
                            —JULIANA OF NORWICH,
                            Revelations of Divine Love

Nam homo proponit, sed Deus disponit.
For man proposes, but God disposes.
    —THOMAS À KEMPIS, *Of the Imitation of Christ*

A man with God is always in the majority.
        —JOHN KNOX,
            inscription on the Reformation Monument
            in Geneva

[See also Andrew Jackson under COURAGE.]

He is the first and the last, the manifest and the hidden: and He knoweth all things.   —KORAN

Though the mills of God grind slowly, yet they grind
exceedingly small.
    —FRIEDRICH VON LOGAU, *Retribution*, translated
        by Henry Wadsworth Longfellow

[Cf. Zenobius, below.]

A mighty fortress is our God.
A bulwark never failing.
                —MARTIN LUTHER, *A Mighty Fortress*

A safe stronghold our God is still,
A trusty shield and weapon.   —*Ibid.*

It takes a long while for a naturally trustful person to reconcile himself to the idea that after all God will not help him.   —H. L. MENCKEN, *Minority Report*

There is a very good saying that if triangles invented a god, they would make him three-sided.
—MONTESQUIEU, *Lettres persanes*

God is dead: but considering the state the species Man is in, there will perhaps be caves, for ages yet, in which his shadow will be shown.
—FRIEDRICH NIETZSCHE,
Die fröhliche Wissenschaft

It is convenient that there be gods, and, as it is convenient, let us believe there are.
—OVID, *Ars amatoria*

Be comforted. You would not be seeking Me if you had not found Me.   —PASCAL, *Pensées*

He was a wise man who invented God.
—PLATO, *Sisyphus*
[See also Voltaire, below.]

Lo, the poor Indian! whose untutored mind
Sees God in clouds, or hears him in the wind;
His soul proud science never taught to stray
Far as the solar walk, or milky way.
—ALEXANDER POPE, *Essay on Man*

As flies to wanton boys are we to the gods
They kill us for their sport.
SHAKESPEARE, *King Lear*, IV, i

A god does not change his ways.
—TERTULLIAN, *The Christian's Defense*

I fled Him, down the nights and down the days;
I fled Him, down the arches of the years;
I fled Him, down the labyrinthine ways
Of my own mind.
—FRANCIS J. THOMPSON, *The Hound of Heaven*

If God did not exist, it would be necessary to invent him. —VOLTAIRE, *A l'auteur du livre des trois imposteurs*

If God made us in His image, we have certainly returned the compliment. —VOLTAIRE, *Le Sottisier*

Jupiter is slow looking into his notebook, but he always looks. —ZENOBIUS, *Sententiae*

GOOD-BYES See FAREWELLS

GOODNESS See VIRTUE

GOVERNMENT See also DIPLOMACY; HIGH POSITION: RULERS & LEADERS; LAW; LAWYERS; POLITICS; SECURITY; TAXES; TYRANNY & TOTALITARIANISM

Divide et impera.
Divide and rule.
—ANONYMOUS (LATIN PROVERB)
[Also appears as *Divide ut regnes*—"Divide in order to rule."]

Government is a contrivance of human wisdom to provide for human wants. Men have a right that these wants should be provided for by this wisdom.
—EDMUND BURKE, *Reflections on the Revolution in France*
[For Burke on government and compromise, see under Bismarck at POLITICS, the second quote.]

No man should be in public office who can't make more money in private life.
—THOMAS E. DEWEY, maxim, cited in Richard Norton Smith, *Thomas E. Dewey*

The less government we have, the better.
—RALPH WALDO EMERSON, *Politics*

In every society some men are born to rule, and some to advise. —RALPH WALDO EMERSON, *The Young American*

A government that is big enough to give you all you want is big enough to take it all away.
—BARRY GOLDWATER, speech, Oct. 21, 1964

A civil servant doesn't make jokes.
—EUGENE IONESCO, *The Killer*

The natural progress of things is for liberty to yield and government to gain ground.
—THOMAS JEFFERSON, letter to Colonel Edward Carrington, 1788

The whole art of government consists in being honest.
—THOMAS JEFFERSON, *Works*, VI, 186

The great task remaining before us . . . that government of the people, by the people, for the people, shall not perish from the earth.
—ABRAHAM LINCOLN, Address at Gettysburg, Nov. 19, 1863
[Lincoln may have been familiar with Daniel Webster's reference to "the people's government, made for the people, made by the people, and answerable to the people," speech, Jan. 26, 1830. A possible earlier source is said to be the prologue to John Wycliffe's translation of the Bible in 1382: "This Bible is for the government of the people, by the people, and for the people." However, this attribution remains unverified.]

It is perfectly true that the government is best which governs least. It is equally true that the government is best which provides most.
—WALTER LIPPMANN, *A Preface to Politics*
[The reference is to John O'Sullivan's maxim, see below.]

Every nation has the government that it deserves.
—JOSEPH DE MAISTRE, letter to X, Aug. 1811

The worst government is the most moral. One composed of cynics is often very tolerant and humane. But when fanatics are on top there is no limit to oppression.
—H. L. MENCKEN, *Notebooks*

All government is evil. . . . The best government is that which governs least.
—JOHN L. O'SULLIVAN, Introduction, *The United States Magazine and Democratic Review*, 1837
[For a response, see Walter Lippmann, above.]

Society in every state is a blessing, but government even in its best state, is but a necessary evil; in its worst state, an intolerable one.
—THOMAS PAINE, *Common Sense*

For forms of government let fools contest,
Whate'er is best administered is best.
—ALEXANDER POPE, *Essay on Man*

Government can easily exist without law, but law cannot exist without government.
—BERTRAND RUSSELL, *Unpopular Essays*

GRACE   See also BEAUTY; CHARM;
                                         STYLE; VIRTUE

A soft answer turneth away wrath.
—BIBLE, *Proverbs* 15:1

There be three things which are too wonderful for me, yea, four which I know not.
    The way of an eagle in the air; the way of a serpent upon a rock; the way of a ship in the midst of the sea; and the way of a man with a maid.
—*Ibid.*, 30:18, 19

Whatever is worth doing at all, is worth doing well.
—EARL OF CHESTERFIELD, letter to his son,
March 10, 1746

To learn to dance by practicing dancing or to live by practicing living, the principles are the same. . . . One becomes, in some area, an athlete of God.
—MARTHA GRAHAM, May 15, 1945

Grace is the absence of everything that indicates pain or difficulty, hesitation or incongruity.
—WILLIAM HAZLITT, *On Beauty*

Grace under pressure.
—ERNEST HEMINGWAY, definition of *guts*, quoted in John F. Kennedy, *Profiles in Courage* [According to Dorothy Parker, in "The Artist's Reward," *The New Yorker*, Nov. 20, 1929, Hemingway used the phrase originally in 1926 to describe Gerald Murphy's first efforts at downhill skiing. Later, describing the bullfighter Antonio Ordoñez, Hemingway wrote: "He had the three great requisites of a matador: courage, skill in his profession, and grace in the presence of the danger of death," *The Dangerous Summer*.]

Do every act of your life as if it were your last.
—MARCUS AURELIUS, *Meditations*

To know how to live is my trade and my art.
—MONTAIGNE, *Essays*

GRACE, DIVINE   See FAITH; PROVIDENCE, DIVINE

GREATNESS   See also AMBITION; GENIUS; HEROES; HIGH POSITION: RULERS & LEADERS; SUCCESS & FAME

A great man is always willing to be little.
—RALPH WALDO EMERSON, *Compensation*

To be great is to be misunderstood.
—RALPH WALDO EMERSON, *Self-Reliance*

Great deeds are usually wrought at great risks.
—HERODOTUS, *Histories*

Four things greater than all things are,—
Women and Horses and Power and War.
—RUDYARD KIPLING, *The Ballad of the King's Jest*

The great man is he who does not lose his child's heart.　　　　　　　　　　　—MENCIUS, *Works*

Great men can't be ruled.
　　　　　　　　　—AYN RAND, *The Fountainhead*

Be not afraid of greatness. Some are born great, some achieve greatness, and some have greatness thrust upon them.　　　　　—SHAKESPEARE, *Twelfth Night*, II, v

In order to carry out great enterprises, one must live as if one will never have to die.
　　　　　　　—MARQUIS DE VAUVENARGUES,
　　　　　　　　Réflexions et maximes

Le mieux est l'ennemi du bien.
The best is the enemy of the good.
　　　　　　　—VOLTAIRE, *Dictionnaire philosophique*,
　　　　　　　　"Art dramatique"

GREECE　　　　　　　　　　　See NATIONS

GREED　　　　　　　　　See SELF-INTEREST

GUILT　　　　　　See also CRIME; EVIDENCE;
　　　　　　　　　　　　EVIL; INNOCENCE

The wicked flee when no man pursueth.
　　　　　　　　　—BIBLE, *Proverbs* 28:1
[Often misquoted as "The guilty flee . . . ," for example by Robert Bork in his Supreme Court nomination confirmation hearings, 1987.]

The guilty think all talk is of themselves.
　　　　　　　—CHAUCER, *The Canterbury Tales*

Where guilt is, rage and courage doth abound.
　　　　　　　　　—BEN JONSON, *Sejanus*

Alas! how difficult it is not to betray guilt by our countenance.　　　　　—OVID, *Metamorphoses*

Nobody becomes guilty by fate.
　　　　　　　　　—SENECA, *Oedipus*

The lady doth protest too much, methinks.
                    —SHAKESPEARE, *Hamlet*, III, ii

Here's the smell of the blood still. All the perfumes of Arabia will not sweeten this little hand.
                    —SHAKESPEARE, *Macbeth*, V, i

H

HABIT   See also CUSTOM

The nature of men is always the same; it is their habits that separate them.   —CONFUCIUS, *Analects*

Nothing is more powerful than habit.
                                —OVID, *Ars amatoria*

Habit is a second nature that prevents us from knowing the first, of which it has neither the cruelties nor the enchantments.
   —MARCEL PROUST, *Remembrance of Things Past: The Guermantes Way*

To fall into a habit is to begin to cease to be.
                                —MIGUEL DE UNAMUNO,
                                The Tragic Sense of Life

Rigid, the skeleton of habit alone upholds the human frame.   —VIRGINIA WOOLF, *Mrs. Dalloway*

HAPPINESS   See also ETHICS & MORALITY;
                      HAPPINESS, EXPRESSIONS OF; HEDONISM;
                                      LOVE, EXPRESSIONS OF

A joy that's shared is a joy made double.
       —ANONYMOUS (ENGLISH PROVERB), recorded
          by John Ray, *English Proverbs*

One half of the world cannot understand the pleasures of the other.   —JANE AUSTEN, *Mansfield Park*

Weeping may endure for a night, but joy cometh in the morning.   —BIBLE, *Psalms* 30:5

Judge none blessed before his death.
                    —BIBLE, *Ecclesiasticus* 11:28
[This concept was expressed by other ancient writers, including Solon; see below.]

The joyfulness of a man prolongeth his days.
                    —*Ibid.*, 30:22

The secret of happiness is to admire without desiring. And that is not happiness.
                    —F. H. BRADLEY, *Aphorisms*

Make us happy and you make us good.
                    —ROBERT BROWNING, *The Ring and the Book*

Follow your bliss.   —JOSEPH CAMPBELL, motto

The latter end of joy is woe.
                    —GEOFFREY CHAUCER, *The Canterbury Tales*

All seek joy, but it is not found on earth
                    —ST. JOHN CHRYSOSTOM, *Homilies*

Great joys must be controlled.
                    —COLETTE, *The Seamstress*

It is neither wealth nor splendor, but tranquillity and occupation, which give happiness.
                    —THOMAS JEFFERSON, letter to
                    Mrs. A. S. Marks, 1788

One is never as fortunate or as unfortunate as one imagines.   —LA ROCHEFOUCAULD, *Maxims*

To live happily is an inward power of the soul.
                    —MARCUS AURELIUS, *Meditations*

toujours gai, archy, toujours gai.
                    —DON MARQUIS, *archy's life of mehitabel*

Ask yourself whether you are happy, and you will cease to be so.

—JOHN STUART MILL, *Autobiography*

The secret of happiness is to face the fact that the world is horrible, horrible, *horrible*.

—BERTRAND RUSSELL, quoted in Alan Wood, *Bertrand Russell: The Passionate Skeptic*

Happiness is the only sanction in life; where happiness fails, existence remains a mad and lamentable experiment.

—GEORGE SANTAYANA, *The Life of Reason*

We have no more right to consume happiness without producing it than to consume wealth without producing it.   —GEORGE BERNARD SHAW, *Candida*

A lifetime of happiness! No man alive could bear it: it would be hell on earth.

—GEORGE BERNARD SHAW, *Man and Superman*

There are two things to aim at in life: first, to get what you want; and, after that, to enjoy it. Only the wisest of mankind achieve the second.

—LOGAN PEARSALL SMITH, *Afterthoughts*

Call no man happy until he dies; he is at best but fortunate.

—SOLON, quoted in Herodotus, *Histories*

Our happiness depends on wisdom all the way.

—SOPHOCLES, *Antigone*

The world is so full of a number of things.
I'm sure we should all be as happy as kings.

—ROBERT LOUIS STEVENSON,
"Happy Thought," in
A Child's Garden of Verses

Happiness is an imaginary condition formerly often attributed by the living to the dead, now usually attributed by adults to children, and by children to adults.

—THOMAS SZASZ, "Emotions," in
The Second Sin

HAPPINESS, EXPRESSIONS OF   See also
                HAPPINESS; LOVE, EXPRESSIONS OF

The morning stars sang together, and all the sons of
God shouted for joy.   —BIBLE, *Job* 38:7

"And hast thou slain the Jabberwock?
Come to my arms, my beamish boy!
O frabjous day! Callooh! Callay!"
He chortled in his joy.
            —LEWIS CARROLL, "Jabberwocky," in
            Through the Looking-Glass

Everyone suddenly burst out singing.
            —SIEGFRIED SASSOON, *Everyone Sang*

O wonderful, wonderful, and most wonderful! and
yet again wonderful, and after that, out of all whooping!
            —SHAKESPEARE, *As You Like It*, III, ii

HARLEM   See CITIES

HASTE

Festina lente.
Hasten slowly.   —ANONYMOUS (PROVERB)

What is done well is done quickly enough.
            —AUGUSTUS CAESAR, favorite
            proverbial saying, quoted in Suetonius,
            Lives of the Caesars

No man who is in a hurry is quite civilized.
            —WILL DURANT, *What Is Civilization?*

Nothing is more vulgar than haste.
            —RALPH WALDO EMERSON,
            The Conduct of Life

Haste in every business brings failures.
—HERODOTUS, *Histories*

We haven't the time to take our time.
—EUGÈNE IONESCO, *Exit the King*

Wisely and slowly; they stumble that run fast.
—SHAKESPEARE, *Romeo and Juliet*, II, iii

More haste, less speed.   —THEOGNIS, fragment

Never hurry and never worry!
—E. B. WHITE, *Charlotte's Web*
[Charlotte's advice to Wilbur.]

HATE   See also ANGER; REVENGE

Hatred watches while friendship sleeps.
—ANONYMOUS (FRENCH PROVERB)

Thou shalt not hate thy brother in thy heart.
—BIBLE, *Leviticus* 19:17

The bloodthirsty hate the upright.
—BIBLE, *Proverbs* 29:10

Now hatred is by far the longest pleasure;
Men love in haste, but they detest at leisure.
—LORD BYRON, *Don Juan*

I tell you there is such a thing as creative hate.
—WILLA CATHER, *The Song of the Lark*

Heaven has no rage like love to hatred turned,
Nor hell a fury like a woman scorned.
—WILLIAM CONGREVE, *The Mourning Bride*

Violent antipathies are always suspicious, and betray
a secret affinity.   —WILLIAM HAZLITT, *Table-Talk*

We can scarcely hate anyone that we know.
—WILLIAM HAZLITT, *On Criticism*

Hate is the coward's revenge for being humiliated.
—GEORGE BERNARD SHAW, *Major Barbara*

It is human to hate those whom we have injured.
—TACITUS, *Life of Agricola*

HAVES & HAVE-NOTS See also COMPASSION & PITY;
MONEY; POVERTY & HUNGER; POWER;
RUIN; WINNING & LOSING, VICTORY & DEFEAT

The rich would have to eat money, but luckily the poor provide food.
—ANONYMOUS (RUSSIAN PROVERB)

The poor is hated even of his own neighbor, but the rich have many friends. —BIBLE, *Proverbs* 14:20

For unto everyone that hath shall be given, and he shall have abundance: but from him that hath not shall be taken even that which he hath.
—BIBLE, *Matthew* 25:29

There are only two families in the world, my old grandmother used to say, the *Haves* and the *Have-nots*.
—CERVANTES, *Don Quixote*

I was told . . . that an impassable gulf divided the Rich from the Poor; I was told that the Privileged and the People formed Two Nations.
—BENJAMIN DISRAELI, *Sybil*

The meek shall inherit the earth but not the mineral rights. —J. PAUL GETTY, attributed

If you are poor today, you will always be poor. Only the rich acquire riches. —MARTIAL, *Epigrams*

Wealth . . . and poverty; . . . the one is the parent of luxury and idolence, and the other of meanness and viciousness, and both of discontent.
—PLATO, *The Republic*
[More at ARTS.]

Half the world does not know how the other half lives.   —RABELAIS, *Pantagruel*

Really, if the lower orders don't set us a good example, what on earth is the use of them?
                    —OSCAR WILDE,
                         The Importance of Being Earnest

HEALTH   See also DOCTORS & THE PRACTICE OF
                    MEDICINE; ILLNESS & REMEDIES;
                    MADNESS; PHYSICAL FITNESS

There is a limit to the best of health: disease is always a near neighbor.   —AESCHYLUS, *Agamemnon*

Health and good estate of body are above all good.
                    —BIBLE, *Ecclesiasticus* 30:15

Early to bed and early to rise, makes a man healthy, wealthy, and wise.   —BENJAMIN FRANKLIN,
                         Poor Richard's Almanac

Orandum est ut sit mens sana in corpore sano.
We should pray for a sound mind in a sound body.
                    —JUVENAL, *Satires*

A sound mind in a sound body is a short but full description of a happy state in this world.
                    —JOHN LOCKE,
                         Some Thoughts Concerning Education

Non est vivere, sed valera vita est.
Life is not merely living but living in health.
                    —MARTIAL, *Epigrams*

Too much attention to health is a hindrance to learning, to invention, and to studies of any kind, for we are always feeling suspicious shootings and swimmings in our heads, and we are prone to blame our studies for them.   —PLATO, *The Republic*

People who feel well are sick people neglecting themselves.   —JULES ROMAINS,
                         *Knock, où le triomphe
                         de la mèdecine*

Use your health, even to the point of wearing it out. That is what it is for. Spend all you have before you die; and do not outlive yourself.
—GEORGE BERNARD SHAW,
The Doctor's Dilemma

Keep breathing [key to longevity.]
—SOPHIE TUCKER,
newspaper reports,
Jan. 13, 1964

HEART   See also EMOTIONS; LOVE

When I was one-and-twenty
I heard a wise man say,
Give crowns and pounds and guineas
But not your heart away.
—A. E. HOUSMAN, *A Shropshire Lad*

The intellect is always fooled by the heart.
—LA ROCHEFOUCAULD, *Maxims*

In the human heart, there is a ceaseless birth of passions, so that the destruction of one is almost always the establishment of another.   —*Ibid.*

The human heart is like a ship on a stormy sea driven about by winds blowing from all four corners of heaven.
—MARTIN LUTHER, preface to his
translation of the *Psalms*

My heart is a lonely hunter that hunts on a lonely hill.   —FIONA MACLEOD, *The Lonely Hunter*

La coeur a ses raisons que la raison ne connaît point.
The heart has its reasons which reason does not know at all.
—PASCAL, *Pensées*

I follow my heart for I can trust it.
—J. C. F. VON SCHILLER,
Wallensteins Tod

Great thoughts always come from the heart.
> —MARQUIS DE VAUVENARGUES,
> *Réflexions et maximes*

Now that my ladder's gone,
I must lie down where all the ladders start,
In the foul rag-and-bone shop of the heart.
> —WILLIAM BUTLER YEATS,
> *The Circus Animals' Desertion*

[These famous lines were written in the poet's old age; the missing "ladder" is the power of "pure mind" to create masterful themes out of the refuse of experience.]

HEAVEN   See IMMORTALITY; LAST JUDGMENT & THE HEREAFTER

HEAVENS, THE   See NATURE: THE HEAVENS, THE SKY

HEDONISM   See also EXCESS; HAPPINESS; SEX & SENSUALITY

Who loves not wine, women, and song
Remains a fool his whole life long.
> —ANONYMOUS

[Traditionally but probably wrongly attributed to Martin Luther.]

Let us eat and drink; for tomorrow we shall die.
> —BIBLE, *Isaiah* 22:13

[The same is found at *I Corinthians* 15:32, "Let us eat and drink; for tomorrow we die."]

Gather ye rosebuds while ye may,
Old Time is still a-flying;
And this same flower that smiles today,
Tomorrow will be dying.
> —ROBERT HERRICK, *To the Virgins,*
> *To Make Much of Time*

[For "the days of wine and roses," see under Dawson at YOUTH.]

Had we but world enough, and time,
This coyness, Lady, were no crime.
    —ANDREW MARVELL, *To His Coy Mistress*

But at my back I always hear
Time's wingèd chariot hurrying near;
And yonder all before us lie
Deserts of vast eternity.   *—Ibid.*

The grave's a fine and private place,
But none, I think, do there embrace.   *—Ibid.*

I seek the utmost pleasure and the least pain.
    —PLAUTUS, *Captivi*

Fait ce que voudras.
Do what you will.
    —RABELAIS, *Gargantua and Pantagruel*

Pleasure is the only thing to live for. Nothing ages
like happiness. —OSCAR WILDE, *An Ideal Husband*

Give me the luxuries of life and I will willingly do
without the necessities.
    —FRANK LLOYD WRIGHT, quoted in
    The New York Times, obituary, April 9, 1959
[Similarly, *The New York Times* reported that an aphorism favored by painter Elaine de Kooning was "Take
care of the luxuries, the necessities will take care of
themselves." A person of great grace, Mrs. de Kooning
was once asked what it was like to live in the "shadow"
of her husband, abstract expressionist Willem de Kooning. "I live in his light," she replied.]

HELL   See also DEVIL; EVIL;
                LAST JUDGMENT & THE HEREAFTER

Hell, madame, is to love no more.
    —GEORGES BERNANOS,
      The Diary of a Country Priest

All hope abandon, ye who enter here!
—DANTE, *Inferno,* in *The Divine Comedy*

Hell is oneself.   —T. S. ELIOT, *The Cocktail Party*

When all the world dissolves,
And every creature shall be purified,
All place shall be hell that is not heaven.
—CHRISTOPHER MARLOWE, *Dr. Faustus*

The road to Hell is paved with good intentions.
—KARL MARX, *Capital*
[Essentially proverbial. Also attributed to St. Bernard
—"Hell is full of good intentions and desires"—and
others.]

Long is the way
And hard, that out of hell leads up to light.
—JOHN MILTON, *Paradise Lost*

Which way I fly is hell; myself am hell;
And in the lowest deep a lower deep
Still threatening to devour me opens wide,
To which the hell I suffer seems a heaven.
—*Ibid.*

Hell has no terrors for pagans.
—ARTHUR RIMBAUD,
Mauvais Sang

To work hard, to live hard, to die hard, and then to
go to hell after all would be too damned hard.
—CARL SANDBURG, *The People, Yes*

Hell is other people.
—JEAN-PAUL SARTRE, *No Exit*

The way down to hell [Hades] is easy.
The gates of black Dis stand open night and day.
But to retrace one's steps and escape to the upper
air
That is toil, that is labor.   —VIRGIL, *Aeneid*

HEROES See also COURAGE; GREATNESS;
HIGH POSITION: RULERS & LEADERS

No hero is mortal till he dies.
—W. H. AUDEN, *A Short Ode to a Philologist*

Unhappy the land that needs heroes.
—BERTOLT BRECHT, *Galileo*
[See also Plato under TYRANNY & TOTALITARIANISM.]

Down these mean streets a man must go who is not
himself mean; who is neither tarnished nor afraid.
—RAYMOND CHANDLER,
The Simple Art of Murder

Every hero becomes a bore at last.
—RALPH WALDO EMERSON, *Representative Men*

Show me a hero and I will write you a tragedy.
—F. SCOTT FITZGERALD, *Notebooks*

The boy stood on the burning deck
Whence all but he had fled.
—FELICIA HEMANS, *Casabianca*
[The boy was Giacomo Casabianca, who died during
the Battle of the Nile on the French flagship *L'Orient*.
His father, Louis, the ship's commander, was also
killed.]

Listen, my children, and you shall hear,
Of the midnight ride of Paul Revere,
On the eighteenth of April, in Seventy-five;
Hardly a man is now alive
Who remembers that famous day and year.
—HENRY WADSWORTH LONGFELLOW,
"Paul Revere's Ride," in
Tales of a Wayside Inn

One if by land, and two if by sea;
And I on the opposite shore will be,
Ready to ride and spread the alarm
Through every Middlesex village and farm.
—*Ibid.*

Then out spake brave Horatius,
The Captain of the Gate:
"To every man upon this earth
Death cometh soon or late.
And how can man die better
Than facing fearful odds,
For the ashes of his fathers,
And the temples of his Gods?"
—THOMAS BABINGTON MACAULAY,
"Horatius," in
Lays of Ancient Rome

See, the conquering hero comes!
Sound the trumpets, beat the drums!
—THOMAS MORRELL, *Joshua*

We seek him here, we seek him there,
Those Frenchies seek him everywhere.
Is he in heaven?
Is he in hell?
That demmed, elusive Pimpernel.
—BARONESS ORCZY, *The Scarlet Pimpernel*
[The Masterpiece Theater series on the Pankhurst family reported that when feminist Christabel Pankhurst was in hiding to avoid arrest this bit of doggerel surfaced: "Is she in heaven? Is she in hell? / That damned, elusive Christabel!"]

The hero is strangely akin to those who die young.
—RAINER MARIA RILKE, *Duino Elegies*

He was born with the gift of laughter and a sense that the world was mad.
—RAFAEL SABATINI, *Scaramouche*

Hail to the chief who in triumph advances!
—SIR WALTER SCOTT, *The Lady of the Lake*

O, young Lochinvar is come out of the west.
—SIR WALTER SCOTT, *Marmion*

He was a man, take him for all in all.
I shall not look upon his like again.
—SHAKESPEARE, *Hamlet*, I, ii

This was the noblest Roman of them all.
—SHAKESPEARE, *Julius Caesar*, V, v
[The reference is to Brutus.]

His life was gentle, and the elements
So mixed in him that Nature might stand up
And say to all the world, "This was a man."
—*Ibid.*

Arms and the man I sing, the first who came,
Compelled by fate, an exile out of Troy,
To Italy and the Lavinian coast.
—VIRGIL, *The Aeneid*

HIGHLANDS OF SCOTLAND   See NATIONS

HIGH POSITION: See also GOVERNMENT; HEROES;
RULERS & LEADERS   MILITARY, THE; POLITICS;
                           POWER; SUCCESS & FAME

Princes are like to heavenly bodies, which cause good
or evil times, and which have much veneration but no
rest.   —FRANCIS BACON, *Of Empire*

It is a miserable state of mind to have few things to
desire, and many things to fear; and yet that commonly
is the case of kings.   —*Ibid.*

The people's leaders have taken the wrong turning,
and those who are led are lost.
—BIBLE, *Isaiah* 9:16

Put not your trust in princes.
—BIBLE, *Psalms* 146:3

I have to be seen to be believed.
—ELIZABETH II, saying,
quoted in *The Wall Street Journal*,
April 21, 1986.

Caesar's wife must be above suspicion.
>—JULIUS CAESAR, attributed, based
>on Plutarch's biography of Caesar

I had rather be right than be President.
>—HENRY CLAY, Senate speech, 1850

To be a leader of men one must turn one's back on
men. —HAVELOCK ELLIS, Introduction to,
>*A Rebours*, by J. K. Huysmans

A president's hardest task is not to do what is right
but to know what is right.
>—LYNDON B. JOHNSON,
>State of the Union speech, 1965

Noblesse oblige.
Nobility [or, rank] has its obligations.
>—DUC DE LÉVIS, *Maxims and Reflections*

L'état c'est moi.
I am the state. —LOUIS XIV
[Reputedly said in a speech on April 13, 1665, but very
possibly apocryphal—see also Napoleon Bonaparte at
TYRANNY & TOTALITARIANISM.]

A prince who desires to maintain his position must
learn to be not always good, but to be so or not, as
needs require. —MACHIAVELLI, *The Prince*

A prince who is a man of courage and is able to
command, who knows how to preserve order in his
state, need never regret having founded his security on
the affection of the people. —*Ibid.*

A leader is a dealer in hope.
>—NAPOLEON BONAPARTE, *Maxims*

Uneasy lies the head that wears a crown.
>—SHAKESPEARE, *Henry IV, Part II*, III, i

And what have kings that privates have not too,
Save ceremony, save general ceremony.
>—SHAKESPEARE, *Henry V*, IV, i

Nice customs curtsey to great kings.   —*Ibid.*, V, ii

I would not be a queen
For all the world.
                        —SHAKESPEARE, *Henry VIII*, II, iii

For God's sake, let us sit upon the ground
And tell sad stories of the death of kings.
                        —SHAKESPEARE, *Richard II*, III, ii.

Now is the winter of our discontent
Made glorious summer by this sun of York.
                        —SHAKESPEARE, *Richard III*, I, i

I met a traveler from an antique land
Who said: "Two vast and trunkless legs of stone
Stand in the desert. . . . Near them, on the sand,
Half sunk, a shattered visage lies, whose frown,
And wrinkled lip, and sneer of cold command,
Tell that its sculptor well those passions read."
                        —PERCY BYSSHE SHELLEY, *Ozymandias*

"My name is Ozymandias, king of kings:
Look on my works, ye Mighty, and despair!"
Nothing beside remains. Round the decay
Of that colossal wreck, boundless and bare,
The lone and level sands stretch far away.   —*Ibid.*

To know nor faith, nor love nor law; to be
Omnipotent but friendless is to reign.
  —PERCY BYSSHE SHELLEY, *Prometheus Unbound*

The only emperor is the emperor of ice-cream.
  —WALLACE STEVENS, *The Emperor of Ice-Cream*

All kings is mostly rapscallions.
                        —MARK TWAIN, *The Adventures of
                        Huckleberry Finn*

O Captain! my Captain! our fearful trip is done,
  The ship has weathered every rack, the prize we
sought is won.
                        —WALT WHITMAN, *O Captain! My Captain!*

[Whitman was writing of the Civil War and Lincoln's death. The poem ends ". . . on the deck my Captain lies, / Fallen cold and dead."]

HISTORY See also PAST, THE

Man is a history-making creature who can neither repeat his past nor leave it behind.
—W. H. AUDEN, *The Dyer's Hand*

History, n. an account mostly false, of events mostly unimportant, which are brought about by rulers, mostly knaves, and soldiers, mostly fools.
—AMBROSE BIERCE, *The Devil's Dictionary*

Happy the people whose annals are blank in history books! —THOMAS CARLYLE, *Frederick the Great*

The history of the world is but the biography of great men.
—THOMAS CARLYLE, *Heroes and Hero Worship*

History has many cunning passages, contrived corridors and issues. —T. S. ELIOT, *Gerontion*

History is more or less bunk.
—HENRY FORD, quoted in *Chicago Tribune*,
May 25, 1916
[In context, what Ford meant was that history as traditionally taught by academics is fairly useless.]

History . . . is little more than the register of the crimes, follies, and misfortunes of mankind.
—EDWARD GIBBON, *The Decline and Fall of the Roman Empire*

People and governments never have learned anything from history.
—HEGEL, *Philosophy of History*, Introduction

History is the autobiography of a madman.
—ALEXANDER HERZEN, *Dr. Krupov*

It is not the neutrals or the lukewarms who make history. —ADOLF HITLER, speech, April 23, 1933

History, Stephen said, is a nightmare from which I am trying to awake.   —JAMES JOYCE, *Ulysses*

The history of all hitherto existing society is the history of class struggles.
—KARL MARX, *The Communist Manifesto*

Hegel remarks somewhere that all great historical facts and personages occur, as it were, twice. He has forgotten to add: the first time as tragedy, the second time as farce.
—KARL MARX, *The Eighteenth Brumaire of Louis Bonaparte*, opening sentences

Men make their own history, but they do not make it just as they please.   —KARL MARX, *Ibid.*

World history is the world's verdict.
—J. C. F. VON SCHILLER, *Resignation*

A historian is a prophet in reverse.
—FRIEDRICH VON SCHLEGEL, *Athenaeum*

History is no more than the portrayal of crimes and misfortunes.   —VOLTAIRE, *L'Ingénu*

History can be well written only in a free country.
—VOLTAIRE, letter to Frederick the Great, May 27, 1773

Human history becomes more and more a race between education and catastrophe.
—H. G. WELLS, *The Outline of History*

Nothing has really happened until it has been recorded.   —VIRGINIA WOOLF, quoted in Harold Nicolson, *Diaries*

HOLIDAYS   See CHRISTMAS; NEW YEAR

HOME   See also FAMILY; MARRIAGE; PRIVACY; TRAVEL

To make a happy fireside clime
To wean and wife,

That's the true pathos and sublime
Of human life.
>   —ROBERT BURNS, *To Dr. Blacklock*

Home is where one starts from.
>   —T. S. ELIOT, *East Coker*

Home is the place where when you have to go there
They have to take you in.
>   —ROBERT FROST, *The Death of the Hired Man*

I remember, I remember,
The house where I was born,
The little window where the sun
Came peeping in at morn.
>   —THOMAS HOOD, *I Remember*

A man travels the world over in search of what he
needs and returns home to find it.
>   —GEORGE MOORE, *The Brook Kerith*

Happy the man whose wish and care
A few paternal acres bound,
Content to breathe his native air
In his own ground.
>   —ALEXANDER POPE, *Ode on Solitude*

Home is the girl's prison and the woman's work-
house.   —GEORGE BERNARD SHAW, *Man and
Superman*, "Maxims for Revolutionists"

You Can't Go Home Again.   —THOMAS WOLFE

HONESTY & SINCERITY   See also TRUTH

An honest man's word is as good as his bond.
>   —CERVANTES, *Don Quixote*

A few honest men are better than numbers.
>   —OLIVER CROMWELL, letter to
Sir W. Spring, Sept. 1643

Being entirely honest with oneself is a good exercise.
—FREUD, letter to Wilhelm Fliess,
Oct. 15, 1897

He that resolves to deal with none but honest men
must leave off dealing.
—THOMAS FULLER, *Gnomologia*

The secret of success is sincerity. Once you can fake
that, you've got it made.
—JEAN GIRAUDOUX, quoted by
A. Bloch, *Murphy's Law Book Two*
[Also attributed to Samuel Goldwyn.]

Honesty is praised and starves.
—JUVENAL, *Satires*

We only confess our little faults to persuade people
that we have no large ones.
—LA ROCHEFOUCAULD, *Maxims*

Children and fools speak true.
—JOHN LYLY, *Endymion*

Some persons are likeable in spite of their unswerving
integrity.
—DON MARQUIS, quoted by Edward Anthony,
O Rare Don Marquis

It's annoying to be honest for nothing.
—OVID, *Ex ponto*

Honesty is for the most part less profitable than
dishonesty.   —PLATO, *The Republic*

An honest man's the noblest work of God.
—ALEXANDER POPE, *An Essay on Man*

God looks at the clean hands, not the full ones.
—PUBLILIUS SYRUS, *Moral Sayings*

Men should be what they seem.
—SHAKESPEARE, *Othello*, III, iii

Take note, take note, O world!
To be direct and honest is not safe.   *—Ibid.*

Every man has his fault, and honesty is his.
    —SHAKESPEARE, *Timon of Athens*, III, i

I hold the maxim no less applicable to public than to
private affairs, that honesty is the best policy.
    —GEORGE WASHINGTON, *Farewell Address*, 1796
[The maxim was already time-honored; Cervantes also
used it in *Don Quixote*.]

A little sincerity is a dangerous thing, and a great
deal of it is absolutely fatal.
    —OSCAR WILDE, *The Picture of Dorian Gray*

If you do not tell the truth about yourself you cannot
tell it about other people.
    —VIRGINIA WOOLF, *The Moment
    and Other Essays*

HONOR   See REPUTATION; VIRTUE

HOPE   See also OPTIMISM & PESSIMISM

Hope is a waking dream.
    —ARISTOTLE, quoted in Diogenes Laërtius,
    Lives of Eminent Philosophers
[Cf. Matthew Prior, below.]

Hope is a good breakfast, but it is a bad supper.
    —FRANCIS BACON, *Apophthegms*

He that lives upon hope will die fasting.
    —BENJAMIN FRANKLIN, *Poor Richard's
    Almanac*, Preface

If it were not for hopes, the heart would break.
    —THOMAS FULLER, *Gnomologia*

Hope, like the gleaming taper's light,
Adorns and cheers our way;
And still, as darker grows the night,
Emits a lighter ray.   —OLIVER GOLDSMITH,
    The Captivity

Hope springs eternal in the human breast:
Man never is, but always to be blest.
—ALEXANDER POPE, *An Essay on Man*

For hope is but the dream of those that wake.
—MATTHEW PRIOR, *Solomon*
[Cf. Aristotle, above.]

Extreme hopes are born of extreme misery.
—BERTRAND RUSSELL, *The Future of Mankind*, in *Unpopular Essays*

True hope is swift and flies with swallow's wings;
Kings it makes Gods, and meaner creatures kings.
—SHAKESPEARE, *Richard III*, V, ii

Hope deceives more men than cunning can.
—MARQUIS DE VAUVENARGUES, *Réflexions et maximes*

HORSES   See NATURE: ANIMALS

HOSPITALITY

What is there more kindly than the feelings between host and guest?
—AESCHYLUS, *The Libation Bearers*

One cannot have too large a party.
—JANE AUSTEN, *Emma*

Go out into the highways and hedges, and compel them to come in, that my house may be filled.
—BIBLE, *Luke* 14:23

Use hospitality one to another without grudging.
—BIBLE, *I Peter* 4:9

Hospitality consists in a little fire, a little food, and an immense quiet.
—RALPH WALDO EMERSON, *Journal*, 1856

Why don't you come up sometime, 'n see me?
—MAE WEST, *She Done Him Wrong*

HUMAN BODY   See BODY, HUMAN

HUMANS & HUMAN NATURE   See also LIFE;
MEN; MIND; MISANTHROPY;
WOMEN

For Mercy has a human heart,
Pity a human face,
And Love, the human form divine,
And Secrecy, the human dress.
        —WILLIAM BLAKE, *The Divine Image*, in
            Songs of Innocence

Cruelty has a human heart,
And Jealousy a human face;
Terror, the human form divine,
And Secrecy, the human dress.
        —WILLIAM BLAKE, *A Divine Image*, in
            Songs of Experience

Man's inhumanity to man makes countless thousands
mourn.
        —ROBERT BURNS, *Man Was Made to Mourn*

Man is a tool-using animal. . . . Without tools he is
nothing, with tools, he is all.
        —THOMAS CARLYLE, *Sartor Resartus*
[Earlier, James Boswell ascribed the definition of man
as "a tool-making animal" to Benjamin Franklin (*The
Life of Johnson*, April 17, 1778). Johnson retorted:
"But many a man never made a tool; and suppose a
man without arms, he could not make a tool."]

Human nature is the same all over the world.
        —EARL OF CHESTERFIELD, letter to his son,
            Oct. 2, 1747

No man is an island entire of itself; every man is a
part of the continent, a part of the main.
        —JOHN DONNE, *Devotions XVII*

Any man's death diminishes me, because I am involved in mankind. And therefore never send to know
for whom the bell tolls. It tolls for thee.   —*Ibid.*

Man is slightly nearer to the atom than the star.
... From his central position man can survey the grand-
est works of nature with the astronomer, or the minutest
works with the physicist.
—Sir Arthur Eddington, *Stars and Atoms*

In spite of everything I still believe that people are
really good at heart.   —Anne Frank, *The Diary
of a Young Girl*

Men and melons are hard to know.
—Benjamin Franklin,
Poor Richard's Almanac

Wild animals never kill for sport. Man is the only one
to whom the torture and death of his fellow creatures
is amusing in itself.   —James A. Froude, *Oceana*

When God at first made man,
Having a glass of blessings standing by,
Let us, said he, pour on him all we can.
Let the world's riches, which dispersèd lie,
Contract into a span.
[But God withholds one gift: rest.]
—George Herbert, "The Pulley,"
in *The Temple*

At last,
If goodness lead him not, yet weariness
May toss him to My breast.   —*Ibid.*

Out of the crooked timber of humanity no straight
thing ever can be made.
—Immanuel Kant, *Idee
zu Einer Allgemeinen
Geschichte in Weltgebürglicher Absicht*

We has met the enemy, and it is us.
—Walt Kelly, *Pogo*
[For Oliver Hazard Perry's version, see under american
history: memorable moments.]

I teach you the superman. Man is something to be
surpassed.   —Friedrich Nietzsche,
Thus Spake Zarathustra

Man is the measure of all things, of things that are,
that they are, of things that are not, that they are not.
　　　—PROTAGORAS, quoted in Diogenes Laërtius,
　　　　Lives of Eminent Philosophers

Everything is good when it leaves the Creator's
hands; everything degenerates in the hands of man.
　　　　　—JEAN JACQUES ROUSSEAU, *Émile*

Brief and powerless is man's life; on him and all his
race the slow, sure doom falls pitiless and dark.
　　　—BERTRAND RUSSELL, *The Free Man's Worship*

We are such stuff
As dreams are made on, and our little life
Is rounded with a sleep.　　　—SHAKESPEARE,
　　　　　　　　　　　　The Tempest, IV, i

How beauteous mankind is! O brave new world,
That has such people in it.　　　　—*Ibid.*, V, i

Wonders are many, and none is more wonderful than
man.　　　　　　　　—SOPHOCLES, *Antigone*

Man is a social animal.　　　　—SPINOZA, *Ethics*

We feel and know that we are eternal.　　　—*Ibid.*

I am a man; nothing human is alien to me.
　　　—TERENCE, *Heuton timoroumenos*

Man is the only animal that blushes. Or needs to.
　　　—MARK TWAIN, "Pudd'nhead Wilson's
　　　　New Calendar," in *Following the Equator*

If you pick up a starving dog and make him prosperous, he will not bite you. This is the principal difference between a dog and a man.
　　　—MARK TWAIN, "Pudd'nhead Wilson's Calendar,"
　　　in *Pudd'nhead Wilson*

The still, sad music of humanity.
　　　　　—WILLIAM WORDSWORTH, *Tintern Abbey*

HUMOR   See also LAUGHTER

A man who could make so vile a pun would not scruple to pick a pocket.
—JOHN DENNIS, *The Gentleman's Magazine*, 1781

There is no better role to play among the great than that of jester.   —DENIS DIDEROT, *Le Neveu de Rameau*

A difference of taste in jokes is a great strain on the affections.   —GEORGE ELIOT, *Daniel Deronda*

Wit makes its own welcome and levels all distinctions.
—RALPH WALDO EMERSON, *The Comic*

Humor is an affirmation of dignity, a declaration of man's superiority to all that befalls him.
—ROMAIN GARY, *Promise at Dawn*

You can pretend to be serious; but you can't pretend to be witty.
—SACHA GUITRY, quoted in *Workshop on World Humor*, Nov. 1984, cited by Donal Henahan in *The New York Times*, March 17, 1985.

Leave jesting while it pleaseth, lest it turn to earnest.
—GEORGE HERBERT, *Jacula prudentum*

Impropriety is the soul of wit.
—SOMERSET MAUGHAM, *The Moon and Sixpence*
[For Shakespeare on the soul of wit, see ARTS: STYLE IN WRITING & EXPRESSION.]

Everybody likes a kidder, but nobody lends him money.   —ARTHUR MILLER, *Death of a Salesman*

Wit is the epitaph of an emotion.
—FRIEDRICH NIETZSCHE, *Miscellaneous Maxims and Opinions*

Even the gods love their jokes.   —PLATO, *Cratylus*

Everything is funny as long as it happens to somebody else. —WILL ROGERS, "Warning to Jokers: Lay Off the Prince," in *The Illiterate Digest*

The quality of wit inspires more admiration than confidence. —GEORGE SANTAYANA, "Wit," in *The Sense of Beauty*

Comedy is the last refuge of the nonconformist mind. —GILBERT SELDES, *The New Republic*, Dec. 20, 1954

My way of joking is to tell the truth. —GEORGE BERNARD SHAW, *John Bull's Other Island*

The wit makes fun of other persons; the satirist makes fun of the world; the humorist makes fun of himself. —JAMES THURBER, in Edward R. Murrow television interview

Humor . . . is emotional chaos remembered in tranquillity. —JAMES THURBER, *New York Post*, Feb. 29, 1960 [Thurber was referring here of course to Wordsworth's immortal definition of poetry; see under ARTS: POETRY & POETS.]

The secret source of humor itself is not joy but sorrow. There is no humor in heaven. —MARK TWAIN, "Pudd'nhead Wilson's New Calendar," in *Following the Equator* [Samuel Beckett, in *Endgame*, expressed a similar thought: "Nothing is funnier than unhappiness."]

We are not amused. —QUEEN VICTORIA, after seeing an imitation of herself by a groom-in-waiting, in *Notebooks of a Spinster*, Jan. 2, 1900

It's hard to be funny when you have to be clean. —MAE WEST, quoted in Joseph Weintraub, ed., *The Wit and Wisdom of Mae West*

HUNGER	See FOOD, WINE, & EATING; POVERTY & HUNGER
HURRYING	See HASTE
HYPOCRISY	See also CRAFTINESS; DISHONESTY & LIES

Only the hypocrite is really rotten to the core.
—HANNAH ARENDT, *On Revolution*

And when thou prayest, thou shalt not be as the hypocrites are: for they love to pray standing in the synagogues and in the corners of the streets, that they may be seen of men.   —BIBLE, *Matthew* 6:6

Beware of false prophets, which come to you in sheep's clothing, but inwardly they are ravening wolves.   —*Ibid.*, 7:15

Woe unto you, scribes and Pharisees, hypocrites! for ye are like unto whitened sepulchres, which indeed appear beautiful outward, but are within full of dead men's bones, and of all uncleanness.   —*Ibid.*, 23:27

Be a hypocrite if you like; but don't talk like one!
—DENIS DIDEROT, *Le Neveu de Rameau*

I detest that man who hides one thing in the depth of his heart and speaks forth another.

—HOMER, *Iliad*

No man is a hypocrite in his pleasures.
—SAMUEL JOHNSON, quoted in James Boswell, *Life of Johnson*, June 19, 1784

Hypocrisy is the homage which vice pays to virtue.
—LA ROCHEFOUCAULD, *Maxims*

A hypocrite is a person who . . . but who isn't?
—DON MARQUIS, quoted by Frederick B. Wilcox, *A Little Book of Aphorisms*

For neither man nor angel can discern
Hypocrisy, the only evil that walks
Invisible, except to God alone.

—JOHN MILTON,
Paradise Lost

Being a hypocrite has marvelous advantages!
—MOLIÈRE,
Don Juan

With devotion's usage
And pious action we do sugar o'er
The devil himself.

—SHAKESPEARE, *Hamlet*, III, i

A nice man is a man of nasty ideas.
—JONATHAN SWIFT, *A Critical
Essay upon the Faculties of the Mind*

As for conforming outwardly, and living your own
life inwardly, I don't think much of that.
—HENRY DAVID THOREAU, *Excursions* (letter to
Harrison Blake, Aug. 9, 1850)

I

IDEAS & IDEALS   See also ETHICS & MORALITY;
                                  MIND, THOUGHT, &
                                  UNDERSTANDING; VISION
                                  & VISIONARIES

If you believe in an ideal, you don't own you, it owns
you.   —RAYMOND CHANDLER, quoted
                          by F. MacShane,
                          The Life of Raymond Chandler

You can't shoot an idea.
                        —THOMAS E. DEWEY, debate with
                          Harold Stassen on whether to outlaw
                          the Communist party, 1948

An invasion of armies can be resisted, but not an idea
whose time has come.   —VICTOR HUGO, *Histoire
                                 d'un crime*
[This famous line is a free translation of the original,
which does not contain the phrase "whose time has
come."]

An idea isn't responsible for the people who believe
in it.   —DON MARQUIS, *The Sun Dial*

To die for an idea: it is unquestionably noble. But
how much nobler would it be if men died for ideas that
were true.

—H. L. MENCKEN, *Prejudices: Fifth Series*

As there are misanthropists, or haters of mankind,
so there are mislogists, or haters of ideas.   —PLATO,
                                                    Phaedo

Loyalty to petrified opinion never yet broke a chain or freed a human soul.
> —MARK TWAIN, attributed, inscribed
> beneath his bust in the Hall of Fame

Serious people have few ideas. People with ideas are never serious. —PAUL VALÉRY, *Mauvaises pensées*

The true God, the mighty God, is the God of ideas.
> —ALFRED DE VIGNY, *La Bouteille à la mer*

All great ideas are dangerous.
> —OSCAR WILDE, *De Profundis*

IDLENESS See LAZINESS; LEISURE; PROCRASTINATION

ILLNESS & REMEDIES See also DEATH; DOCTORS &
THE PRACTICE OF MEDICINE;
HEALTH; MADNESS

Illness tells us what we are.
> —ANONYMOUS (ITALIAN PROVERB)

The greatest evil is physical pain.
> —ST. AUGUSTINE, *Soliloquies*

Look into the depths of your own soul and learn first to know yourself, then you will understand why this illness was bound to come upon you and perhaps you will thenceforth avoid falling ill.
> —FREUD, *One of the Difficulties
> of Psychoanalysis*

Natural forces within us are the true healers of disease. —HIPPOCRATES, *Aphorisms*

The patient must combat the disease along with the physician. —*Ibid.*

To live by medicine is to live horribly.
> —LINNAEUS, *Diaeta naturalis*, Introduction

Illness is not something a person *has*. It's another way of being.
>   —JONATHAN MILLER, *The Body in Question*

Nearly all men die of their medicines, and not of their illnesses.   —MOLIÈRE, *La Malade imaginaire*

Brightness falls from the air;
Queens have died young and fair;
Dust hath closed Helen's eye.
I am sick, I must die.
Lord have mercy on us.
>   —THOMAS NASH, *Litany in Time of Plague*

["Brightness falls" was used by James Joyce in *A Portrait of the Artist as a Young Man*, and by Jay McInerney as the title of a 1992 novel. In that novel, one of the characters refers to scholarly speculation that the opening line originally read, "Brightness falls from the hair."]

Everything great that we know has come to us from neurotics. They alone have founded our religions and created our masterpieces. Never will the world be aware of how much it owes to them, nor above all what they have suffered in order to bestow their gifts on it.
>   —MARCEL PROUST, *Remembrance of
>   Things Past: The Guermantes Way*

There are maladies we must not seek to cure because they alone protect us from others that are more serious.   —*Ibid.*

There are some remedies worse than the disease.
>   —PUBLILIUS SYRUS, *Moral Sayings*

[Also, Francis Bacon in *Of Seditions and Troubles:* "The remedy is worse than the disease."]

Everyone who is born holds dual citizenship, in the kingdom of the well and the kingdom of the sick.
>   —SUSAN SONTAG,
>   *Illness as Metaphor*

There never was yet philosopher
That could endure the toothache patiently.
                              —SHAKESPEARE, *Much Ado About
                              Nothing*, V, i

ILLUSIONS   See REALITY & ILLUSIONS

IMAGINATION   See MIND, THOUGHT &
                              UNDERSTANDING; VISION &
                              VISIONARIES

IMMORTALITY   See also DEATH; LAST JUDGMENT &
                              THE HEREAFTER; LIFE

A man should have a child, plant a tree, and write a
book.   —ANONYMOUS (CHINESE PROVERB)

God created man to be immortal, and made him to
be an image of his own eternity.
                              —BIBLE, *The Wisdom
                              of Solomon*

When all the desires that enter one's heart are aban-
doned, then does the mortal become immortal.
                              —BRIHADARANYAKA UPANISHAD

If I err in my belief that the souls of men are immortal,
I err gladly, and do not wish to lose so delightful an
error.   —CICERO, *De senectute*

I shall see the Son of God, the Sun of glory, and shine
myself, as that sun shines.   —JOHN DONNE, *Sermons*

I long to believe in immortality.
                              —JOHN KEATS, letter to
                              Fanny Brawne, 1818

INACTION   See LAZINESS; PROCRASTINATION

INDIANS   See RACES & PEOPLES

INITIATIVE   See BOLDNESS & INITIATIVE;
                            SELF-RELIANCE

INNOCENCE   See also CHILDREN & CHILDHOOD;
                             VIRTUE

Where, my God, where, Oh Lord, where or when
was I, Your servant, innocent?   —ST. AUGUSTINE,
                                  Confessions

God will not cast away an innocent man.
                           —BIBLE, *Job* 8:20

Blessed are the pure in heart: for they shall see God.
                     —BIBLE, *Matthew* 5:8
[For other verses from the Sermon on the Mount see
VIRTUE.]

Except ye be converted and become as little children,
ye shall not enter into the kingdom of heaven.
                             —*Ibid.*, 18:3

Innocence dwells with wisdom, but never with
ignorance.   —WILLIAM BLAKE,
                             The Four Zoas

The innocent are God's elect.
   —ST. CLEMENT, *First Epistle to the Corinthians*

Teach us delight in simple things,
And mirth that has no bitter springs.
                     —RUDYARD KIPLING,
                         The Children's Song

Innocence is ashamed of nothing.
             —JEAN JACQUES ROUSSEAU,
                        Émile

If you carry with you your childhood, you never become older.   —ABRAHAM SUTZKEVER, interview,
The New York Times,
March 17, 1985
[The slightly eccentric syntax reflects Sutzkever's linguistic orientation—he is probably the foremost modern Yiddish poet.]

I used to be Snow White—but I drifted.
        —MAE WEST, quoted in Joseph Weintraub, ed.,
The Wit and Wisdom of Mae West

INNOVATION   See NEW THINGS;
SCIENCE: DISCOVERY

INSANITY   See MADNESS

INSIGHT   See MIND, THOUGHT, &
UNDERSTANDING; SCIENCE: DISCOVERY;
VISION & VISIONARIES

INSULTS & PUT-DOWNS   See also MANNERS

California is a great place to live—if you happen to be an orange.   —FRED ALLEN, attributed

There is less in this than meets the eye.
        —TALLULAH BANKHEAD
[*Bartlett's* says that she made this remark to Alexander Woollcott at Maurice Maeterlinck's play *Aglavaine and Selysette*.]

There goes the famous good time that was had by all.   —BETTE DAVIS, speaking of a starlet,
quoted in Leslie Halliwell,
The Filmgoer's Book of Quotes

I went to Philadelphia one Sunday. The place was closed.   —W. C. FIELDS, attributed
[One of many cracks at Philadelphia by Fields; see also under CITIES.]

Another damned, thick square book! Always scribble, scribble, scribble! Eh! Mr. Gibbon?
>—WILLIAM HENRY, DUKE OF GLOUCESTER,
>upon receiving from Edward Gibbon
>Vol. II of *Decline and Fall of the Roman
>Empire*, quoted in note to James
>Boswell's *Life of Johnson*

I could carve out of a banana a judge with more backbone than that.
>—OLIVER WENDELL HOLMES, JR.,
>quoted in *The New York Times*, Feb. 23, 1984

They teach the morals of a whore, and the manners of a dancing master.
>—SAMUEL JOHNSON, speaking of
>the Earl of Chesterfield's letters, in James
>Boswell, *Life of Johnson*, 1754

The noblest prospect that a Scotchman ever sees is the high road that leads to London.
>—SAMUEL JOHNSON, quoted by James Boswell,
>*Tour to the Hebrides*, Nov. 10, 1773

Sir, a woman's preaching is like a dog's walking on his hinder legs. It is not done well; but you are surprised to find it done at all.   —*Ibid.*, July 31, 1763

Mad, bad, and dangerous to know.
>—LADY CAROLINE LAMB, speaking of
>Lord Byron, *Journal*

She looked as though butter wouldn't melt in her mouth—or anywhere else.
>—ELSA LANCHESTER, cited in
>Leslie Halliwell, *The Filmgoer's Book of Quotes*

My dear, I don't give a damn.
>—MARGARET MITCHELL, *Gone with the Wind*
[In the movie, the line is "Frankly, my dear, I don't give a damn." Producer David O. Selznick had to fight for the "damn," and pay a $5,000 fine for breaking the Motion Picture Production Code.]

She ran the whole gamut of emotions from A to B.
  —DOROTHY PARKER, re Katharine Hepburn,
    in *The Lake*

It is not a novel to be thrown aside lightly. It should
be thrown aside with great force.
  —DOROTHY PARKER, book review, quoted by
    A. Johnston, "Legend of a Sport," in *The New
    Yorker*

House Beautiful is the play lousy.
  —DOROTHY PARKER, theater review

He never said a foolish thing
Nor never did a wise one.
  —EARL OF ROCHESTER, *The King's Epitaph*,
    for Charles II

You blocks, you stones, you worse than senseless
things!   —SHAKESPEARE, *Julius Caesar*, I, i

Dear Sir, Your profession has, as usual, destroyed
your brain.
  —GEORGE BERNARD SHAW, letter to a journalist,
    Collected Letters, Dan H. Laurence, ed.

No matter how thin you slice it, it's still baloney.
  —ALFRED E. SMITH, campaign speeches, 1936

I am just going to pray for you at St. Paul's, but with
no very lively hope of success.
  —REV. SYDNEY SMITH, quoted by H. Pearson,
    The Smith of Smiths

I regard you with an indifference closely bordering
on aversion.   —ROBERT LOUIS STEVENSON,
                  "Story of the Bandbox," in
                  New Arabian Nights

INTEGRITY See HONESTY & SINCERITY;
SELF; VIRTUE

INTELLIGENCE See GENIUS; MIND,
THOUGHT, & UNDERSTANDING

INTIMACY & FAMILIARITY

Familiarity breeds contempt.
—AESOP, *The Fox and the Lion*
[See Mark Twain's amendment, below.]

No man is a hero to his valet.
—ANNE BIGOT DU CORNUEL, quoted in
Lettres de Mme. Aissé, Aug. 13, 1728

Many a man has been a wonder to the world, whose
wife and valet have seen nothing in him that was even
remarkable. Few men have been admired by their
servants. —MONTAIGNE, *Essays*

Familiarity breeds contempt—and children.
—MARK TWAIN, *Notebooks*

INVENTION See NEW THINGS; SCIENCE:
DISCOVERY; TECHNOLOGY

IRELAND See NATIONS

ITALY See NATIONS

J

JAPAN   See NATIONS

JEALOUSY

Jealousy is nothing but the foolish child of pride.
—PIERRE-AUGUSTIN DE BEAUMARCHAIS,
The Marriage of Figaro

Love is as strong as death; jealousy is as cruel as the grave.   —BIBLE, *Song of Solomon* 8:6

It is not love that is blind, but jealousy.
—LAWRENCE DURRELL, *Justine*

Jealousy is always born with love, but does not always die with it.   —LA ROCHEFOUCAULD, *Maxims*

O! beware, my lord, of jealousy.
It is the green-eyed monster which doth mock the meat it feeds on.   —SHAKESPEARE, *Othello*, III, iii

There is no greater glory than love, nor any greater punishment than jealousy.
—LOPE DE VEGA, *Cantorcillo de la Virgen*

JERUSALEM   See CITIES

JESUS   See also CHRISTMAS;
                              PROVIDENCE, DIVINE

And the angel came in unto her, and said, Hail, thou that art highly favored, the Lord is with thee; blessed art thou among women.   —BIBLE, *Luke* 1:28

Thou shalt conceive in thy womb, and bring forth a son, and shalt call his name *Jesus*.   —*Ibid.*, 1:31

In the beginning was the Word, and the Word was with God, and the Word was God.
                                        —BIBLE, *John* 1:1

In him was life; and the life was the light of men.
And the light shineth in darkness; and the darkness comprehended it not.   —*Ibid.*, 1:4,5

And the Word was made flesh, and dwelt among us (and we beheld his glory, the glory as of the only begotten of the Father), full of grace and truth.
                                        —*Ibid.*, 1:14

For God so loveth the world, that he gave his only begotten son, that whosoever believeth in him should not perish, but have everlasting life.   —*Ibid.*, 3:16

I am the good shepherd. The good shepherd giveth his life for the sheep.   —*Ibid.*, 10:11

Thou hast conquered, Galilean!
                —JULIAN THE APOSTATE,
                    attributed deathbed words

Jesus died too soon. He would have repudiated his doctrine if he had lived to my age.
—FRIEDRICH NIETZSCHE, *Thus Spake Zarathustra*

Thou hast conquered, O pale Galilean; the world has grown gray from thy breath;
We have drunken of things Lethean, and fed on the fullness of death.   —ALGERNON C. SWINBURNE,
                    Hymn to Prosperine

Christ is God clothed with human nature.
                —BENJAMIN WHICHCOTE,
                    Moral and Religious Aphorisms

JEWS   See RACES & PEOPLES

JOY   See HAPPINESS; HAPPINESS,
                                              EXPRESSIONS OF

JUDGES   See also JUSTICE; LAW

Tell God the truth, but give the judge money.
> —ANONYMOUS (RUSSIAN PROVERB)

Oh that I were made judge.
> —BIBLE, *II Samuel* 15:4

[A heartfelt prayer as common today as in ancient times. The speaker here is Absalom, whose wish is granted and who uses the position to win allies in his ill-fated rebellion against his father, King David.]

Judges are the weakest link in our system of justice, and they are also the most protected.
> —ALAN DERSHOWITZ, *Newsweek*, Feb. 20, 1978

[See also Oliver Wendell Holmes, Jr., on a weak judge, under INSULTS & PUT-DOWNS.]

Even judges sometimes progress.
> —EMMA GOLDMAN, *The Social Aspects of Birth Control*

The acme of judicial distinction means the ability to look a lawyer straight in the eyes for two hours and not to hear a damned word he says.
> —JOHN MARSHALL, quoted in Albert J. Beveridge, *The Life of John Marshall*

We must never forget that the only real source of power that we as judges can tap is the respect of the people.
> —THURGOOD MARSHALL, *Chicago Tribune*, Aug. 15, 1981

A judge is not supposed to know anything about the facts of life until they have been presented into evidence and explained to him at least three times.
> —LORD CHIEF JUSTICE PARKER, quoted in the *Observer*, March 12, 1961

When a judge sits in judgment over a fellow man, he should feel as if a sword is pointed at his own heart.
—TALMUD, *Sanhedrin*

Disaster comes because of the kind of judges we have.
—TALMUD, *Shabbat*

JUDGING OTHERS   See EVIDENCE; FORGIVENESS & MERCY; JUDGES; JUSTICE; TOLERANCE & UNDERSTANDING

JUNE   See NATURE: SEASONS

JUSTICE   See also EVIDENCE; FORGIVENESS & MERCY; JUDGES; LAW; LAWYERS; PUNISHMENT; REVENGE

All virtue is summed up in dealing justly.
—ARISTOTLE, *Nicomachean Ethics*

With what measure ye mete, it shall be meted to you.
—BIBLE, *Mark* 4:24

God is not mocked: for whatsoever a man soweth, that shall he also reap.   —BIBLE, *Galatians* 6:7

Let judgment run down as waters, and righteousness as a mighty stream.   —BIBLE, *Amos* 5:24
[See Martin Luther King's paraphrase under RACES & PEOPLES.]

Justice is not to be taken by storm. She is to be wooed by slow advances.   —BENJAMIN N. CARDOZO, *The Growth of the Law*

Justice is the crowning glory of the virtues.
—CICERO, *De officiis*

There is no such thing as justice—in or out of court.
—CLARENCE DARROW, interview, *The New York Times*, April 19, 1936

Justice is truth in action.
>—BENJAMIN DISRAELI, speech, Feb. 11, 1851

Justice . . . is a kind of compact not to harm or be harmed. —EPICURUS, *Principal Doctrines*

Only the just man enjoys peace of mind.
>—EPICURUS, fragment

A fox should not be of the jury at a goose's trial.
>—THOMAS FULLER, *Gnomologia*

Thou shalt not ration justice.
>—LEARNED HAND, speech
>to the Legal Aid Society of
>New York, Feb. 16, 1951

Justice consists in taking from no man what is his.
>—THOMAS HOBBES, *Leviathan*

Injustice anywhere is a threat to justice everywhere.
>—MARTIN LUTHER KING, JR., letter from
>the Birmingham, Ala., jail, 1963

Love of justice in most men is no more than the fear of suffering injustice. —LA ROCHEFOUCAULD, *Maxims*

Your justice would freeze beer!
>—ARTHUR MILLER, *The Crucible*

I shall temper . . . justice with mercy.
>—JOHN MILTON, *Paradise Lost*

Justice without force is impotent; force without justice is tyranny. —PASCAL, *Pensées*

Everywhere there is one principle of justice, which is the interest of the stronger.
>—PLATO, *The Republic*

All justice comes from God—he alone is its source.
>—JEAN JACQUES ROUSSEAU,
>*The Social Contract*

There are times when even justice brings harm with it. —SOPHOCLES, *Electra*

If they are just, they are better than clever.
—SOPHOCLES, *Philoctetes*

There is one universal law. . . . That law is justice. Justice forms the cornerstone of each nation's law.
—ALEXIS DE TOCQUEVILLE,
Democracy in America

The laws of changeless justice bind
Oppressor and oppressed;
And close as sin and suffering joined,
We march to fate abreast.
—JOHN GREENLEAF WHITTIER, *At Port Royal*

The good ended happily, and the bad unhappily. That is what Fiction means.
—OSCAR WILDE, *The Importance of Being Earnest*

K

KINDNESS   See COMPASSION; VIRTUE

KINGS   See HIGH POSITION:
                              RULERS & LEADERS

KNOWLEDGE   See EDUCATION & LEARNING;
                                      SCIENCE

L

LABOR   See WORK & WORKERS

LAISSEZ-FAIRE   See CAPITALISM

LANGUAGE   See also ARTS: STYLE IN WRITING &
& WORDS   EXPRESSION; ARTS: WRITING; CONVERSA-
                    TION; SILENCE; TALK

Words are slippery.
           —HENRY BROOKS ADAMS,
             The Education of Henry Adams

By thy words thou shalt be justified, and by thy words
thou shalt be condemned.   —BIBLE, *Matthew* 12:37
[More at TALK.]

What so wild as words are?
        —ROBERT BROWNING, *A Woman's Last Word*

A blow with a word strikes deeper than a blow with
a sword.
        —ROBERT BURTON, *The Anatomy of Melancholy*

"When I use a word," Humpty Dumpty said, in a
rather scornful tone, "it means just what I choose it to
mean—neither more nor less."
    "The question is," said Alice, "whether you can
make words mean so many different things."
    "The question is," said Humpty Dumpty, "which
is to be master—that's all."
                   —LEWIS CARROLL,
                   Through the Looking-Glass

I speak Spanish to God, Italian to women, French to men, and German to my horse.
—EMPEROR CHARLES V, attributed

A word is dead
When it is said,
Some say.
I say it just
Begins to live
That day. —EMILY DICKINSON, poem no. 1212

Language is the archives of history.
—RALPH WALDO EMERSON, *The Poet*

The chief merit of language is clarity, and we know that nothing detracts so much from this as do unfamiliar terms. —GALEN, *On the Natural Faculties*

Fair words cost nothing. —JOHN GAY,
The Mohocks

Words are mere sound and smoke, dimming the heavenly light. —GOETHE, *Faust*

In two words: im–possible. —SAMUEL GOLDWYN,
attributed

The tongue of man is a twisty thing. —HOMER,
Iliad

Once a word has been allowed to escape, it can never be recalled. —HORACE, *Epistles*, I, 18

Language is the dress of thought.
—SAMUEL JOHNSON, *Lives of the English Poets*
[See also Wesley at ARTS: STYLE IN WRITING & EXPRESSION.]

My heavens! I've been talking prose for the last forty years without knowing it.
—MOLIÈRE, *Le Bourgeois Gentilhomme*

Every word is a preconceived judgment.
—FRIEDRICH NIETZSCHE,
Human All-Too-Human

The use of language is all we have to pit against death
and silence.   —JOYCE CAROL OATES, speech,
                           National Book Awards, 1969

Words are weapons, and it is dangerous . . . to borrow
them from the arsenal of the enemy.
                    —GEORGE SANTAYANA, *Obiter Scripta*

These are but wild and whirling words.
                           —SHAKESPEARE, *Hamlet*, I, v

Taffeta phrases, silken terms precise,
Three-piled hyperboles, spruce affectation,
Figures pedantical.   —SHAKESPEARE,
                           Love's Labour's Lost, V, ii

What's in a name? That which we call a rose
By any other name would smell as sweet.
                    —SHAKESPEARE, *Romeo and Juliet*, II, ii

Words pay no debts.
          —SHAKESPEARE, *Troilus and Cressida*, III, ii
[Also, "Words are no deeds." *Henry VIII*, III, ii.]

Silence hides nothing. Words conceal.
                    —AUGUST STRINDBERG, *Ghost Sonata*

An idea does not pass from one language to another
without change.   —MIGUEL DE UNAMUNO,
                           The Tragic Sense of Life

The limits of my language mean the limits of my
world.   —LUDWIG WITTGENSTEIN,
                    Tractatus logico-philosophicus

LAST JUDGMENT   See also HELL; IMMORTALITY;
& THE HEREAFTER   WORLD, END OF

But many that are first shall be last; and the last shall
be first.   —BIBLE, *Matthew* 19:30

And whosoever shall exalt himself shall be abased;
and he that shall humble himself shall be exalted.
                           —*Ibid.*, 23:12

He shall separate them one from another, as a shepherd divideth his sheep from his goats.

—*Ibid.*, 25:32

Don't wait for the Last Judgment. It takes place every day. —ALBERT CAMUS, *The Fall*

Abou Ben Adhem (may his tribe increase!)
Awoke one night from a deep dream of peace,
And saw, within the moonlight of the room,
Making it rich, and like a lily in bloom,
An angel writing in a book of gold.

—LEIGH HUNT, *Abou Ben Adhem
and the Angel*

Write me as one that loves his fellow men. —*Ibid.*

The angel wrote, and vanished. The next night
It came again with a great wakening light,
And showed the names whom love of God had
blessed
And lo! Ben Adhem's name led all the rest.

—*Ibid.*

The bottom line is in heaven.

—EDWIN HERBERT LAND, shareholders'
meeting, Polaroid Corp., April 26, 1977

Now hast thou but one bare hour to live
And then thou must be damned perpetually!
Stand still you ever-moving spheres of heaven,
That time may cease and midnight never come.

—CHRISTOPHER MARLOWE, *Dr. Faustus*

LAUGHTER   See also HUMOR

Meaningless laughter is a sign of ill-breeding.

—ANONYMOUS (ARAB PROVERB)

A maid that laughs is half taken.

—ANONYMOUS (ENGLISH PROVERB), quoted in
John Ray, *English Proverbs*

[St. John Chrysostom may have had this in mind when
he related laughter to sin; see below.]

He laughs best who laughs last.
>   —ANONYMOUS (ENGLISH PROVERB)

[H. L. Mencken noted that this appears to be proverbial in all European languages.]

Man thinks. God laughs.   —ANONYMOUS (JEWISH
>   PROVERB)

I force myself to laugh at everything for fear of being obliged to weep.
>   —PIERRE-AUGUSTIN DE BEAUMARCHAIS,
>   *The Barber of Seville*

Laughter has no greater enemy than emotion.
>   —HENRI BERGSON, *Laughter*

[Bergson went on to say that laughter requires "a momentary anesthesia of the heart."]

No man who has once heartily and wholly laughed can be altogether irreclaimably bad.
>   —THOMAS CARLYLE, *Sartor Resartus*

Nothing is sillier than silly laughter.   —CATULLUS,
>   *Carmina*

The most wasted of all days is that in which we have not laughed.   —SÉBASTIEN R. N. CHAMFORT,
>   *Maximes et pensées*

In my mind, there is nothing so illiberal and so ill-bred as audible laughter.
>   —EARL OF CHESTERFIELD, letter to his
>   son, March 9, 1748

Laughter does not seem to be a sin, but it leads to sin.   —ST. JOHN CHRYSOSTOM, *Homilies*

One must laugh before one is happy or one may die without ever having laughed at all.
>   —LA BRUYÈRE, *Les Caractères*

Laugh, and the world laughs with you;
Weep, and you weep alone.
>   —ELLA WHEELER WILCOX, *Solitude*

LAW   See also EVIDENCE; GOVERNMENT; JUDGES;
                  JUSTICE; LAWYERS

A government of laws, and not of men.
           —JOHN ADAMS, *Novanglus*, 1775.
[Adams credited the phrase to the seventeenth-century writer James Harrington. It was used in 1780 in the Massachusetts Constitution.]

Go to law for a sheep and lose your cow.
           —ANONYMOUS (GERMAN PROVERB)

Law is a bottomless pit.
           —JOHN ARBUTHNOT, pamphlet title

Law means good order.   —ARISTOTLE, *Politics*

All law has for its object to confirm and exalt into a system the exploitation of the workers by a ruling class.
           —MIKHAIL A. BAKUNIN, *Dieu et l'état*

If you like laws and sausage, you should never watch either being made.   —OTTO VON BISMARCK,
                     attributed
[In *Respectfully Quoted*, published by the Library of Congress, this comment, widely attributed to Bismarck, is described as unverified.]

It is better that ten guilty persons escape than one innocent suffer.
           —WILLIAM BLACKSTONE, *Commentaries on
            the Laws of England*
[See also Voltaire, below.]

One law for the lion and ox is oppression.
           —WILLIAM BLAKE,
              The Marriage of Heaven and Hell

If we would guide by the light of reason, we must let our minds be bold.
           —LOUIS D. BRANDEIS, *N.Y. State Ice Co.*
           v. *Liebmann*, 1932

The people's good is the highest law.
           —CICERO, *De legibus*

Conscience and law never go together.
—WILLIAM CONGREVE, *The Double Dealer*

One with the law is a majority.
—CALVIN COOLIDGE, speech, July 27, 1920

Law [is] a horrible business.
—CLARENCE DARROW, interview,
The New York Times, April 19, 1936

The law is bigger than money—but only if the law works hard enough.
—THOMAS E. DEWEY, quoted in
Richard Norton Smith, *Thomas E. Dewey*

"If the law supposes that," said Mr. Bumble . . . "the law is a ass—a idiot."
—CHARLES DICKENS,
Oliver Twist

Good men must not obey the laws too well.
—RALPH WALDO EMERSON, *Politics*

Public opinion is always in advance of the law.
—JOHN GALSWORTHY, *Windows*

There is no better way of exercising the imagination than the study of law. No poet ever interpreted nature as freely as a lawyer interprets the truth.
—JEAN GIRAUDOUX, *Tiger at the Gates*

Law is mighty, mightier necessity.
—GOETHE, *Faust*
[For more on necessity and law, see under NECESSITY.]

Laws grind the poor, and rich men rule the law.
—OLIVER GOLDSMITH, *The Traveller*

A verbal contract isn't worth the paper it's printed on.
—SAMUEL GOLDWYN, attributed

The law is not the same at morning and at night.
—GEORGE HERBERT, *Jacula prudentum*

The life of the law has not been logic; it has been experience.
—OLIVER WENDELL HOLMES, JR.,
The Common Law

Great cases like hard cases make bad law.
>—OLIVER WENDELL HOLMES, JR.,
>*Northern Securities Co.* v. *U.S.*, 1904

[Holmes is alluding to the legal byword: "Hard cases make bad law."]

The execution of the laws is more important than the making them. —THOMAS JEFFERSON, letter to the
>Abbé Arnond, 1789

It is a fortunate thing for society that the courts do not get the same chance at the Ten Commandments as they do at the Constitution of the United States.
>—PHILANDER C. JOHNSON,
>*Senator Sorghum's Primer of Politics*

Morality cannot be legislated but behavior can be regulated. Judicial decrees may not change the heart, but they can restrain the heartless.
>—MARTIN LUTHER KING, JR., *Strength to Love*

Wherever law ends, tyranny begins.
>—JOHN LOCKE, *Two Treatises on Government*

[The almost identical observation was made, or borrowed, by William Pitt, see below.]

Useless laws weaken the necessary laws.
>—MONTESQUIEU, *De l'esprit des lois*

Laws were made to be broken.
>—CHRISTOPHER NORTH, *Noctes Ambrosianae*

Where laws end, tyranny begins.
>—WILLIAM PITT, EARL OF CHATHAM, speech,
>Jan. 9, 1770, on the Wilkes case

[Note similarity to John Locke's comment, above.]

The law must be stable, but it must not stand still.
>—ROSCOE POUND,
>*Introduction to the Philosophy of Law*

The law does not generate justice. The law is nothing but a declaration and application of what is just.
>—PIERRE-JOSEPH PROUDHON, *De la justice dans la révolution*

No man is above the law and no man is below it; nor do we ask any man's permission when we require him to obey it.
                    —THEODORE ROOSEVELT, speech, Jan. 1904

Laws are always useful to persons of property and hurtful to those who have none.
        —JEAN JACQUES ROUSSEAU, *The Social Contract*

Ignorance of the law excuses no man: not that all men know the law, but because 'tis an excuse every man will plead, and no man can tell how to refute him.
            —JOHN SELDEN, "Judgments," in *Table Talk*

Pity is the virtue of the law.
                —SHAKESPEARE, *Timon of Athens*, III, v
[The meaning is that pity, or mercy, is the best characteristic of law.]

Laws are like spiders' webs: If some poor weak creature come up against them, it is caught; but a big one can break through and get away.
                        —SOLON, quoted in Diogenes
                        Laërtius, *Lives of Eminent
                        Philosophers*

Extreme law is often extreme injustice.
                —TERENCE, *Heauton timoroumenos*

It is better to risk saving a guilty man than to condemn an innocent one.   —VOLTAIRE, *Zadig*
[The idea is probably better known in Blackstone's formulation, see above.]

LAWYERS   See also LAW

The Pharisees and lawyers rejected the counsel of God.   —BIBLE, *Luke* 7:30

Lawyer, n. One skilled in circumvention of the law.
            —AMBROSE BIERCE, *The Devil's Dictionary*

Our wrangling lawyers . . . are so litigious and busy here on earth, that I think they will plead their clients' causes hereafter, some of them in hell.
                    —ROBERT BURTON,
                    The Anatomy of Melancholy

Resolve to be honest at all events: and if in your judgment you cannot be an honest lawyer, resolve to be honest without being a lawyer. Choose some other occupation. —ABRAHAM LINCOLN,
notes for a lecture, 1850

They have no lawyers among them [in Utopia] for they consider them as the sort of people whose profession it is to disguise matters. —THOMAS MORE,
Utopia

The first thing we do, let's kill all the lawyers.
—SHAKESPEARE, *Henry VI, Part II*, IV, ii

I'm not a potted plant.
—BRENDAN SULLIVAN, Senate hearing,
July 9, 1987
[Attorney Sullivan was justifying his aggressive tactics in defense of his client, Col. Oliver North.]

LAZINESS See also LEISURE; PHYSICAL FITNESS;
PROCRASTINATION; PRUDENCE &
PRACTICAL WISDOM

Laziness is often mistaken for patience.
—ANONYMOUS (FRENCH PROVERB)

Go to the ant, thou sluggard; consider her ways, and be wise. —BIBLE, *Proverbs* 6:6
[More at WORK & WORKERS.]

Laziness travels so slowly that poverty soon overtakes him.
—BENJAMIN FRANKLIN, *Poor Richard's Almanac*

Idle men are dead all their life long.
—THOMAS FULLER, *Gnomologia*

I have all my life long been lying [in bed] till noon; yet I tell all young men, and tell them with great sincerity, that nobody who does not rise early will ever do any good.
—SAMUEL JOHNSON, quoted by James Boswell,
Tour to the Hebrides, Sept. 14, 1773

Lazy people are always looking for something to do.
> —MARQUIS DE VAUVENARGUES,
> *Maximes et pensées*

Iron rusts from disuse, stagnant water loses its purity and in cold weather becomes frozen; even so does inaction sap the vigors of the mind.
> —LEONARDO DA VINCI, *Notebooks*

[See also "rust" quote from Sir Walter Scott at LEISURE.]

LEADERS   See HIGH POSITION: RULERS & LEADERS

LEARNING   See EDUCATION & LEARNING

LEISURE   See also LAZINESS; WORK & WORKERS

Better to idle well than to work badly.
> —ANONYMOUS (SPANISH PROVERB)

Rest is for the dead.
> —THOMAS CARLYLE, *Journal*, June 22, 1830

What is this life, if full of care,
We have no time to stand and stare.
> —W. H. DAVIES, *Leisure*

[Davies was a well-traveled vagrant; see his classic *Autobiography of a Super-Tramp*, 1908. Bernard Shaw, in 1905, had recognized his talent and set him on the road to fame.]

The occupation most becoming a civilized man is to do nothing.
> —THÉOPHILE GAUTIER, *Whims and Zigzags*

Too much rest itself becomes a pain.   —HOMER,
> *Odyssey*

Too much rest is rust.   —SIR WALTER SCOTT,
> *The Betrothed*

[A saying that has been widely used. Wilhelm II of Germany as a youth adopted the motto, "If I rest, I rust." See also the Leonardo da Vinci passage at LAZINESS.]

The man who does not betake himself at once and desperately to sawing is called a loafer, though he may be knocking at the doors of heaven all the while.
—HENRY DAVID THOREAU, *Winter*

For Satan finds some mischief still
For idle hand to do.
—ISAAC WATTS, *Against Idleness and Mischief*

LIBERTY   See FREEDOM

LIES   See DISHONESTY & LIES

LIFE   See also EXPERIENCE; GENERATIONS; HEDONISM

And we are here as on a darkling plain
Swept with confused alarms of struggle and flight,
Where ignorant armies clash by night.
—MATTHEW ARNOLD, *Dover Beach*

To every thing there is a season, and a time to every purpose under the heaven:
A time to be born and a time to die; a time to plant, and a time to pluck up that which is planted;
A time to kill, and a time to heal; a time to break down, and a time to build up;
A time to weep, and a time to laugh; a time to mourn, and a time to dance;
A time to cast away stones, and a time to gather stones together; a time to embrace, and a time to refrain from embracing;
A time to get, and a time to lose; a time to keep, and a time to cast away;
A time to rend, and a time to sew; a time to keep silence, and a time to speak;
A time to love, and a time to hate; a time of war, and a time of peace.   —BIBLE, *Ecclesiastes* 3:1–8

Oh, the wild joys of living!
—ROBERT BROWNING, *Saul*

How good is man's life, the mere living! how fit to employ

All the heart and the soul and the sense for ever in
joy!   —*Ibid.*

We are involved in a life that passes understanding
and our highest business is our daily life.
> —JOHN CAGE, "Where Are We Going and
> What Are We Doing?" in *Silence*

There are only two or three human stories, and they
go on repeating themselves as fiercely as if they had
never happened before.
> —WILLA CATHER, *O Pioneers!*

If life had a second edition, how I would correct the
proofs.   —JOHN CLARE, letter to a friend, quoted
> in J. W. Tibble and Anne Tibble,
> *John Clare: A Life*

What is life? It is a flash of a firefly in the night. It
is the breath of a buffalo in the wintertime. It is the
little shadow which runs across the grass and loses itself
in the sunset.   —CROWFOOT, last words

That it will never come again
Is what makes life so sweet.
> —EMILY DICKINSON, poem no. 1741

What we anticipate seldom occurs; what we least expected generally happens.
> —BENJAMIN DISRAELI, *Henrietta Temple*

I have measured out my life with coffee spoons.
> —T. S. ELIOT, *Love Song of J. Alfred Prufrock*

Birth, copulation, and death.
That's all the facts when you come to brass tacks.
> —T. S. ELIOT, *Sweeney Agonistes*

We are always getting ready to live but never living.
> —RALPH WALDO EMERSON, *Journals*, 1834

Life consists in what a man is thinking of all day.
> —*Ibid.*, 1847

Only connect . . .   —E. M. FORSTER,
                                    Howards End, epigraph
[What Forster had in mind is conveyed in this passage
in the book: "Only connect! That was the whole of her
sermon. Only connect the prose and the passion, and
both will be exalted, and human love will be seen at its
height. Live in fragments no longer. Only connect, and
the beast and the monk, robbed of the isolation that is
life to either, will die."]

Life is a jest; and all things show it.
I thought so once; but now I know it.
                          —JOHN GAY, *My Own Epitaph*

A useless life is an early death.
                          —GOETHE, *Iphigenie auf Tauris*

Life is short, art long, opportunity fleeting, experience treacherous, judgment difficult.
                          —HIPPOCRATES, *Aphorisms*
[For the proverbial version, see under ARTS, the first
quote. See also Hippocrates at WORK.]

The condition of man . . . is a condition of war of
everyone against everyone.   —THOMAS HOBBES,
                                              Leviathan

. . . the life of man, solitary, poor, nasty, brutish,
and short.   —*Ibid.*

Life is just one damn thing after another.
—ELBERT HUBBARD, *Thousand and One Epigrams*
[For Edna St. Vincent Millay's response, see below.]

Life is an abnormal business.
                          —EUGÈNE IONESCO, *Rhinoceros*

How small it's all.
                          —JAMES JOYCE, *Finnegans Wake*

There is always inequity in life. Some men are killed
in a war and some men are wounded, and some men
never leave the country. . . . Life is unfair.
                          —JOHN F. KENNEDY,
                          press conference, March 23, 1962

Life can only be understood backwards, but it must be lived forwards. —SÖREN KIERKEGAARD, *Life*

For men must work and women must weep,
And the sooner it's over, the sooner to sleep.
  —CHARLES KINGSLEY, *The Three Fishers*

Ships that pass in the night, and speak each other in
    passing;
Only a signal shown and a distant voice in the
    darkness;
So on the ocean of life we pass and speak one another,
Only a look and a voice; then darkness again and a
    silence.
  —HENRY WADSWORTH LONGFELLOW,
    "The Theologian's Tale," in
    Tales of a Wayside Inn

Life is one long struggle in the dark.
  —LUCRETIUS, *De rerum natura*

The world has always been the same; and there has always been as much good fortune as bad in it.
  —MACHIAVELLI, *Discorsi*, Introduction

It is not true that life is one damned thing after another—it is one damn thing over and over.
  —EDNA ST. VINCENT MILLAY,
    Letters of Edna St. Vincent Millay,
    edited by Allen R. Macdougal

The value of life lies not in the length of days, but in the use we make of them; a man may live long yet live very little. —MONTAIGNE, *Essays*

Those who have compared life to a dream were right.
. . . We sleep when we are awake, and awake when sleeping. —*Ibid.*

La vie est vaine:
Un peu d'amour,
Un peu de haine,
Et puis—bonjour!

La vie est brève:
Un peu d'espoir,
Un peu de rève,
Et puis—bon soir!

Life is aimless: a little love, a little hate, and then—good day! Life is short: a little hope, a little dreaming, and then—goodnight!

—LÉON MONTENAEKEN, *Peu de chose*

Human life is but a series of footnotes to a vast obscure unfinished masterpiece.

—VLADIMIR NABOKOV, *Pale Fire*

To burn always with this hard gem-like flame, to maintain this ecstasy, is success in life.

—WALTER PATER, *The Renaissance*, "Conclusion"

The world itself is but a large prison out of which some daily are led to execution.

—SIR WALTER RALEIGH

[Sir Walter made this comment while being led back to prison after his trial.]

There is no wealth but life.   —JOHN RUSKIN,
Unto This Last

There must be more to life than having everything!

—MAURICE SENDAK, *Higglety Pigglety Pop!*

All the world's a stage,
and all the men and women merely players.

—SHAKESPEARE, *As You Like It*, II, vii

Life is as tedious as a twice-told tale
Vexing the dull ear of a drowsy man.

—SHAKESPEARE, *King John*, III, iv

When we are born, we cry that we are come
To this great stage of fools.   —SHAKESPEARE,
King Lear, IV, vi

Life's but a walking shadow, a poor player
That struts and frets his hour upon the stage
And then is heard no more. It is a tale
Told by an idiot, full of sound and fury,
Signifying nothing.

—SHAKESPEARE, *Macbeth*, V, v

Dying is no big deal. The least of us will manage that. Living is the trick.
> —WALTER ("RED") SMITH, funeral eulogy
> for golf impresario Fred Corcoran

Old and young, we are all on our last cruise.
> —ROBERT LOUIS STEVENSON,
> *Crabbed Age and Youth*

If a person saves one life it is as if he had saved the whole world.   —TALMUD

While there's life, there's hope.
> —TERENCE, *Heauton timoroumenos*

The mass of men lead lives of quiet desperation.
> —HENRY DAVID THOREAU, *Walden*

Life is so unlike theory.   —ANTHONY TROLLOPE,
> *Phineas Finn*

The world is a comedy to those that think, a tragedy to those that feel.
> —HORACE WALPOLE, letter to the
> Countess of Upper Ossory, Aug. 16, 1776

Life is an offensive, directed against the repetitious mechanism of the universe.
> —ALFRED NORTH WHITEHEAD,
> *Adventures of Ideas*

Life imitates art far more than art imitates life.
> —OSCAR WILDE, "The Decay of
> Lying" in *Intentions*
[Cf. Seneca on art, under ARTS, and Marshall McLuhan at REALITY & ILLUSION.]

The world is too much with us; late and soon,
Getting and spending, we lay waste our powers:
Little we see in Nature that is ours;
We have given our hearts away.
> —WILLIAM WORDSWORTH,
> *The World Is Too Much with Us*

Cast a cold eye
On life, on death.
Horseman, pass by!   —WILLIAM BUTLER YEATS,
                                    Under Ben Bulben

LIMITS   See also FAILINGS

A man cannot jump over his own shadow.
                    —ANONYMOUS (YIDDISH PROVERB)
[Sometimes used in the sense: one cannot escape the
consequences of one's acts.]

Tempt us not to bear above our power!
                              —SHAKESPEARE,
                              King John, V, vi

LITERATURE   See ARTS entries;
                                   BOOKS & READING

LITTLE THINGS   See DETAILS & OTHER
                                   SMALL THINGS; THINGS
                                   & POSSESSIONS

LIVING WELL   See GRACE; HEDONISM; LIFE

LOGIC   See MIND; PHILOSOPHY; REASON & REASONS;
                    REASONABLE & UNREASONABLE PEOPLE

LONDON   See CITIES

LONELINESS   See SOLITUDE

LOSERS   See HAVES AND HAVE-NOTS; RUIN;
                                   WINNING & LOSING,
                                   VICTORY & DEFEAT

LOVE   See also HEART; JEALOUSY; LOVE, EXPRESSIONS
          OF; LOVE & CHARITY: BIBLICAL REFERENCES;
          MARRIAGE; SEX & SENSUALITY; WOMEN & MEN

Love teaches even asses to dance.
> —ANONYMOUS (FRENCH PROVERB)

The heart that loves is always young.
> —ANONYMOUS (GREEK PROVERB)

It is impossible to love and be wise.
> —FRANCIS BACON, *Of Love*

Absence makes the heart grow fonder.
> —T. H. BAYLY, *Isle of Beauty*

Where love is concerned, too much is not even enough.   —PIERRE-AUGUSTIN DE BEAUMARCHAIS, *The Marriage of Figaro*

Who can give law to lovers? Love is a greater law to itself.   —BOETHIUS, *De consolatione philosophiae*
[See also John Lyly, below.]

Man's love is of man's life a thing apart,
'Tis woman's whole existence.
> —LORD BYRON, *Don Juan*

In her first passion woman loves her lover,
In all the others, all she loves is love.   —*Ibid.*
[Byron might have credited La Rochefoucauld, see below.]

Love, such as it is in society, is only the exchange of two fantasies, and the contact of two bodies.
> —SÉBASTIEN R. N. CHAMFORT, *Maximes et pensées*

Great loves too must be endured.
> —COCO CHANEL, quoted in Marcel Haedrich, *Coco Chanel, Her Life, Her Secrets*

Love is blind.
> —GEOFFREY CHAUCER, *The Merchant's Tale*, in *The Canterbury Tales*
[Essentially proverbial; see variations by Menander and Shakespeare, below.]

Can there be a love which does not make demands on its object? ——CONFUCIUS, *Analects*

Love and murder will out.
—WILLIAM CONGREVE, *The Double Dealer*
[For more on the alleged tendency of murder to be discovered, see under CRIME.]

Love, all alike, no season knows, nor clime,
Nor hours, days, months, which are the rags of time.
—JOHN DONNE, *The Sun Rising*

For heaven be thanked, we live in such an age,
When no man dies for love, but on the stage.
—JOHN DRYDEN, *Mithridates*, Epilogue

All mankind love a lover.
—RALPH WALDO EMERSON, *Love*

Love is all we have, the only way that each can help the other. —EURIPIDES, *Orestes*

The only regret I will have in dying is if it is not for love. —GABRIEL GARCÍA MARQUEZ,
Love in the Time of Cholera
[Speaking of "the Latin way of loving and dying" in a *New York Times* interview, Aug. 21, 1991, García Marquez remarked that the Latin view of love was well put by Brazilian songwriter Vinicius de Moralis: "Love is eternal as long as it lasts."]

She who has never loved has never lived.
—JOHN GAY, *Captives*

It's love that makes the world go round!
—W. S. GILBERT, *Iolanthe*
[Probably proverbial. The French say, *"L'amour fait tourner le monde."*]

Love knows nothing of order.
—ST. JEROME, letter 7

Love is swift, sincere, pious, pleasant, generous, strong, patient, faithful, prudent, long-suffering, manly,

and never seeking her own; for wheresoever a man seeketh his own, there he falleth from love.
—THOMAS À KEMPIS, *Imitation of Christ*

A fool there was and he made his prayer
(Even as you and I!)
To a rag and a bone and a hank of hair
(We called her the woman who did not care)
But the fool he called her his lady fair—
Even as you and I.
—RUDYARD KIPLING, *The Vampire*

If one judges love by the majority of its effects, it is more like hatred than friendship.
—LA ROCHEFOUCAULD, *Maxims*

There is no disguise which can hide love for long where it exists, or simulate it where it does not.
—*Ibid.*

In their first passion, women love their lovers; in all the others, they love love.   —*Ibid.*
[See also Byron, above.]

It requires far more genius to make love than to command armies.   —NINON DE LENCLOS, ascribed

Two souls with but a single thought,
Two hearts that beat as one.
—MARIA LOVELL, *Ingomar the Barbarian*

Love is a product of habit.   —LUCRETIUS,
De rerum natura
[A similar thought occurred to Jane Austen: "I am pleased that you have learned to love a hyacinth, the mere habit of learning to love is the thing."]

Love knoweth no laws.   —JOHN LYLY, *Euphues*
[See also Boethius, above.]

Delicacy is to love what grace is to beauty.
—MADAME DE MAINTENON, *Maximes de Mme. de Maintenon*

It is love, not reason, that is stronger than death.
> —THOMAS MANN, *The Magic Mountain*

Who ever loved that loved not at first sight?
> —CHRISTOPHER MARLOWE, *Hero and Leander*

When you have loved as she has loved, you grow old beautifully.
> —W. SOMERSET MAUGHAM, *The Circle*

Love blinds all men alike, both the reasonable and the foolish.   —MENANDER, *Andria*

We are easily duped by those we love.
> —MOLIÈRE, *Tartuffe*

No, there's nothing half so sweet in life
As love's young dream.
> —THOMAS MOORE, *Love's Young Dream*

This is the hardest of all: to close the open hand out of love, and to keep modest as a giver.
> —FRIEDRICH NIETZSCHE, *Thus Spake Zarathustra*

Love is a kind of warfare.
> —OVID, *Ars amatoria*

Oh, life is a glorious cycle of song,
A medley of extemporanea;
And love is a thing that can never go wrong,
And I am Marie of Roumania.
> —DOROTHY PARKER, *Comment*

By the time you swear you're his
Shivering and sighing,
And he vows his passion is
Infinite, undying—
Lady make a note of this:
One of you is lying.
> —DOROTHY PARKER,
> *Unfortunate*
> *Coincidence*

[Love is] the joy of the good, the wonder of the wise, the amazement of the gods.
—PLATO, *The Symposium*

There can be no peace of mind in love since the advantage one has secured is never anything but a fresh starting point for further desire.
—MARCEL PROUST, *Remembrance of Things Past: Within a Budding Grove*

What is life without the radiance of love?
—J. C. F. VON SCHILLER, *Wallensteins Tod*

Love means never having to say you're sorry.
—ERICH SEGAL, *Love Story*

Men have died from time to time and worms have eaten them, but not for love.
—SHAKESPEARE, *As You Like It*, IV, i

Love is a familiar. Love is a devil. There is no evil angel but Love.
—SHAKESPEARE, *Love's Labour's Lost*, I, ii

But love is blind, and lovers cannot see
The pretty follies that themselves commit.
—SHAKESPEARE, *The Merchant of Venice*, II, vi

The course of true love never did run smooth.
—SHAKESPEARE, *A Midsummer Night's Dream*, I, i

Speak low, if you speak love.
—SHAKESPEARE, *Much Ado About Nothing*, II, i

Speak of me as I am . . . one that loved not wisely but too well.   —SHAKESPEARE, *Othello*, V, ii

They do not love that do not show their love.
—SHAKESPEARE, *The Two Gentlemen of Verona*, I, ii
[An old saying; Shakespeare used proverbial comments freely.]

Let me not to the marriage of true minds
Admit impediments. Love is not love
Which alters when it alteration finds,
Or bends with the remover to remove.
Oh no! It is an ever-fixèd mark
That looks on tempests and is never shaken.
It is the star to every wandering bark,
Whose worth's unknown, although his height be
    taken.   —SHAKESPEARE, sonnet 116

Love comforteth like sunshine after rain.
          —SHAKESPEARE, *Venus and Adonis*

Familiar acts are beautiful through love.
    —PERCY BYSSHE SHELLEY, *Prometheus Unbound*

All love is sweet,
Given or returned. Common as light is love,
And its familiar voice wearies not ever.   *—Ibid.*

All's fair in love and war.
          —FRANCIS EDWARD SMEDLEY,
          Frank Fairlegh

One word frees us of all the weight and pain of life:
That word is love.
        —SOPHOCLES, *Oedipus at Colonus*

'Tis better to have loved and lost
Than never to have loved at all.
    —ALFRED, LORD TENNYSON, *In Memoriam*

O, tell her, brief is life but love is long.
    —ALFRED, LORD TENNYSON, *The Princess*

All, everything that I understand, I understand only
because I love.   —LEO TOLSTOY, *War and Peace*

Omnia vincit Amor: et nos cedamus Amori.
Love conquers all: and let us too surrender to love.
          —VIRGIL, *Eclogues*

Love those who love you.
    —VOLTAIRE, letter to d'Alembert, Nov. 28, 1762
[This is the last, often overlooked phrase in the noted
écrasez l'infâme exhortation, cited in full at RELIGION.]

'Tis said that some have died for love.
—WILLIAM WORDSWORTH,
'Tis Said That Some Have Died

A pity beyond all telling
Is hid in the heart of love.
—WILLIAM BUTLER YEATS, *The Pity of Love*

LOVE & CHARITY: See also LOVE
BIBLICAL REFERENCES

Thou shalt love thy neighbor as thyself.
—BIBLE, *Leviticus* 19:18
[Also found in several other places in the Bible, including most notably *Matthew* 22:39, where in the next verse it is described as one of the two essential commandments, along with the commandment to love God—see under GOD.]

A new commandment I give unto you, that you love one another.   —BIBLE, *John* 13:34

Though I speak with the tongues of men and of angels, and have not charity, I am become as sounding brass, or a tinkling cymbal.
—BIBLE, *I Corinthians* 13:1

Charity suffereth long and is kind; charity envieth not; charity vaunteth not itself, is not puffed up.
—*Ibid.*, 13:4

And now abideth faith, hope, and charity, these three; but the greatest of these is charity.
—*Ibid.*, 13:13

There is no fear in love; but perfect love casteth out fear.   —BIBLE, *I John*, 4:18

He that loveth not his brother whom he hath seen, how can he love God whom he hath not seen?
—*Ibid.*, 4:20

LOVE, EXPRESSIONS OF   See also HEDONISM;
   LOVE; MARRIAGE; WOMEN, BEAUTIFUL & HOMELY

Western Wind, when wilt thou blow,
That the small rain down can rain?
Christ if my love were in my arms
And I in my bed again.   —ANONYMOUS

Arise, my love, my fair one, and come away.
         —BIBLE, *The Song of Solomon* 2:10–13
[The quote is given in full at NATURE: SEASONS.]

If ever two were one, then surely we.
If ever man were loved by wife, then thee.
         —ANNE BRADSTREET,
            To My Dear and Loving Husband

These I have loved:
White plates and cups, clean-gleaming,
Ringed with blue lines.   —RUPERT BROOKE,
                  The Great Lover

Then, the cool kindliness of sheets, that soon
Smooth away trouble; and the rough male kiss
Of blankets; grainy wood; live hair that is
Shining and free; blue massing clouds; the keen
Unpassioned beauty of a great machine.   —*Ibid.*

How do I love thee? Let me count the ways.
I love thee to the depth and breadth and height
My soul can reach, when feeling out of sight
For the ends of being and ideal grace.
         —ELIZABETH BARRETT BROWNING,
            Sonnets from the Portuguese, 43

I love thee with the breath,
Smiles, tears, of all my life!—and, if God choose,
I shall but love thee better after death.   —*Ibid.*

But to see her was to love her,
Love but her, and love for ever.
                  —ROBERT BURNS, *Ae Fond Kiss*
[Yes, Burns wrote almost identical lines in another
poem:

To see her is to love her,
And love but her for ever:
For Nature made her what she is, and never made
     sic anither!   —*Bonnie Lesley*.]

O, my luve's like a red red rose
That's newly sprung in June:
O my luve's like the melodie
That's sweetly played in tune.
                    —ROBERT BURNS,
                         My Love Is Like a Red Red Rose

O whistle an' I'll come to ye, my lad,
O whistle an' I'll come to ye, my lad,
Tho' father an' mother an' a' should gae mad,
O whistle an' I'll come to ye, my lad.
                    —ROBERT BURNS, *O Whistle an'*
                         I'll Come to Ye, My Lad

Come live with me, and be my love,
And we will some new pleasures prove
Of golden sands, and crystal brooks,
With silken lines, and silver hooks.
                    —JOHN DONNE, *The Bait*
[The similar but more famous verse is by Christopher
Marlowe, see below.]

I have found it impossible to carry the heavy burden
of responsibility and to discharge my duties as king as
I would wish without the help and support of the woman
I love.
 —EDWARD VIII, abdication speech, Dec. 11, 1936

A book of verses underneath the bough
A jug of wine, a loaf of bread—and thou
Beside me singing in the wilderness.
                    —EDWARD FITZGERALD,
                         The Rubáiyát of Omar Khayyám

Why don't you speak for yourself, John?
                    —HENRY WADSWORTH LONGFELLOW,
                         The Courtship of Miles Standish

[Priscilla Mullins to John Alden, who had been speaking for his friend Miles Standish. Longfellow was descended from John and Priscilla.]

Come live with me and be my love,
And we will all the pleasures prove
That valleys, groves, hills, and fields,
Woods or steepy mountain yields.
　　　　　—CHRISTOPHER MARLOWE,
　　　　　　The Passionate Shepherd to His Love
[Cf. John Donne, above.]

I was a child and she was a child,
In this kingdom by the sea;
But we loved with a love that was more than love—
I and my Annabel Lee.
　　　　　—EDGAR ALLAN POE, *Annabel Lee*

What's mine is yours, and what is yours is mine.
　　　　　—SHAKESPEARE, *Measure for Measure*, V, i
[Plautus used the same line.]

But, soft! What light through yonder window breaks?
It is the east, and Juliet is the sun.
　　　　　—SHAKESPEARE, *Romeo and Juliet*, II, ii

See how she leans her cheek upon her hand!
Oh, that I were a glove upon that hand,
That I might touch that cheek!　　　　—*Ibid.*

O Romeo, Romeo, wherefore art thou Romeo?
Deny thy father and refuse thy name,
Or, if thou wilt not, be but sworn my love
And I'll no longer be a Capulet.　　　—*Ibid.*

Goodnight! goodnight!
Parting is such sweet sorrow
That I shall say goodnight till it be morrow.
　　　　　—*Ibid.*

When he shall die,
Take him and cut him out in little stars,
And he will make the face of heaven so fine
That all the world will be in love with night.
　　　　　—*Ibid.*, III, ii

Kiss me, Kate!
—SHAKESPEARE, *The Taming of the Shrew*, II, i

Shall I compare thee to a summer's day?
Thou art more lovely and more temperate.
—SHAKESPEARE, sonnet 18

Nothing in the world is single;
All things by a law divine
In one spirit meet and mingle.
Why not I with thine?
—PERCY BYSSHE SHELLEY, *Love's Philosophy*

One can't live on love alone; and I am so stupid that
I can do nothing but think of him.
—SOPHIE TOLSTOY, *A Diary*

When you are old and gray and full of sleep
And nodding by the fire, take down this book,
And slowly read.
—WILLIAM BUTLER YEATS, *When You Are Old*

How many loved your moments of glad grace,
And loved your beauty with love false or true;
But one man loved the pilgrim soul in you,
And loved the sorrows of your changing face.
—*Ibid.*

LOYALTY   See UNITY AND LOYALTY

LUCK   See also FATE

Throw a lucky man in the sea, and he will come up
with a fish in his mouth.
—ANONYMOUS (ARAB PROVERB)

The race is not to the swift, nor the battle to the
strong, neither yet bread to the wise, nor yet riches to
men of understanding, nor yet favor to men of skill;
but time and chance happeneth to them all.
—BIBLE, *Ecclesiastes* 9:11

Who has good luck is good. Who has bad luck is bad.
  —BERTOLT BRECHT, *The Exception and the Rule*

Heaven's help is better than early rising.
    —CERVANTES, *Don Quixote*
[Probably proverbial—Mencken cites as an Irish proverb, "Good luck beats early rising."]

Luck is not chance—
It's toil—
Fortune's expensive smile
Is earned.   —EMILY DICKINSON, poem no. 1350

The lucky person passes for a genius.
        —EURIPIDES, *Herakleidai*

Have but luck, and you will have the rest; be fortunate, and you will be thought great.
        —VICTOR HUGO, *Les Misérables*

A lucky man is rarer than a white cow.
        —JUVENAL, *Satires*

If it wasn't for bad luck, I wouldn't have no luck at all.   —ALBERT KING, *Born Under a Bad Sign*
[A folk saying that appears in many forms, including King's blues classic, cited here.]

Now and then
there is a person born
who is so unlucky
that he runs into accidents
which started out to happen to somebody else.
        —DON MARQUIS, *archy says*

Luck is the Residue of Design.
        —BRANCH RICKEY, lecture title, 1950
[At the time, Rickey was running the Brooklyn Dodgers.]

Luck never made a man wise.
        —SENECA, *Letters to Lucilius*

Fortune favors the brave.   —TERENCE, *Phormio*

'Tis better to be fortunate than wise.
                        —JOHN WEBSTER, *The White Devil*
[More at FATE.]

Luck is not something you can mention in the presence of self-made men.
                        —E. B. WHITE, "Control," in *One Man's Meat*

LUXURY   See EXCESS; HEDONISM

LYING   See DISHONESTY & LIES

M

MACHINES See TECHNOLOGY

MADNESS See also DESPAIR, DEPRESSION, MISERY; ILLNESS & REMEDIES; SCIENCE: PSYCHOLOGY & PSYCHOANALYSIS

We are all born mad. Some remain so.
——SAMUEL BECKETT, *Waiting for Godot*

My name is Legion: for we are many.
——BIBLE, *Mark* 5:9
[The speaker is a devil inhabiting a madman of the Gadarenes. Jesus sent the devils to enter a herd of two thousand swine.]

There is a pleasure sure
In being mad, which none but madmen know.
——JOHN DRYDEN, *The Spanish Friar*

Those whom God wishes to destroy, he first makes mad. ——EURIPIDES, fragment
[This became a proverbial comment, and is found in several other sources. In a famous revision, Cyril Connolly wrote, "Whom the gods wish to destroy they first call promising," *Enemies of Promise*.]

Everyone is more or less mad on one point.
——RUDYARD KIPLING, "On the Strength of a Likeness," in *Plain Tales from the Hills*

Men . . . go mad in herds, while they only recover
their senses slowly, and one by one.
                    —CHARLES MACKAY,
                        *Extraordinary Popular Delusions
                        and the Madness of Crowds*

As I was going up the stair,
I met a man who wasn't there.
He wasn't there again today.
I wish, I wish he'd stay away.
                    —HUGHES MEARNS, *The Psychoed*

From childhood's hour I have not been
As others were—I have not seen
As others saw.   —EDGAR ALLAN POE, *Alone*

There is no great genius without some touch of
madness.   —SENECA, *On Tranquillity of the Mind*

Madness in great ones must not unwatched go.
                    —SHAKESPEARE, *Hamlet*, III, i
[See also METHOD.]

Is this a dagger which I see before me,
The handle toward my hand? Come let me clutch
    thee.   —SHAKESPEARE, *Macbeth*, II, i

Art thou but
A dagger of the mind, a false creation
Proceeding from the heat-oppressed brain?
                                    —*Ibid.*

It is an accustomed action with her to seem thus wash-
ing her hands. I have known her continue in this a
quarter of an hour.   —*Ibid.*, V, i

Out, damned spot! Out, I say! One, two, why, then
'tis time to do't. Hell is murky!   —*Ibid.*
[Lady Macbeth also appears under GUILT.]

When we remember that we are all mad, the mysteries disappear and life stands explained.
                    —MARK TWAIN, *Notebook*

My apprehensions come in crowds;
I dread the rustling of the grass;
The very shadows of the clouds
Have power to shake me as they pass:
I question things and do not find
One that will answer to my mind;
And all the world appears unkind.
　　　　　　　　—WILLIAM WORDSWORTH,
　　　　　　　　The Affliction of Margaret

MAGIC　　　　　　　　　　See OCCULT, THE

MAJORITY　　　　　　　　　See PEOPLE, THE

MALAYA　　　　　　　　　　See ORIENT, THE

MANDALAY　　　　　　　　　See ORIENT, THE

MANKIND　　　　　See HUMANS & HUMAN NATURE;
　　　　　　　　　　MEN; WOMEN & MEN

MANNERS　　　See also CUSTOM; GRACE; HOSPITALITY;
　　　　　　　　　　INSULTS & PUT-DOWNS

Whatsoever ye would that men should do to you, do
ye even so to them.　　　　　—BIBLE, *Matthew* 7:12
[Often paraphrased; known as the Golden Rule. See
also related quotes from Confucius and Shaw, below.]

An injury is much sooner forgotten than an insult.
　　　　　—EARL OF CHESTERFIELD, letter to his son,
　　　　　　　　Oct. 9, 1746

Take the tone of the company you are in.
　　　　　　　　　—*Ibid.*, Oct. 9, 1747
[See also St. Ambrose at TRAVEL.]

O tempora! O mores!
O the times! O the manners!
　　　　　　　　　—CICERO, *In catilinam*

To be audacious with tact, you have to know to what
point you can go too far.
　　　　　　　　—JEAN COCTEAU, *Le Coq et l'Harlequin*

[The phrase "to know to what point you can go too far"—*savoir jusqu'où on peut aller trop loin*—has become a common expression among French speakers.]

It is good manners which make the excellence of a neighborhood. No wise man will settle where they are lacking.   —CONFUCIUS, *Analects*

Behave to everyone as if you were receiving a great guest; . . . [do not] do to others what you would not wish done to yourself.   —CONFUCIUS, *Ibid.*

The trouble with treating people as equals is that the first thing you know they may be doing the same thing to you.   —PETER DE VRIES, *The Prick of Noon*

The art of pleasing consists in being pleased.
                          —WILLIAM HAZLITT, *On Manners*
[See also Johnson, below.]

You never want to give a man a present when he's feeling good. You want to do it when he's down.
   —LYNDON B. JOHNSON, quoted in Doris Kearns,
      Lyndon Johnson and the American Dream

He who endeavors to please must appear to be pleased.
   —SAMUEL JOHNSON, *The Rambler,* Aug. 31, 1751

Punctuality is the politeness of kings.
                          —LOUIS XVIII, attributed

My father used to say
"Superior people never make long visits."
                          —MARIANNE MOORE, *Silence*

It is almost a definition of a gentleman to say that he is one who never inflicts pain.
   —CARDINAL NEWMAN, *The Idea of a University*

Manners go on deteriorating.
                          —PLAUTUS, *Mercator*

Etiquette can be at the same time a means of approaching people and of staying clear of them.
—DAVID RIESMAN, *The Lonely Crowd*

Rudeness is better than any argument; it totally eclipses intellect.
—ARTHUR SCHOPENHAUER, *Position*

Is there no respect of place, persons, nor time, in you? SHAKESPEARE, *Twelfth Night*, II, iii

Do not do unto others as you would they should do unto you. Their tastes may not be the same.
—GEORGE BERNARD SHAW, *Man and Superman*, "Maxims for Revolutionists"

Good breeding consists in concealing how much we think of ourselves and how little we think of the other person. —MARK TWAIN, *Notebooks*

MARRIAGE See also FAMILY; HOME; LOVE; WOMEN & MEN

Those marriages generally abound most with love and constancy that are preceded by a long courtship.
—JOSEPH ADDISON, *The Spectator*, Dec. 29, 1711

When a match has equal partners, then I fear not.
—AESCHYLUS, *Prometheus Bound*

Autant de mariages, autant ménages.
As many as there are marriages, so many living arrangements. —ANONYMOUS (FRENCH PROVERB)

Se marie, c'est apprendre être seul.
To marry is to learn to be alone.
—ANONYMOUS (FRENCH PROVERB)

Marriage, to woman as to men, must be a luxury, not a necessity; an incident of life, not all of it.
—SUSAN B. ANTHONY, speech, 1875

I married beneath me—all women do.
—NANCY ASTOR, speech, Oldham, England, 1951

It is a truth universally acknowledged, that a single man in possession of good fortune, must be in want of a wife.   —JANE AUSTEN, *Pride and Prejudice*
[For more on this line, see Austen at WOMEN & MEN.]

It is better to marry than to burn.
—BIBLE, *I Corinthians* 7:9

One was never married, and that's his hell; another is, and that's his plague.
—ROBERT BURTON,
The Anatomy of Melancholy

Polygamy may well be held in dread,
Not only as a sin but as a bore.
—LORD BYRON, *Don Juan*

Marriage is a result of the longing for the deep, deep peace of the double bed after the hurly-burly of the chaise-longue.
—MRS. PATRICK CAMPBELL, quoted in
Ralph G. Martin, *Jenny*

The divorce will be gayer than the wedding.
—COLETTE,
Cheri

I am not against hasty marriages, where a mutual flame is fanned by an adequate income.
—WILKIE COLLINS, *No Name*

Married in haste, we may repent at leisure.
—WILLIAM CONGREVE, *The Old Bachelor*
[The proverb—"Marry in haste, repent at leisure"—predates Congreve.]

A single man . . . is an incomplete animal. He resembles the odd half of a pair of scissors.
—BENJAMIN FRANKLIN,
letter to a young man,
June 25, 1745

Where there's marriage without love, there will be love without marriage.
—BENJAMIN FRANKLIN, *Poor Richard's Almanac*

I think it can be stated without denial that no man ever saw a man he would be willing to marry if he were a woman.   —GEORGE GIBBS, *How to Stay Married*

Let there be spaces in your togetherness.
—KAHLIL GIBRAN, *The Prophet*

A wife loves out of duty, and duty leads to constraint, and constraint kills desire.
—JEAN GIRAUDOUX, *Amphitryon 38*

Faithful women are all alike. They think only of their fidelity and not of their husbands.   —*Ibid.*

When a woman gets married, it's like jumping into a hole in the ice in the middle of winter: you do it once and you remember it the rest of your days.
—MAXIM GORKY, *The Lower Depths*

A gentleman who had been very unhappy in marriage, married immediately after his wife died: Johnson said it was the triumph of hope over experience.
—SAMUEL JOHNSON, quoted in
James Boswell, *Life of Johnson*, 1770

Marriage has many pains, but celibacy has no pleasures.   —SAMUEL JOHNSON, *Rasselas*

There are some good marriages, but no delightful ones.   —LA ROCHEFOUCAULD, *Maxims*

There is no more lovely, friendly, and charming relationship, communion, or company than a good marriage.   —MARTIN LUTHER, *Table Talk*

Marriages are made in heaven.
—JOHN LYLY, *Euphues and His England*

"That's bigamy."
"Yes and it's big of me, too. It's big of all of us. I'm sick of these conventional marriages. One woman and

one man was good enough for your grandmother. But who wants to marry your grandmother?"
　　　　　　　—GROUCHO MARX, *Animal Crackers*

Marriage, to tell the truth, is an evil, but it is a necessary evil.　　　　—MENANDER, fragment

It [marriage] is like a cage; one sees the birds outside desperate to get in, and those inside desperate to get out.　　　　　　　—MONTAIGNE, *Essays*

Not louder shrieks to pitying heaven are cast,
When husbands or when lapdogs breathe their last.
　　　　—ALEXANDER POPE, *The Rape of the Lock*

A good marriage is that in which each appoints the other the guardian of his solitude.
　　　　　　　—RAINER MARIA RILKE, *Letters*

It doesn't much signify whom one marries, for one is sure to find out the next morning that it was someone else.　　　　　—SAMUEL ROGERS, *Table Talk*

Love, the quest; marriage, the conquest; divorce, the inquest.　　　—HELEN ROWLAND, *A Guide to Men*

Marriage is for woman the commonest mode of livelihood, and the total amount of undesired sex endured by women is probably greater in marriage than in prostitution.
　　　　—BERTRAND RUSSELL, *Marriage and Morals*

It takes patience to appreciate domestic bliss; volatile spirits prefer unhappiness.
　　　　—GEORGE SANTAYANA, *The Life of Reason*

To marry is to halve your rights and double your duties.　　　　　　—ARTHUR SCHOPENHAUER,
　　　　　　　　　The World as Will and Idea

Marriage is a desperate thing.
　　　　　　　—JOHN SELDEN, *Marriage*

The ancient saying is no heresy,
Hanging and wiving goes by destiny.
　　　—SHAKESPEARE, *The Merchant of Venice*, II, ix

[Another form of this proverb was cited by John Heywood:
Wedding is destiny,
And hanging likewise.]

A light wife doth make a heavy husband.
—*Ibid.*, V, i

Item: I give unto my wife my second best bed.
—SHAKESPEARE, his will

It is a woman's business to get married as soon as possible, and a man's to keep unmarried as long as he can.
—GEORGE BERNARD SHAW, *Man and Superman*

Marriage is popular because it combines the maximum of temptation with the maximum of opportunity.
—*Ibid.*, "Maxims for Revolutionists"

The married state is the completest image of heaven and hell we are capable of receiving in this life.
—RICHARD STEELE, *The Spectator*,
no. 479, 1711–12

In marriage, a man becomes slack and selfish, and undergoes a fatty degeneration of his moral being.
—ROBERT LOUIS STEVENSON,
Virginibus Puerisque

Oh husbands, oh, my married friends, what comfort is there to be derived from a wife well obeyed!
—ANTHONY TROLLOPE, *Barchester Towers*

In married life, three is company and two is none.
—OSCAR WILDE, *The Importance
of Being Earnest*

The world has grown suspicious of anything that looks like a happy married life.
—OSCAR WILDE, *Lady Windermere's Fan*

MARXISM	See COMMUNISM
MASSES	See PEOPLE, THE
MATHEMATICS	See SCIENCE: MATHEMATICS & STATISTICS
MAXIMS	See QUOTATIONS, MAXIMS, & PROVERBS
MAY	See NATURE: SEASONS
MEANS	See ENDS & MEANS
MEDIA	See also ADVERTISING; PRESS, THE

One picture is worth a thousand words.
—FRED R. BARNARD,
in *Printers' Ink*,
March 10, 1927
[Barnard called this a Chinese proverb, but actually it is a rewrite of an earlier Barnard maxim, "One look is worth a thousand words," *Printers' Ink*, Dec. 8, 1921.]

The printing press is either the greatest blessing or the greatest curse of modern times, one sometimes forgets which. —J. M. BARRIE, *Sentimental Tommy*

Some television programs are so much chewing gum for the eyes.
—JOHN MASON BROWN, interview, July 28, 1955
[This also has been attributed to Frank Lloyd Wright and Fred Allen.]

Now Barabbas was a publisher.
—LORD BYRON, traditional attribution
[Some feel that a more likely source is Thomas Campbell.]

Television is a form of soliloquy.
—SIR KENNETH CLARK, in the *Guardian*,
Nov. 26, 1977

Because television can make so much money doing its worst, it often cannot afford to do its best.
—FRED W. FRIENDLY,
Due to Circumstances Beyond Our Control

The hand that rules the press, the radio, the screen, and the far-spread magazine rules the country.
—LEARNED HAND, speech, Dec. 21, 1942

[Television:] a medium, so called because it is neither rare nor well done.
—ERNIE KOVACS, quoted in Leslie Halliwell, *The Filmgoer's Book of Quotes*

The new electronic interdependence re-creates the world in the image of a global village.
—MARSHALL MCLUHAN, *The Gutenberg Galaxy*

The medium is the message.
—MARSHALL MCLUHAN, *Understanding Media*

[If you watch television from morning to night] I can assure you that you will observe a vast wasteland.
—NEWTON MINOW, speech to the National Association of Broadcasters, May 9, 1961

It is not enough to cater to the nation's whims—you must also serve the nation's needs.   —*Ibid.*

The more we elaborate our means of communication, the less we communicate.
—J. B. PRIESTLEY, "Televiewing," in *Thoughts in the Wilderness*

The New Yorker will be the magazine that is not edited for the old lady in Dubuque.
—HAROLD R. ROSS, prospectus for *The New Yorker*, 1924

I believe television is going to be the test of the modern world, and that in this new opportunity to see beyond the range of our vision we shall discover either a new and unbearable disturbance of the general peace

or a saving radiance in the sky. We shall stand or fall by television.
> —E. B. WHITE, "Removal," in *One Man's Meat*
[Written in 1938 for *Harper's* magazine.]

MEDICINE   See DOCTORS & THE PRACTICE OF
                             MEDICINE; ILLNESS & REMEDIES;
                             MADNESS; SCIENCE: PSYCHOLOGY
                             & PSYCHOANALYSIS

MEDIOCRITY

Be not righteous over much; neither make thyself over wise.   —BIBLE, *Ecclesiastes* 7:16

The world is a republic of mediocrities, and always was.   —THOMAS CARLYLE, letter to Emerson, May 13, 1853

The only sin is mediocrity.
> —MARTHA GRAHAM, quoted in
> *The New York Times*, March 31, 1985

The way to get on in the world is to be neither more nor less wise, neither better nor worse than your neighbors.   —WILLIAM HAZLITT,
> *On Knowledge of the World*

Some men are born mediocre, some men achieve mediocrity, and some men have mediocrity thrust upon them. With Major Major it had been all three.
> —JOSEPH HELLER,
> *Catch-22*
[See also Shakespeare at GREATNESS.]

Even if he is mediocre, there are lots of mediocre judges, and people, and lawyers. They are entitled to a little representation, too, aren't they?
> —ROMAN L. HRUSKA, Senate hearings
> on the nomination of G. Harrold Carswell
> to the Supreme Court, 1970
[Hruska, a Republican senator from Nebraska, was attempting to defend President Richard Nixon's nominee.

The comment, however, was not helpful. The Senate rejected Judge Carswell.]

There are certain things in which mediocrity is insupportable—poetry, music, painting, public speaking. —LA BRUYÈRE, *Les Caractères*

MELANCHOLY See DESPAIR, DEPRESSION, MISERY; SORROW, SADNESS, & SUFFERING

MEMORY See also PAST, THE

Memory is the mother of all wisdom.
—AESCHYLUS, *Prometheus Bound*

I have more memories than if I were a thousand years old. —CHARLES BAUDELAIRE, *Spleen et idéal*

Some memories are realities, and are better than anything that can ever happen to one again.
—WILLA CATHER, *My Antonia*

Memory is the treasury and guardian of all things.
—CICERO, *De Oratore*

It is an art to recollect. —SÖREN KIERKEGAARD, *Stages on Life's Way*

Good memories are lost jewels.
—PAUL VALÉRY, *Mauvaises Pensées*

In memory everything seems to happen to music.
—TENNESSEE WILLIAMS, *The Glass Menagerie*

MEN See also HUMANS & HUMAN NATURE; WOMEN & MEN

If there is anything disagreeable going on, men are sure to get out of it.
—JANE AUSTEN, *Northanger Abbey*

As long as you know that most men are like children, you know everything.
—COCO CHANEL, attributed

A man is a god in ruins.
> —RALPH WALDO EMERSON, *Nature*

Every man has a wild animal in him.
> —FREDERICK THE GREAT,
> letter to Voltaire, 1759

There's nothing so stubborn as a man when you want him to do something.
> —JEAN GIRAUDOUX, *The Madwoman of Chaillot*

What a piece of work is a man! How noble in reason! How infinite in faculty! In form, in moving, how express and admirable! In action how like an angel! In apprehension how like a god! The beauty of the world! The paragon of animals!
> —SHAKESPEARE, *Hamlet*, II, ii

Sigh no more, ladies, sigh no more,
Men were deceivers ever;
One foot in sea, and one on shore,
To one thing constant never.
> —SHAKESPEARE, *Much Ado About Nothing*,
> II, iii

Every man over forty is a scoundrel.
> —GEORGE BERNARD SHAW, *Man and Superman*,
> "Maxims for Revolutionists"

A man in the house is worth two in the street.
> —MAE WEST, *Belle of the Nineties*

MERCY   See FORGIVENESS &
                              MERCY; JUSTICE

METAPHYSICS   See ETHICS &
                          MORALITY; PHILOSOPHY

METHOD   See also ENDS & MEANS; WORK & WORKERS

If there are obstacles, the shortest line between two points may be the crooked line.
> —BERTOLT BRECHT, *Galileo*

There are some enterprises in which a careful disorderliness is the true method.
—HERMAN MELVILLE, *Moby-Dick*

Though this be madness, yet there is method in it.
—SHAKESPEARE, *Hamlet*, II, ii

MEXICO   See NATIONS

MIDDLE AGE & MID-LIFE CRISIS

Midway in our life's journey, I went astray from the straight road and woke to find myself alone in a dark wood.   —DANTE, *Inferno*, in *The Divine Comedy*

After thirty, a man wakes up sad every morning, excepting perhaps five or six, until the day of his death.
—RALPH WALDO EMERSON, *Journals*, 1834

By the time a person has achieved years adequate for choosing a direction, the die is cast and the moment has long since passed which determined the future.
—ZELDA FITZGERALD, *Save Me the Waltz*

Whoever, in middle age, attempts to realize the wishes and hopes of his early youth invariably deceives himself. Each ten years of a man's life has its own fortunes, its own hopes, its own desires.
—GOETHE, *Elective Affinities*

Men, like peaches and pears, grow sweet a little while before they begin to decay.
—OLIVER WENDELL HOLMES, SR.,
The Autocrat of the Breakfast Table

The long dull monotonous years of middle-aged prosperity or middle-aged adversity are excellent campaigning weather for the Devil.
—C. S. LEWIS, *The Screwtape Letters*

[Middle age is] the time when a man is always thinking that in a week or two he'll feel just as good as ever.
—DON MARQUIS, quoted in B. Wilcox,
A Little Book of Aphorisms

Maturity hath her defects, as well as greenness, or worse. —MONTAIGNE, *Essays*

From forty to fifty, a man is at heart either a stoic or a satyr.
—A. W. PINERO, *The Second Mrs. Tanqueray*

Life begins at forty.
—WALTER PITKIN, book title, 1932

What is the prime of life? May it not be defined as a period of about twenty years in a woman's life, and thirty in a man's? —PLATO, *The Republic*

One's prime is elusive.
—MURIEL SPARK,
The Prime of Miss Jean Brodie

MIGHT See STRENGTH;
VIOLENCE & FORCE

MILITARY, THE See also MILITARY BATTLES; WAR

If it moves, salute it. If it doesn't move, pick it up. If you can't pick it up, paint it. —ANONYMOUS

If the trumpet give an uncertain sound, who shall prepare himself to the battle?
—BIBLE, *I Corinthians* 14:8

Don't talk to me about naval tradition. It's nothing but rum, sodomy, and the lash.
—WINSTON CHURCHILL, quoted by
Sir Peter Gretton, *Former Naval Person*

The services in wartime are fit only for desperadoes, but in peace are fit only for fools.
—BENJAMIN DISRAELI, *Vivian Grey*

There are all sorts of things to be done in this country. . . . I see no reason why the sums which are now going into these sterile, negative mechanisms that we call war munitions shouldn't go into something positive.
—DWIGHT D. EISENHOWER, quoted in
Stephen E. Ambrose,
Eisenhower: The President

[For the renowned "military-industrial establishment" speech, see AMERICAN HISTORY: MEMORABLE MOMENTS.]

A large army is always disorderly.
—EURIPIDES, *Heruba*

Stick close to your desks and *never go to sea*,
And you all may be Rulers of the Queen's Navee!
—W. S. GILBERT, *H.M.S. Pinafore*

Ask any soldier. To kill a man is to merit a woman.
—JEAN GIRAUDOUX, *Tiger at the Gates*

For a people who are free, and who mean to remain so, a well-organized and armed militia is their best security.
—THOMAS JEFFERSON, message to Congress, Nov. 1808

Every citizen [should] be a soldier. This was the case with the Greeks and the Romans, and must be that of every free state. —THOMAS JEFFERSON, letter to James Monroe, 1813

The people are like water and the army is like fish.
—MAO ZEDUNG, *Aspects of China's Anti-Japanese Struggle*

The greatest general is he who makes the fewest mistakes. —NAPOLEON BONAPARTE, *Maxims*

Soldiers generally win battles; generals generally get credit for them. —NAPOLEON BONAPARTE, to Gaspard Gourgaud at St. Helena

An army marches on its stomach.
—NAPOLEON BONAPARTE, traditional attribution

Russia has two generals whom she can trust—Generals Janvier and Février [Generals January and February].
—NICHOLAS I, quoted in *Punch*, March 10, 1853

I never expect a soldier to think.
—GEORGE BERNARD SHAW, *The Devil's Disciple*

The British soldier can stand up to anything except the British War Office. —*Ibid.*

To fight and conquer in all your battles is not supreme excellence; supreme excellence consists in breaking the enemy's resistance without fighting.
—SUN TZE, *Sun Tze Ping Fa*

Theirs not to reason why.
Theirs but to do and die.
—ALFRED, LORD TENNYSON,
The Charge of the Light Brigade
[For more, see under MILITARY BATTLES, below.]

The strength of an army lies in strict discipline and undeviating obedience to its officers.
—THUCYDIDES, *The History of the Peloponnesian War*

The chief attraction of military service has consisted and will consist in this compulsory and irreproachable idleness. —LEO TOLSTOY, *War and Peace*

God is always on the side of the big battalions.
—MARSHAL TURENNNE, attributed
[Sometimes also attributed to Voltaire, Frederick the Great, and others, but the saying was already established by then. *Bartlett's* suggests that it may date from Tacitus; see under STRENGTH.]

The army is a nation within the nation: it is a vice of our time. —ALFRED DE VIGNY,
Servitude et grandeur militaires

Military intelligence—a contradiction in terms.
>—OSWALD GARRISON VILLARD, lecture,
>about 1920, personal report by a
>member of the audience

In this country we find it pays to shoot an admiral from time to time to encourage the others.
>—VOLTAIRE, *Candide*

Discipline is the soul of an army. It makes small numbers formidable; procures success to the weak and esteem to all.   —GEORGE WASHINGTON, letter to the
>Captains of the Virginia Regiments,
>July 1759

Who is this happy warrior? Who is he
That every man in arms should wish to be?
>—WILLIAM WORDSWORTH,
>*Character of the Happy Warrior*

MILITARY BATTLES   See also AMERICAN
>HISTORY: MEMORABLE MOMENTS;
>ENGLAND; MILITARY, THE; WAR

Veni, vidi, vici.
I came, I saw, I conquered.
>—JULIUS CAESAR, quoted in Suetonius,
>*Lives of the Caesars*

Gentlemen, we are being killed on the beaches. Let's go inland and be killed.
>—GEN. NORMAN COTA, Omaha Beach, 1944

My center is giving way, my right is in retreat; situation excellent. I am attacking.
>—MARSHAL FERDINAND FOCH, attributed
[Sources vary as to the date; it is most often reported as Sept. 1914, the Battle of the Marne. The quote is probably apocryphal but does reflect Foch's characteristic approach to battle.]

Get there first with the most men.
>—NATHAN BEDFORD FORREST,
>quoted by Gen. Basil Duke &
>Gen. Richard Taylor

[Gen. Forrest, a Confederate cavalry commander, evidently did not speak in the rural style popularly attributed to him, as in "Git thar firstest with the mostest."]

Die hard, men, die hard!
>—WILLIAM INGLIS, battle of Albuera,
>   Spain, May 16, 1811

[Because of this order by Col. Inglis, the 57th Foot Regiment of Middlesex came to be known as "the Diehards." In the battle, a combined force of British, Portuguese and Spanish defeated the French.]

Sighted sub, sank same.
>—DONALD F. MASON, radio
>   dispatch, Jan. 28, 1942

Soldiers, consider that from the summit of these pyramids, forty centuries look down upon you.
>—NAPOLEON BONAPARTE, address to the troops
>   before the Battle of the Pyramids, July 1798

Ils ne passeront pas.
They shall not pass.
>—ROBERT-GEORGES NIVELLE, Verdun, 1916

[In this form, the order became a slogan, however, the actual wording was, *"Vous ne laisserez pas passer"*— "You shall not let them pass." In the Spanish Civil War, the Republicans used *No pasarán*; see under Ibarruri at APPEASEMENT VS. RESISTANCE.]

Don't cheer, men, those poor devils are dying.
>—REAR ADM. JOHN WOODWARD PHILIP,
>   the Battle of Santiago, 1898

One more such victory, and we are undone.
>—KING PYRRHUS OF EPIRUS, after fighting the
>   Romans at Asculum, 279 B.C.

Go, tell the Spartans, thou who passeth by:
Carrying out their orders, here we lie.
>—SIMONIDES, epitaph for the Spartan dead at
>   Thermopylae, quoted in Herodotus, *Histories*

It is the beginning of the end.
>—TALLEYRAND, after the Battle of Borodino, 1812

Half a league, half a league,
Half a league onward,
All in the valley of Death
Rode the six hundred.
                    —ALFRED, LORD TENNYSON,
                         The Charge of the Light Brigade

Cannon to right of them
Cannon to left of them,
Cannon behind them
Volleyed and thundered.   —*Ibid.*

Into the jaws of death,
Into the mouth of hell
Rode the six hundred.   —*Ibid.*

Nothing except a battle lost can be half so melancholy
as a battle won.   —DUKE OF WELLINGTON,
                         dispatch from Waterloo, 1815

The battle of Waterloo was won on the playing fields
of Eton.
     —DUKE OF WELLINGTON, traditional attribution
       but apparently invented several years after
       Wellington's death

MIND, THOUGHT,   See also GENIUS;
& UNDERSTANDING   IDEAS & IDEALS; MADNESS;
                    REASON & REASONS; REASONABLE &
UNREASONABLE PEOPLE; SOUL; VISION & VISIONARIES

The empires of the future are the empires of the mind.
                    —WINSTON CHURCHILL, address at
                         Harvard University, Sept. 6, 1943

Cogito ergo sum.
I think therefore I am.
               —RENÉ DESCARTES, *Discourse on Method*
[Probably the most famous maxim in the history of philosophy. Folklorist Roger Welsch, in the September
1992 issue of *Natural History*, reported seeing on a new-
lywed's car: *Coito ergo sum.*]

Being and thought are one.
> —JEAN DUBUFFET, quoted in his obituary,
> *The New York Times*, May 15, 1985

What once was thought can never be undone.
> —FRIEDRICH DÜRRENMATT, *The Physicist*

Imagination is more important than knowledge.
> —ALBERT EINSTEIN, *On Science*

On earth there is nothing great but man; in man there is nothing great but mind.
> —SIR WILLIAM HAMILTON,
> *Lectures on Metaphysics*

What we call a mind is nothing but a heap or collection of different perceptions, united together by certain relations and supposed, though falsely, to be endowed with a perfect simplicity and identity.
> —DAVID HUME, *A Treatise of Human Nature*

Sooner or later, false thinking brings wrong conduct.
> —JULIAN HUXLEY, *Essays of a Biologist*

Meditation is not a means to an end. It is both the means and the end.
> —KRISHNAMURTI, *The Second Penguin Krishnamurti Reader*

Intelligence forbids tears.
> —DORIS LESSING, "To Room 19,"
> in *A Man and Two Women*

Stone walls do not a prison make
Nor iron bars a cage.
> —RICHARD LOVELACE, *To Althea, From Prison*

Our life is what our thoughts make it.
> —MARCUS AURELIUS, *Meditations*

It is not the consciousness of men that determines their existence, but on the contrary, their social existence determines their consciousness.
> —KARL MARX, *Critique of Political Economy*

The mind is its own place, and in itself
Can make a heaven of Hell, a hell of Heaven.
     —JOHN MILTON, *Paradise Lost*

[There is no] Ghost in the Machine.
    —GILBERT RYLE, *The Concept of Mind*

Our dignity is not in what we do but what we understand. The whole world is doing things.
    —GEORGE SANTAYANA, *Winds of Doctrine*

A good mind is a lord of a kingdom.
     —SENECA, *Thyestes*

There is nothing either good or bad but thinking
makes it so. —SHAKESPEARE, *Hamlet*, II, ii

Thy wish was father, Harry, to that thought.
    —SHAKESPEARE, *Henry IV, Part II*, IV, v
[Prince Henry has just said to his aged father, the king,
who appeared to have died in his sleep, "I never thought
to hear you speak again."]

He gave man speech, and speech created thought,
Which is the measure of the universe.
  —PERCY BYSSHE SHELLEY, *Prometheus Unbound*

It is the mind that maketh good or ill,
That maketh wretch or happy, rich or poor.
    —EDMUND SPENSER, *The Faerie Queene*

Intellect does not attain its full force until it attacks
power.
  —MADAME DE STAËL, *De la littérature considerée
dans ses rapports avec les institutions sociales*

Consciousness is a disease.
    —MIGUEL DE UNAMUNO,
    The Tragic Sense of Life

Intellectual passion drives out sensuality.
                              —LEONARDO DA VINCI, *Notebooks*

MINORITIES   See RACES & PEOPLE

MIRACLES

Rise, take up thy bed, and walk.
                              —BIBLE, *John* 5:8

The distance is nothing. It's only the first step that's
important.   —MARQUISE DU DEFFAND [comment
                              on the legend that St. Denis walked
                              six miles with his head in his hand],
                              letter to d'Alembert, July 7, 1763

Everything is miraculous. It is miraculous that one
does not melt in one's bath.   —PICASSO, attributed
[*The Penguin Dictionary of Modern Quotations* indicates that Cocteau reported this delightful observation.]

There have been rains of milk, blood, flesh, iron,
sponges, wool, and baked bricks.
                              —PLINY, *Natural History*
[As Pliny notes, quite a variety of miraculous omens
from heaven were reported in ancient times.]

Miracles are propitious accidents, the natural causes
of which are too complicated to be readily understood.
                              —GEORGE SANTAYANA, *The Ethics of Spinoza*

They say miracles are past.
    —SHAKESPEARE, *All's Well That Ends Well*, II, iii
[For the modern "age of miracles" see Carlyle at
MODERN TIMES.]

Macbeth shall never vanquished be until
Great Birnam Wood to High Dunsinane Hill
Shall come against him.
                              —SHAKESPEARE, *Macbeth*, IV, i
[Macbeth, bolstered by this prophecy, later boasts,
    I will not be afraid of death and bane
    Till Birnham Forest come to Dunsinane.

He expects neither a miracle nor a trick. For more on wonders and the weird sisters, see OCCULT, THE.]

MISANTHROPY

I do not want people to be very agreeable, as it saves me the trouble of liking them a great deal.
> —JANE AUSTEN, letter to her sister Cassandra, Dec. 24, 1798

[The date suggests the author may have been suffering a holiday depression.]

I do not love thee, Doctor Fell.
The reason why I cannot tell.
But this alone I know full well.
I do not love thee, Doctor Fell.
> —THOMAS ("TOM") BROWN, Oxford University student

I wish I loved the human race;
I wish I loved its silly face;
I wish I loved the way it walks;
I wish I loved the way it talks;
And when I'm introduced to one,
I wish I thought *What jolly fun.*
> —SIR WALTER A. RALEIGH, *Wishes of an Elderly Man*

Any man who hates dogs and babies can't be all bad.
> —LEO C. ROSTEN, speaking of W. C. Fields, Masquer's Club, 1939

[Often attributed to Fields in the form: "Anyone who hates children and dogs can't be all bad." William Safire, thanks to a correspondent, unearthed an earlier version, from *Harper's* magazine, 1937, penned by Cedric Worth: "No man who hates dogs and children can be all bad."]

Plus je connais les hommes, plus j'aime mon chien.
The more I know men, the more I like my dog.
> —MADAME DE SÉVIGNÉ, attributed

Man delights not me; no, nor woman either.
—SHAKESPEARE, *Hamlet*, II, ii

MISERY   See DESPAIR, DEPRESSION,
   MISERY; SORROW, SADNESS, & SUFFERING; TROUBLE

MISFORTUNE   See LUCK; RUIN; TROUBLE

MISTAKES   See also FAILINGS

He is always right who suspects that he makes
mistakes.   —ANONYMOUS (SPANISH PROVERB)

C'est pire qu'un crime, c'est une faute.
It's worse than a crime, it's a blunder.
   —ANTOINE BOULAY DE LA MEURTHE,
      on the execution of the Duc d'Enghien, 1804
[Attributed also to Talleyrand and Joseph Fouché.]

It is the true nature of mankind to learn from mistakes, not from example.
               —FRED HOYLE, *Into Deepest Space*

When I make a mistake, it's a beaut!
      —FIORELLO LA GUARDIA, attributed remark
         referring to a bad appointment

The only one who makes no mistakes is one who
never does anything!
—THEODORE ROOSEVELT, saying inscribed on the
Theodore Roosevelt Birthplace National Historic Site,
New York City

A life spent in making mistakes is not only more
honorable but more useful than a life spent doing
nothing.   —GEORGE BERNARD SHAW,
                  The Doctor's Dilemma, Preface

Mistakes live in the neighborhood of truth and therefore delude us.
               —RABINDRANATH TAGORE, *Fireflies*

MODERATION   See PRUDENCE & PRACTICAL WISDOM

MODERN TIMES   See also CIVILIZATION;
                                ENVIRONMENT; MEDIA;
        PROGRESS; TECHNOLOGY; TURBULENT TIMES

In the nightmare of the dark
All the dogs of Europe bark,
And the living nations wait,
Each sequestered in its hate.
          —W. H. AUDEN, *In Memory of W. B. Yeats*

We have grasped the mystery of the atom and rejected the Sermon on the Mount.
               —GEN. OMAR BRADLEY, speech,
                  Armistice Day, 1948

The age of chivalry is gone. That of sophisters, economists, and calculators has succeeded, and the glory of Europe is extinguished forever.
          —EDMUND BURKE, *Reflections on the
               Revolution in France*

The age of miracles is forever here!
          —THOMAS CARLYLE, *The Hero as Priest*
[But see Shakespeare at MIRACLES.]

Perfection of means and confusion of goals seem, in my opinion, to characterize our age.
          —ALBERT EINSTEIN, *Out of My Later Years*

I saw the best minds of my generation destroyed by madness.   —ALLEN GINSBERG, *Howl*

The lamps are going out all over Europe; we shall not see them lit again in our lifetime.
          —VISCOUNT GREY OF FALLODEN, Aug. 3, 1914
[The remark was made while Grey was standing at a window in the Foreign Office, London, watching lamplighters at work. War was declared the next day.]

One of the crying needs of the time is for a suitable burial service for the admittedly damned.
—H. L. MENCKEN, *Prejudices*

There are evidently limits to the achievements of science; and there are irresolvable contradictions both between prosperity and virtue, and between happiness and "the good life," which had not been anticipated in our philosophy. The discovery of these contradictions threatens our culture with despair.
—REINHOLD NIEBUHR, *The Irony of American History*

Morality in Europe today is herd morality.
—FRIEDRICH NIETZSCHE, *Beyond Good and Evil*

Today violence is the rhetoric of the period.
—ORTEGA Y GASSET, *The Revolt of the Masses*

We are suffering today from a greed for knowledge of evil.   —CHRISTABEL PANKHURST, speech, 1930, quoted in David Mitchell, *The Fighting Pankhursts*

All the modern inconveniences.
—MARK TWAIN, *Life on the Mississippi*

The century on which we are entering can be and must be the century of the common man.
—HENRY A. WALLACE, speech, May 8, 1942

Plain living and high thinking are no more.
—WILLIAM WORDSWORTH, *Written in London*, Sept. 1802

Things fall apart; the center cannot hold;
Mere anarchy is loosed upon the world.
—WILLIAM BUTLER YEATS, *The Second Coming*

The best lack all conviction, while the worst
Are full of passionate intensity.   —*Ibid.*

MONEY   See also CAPITALISM; ECONOMICS; HAVES &
HAVE-NOTS; POVERTY & HUNGER;
SELF INTEREST

Money disappears like magic.
—ANONYMOUS (ARAB PROVERB)

Every man thinks God is on his side. The rich and
powerful know he is.   —JEAN ANOUILH, *The Lark*

It is very difficult for the prosperous to be humble.
—JANE AUSTEN, *Emma*
[Cf. Epictetus, below.]

A large income is the best recipe for happiness I ever
heard of.   —JANE AUSTEN, *Northanger Abbey*

Money is like muck, not good except it be spread.
—FRANCIS BACON, *Of Seditions and Troubles*

Money, it turned out, was exactly like sex. You
thought of nothing else if you didn't have it and thought
of other things if you did.
—JAMES BALDWIN, "The Black Boy Looks at the
White Boy," in *Nobody Knows My Name*

If you want to know what the Lord God thinks of
money, you have only to look at those to whom he gives
it.
—MAURICE BARING, quoted by Dorothy Parker,
Writers at Work: First Series

Wealth maketh many friends.
—BIBLE, *Proverbs* 19:4

He that maketh haste to be rich shall not be innocent.
—*Ibid.*, 28:20

A feast is made for laughter, and wine maketh merry:
but money answereth all things.
—BIBLE, *Ecclesiastes* 10:19

It is easier for a camel to go through the eye of a
needle, than for a rich man to enter into the kingdom
of God.   —BIBLE, *Matthew* 19:24

[Also *Mark* 10:25, and *Luke* 18:25. The "needle" was actually a narrow city gate—too narrow for a camel loaded with baggage.]

The love of money is the root of all evil.
—BIBLE, *I Timothy* 6:10

Money, n. A blessing that is of no advantage to us excepting when we part with it.
—AMBROSE BIERCE,
The Devil's Dictionary

A rich man's joke is always funny.
—THOMAS E. BROWNE, *The Doctor*

It has been said that the love of money is the root of all evil. The want of money is so quite as truly.
—SAMUEL BUTLER, *Erewhon*
[Cf. George Bernard Shaw, below.]

Ready money is Aladdin's lamp.   —LORD BYRON,
Don Juan

Money you know will hide many faults.
—CERVANTES, *Don Quixote*

I knew once a very covetous, sordid fellow, who used to say, "Take care of the pence, for the pounds will take care of themselves."
—EARL OF CHESTERFIELD,
letter to his son, Nov. 6, 1747

To be clever enough to get all the money, one must be stupid enough to want it.
—G. K. CHESTERTON,
The Innocence of Father Brown

Annual income twenty pounds, annual expenditure nineteen pounds six, result happiness. Annual income twenty pounds, annual expenditure twenty pounds ought and six, result misery.
—CHARLES DICKENS, *David Copperfield*

A billion here and a billion there and pretty soon you're talking big money.
> —SEN. EVERETT DIRKSEN, attributed
> [*The Wall Street Journal* reported on January 1, 1985, that the curator of the Dirksen Congressional Center could not track down the quote, but had noted, "That doesn't mean he didn't say it."]

All heiresses are beautiful.
> —JOHN DRYDEN,
> *King Arthur*

Money, which represents the prose of life . . . is, in its effects and laws, as beautiful as roses.
> —RALPH WALDO EMERSON, *Nominalist and Realist*

It is difficult for a rich person to be modest, or a modest person rich.
> —EPICTETUS, *Enchiridion*
> [Cf. Jane Austen, above.]

Money's the wise man's religion.
> —EURIPIDES, *The Cyclops*

Money is far more persuasive than logical arguments.
> —EURIPIDES, *Medea*

Ah, take the Cash, and let the Credit go,
Nor heed the rumble of a distant Drum.
> —EDWARD FITZGERALD,
> *The Rubáiyát of Omar Khayyám*

Let me tell you about the very rich. They are different from you and me.
> —F. SCOTT FITZGERALD,
> *The Rich Boy*

[Ernest Hemingway in "The Snows of Kilimanjaro," published in *Esquire* in 1936, included a witty retort that "someone" made in response to this Fitzgerald comment about the very rich being different. "Yes, they have more money" was the retort. Hemingway himself took credit for being the witty someone, but evidently the remark was made by critic Mary Colum at a lunch in 1936 with Hemingway and famed editor Maxwell Perkins. Ms. Colum's observation reportedly was directed not at Fitzgerald but at Hemingway, who had boasted, "I am getting to know the rich." Colum had replied, "The only difference between the rich and other people is that the rich have more money," Matthew J. Bruccoli, *Scott and Ernest*, 1978. But credit Hemingway for a quotable remark of his own on the rich, also from "The Snows of Kilimanjaro": "The rich were dull and they drank too much."]

Money is like an arm or leg: use it or lose it.
—HENRY FORD,
The New York Times, Nov. 8, 1931

Money is a singular thing. It ranks with love as man's greatest source of joy. And with his death as his greatest source of anxiety.   —JOHN KENNETH GALBRAITH,
The Age of Uncertainty

Honesty is incompatible with amassing a large fortune.   —MOHANDAS GANDHI,
Non-Violence in Peace and War

I am indeed rich since my income is superior to my expenses, and my expense is equal to my wishes.
—EDWARD GIBBON, *Memoirs*

Money is life to us wretched mortals.
—HESIOD, *Works and Days*

He is almost always a slave who cannot live on little.
—HORACE, *Satires*

The almighty dollar, that great object of universal devotion throughout our land.
—WASHINGTON IRVING, *Wolfert's Roost*

There are few ways in which a man can be more innocently employed than in getting money.
—SAMUEL JOHNSON, letter to William Strahan,
March 27, 1775

The human species, according to the best theory I can form of it, is composed of two distinct races, the men who borrow and the men who lend.
—CHARLES LAMB, *The Two Races of Men*

Nothing hurts worse than the loss of money.
　　　　　　　　—LIVY, *History of Rome*

All wealth is the product of labor.
　　　　　　　　—JOHN LOCKE, *Two Treatises of Government*

When a man tells you that he got rich through hard work, ask him: "Whose?"
　　　　　　　　—DON MARQUIS, quoted in Edward Anthony,
　　　　　　　　O Rare Don Marquis

What's a thousand dollars? Mere chicken feed. A poultry matter.　　—GROUCHO MARX, *The Cocoanuts*,
　　　　　　　　screenplay by George S. Kaufman

Money is like a sixth sense without which you cannot make a complete use of the other five.
　　　　　　　　—W. SOMERSET MAUGHAM, *Of Human Bondage*

He must have killed a lot of people to have gotten so rich.　　　　—MOLIÈRE, *La Malade imaginaire*

You can never be too skinny or too rich.
　　　　　　　　—BARBARA "BABE" PALEY, attributed
[Also attributed to the Duchess of Windsor and Gloria Vanderbilt.]

The rich have many consolations.
　　　　　　　　—PLATO, *The Republic*

The tears of an heir are masked laughter.
　　　　　　　　—PUBLILIUS SYRUS, *Moral Sayings*

I believe the power to make money is a gift of God.
　　　　　　　　—JOHN D. ROCKEFELLER, quoted in
　　　　　　　　Matthew Josephson, *The Robber Barons*

A full pocketbook often groans more loudly than an empty stomach.
　　　　　　　　—FRANKLIN D. ROOSEVELT, speech,
　　　　　　　　Nov. 1, 1940

Neither a borrower nor a lender be.
　　　　　　　　—SHAKESPEARE,
　　　　　　　　Hamlet, I, iii

Lack of money is the root of all evil.
—GEORGE BERNARD SHAW, *Man and Superman*,
"Maxims for Revolutionists"
[Cf. Samuel Butler, above.]

The universal regard for money is the one hopeful
fact in our civilization.
—GEORGE BERNARD SHAW,
Major Barbara, Preface

There are few sorrows, however poignant, in which
a good income is of no avail.
—LOGAN PEARSALL SMITH, *Afterthoughts*

For money you would sell your soul.
—SOPHOCLES, *Antigone*

There is nothing in the world so demoralizing as
money.   —*Ibid.*

That man is the richest whose pleasures are the
cheapest.   —HENRY DAVID THOREAU,
Journal, March 3, 1856

In order to stand well in the eyes of the community,
it is necessary to come up to a certain, somewhat in-
definite, conventional standard of wealth.
—THORSTEIN VEBLEN,
The Theory of the Leisure Class

All those men have their price.
—SIR ROBERT WALPOLE, referring to certain
members of Parliament, *Memoirs*
[The popular version is: "Every man has his price."]

Money should circulate like rainwater.
—THORNTON WILDER, *The Matchmaker*

MOON, THE   See NATURE: THE HEAVENS, THE SKY

MORNING   See NATURE: TIMES OF DAY

MORALITY   See ETHICS & MORALITY

MORTALITY   See DEATH; GENERATIONS; HEDONISM;
ILLNESS & REMEDIES; IMMORTALITY; LIFE

MOTHERS   See PARENTS & PARENTHOOD

MURDER   See CRIME

MUSIC   See ARTS: MUSIC & DANCE

MYSTICISM   See also RELIGION

The most beautiful thing we can experience is the
mysterious. It is the source of all true art and science.
—ALBERT EINSTEIN, *What I Believe*

Without mysticism man can achieve nothing great.
—ANDRÉ GIDE, *The Counterfeiters*

The dark night of the soul through which the soul
passes on its way to the Divine Light.
—ST. JOHN OF THE CROSS,
The Ascent of Mount Carmel
[He also used the phrase "The Dark Night of the Soul"
as the title of a treatise. The metaphor is the most
famous expression of the despair that often precedes
intense mystical experience. See also F. Scott Fitzgerald
at DESPAIR, DEPRESSION, MISERY.]

The Way [Tao] that can be told is not the eternal
way.   —LAO-TZU, *Tao Te Ching*

The Way is like an empty vessel that yet may be
drawn from.   —*Ibid.*

Mysticism is, in essence, little more than a certain
intensity and depth of feeling in regard to what is believed about the universe.
—BERTRAND RUSSELL,
Mysticism and Logic, title essay

The more mysterious, the more imperfect: that which
is mystically spoken is but half spoken.
—BENJAMIN WHICHCOTE,
Moral and Religious Aphorisms

N

NAPLES   See CITIES

NATIONS   See also AMERICA & AMERICANS;
                                    CITIES; ENGLAND; ORIENT, THE;
                                    RACES & PEOPLES; TRAVEL

My heart's in the Highlands, my heart is not here,
My heart's in the Highlands a-chasing the deer.
  —ROBERT BURNS, *My Heart's in the Highlands*

England is a paradise for women, and hell for horses;
Italy is a paradise for horses, hell for woman, as the
diverb [proverb] goes.
  —ROBERT BURTON, *The Anatomy of Melancholy*
[See also ENGLAND, the Florio quote.]

Gallia est omnis divisa in partes tres.
All Gaul is divided in three parts.
    —JULIUS CAESAR, *De bello gallico*

France was a long despotism tempered by epigrams.
    —THOMAS CARLYLE,
     History of the French Revolution

I am rather inclined to believe that this is the land
God gave to Cain.
    —JACQUES CARTIER, speaking of Canada,
    La Première Relation

For the great Gaels of Ireland
Are the men that God made mad,
For all their wars are merry,
And all their songs are sad.
    —G. K. CHESTERTON,
    The Ballad of the White Horse

It [Russia] is a riddle wrapped in a mystery inside an engima. —WINSTON CHURCHILL, radio speech, Oct. 1, 1939

Very big, China. —NOËL COWARD, *Private Lives*

How can you be expected to govern a country that has two hundred and forty-six kinds of cheese? —CHARLES DE GAULLE, *Newsweek*, Oct. 1, 1962

Poor Mexico! So far from God and so close to the United States. —PORFIRIO DÍAZ, attributed, in John S. D. Eisenhower, *The U.S. War with Mexico, 1846–48* [Gen. Díaz was president of Mexico from 1877–1911.]

Our fatal troika [modern Russia] dashes on in her headlong flight, perhaps to destruction. —FEODOR DOSTOEVSKI, *The Brothers Karamazov*

The Swiss are not a people so much as a neat clean quite solvent business. —WILLIAM FAULKNER, *Intruder in the Dust*

They [the Greeks] were the first Westerners; the spirit of the West, the modern spirit, is a Greek discovery. —EDITH HAMILTON, *The Greek Way*

What though the spicy breezes
Blow soft o'er Ceylon's isle;
Though every prospect pleases,
And only man is vile.

—REGINALD HEBER, *Missionary Hymn*

The Irish are a fair people;—they never speak well of one another. —SAMUEL JOHNSON, quoted in James Boswell, *Life of Johnson*, March 20, 1775

A man who has not been in Italy is always conscious of an inferiority. —*Ibid.*, April 1776

Ireland is the old sow that eats her farrow.
—JAMES JOYCE, *A Portrait of the Artist as a Young Man*

The wind of change is blowing through this Continent, and whether we like it or not, this growth of national consciousness is a political fact.
—HAROLD MACMILLAN, speech in Cape Town, Feb. 3, 1960
[Macmillan drew on a traditional image here. In his *Political Dictionary*, William Safire cites, among several precedents, Indian Prime Minister Jawaharlal Nehru, "Strong winds are blowing all over Asia," 1947; and British Prime Minister Stanley Baldwin, "There is a wind of nationalism and freedom blowing around the world," 1934.]

A race corrupted by a bad government and a bad religion, long renowned for skill in the arts of voluptuousness, and tolerant of all the caprices of sensuality.
—THOMAS BABINGTON MACAULAY, *Moore's Life of Lord Byron*, in *Edinburgh Review*, June 1831
[An attack on Italians that makes them sound rather appealing.]

Greece is the home of the gods.
—HENRY MILLER, *The Colossus of Maroussi*

I'm troubled, I'm dissatisfied. I'm Irish.
—MARIANNE MOORE, *Spenser's Ireland*

Everything ponderous, viscous, and solemnly clumsy, all long-winded and boring types of style are developed in profuse variety among Germans.
—FRIEDRICH NIETZSCHE, *Beyond Good and Evil*

There is always something new out of Africa.
  —PLINY, *Natural History*

While we spend energy and imagination on new ways of cleaning the floors of our houses, the Japanese solve the problem by not dirtying them in the first place.
  —BERNARD RUDOFSKY, *The Kimono Mind*

The Japanese have perfected good manners and made them indistinguishable from rudeness.
  —PAUL THEROUX, *The Great Railway Bazaar*

We [Greeks] are lovers of the beautiful, yet simple in our tastes, and we cultivate the mind without loss of manliness.
  —THUCYDIDES, *The Peloponnesian War*

I fear the Greeks even when they bring gifts.
  —VIRGIL, *Aeneid*

This agglomeration which was called and still calls itself the Holy Roman Empire was neither holy, nor Roman, nor any empire in any way.
  —VOLTAIRE, *Essai sur les moeurs et l'esprit des nations*

In Italy for thirty years under the Borgias, they had warfare, terror, murder, bloodshed. They produced Michelangelo, Leonardo da Vinci, and the Renaissance. In Switzerland, they had brotherly love, five hundred years of democracy and peace, and what did they produce? The cuckoo clock.
  —ORSON WELLES, *The Third Man*
[The script writer was Graham Greene, but Welles reportedly added this passage himself.]

Romantic Ireland's dead and gone,
It's with O'Leary in the grave.
  —WILLIAM BUTLER YEATS, *Responsibilities*, preliminary poem

NATURE   See also COUNTRY, THE; CREATION,
                    DIVINE; ENVIRONMENT; SEAS & SHIPS,
                  SAILING & BOATING; UNIVERSE; and NATURE
                            subcategories, below

Natura genetrix.
Nature is our mother.   —ANONYMOUS
                                (LATIN PROVERB)

Nature, to be commanded, must be obeyed.
                    —FRANCIS BACON, *Novum Organum*

What I know of the divine science and Holy Scripture
I learnt in woods and fields.   —ST. BERNARD,
                                        Epistle 106

Listen to a man of experience: thou wilt learn more
in the woods than in books.   —*Ibid.*

Speak to the earth, and it shall teach thee.
                              —BIBLE, *Job* 12:8

For the earth is the Lord's, and the fulness thereof.
                    —BIBLE, *I Corinthians* 10:26

To see a world in a grain of sand
And a heaven in a wild flower,
Hold infinity in the palm of your hand
And eternity in an hour.
          —WILLIAM BLAKE, *Auguries of Innocence*

There is a pleasure in the pathless woods,
There is a rapture on the lonely shore,
There is a society where none intrudes,
By the deep sea, and music in its roar:
I love not man the less, but nature more.
          —LORD BYRON, *Childe Harold's Pilgrimage*

The works of nature must all be accounted good.
                    —CICERO, *De senectute*

Earth, with her thousand voices, praises God.
                    —SAMUEL TAYLOR COLERIDGE,
                      Hymn Before Sunrise

Whatever nature has in store for mankind, unpleasant as it may be, men must accept, for ignorance is never better than knowledge.
—ENRICO FERMI, quoted in Laura Fermi, *Atoms in the Family*

Nature goes her own way, and all that to us seems an exception is really according to order.
—GOETHE, quoted in Johann Peter Eckermann, *Conversations with Goethe*

Glory be to God for dappled things.
—GERARD MANLEY HOPKINS, *Pied Beauty*

The world is charged with the grandeur of God.
—GERARD MANLEY HOPKINS, *God's Grandeur*

Though you drive away nature with a pitchfork, she always returns. —HORACE, *Epistles*, I, x

Never does nature say one thing and wisdom another.
—JUVENAL, *Satires*

The poetry of earth is never dead.
—JOHN KEATS, *On the Grasshopper and the Cricket*

The roaring of the wind is my wife and the stars through the window pane are my children.
—JOHN KEATS, letter to
George and Georgina Keats,
Oct. 14, 1818

I demonstrate by means of philosophy that the earth is round, and is inhabited on all sides; that it is insignificantly small, and is borne through the stars.
—JOHANNES KEPLER, *Astronomia nova*

Nature is not human-hearted. —LAO-TZU,
Tao Te Ching

The clearest way into the universe is through a forest wilderness. —JOHN MUIR, *John of the Mountains*

Nature is an infinite sphere of which the center is everywhere and the circumference nowhere.
> —PASCAL, *Pensées*

It were happy if we studied nature more in natural things, and acted according to nature, whose rules are few, plain, and most reasonable.
> —WILLIAM PENN, *Some Fruits of Solitude*

All nature is but art, unknown to thee;
All chance, direction, which thou canst not see;
All discord, harmony not understood;
All partial evil, universal good.
> —ALEXANDER POPE, *An Essay on Man*

Perhaps nature is our best assu   e of immortality.
> —ELEA᾽   ᾳOOSEVELT,
> *My I*   newspaper column,
> Apri᷄   ᷄, 1945

What else is nature but God?   —SENECA,
> *De beneficiis*

One touch of nature makes the whole world kin.
> —SHAKESPEARE, *Troilus and Cressida*, III, iii
[George Eliot offered this variant: "One touch of biliousness makes the whole world kin," Gordon S. Haight, ed., *Selections from George Eliot's Letters*.]

The earth and ocean seem
To sleep in one another's arms, and dream
Of waves, flowers, clouds, woods, rocks, and all that we
Read in their smiles, and call reality.
> —PERCY BYSSHE SHELLEY, *Epipsychidion*

In nature, there is less death and destruction than death and transmutation.   —EDWIN WAY TEALE,
> *Circle of the Seasons*

For men may come and men may go,
But I go on forever.
—ALFRED, LORD TENNYSON, *The Brook*

Nature, red in tooth and claw.
—ALFRED, LORD TENNYSON, *In Memoriam*

I have learned
To look on nature, not as in the hour
Of thoughtless youth; but hearing oftentimes
The still, sad music of humanity.
—WILLIAM WORDSWORTH, *Tintern Abbey*

Nature never did betray the heart that loved her.
—*Ibid.*

NATURE: ANIMALS

The dog was created especially for children. He is
the god of frolic. —HENRY WARD BEECHER,
Proverbs from Plymouth Pulpit

Hast thou given the horse strength? hast though
clothed his neck with thunder? . . .
He paweth in the valley, and rejoiceth in his
strength; he goeth on to meet the armed men. . . .
He saith among the trumpets, Ha, ha; and he smell-
eth the battle afar off, the thunder of the captains, and
the shouting. —BIBLE, *Job* 39:19, 21, 25

A robin red breast in a cage
Puts all heaven in a rage.
—WILLIAM BLAKE, *Auguries of Innocence*

Tiger! Tiger! burning bright
In the forests of the night,
What immortal hand or eye
Could frame thy fearful symmetry?

In what distant deeps or skies
Burnt the fire of thine eyes?

On what wings dare he aspire?
What the hand dare seize the fire?
                    —WILLIAM BLAKE, *The Tiger*

When the stars threw down their spears,
And watered heaven with their tears,
Did he smile his work to see?
Did he who made the Lamb make thee?   —*Ibid.*

That's the wise thrush; he sings each song twice over,
Lest you think he never could recapture
The first fine careless rapture!
                    —ROBERT BROWNING,
                        Home Thoughts from Abroad

An animal's eyes have the power to speak a great
language.   —MARTIN BUBER, *I and Thou*

Wee, sleekit, cow'ring, tim'rous beastie,
O what a panic's in thy breastie!
                    —ROBERT BURNS, *To a Mouse*

A hen is only an egg's way of making another egg.
                    —SAMUEL BUTLER, *Life and Habit*

The greatest pleasure of a dog is that you may make
a fool of yourself with him and not only will he not
scold you, but he will make a fool of himself too.
                    —SAMUEL BUTLER,
                        Higgledy-Piggledy, in *Notebooks*

A canter is the cure for every evil.
                    —BENJAMIN DISRAELI, *The Young Duke*

Animals are such agreeable friends—they ask no
questions, they pass no criticisms.
                    —GEORGE ELIOT, "Mr. Gilfil's Love Story," in
                        Scenes of Clerical Life

The Cat. He walked by himself, and all places were
alike to him.   —RUDYARD KIPLING,
                        The Cat That Walked by Himself

I never saw a wild thing
Sorry for itself.

A small bird will drop frozen dead
From a bough
Without ever having felt sorry for itself.
—D. H. LAWRENCE, *Self Pity*

A wonderful bird is the pelican,
His bill will hold more than his belican.
He can take in his beak
Enough food for a week,
But I'm darned if I know how the helican.
—DIXON MERRITT, *The Pelican*

When I play with my cat, who knows whether she is
not amusing herself with me more than I with her.
—MONTAIGNE, *Essays*

The song of canaries
Never varies,
And when they're moulting
They're pretty revolting.
—OGDEN NASH,
The Canary

Dogs display reluctance and wrath
If you try to give them a bath
They bury bones in hideaways
And half the time they trot sideaways.
—OGDEN NASH, *An Introduction to Dogs*

The trouble with a kitten is
That
Eventually it becomes a
Cat.
—OGDEN NASH, *The Kitten*

There is something about the unselfish and self-
sacrificing love of a brute, which goes directly to the
heart of him who has had frequent occasion to test the
paltry friendship and gossamer fidelity of mere man.
—EDGAR ALLAN POE,
The Black Cat

A horse! A horse! my kingdom for a horse!
—SHAKESPEARE,
Richard III, V, iv

Hail to thee, blithe Spirit!
Bird thou never wert,
That from Heaven, or near it,
Pourest thy full heart
In profuse strains of unpremeditated art.
>   —PERCY BYSSHE SHELLEY, *To a Skylark*

So, naturalists observe, a flea
Hath smaller fleas that on him prey;
And these have smaller fleas to bite 'em
and so proceed *ad infinitum*.
>   —JONATHAN SWIFT, *On Poetry*
[Swift's conclusion, less well-known, is:
> Thus every poet, in his kind,
> Is bit by him that comes behind.]

He clasps the crag with crooked hands;
Close to the sun in lonely lands,
Ringed with the azure world, he stands.
The wrinkled sea beneath him crawls;
He watches from his mountain walls,
And like a thunderbolt he falls.
>   —ALFRED, LORD TENNYSON, *The Eagle*

Cheerfulness is proper to the cock, which rejoices
over every little thing, and crows with varied and lively
movements.   —LEONARDO DA VINCI, *Notebooks*

If a dog jumps in your lap, it is because he is fond
of you; but if a cat does the same thing, it is because
your lap is warmer.
>   —ALFRED NORTH WHITEHEAD, *Dialogues*

I think I could turn and live with animals, they are
    so placid and self-contained,
I stand and look at them long and long.
>   —WALT WHITMAN, *Song of Myself*

The best thing about animals is that they don't talk
much.
>   —THORNTON WILDER, *The Skin of Our Teeth*

NATURE: GARDENS, FLOWERS, & TREES

Flowers are my music.
> —DR. THOMAS ARNOLD, quoted by
> Arthur Stanley, *Life of Dr. Arnold*

God almighty first planted a garden.
> —FRANCIS BACON, *Of Gardens*

Flowers are the sweetest things that God ever made,
and forgot to put a soul into.
> —HENRY WARD BEECHER, *Life Thoughts*

The Lord God planted a garden eastward in Eden.
> —BIBLE, *Genesis* 2:8

Consider the lilies of the field, how they grow; they
toil not, neither do they spin:
    And yet I say unto you, That even Solomon in all
his glory was not arrayed like one of these.
> —BIBLE, *Matthew* 6:28, 29

A garden is a lovesome thing, God wot!
> —THOMAS E. BROWN, *My Garden*

The dandelion's pallid tube
Astonishes the grass,
And winter instantly becomes
An infinite alas.
> —EMILY DICKINSON,
> poem no. 1519

There are fairies at the bottom of our garden.
> —ROSE FYLEMAN, *Fairies*

Verde que te quiero verde
Verde viento. Verde ramas.
Green I love you green.
Green wind. Green branches.
> —GABRIEL GARCÍA LORCA,
> *Romance sonámbulo*

The kiss of the sun for pardon,
The song of the birds for mirth.
One is nearer God's heart in a garden
Than anywhere else on earth.
—DOROTHY GURNEY, *God's Garden*

But though I am an old man, I am but a young
gardener.   —THOMAS JEFFERSON, letter to
Charles Willson Peale,
Aug. 20, 1811

I think that I shall never see
A poem lovely as a tree.   —JOYCE KILMER, *Trees*

Poems are made by fools like me,
But only God can make a tree.   —*Ibid.*

I want death to find me planting my cabbages.
—MONTAIGNE, "To the Reader," in *Essays*

Woodman, spare that tree!
Touch not a single bough!
In youth it sheltered me,
And I'll protect it now.
—GEORGE POPE MORRIS,
Woodman Spare That Tree

Each flower is a soul opening out to nature.
—GÉRARD DE NERVAL, *Vers dorés*

Where'er you walk, cool gales shall fan the glade,
Trees where you sit shall crowd into a shade:
Where'er you tread, the blushing flowers shall rise,
And all things flourish where you turn your eyes.
—ALEXANDER POPE, "Summer," in *Pastorals*

There is material enough in a single flower for the
ornament of a score of cathedrals.
—JOHN RUSKIN, *Stones of Venice*

There's rosemary, that's for remembrance—pray you
love, remember. And there is pansies, that's for
thoughts.   —SHAKESPEARE, *Hamlet*, IV, v

For you there's rosemary and rue, these keep
Seeming and savor all the winter long.
> —SHAKESPEARE, *The Winter's Tale*, IV, iii

The summer's flower is to the summer sweet,
Though to itself it only live and die.
> —SHAKESPEARE, sonnet 94

Rose is a rose is a rose.   —GERTRUDE STEIN,
> *Sacred Emily*

One morning, very early, before the sun was up,
I rose and found the shining dew on every buttercup.
> —ROBERT LOUIS STEVENSON, "A Shadow,"
> in *A Child's Garden of Verses*

Flower in the crannied wall,
I pluck you out of the crannies,
I hold you here, root and all, in my hand,
Little flower—but *if* I could understand
What you are, root and all, and all in all,
I should know what God and man is.
> —ALFRED, LORD TENNYSON,
> *Flower in the Crannied Wall*

To own a bit of ground, to scratch it with a hoe, to
plant seeds and watch their renewal of life—this is the
commonest delight of the race, the most satisfactory
thing a man can do.
> —CHARLES DUDLEY WARNER,
> *My Summer in a Garden*

I wandered lonely as a cloud
That floats on high o'er vales and hills,
When all at once I saw a crowd,
A host of golden daffodils.
> —WILLIAM WORDSWORTH,
> *I Wandered Lonely as a Cloud*

A primrose by a river's brim
A yellow primrose was to him,
And it was nothing more.
> —WILLIAM WORDSWORTH, *Peter Bell*

NATURE: See also SCIENCE:
THE HEAVENS, THE SKY   PHYSICS &
                               COSMOLOGY

I do set my bow in the cloud, and it shall be for a
token of a covenant between me and the earth.
                    —BIBLE, *Genesis* 9:13

The heavens declare the glory of God; and the fir-
mament showeth his handiwork.
                    —BIBLE, *Psalms* 19:1

The moon like a flower
In heaven's high bower,
With silent delight,
Sits and smiles on the night.   —WILLIAM BLAKE,
                                 Night

The moon is a different thing to each one of us.
                    —FRANK BORMAN, from Apollo VIII,
                    Dec. 24, 1968

The heavens call to you, and circle around you, dis-
playing to you their eternal splendours, and your eye
gazes only to earth.
          —DANTE, *Purgatorio*, in *The Divine Comedy*

A man is a small thing, and the night is very large
and full of wonders.   —LORD DUNSANY,
                        The Laughter of the Gods

Space is the stature of God.   —JOSEPH JOUBERT,
                                Pensées

Now the bright morning star, day's harbinger,
Comes dancing from the east.
                    —JOHN MILTON, *On May Morning*

The evening star,
Love's harbinger, appeared.   —JOHN MILTON,
                               Paradise Lost

The moon was a ghostly galleon tossed upon cloudy
skies.   —ALFRED NOYES, *The Highwayman*

The eternal silence of these infinite spaces frightens
me.   —PASCAL, *Pensées*

I have a horror of sunsets, they're so romantic, so
operatic.
   —MARCEL PROUST, *Remembrance of Things Past:
      The Guermantes Way*

My heart leaps up when I behold
A rainbow in the sky.
      —WILLIAM WORDSWORTH, *My Heart Leaps Up*

And pluck till time and times are done
The silver apples of the moon,
The golden apples of the sun.
               —WILLIAM BUTLER YEATS,
                  The Song of the Wandering Aengus

NATURE: THE OCEAN   See also SEAS & SHIPS,
                               SAILING & BOATING

Roll on, thou deep and dark blue ocean—roll!
Ten thousand fleets sweep over thee in vain;
Man marks the earth with ruin—his control
Stops with the shore.
         —LORD BYRON, *Childe Harold's Pilgrimage*

For all at last returns to the sea.
            —RACHEL CARSON, *The Sea Around Us*

The sea never changes and its works, for all the talk
of men, are wrapped in mystery.
                        —JOSEPH CONRAD, *Typhoon*

Never trust her at any time, when the calm sea shows
her false alluring smile.   —LUCRETIUS,
                                    De rerum natura

NATURE: SEASONS

Sumer is icumen in,
Lhude sing cuccu!
Groweth sed, and bloweth med,
And springth the wude nu—
Sing cuccu!   —ANONYMOUS
[Cf. Ezra Pound, below.]

Rise up, my love, my fair one, and come away.
    For lo, the winter is past, the rain is over and gone;
    The flowers appear on the earth; the time of the
singing of birds is come, and the voice of the turtle is
heard in our land;
    The fig tree putteth forth her green figs, and the
vines with the tender grape give a good smell. Arise,
my love, my fair one, and come away.
                —BIBLE, *The Song of Solomon* 2:10–13

Autumn arrives in the early morning, but spring at
the close of a winter day.
        —ELIZABETH BOWEN, *The Death of the Heart*

The year's at the spring
And day's at the morn;
Morning's at seven;
The hillside's dew-pearled;
The lark's on the wing;
The snail's on his thorn:
God's in his heaven—
All's right with the world.
                —ROBERT BROWNING, *Pippa Passes*

Hard is the heart that loved naught in May.
                —GEOFFREY CHAUCER,
                        The Romance of the Rose

April is the cruellest month, breeding
Lilacs out of the dead land, mixing

Memory and desire, stirring
Dull roots with spring rain.
　　　　　　—T. S. ELIOT, *The Waste Land*

Alas, that Spring should vanish with the Rose!
　　　　　—EDWARD FITZGERALD,
　　　　　　　The Rubáiyát of Omar Khayyám
[More of this is at YOUTH.]

Sweet spring, full of sweet days and roses.
　　　　　　—GEORGE HERBERT, *Virtue*, in *The Temple*

I saw old autumn in the misty morn
Stand shadowless like silence, listening
To silence.　　　　　—THOMAS HOOD, *Autumn*

Summer afternoon—summer afternoon; to me those
have always been the two most beautiful words in the
English language.
　　　　　—HENRY JAMES, quoted in Edith Wharton,
　　　　　　A Backward Glance

His soul swooned slowly as he heard the snow falling
faintly through the universe and faintly falling, like the
descent of their last end, upon all the living and the
dead.　　　—JAMES JOYCE, "The Dead," in *Dubliners*

Season of mists and mellow fruitfulness.
　　　　　　—JOHN KEATS, *To Autumn*

In a summer season when soft was the sun.
　　　　　—WILLIAM LANGLAND,
　　　　　　The Vision of Piers the Plowman

What is so rare as a day in June?
Then, if ever, come perfect days.
　　　　　—JAMES RUSSELL LOWELL,
　　　　　　The Vision of Sir Launfal, Prelude

'Tis the last rose of summer
Left blooming alone;
All her lovely companions
Are faded and gone.
　　　　　　—THOMAS MOORE, *'Tis the Last Rose*

It snowed and snowed, the whole world over,
Snow swept the world from end to end.
A candle burned on the table;
A candle burned.   —BORIS PASTERNAK,
                                        Doctor Zhivago

Winter is icumen in,
Lhude sing Goddamm,
Raineth drop and staineth slop,
And how the wind doth ramm!
Sing: Goddamm.   —EZRA POUND, *Ancient Music*
[For the original ancient music, see above, author anon-
ymous.]

O, it sets my heart a-clickin' like the tickin' of a clock,
When the frost is on the punkin and the fodder's in
    the shock.   —JAMES WHITCOMB RILEY,
                        When the Frost Is on the Punkin

The seasons . . . are authentic; there is no mistake
about them, they are what a symphony ought to be:
four perfect movements in intimate harmony with one
another.
                —ARTHUR RUBINSTEIN, *My Young Years*

Summer makes a silence after spring.
                    —VITA SACKVILLE-WEST, *The Land*

November's sky is chill and drear,
November's leaf is red and sear.
        —SIR WALTER SCOTT, *Marmion*, Introduction

Why, this is very midsummer madness.
                    SHAKESPEARE, *Twelfth Night*, III, iv

Rough winds do shake the darling buds of May,
And summer's lease hath all too short a date.
                            —SHAKESPEARE, sonnet 18

If winter comes, can spring be far behind?
    —PERCY BYSSHE SHELLEY, *Ode to the West Wind*

In winter I get up by night
And dress by yellow candlelight.
In summer quite the other way,
I have to go to bed by day.
> —ROBERT LOUIS STEVENSON, "Bed in
> Summer," in *A Child's Garden of Verses*

In the spring a young man's fancy lightly turns to
thoughts of love. —ALFRED, LORD TENNYSON,
Locksley Hall

Years and years and years ago, when I was a boy,
when there were wolves in Wales . . . when we rode
the daft and happy hills bareback, it snowed and it
snowed.
> —DYLAN THOMAS, *A Child's Christmas in Wales*

NATURE: TIMES OF DAY

The morning is wiser than the evening.
> —ANONYMOUS (RUSSIAN PROVERB)

The night
Hath been to me a more familiar face
Than that of man; and in her starry shade
Of dim and solitary loveliness
I learned the languages of another world.
> —LORD BYRON, *Manfred*

Night is the mother of thoughts.
> —JOHN FLORIO, *First Frutes*

Awake! for Morning in the Bowl of Night
Has flung the Stone that puts the Stars to Flight.
> —EDWARD FITZGERALD,
> *The Rubáiyát of Omar Khayyám*

Night is the other half of life, and the better half.
> —GOETHE, *Wilhelm Meisters Lehrjahre*

The curfew tolls the knell of parting day,
The lowing herd wind slowly o'er the lea,

The plowman homeward plods his weary way,
And leaves the world to darkness and to me.
>—THOMAS GRAY, *Elegy Written
>in a Country Churchyard*

The day is done, and the darkness
Falls from the wings of night,
As a feather is wafted downward
From an eagle in his flight.
>—HENRY WADSWORTH LONGFELLOW,
>*The Day Is Done*

Night hath a thousand eyes.
>—JOHN LYLY, *Maides Metamorphose*

Is not the night mournful, sad, and melancholy?
>—RABELAIS, *Gargantua*

Night, when words fade and things come alive.
>—ANTOINE DE SAINT-EXUPÉRY, *Flight to Arras*

Each day is a little life; every waking and rising a
little birth; every fresh morning a little youth; every
going to rest and sleep a little death.
>—ARTHUR SCHOPENHAUER,
>*Our Relation to Ourselves*

'Tis now the very witching time of night,
When churchyards yawn and hell itself breathes out
Contagion to this world.   —SHAKESPEARE,
>*Hamlet*, III, ii

I arise from dreams of thee
In the first sweet sleep of night
When the winds are breathing low,
And the stars are shining bright.
>—PERCY BYSSHE SHELLEY, *The Indian*

Never greet a stranger in the night, for he may be a
demon.
>—TALMUD

NATURE: WIND & WEATHER　　　　　　　See also
　　　　　　　　　　　　　NATURE: TIMES OF DAY

A cloudy day, or a little sunshine have as great an
influence on many constitutions as the most real blessings or misfortunes.
　　　　　　—JOSEPH ADDISON, *The Spectator*, no. 162

It ain't a fit night out for man or beast.
　　　　　　—W. C. FIELDS, *The Fatal Glass of Beer*

Not snow, no, nor rain, nor heat, nor night keeps
them from accomplishing their appointed courses with
all speed.　　　　　　　　—HERODOTUS, *Histories*
[The version inscribed on the main Post Office in Man-
hattan is: "Neither snow, nor rain, nor gloom of night
stays these couriers from the swift completion of their
appointed rounds."]

Who has seen the wind?
Neither you nor I:
But when the trees bow down their heads
The wind is passing by.　　—CHRISTINA ROSSETTI,
　　　　　　　　　　　　　Sing-Song

There is really no such thing as bad weather, only
different kinds of good weather.　　　—JOHN RUSKIN,
　　　　　　　　　　　　　　　　attributed

The fog comes in on little cat feet.
　　　　　　　　　　—CARL SANDBURG, *Fog*

O Wild West Wind, thou breath of Autumn's being,
Thou from whose unseen presence the leaves dead
Are driven like ghosts from an enchanter fleeing,
Yellow and black, and pale, and hectic red,
Pestilence-stricken multitude.
　　　　　　　　　　—PERCY BYSSHE SHELLEY,
　　　　　　　　　　Ode to the West Wind

Thank heaven, the sun has gone in, and I don't have
to go out and enjoy it.
　　　　　　　　　　—LOGAN PEARSALL SMITH,
　　　　　　　　　　Last Words

Sweet and low, sweet and low,
Wind of the western sea.
—ALFRED, LORD TENNYSON,
The Princess

Everybody talks about the weather, but nobody does
anything about it.   —MARK TWAIN, attributed
[The aphorism appeared in print in an unsigned editorial in the *Hartford Courant*, Aug. 24, 1897. Twain
lived in Hartford, so although the attribution is uncertain, the saying may very well have originated with him.
Bartlett's notes that Robert Underwood Johnson, in his
memoirs, quotes Twain as saying, "We all grumble
about the weather, but nothing is *done* about it." On
the other hand, Charles Dudley Warner, associate editor of the *Courant*, was a witty man in his own right.
Or the line could just have been going around town.]

NAVY   See MILITARY, THE

NECESSITY

Necessity, the tyrant's plea.   —JOHN MILTON,
Paradise Lost

The true creator is necessity, which is the mother of
our invention.   —PLATO, *The Republic*
[Jonathan Swift used the modern variant "Necessity is
the mother of invention" in *Gulliver's Travels*.]

Necessity knows no law.   —PUBLILIUS SYRUS,
Moral Sayings
[The adage was used by St. Augustine and Oliver Crom-
well, among others. In *Piers the Plowman*, William
Langland put it: "Need has no law." See also the
Goethe quote under LAW.]

I know this—a man got to do what he got to do.
—JOHN STEINBECK,
The Grapes of Wrath

NEGOTIATION   See also DIPLOMACY

Make sure you leave some fat for the other side.
—ANONYMOUS (CHINESE SAYING)

"Let us agree not to step on each other's feet," said the cock to the horse.   —ANONYMOUS
(ENGLISH PROVERB)

Never hold discussions with the monkey when the organ grinder is in the room.
          —WINSTON CHURCHILL, attributed
[William Safire, in his *Political Dictionary*, writes that Churchill is supposed to have said this in answer to a query from his foreign minister on whether to raise a certain point with Mussolini or Count Ciano, the Italian foreign minister. In another context, in 1957, British Labour leader Aneurin Bevan advised: "If we complain about the tune, there is no reason to attack the monkey while the organ grinder is present."]

Let us never negotiate out of fear, but let us never fear to negotiate.   —JOHN F. KENNEDY,
Inaugural Address, 1961

This offer,
. . . proceeds from policy, not love.
          —SHAKESPEARE,
Henry IV, Part II, IV, l
[Lord Mowbray, expressing doubt as to the good faith of an offer from the king.]

NEUROSIS   See ILLNESS & REMEDIES

NEWS   See also MEDIA; PRESS, THE; RUMOR

How beautiful upon the mountain are the feet of him that bringeth good tidings.   —BIBLE, *Isaiah* 52:7

Though it be honest, it is never good to bring bad news.
          —SHAKESPEARE, *Antony and Cleopatra*, II, v

What news on the Rialto?
          —SHAKESPEARE, *The Merchant of Venice*, I, iii
[The Rialto is a bridge in Venice, formerly a commercial center. The phrase also appears at III, i.]

Nobody likes the bringer of bad news.
                    —SOPHOCLES, *Antigone*

NEW THINGS   See also CHANGE; SCIENCE:
                        DISCOVERY; TECHNOLOGY; VARIETY

He that will not apply new remedies must expect new
evils; for time is the greatest innovator.
                    —FRANCIS BACON, *Of Innovations*

There is nothing new except that which has been
forgotten.   —MLLE. BERTIN, ascribed
[She was the dressmaker of Marie Antoinette.]

There is no new thing under the sun.
                    —BIBLE, *Ecclesiastes* 1:9

Neither do men put new wine into old bottles.
                    —BIBLE, *Matthew* 9:17

Men love . . . newfangledness.
    —GEOFFREY CHAUCER, "The Squire's Tale," in
    The Canterbury Tales

Nothing quite new is perfect.   —CICERO, *Brutus*

Mr. and Mrs. Veneering were bran-new people in a
bran-new house in a bran-new quarter of London.
Everything about the Veneerings was spick-and-span
new. All their furniture was new, all their friends were
new, all their servants were new, their plate was new,
their carriage was new, their harness was new, their
horses were new, their pictures were new, they themselves were new, they were as newly married as was
lawfully compatible with having a bran-new baby, and
if they had set up a great-grandfather, he would have
come in matting from the Pantechnicon, without a
scratch upon him, French polished to the crown of his
head.   —CHARLES DICKENS, *Our Mutual Friend*

If a man write a better book, preach a better sermon,
or make a better mousetrap than his neighbor, tho' he

build his house in the woods, the world will make a beaten path to his door.
>   —RALPH WALDO EMERSON, quoted by
>   Sarah S. B. Yule, *Borrowings*

[*The Concise Oxford Dictionary of Quotations* reports that she took down this remark while listening to a lecture by Emerson; later Elbert Hubbard claimed that he originated the quote.]

It is always the latest song that an audience applauds the most.   —HOMER, *Odyssey*

New opinions are always suspected, and usually opposed, without any other reason but because they are not already common.
>   —JOHN LOCKE,
>   *Essay Concerning Human Understanding*

All good things which exist are the fruit of originality.
>   —JOHN STUART MILL, *On Liberty*

Nothing can be said nowadays which has not already been said.   —TERENCE, *Eunuchus*

NEW YEAR

Now the New Year reviving old Desires,
The thoughtful Soul to Solitude retires.
>   —EDWARD FITZGERALD,
>   *The Rubáiyát of Omar Khayyám*

Ring out, wild bells, to the wild sky,
The flying cloud, the frosty light:
The year is dying in the night;
Ring out wild bells and let him die.

Ring out the old, ring in the new,
Ring, happy bells, across the snow:
The year is going, let him go;
Ring out the false, ring in the true.
>   —ALFRED, LORD TENNYSON,
>   *In Memoriam*

NEW YORK   See CITIES

NIGHT   See NATURE: TIMES OF DAY

NONVIOLENCE   See PACIFISM

NOSTALGIA   See also OLD THINGS, OLD FRIENDS;
                                                PAST, THE

Nostalgia isn't what it used to be.   —ANONYMOUS
[A graffito used as a book title by the French actress
and writer Simone Signoret.]

Play it, Sam. Play "As Time Goes By."
                      —JULIUS J. EPSTEIN,
                      PHILIP G. EPSTEIN,
                      HOWARD KOCH, *Casablanca*

NOVELTY   See NEW THINGS

NOVEMBER   See NATURE: SEASONS

O

OBEDIENCE   See also APPEASEMENT VS. RESISTANCE;
RESISTANCE

Obedience is the mother of success, and the wife of
security.   —AESCHYLUS, *The Seven Against Thebes*

Obedience is in a way the mother of all virtues.
—ST. AUGUSTINE, *On the Good of Marriage*

Nevertheless, not my will, but thine, be done.
—BIBLE, *Luke* 22:42

Obedience is a hard profession.
—PIERRE CORNEILLE, *Nicomède*

It is much safer to obey than to rule.
—THOMAS À KEMPIS, *Imitation of Christ*

It is right that what is just should be obeyed; it is
necessary that what is strongest should be obeyed.
—PASCAL, *Pensées*

He who yields a prudent obedience exercises a partial
control.   —PUBLILIUS SYRUS, *Moral Sayings*

Let them obey that know not how to rule.
—SHAKESPEARE, *Henry VI, Part II*, V, i

Obedience,
Bane of all genius, virtue, freedom, truth,
Makes slaves of men, and, of the human frame,
A mechanized automaton.
—PERCY BYSSHE SHELLEY, *Queen Mab*

Learn to obey before you command.
> —SOLON, quoted in Diogenes Laërtius,
> *Lives of Eminent Philosophers*

OBJECTS   See THINGS & POSSESSIONS

OCCULT, THE   See also MIRACLES

To deny the possibility, nay, the actual existence of witchcraft and sorcery is flatly to contradict the revealed word of God.
> —WILLIAM BLACKSTONE,
> *Commentaries on the Laws of England*

The constellations were consulted for advice, but no one understood them.
> —ELIAS CANETTI,
> *Aufzeichungen*

Go and catch a falling star,
Get a child with mandrake root.
> —JOHN DONNE, *Song:*
> *Go and Catch a Falling Star*

Nature has given us astrology as an adjunct and ally to astronomy.
> —JOHANNES KEPLER,
> *De fundamentis*

Astrology is framed by the devil.
> —MARTIN LUTHER, *Table-Talk*

Millions of spiritual creatures walk the earth
Unseen, both when we wake, and when we sleep.
> —JOHN MILTON, *Paradise Lost*

Magic is detestable, vain and idle . . . though it has what I might call shadows of truth.
> —PLINY, *Natural History*

Once upon a midnight dreary, while I pondered, weak and weary,
Over many a quaint and curious volume of forgotten lore—
While I nodded, nearly napping, suddenly there came a tapping,

As of someone gently rapping, rapping at my chamber door.   —EDGAR ALLAN POE, *The Raven*

Quoth the Raven, "Nevermore."   —*Ibid.*

GLENDOWER: I can call spirits from the vasty deep.
HOTSPUR: Why so can I, or so can any man;
But will they come when you do call for them?
        SHAKESPEARE, *Henry IV, Part I*, III, i

Double, double toil and trouble,
Fire burn and caldron bubble.
        —SHAKESPEARE, *Macbeth*, IV, i

Eye of newt and toe of frog,
Wool of bat and tongue of dog,
Adder's fork and blindworm's sting,
Lizard's leg and owlet's wing,
For a charm of powerful trouble,
Like a hell broth boil and bubble.   —*Ibid.*

I'll break my staff,
Bury it certain fathoms in the earth,
And deeper than did ever plummet sound
I'll drown my book.   —SHAKESPEARE,
                    The Tempest, V, i

OCEAN   See NATURE: THE OCEAN; SEAS & SHIPS,
                        SAILING & BOATING

OLD AGE   See AGE & AGING; OLD THINGS,
                        OLD FRIENDS

OLDEN TIMES   See HISTORY; MEMORY; PAST, THE

OLD THINGS, OLD FRIENDS   See also AGE;
                    NOSTALGIA; PAST, THE

I love everything that's old: old friends, old times,
old manners, old books, old wines.
        —OLIVER GOLDSMITH, *She Stoops to Conquer*

Is not old wine wholesomest, old pippins toothsomest, old wood burn brightest, old linen wash whitest?

Old soldiers, sweethearts, are surest, and old lovers are soundest. —JOHN WEBSTER, *Westward Hoe*

OPPORTUNITY See also BOLDNESS & INITIATIVE

He who sees the last blossom on the plum tree must pick it. —ANONYMOUS (CHINESE PROVERB)

A wise man will make more opportunities than he finds. —FRANCIS BACON, *Essays*

Observe the opportunity. —BIBLE,
Ecclesiasticus 4:20

Seize the day. —HORACE, *Odes*
[More at PRESENT, THE.]

While we stop to think, we often miss our opportunity. —PUBLILIUS SYRUS, *Moral Sayings*

There is a tide in the affairs of men
Which, taken at the flood, leads on to fortune;
Omitted, all the voyage of their life
Is bound in shallows and in miseries.
—SHAKESPEARE, *Julius Caesar*, IV, iii

OPTIMISM & PESSIMISM See also DESPAIR,
DEPRESSION, MISERY; HOPE

The optimist proclaims that we live in the best of all possible worlds; and the pessimist fears this is true.
—JAMES BRANCH CABELL, *The Silver Stallion*

Pessimists have good appetites. —COLETTE, *Gigi*

Cheer up, the worst is yet to come.
—PHILANDER C. JOHNSON, *Shooting Stars*

A pessimist is a person who has had to listen to too many optimists.
—DON MARQUIS, quoted in Frederick B. Wilcox,
A Little Book of Aphorisms

An optimist is a guy that never has had much experience.   —DON MARQUIS, *archy and mehitabel*

To fear the worst oft cures the worse.
          —SHAKESPEARE, *Troilus and Cressida*, III, ii

In this best of all possible worlds . . . all is for the best.   —VOLTAIRE, *Candide*

ORIENT, THE   See also NATIONS; TRAVEL

In Xanadu did Kubla Khan
A stately pleasure dome decree:
Where Alph, the sacred river ran
Through caverns measureless to man
Down to a sunless sea.
          —SAMUEL TAYLOR COLERIDGE, *Kubla Khan*

The mysterious East, perfumed like a flower, silent like death, dark like a grave.   —JOSEPH CONRAD,
                                                        Youth

This is Malaya. Everything takes a long, a very long time in Malaya. Things get done, occasionally, but more often they don't, and the more in a hurry you are, the quicker you break down.
          —HAN SUNYIN, *And the Rain My Drink*

Oh, East is East, and West is West, and never the
     twain shall meet,
Till Earth and Sky stand presently at God's great
     Judgment Seat.
          —RUDYARD KIPLING,
               The Ballad of East and West

On the road to Mandalay,
Where the flyin'-fishes play,
An' the dawn comes up like thunder outer China
     'crost the Bay!
          —RUDYARD KIPLING, *Mandalay*

P

PACIFISM See also APPEASEMENT VS. RESISTANCE;
PEACE; RESIGNATION; VIOLENCE & FORCE; WAR

Resist not evil: but whosoever shall smite thee on thy
right cheek, turn to him the other also.
—BIBLE, *Matthew* 5:39

Be ye therefore wise as serpents, and harmless as
doves. *Ibid.*, 10:16

Non-violence is the first article of my faith. It is also
the last article of my creed.
—MOHANDAS K. GANDHI,
speech in defense against a charge of sedition,
March 23, 1922

Man lives freely only by his readiness to die, if need
be, at the hands of his brother, never by killing him.
—MOHANDAS K. GANDHI, quoted in
S. Hobhouse, ed., *True Patriotism:
Some Sayings of Mahatma Gandhi*

Pacifism is simply undisguised cowardice.
—ADOLF HITLER, speech, Aug. 21, 1926

PAINTING See ARTS: PAINTING

PARENTS & See also CHILDREN & CHILDHOOD;
PARENTHOOD FAMILY; GENERATIONS

The joys of parents are secret, and so are their griefs
and fears: they cannot utter the one, nor will they utter
the other.
—FRANCIS BACON, *Of Parents and Children*

There is no slave out of heaven like a loving woman; and, of all loving women, there is no such slave as a mother. —HENRY WARD BEECHER, *Proverbs from Plymouth Pulpit*

What the mother sings to the cradle goes all the way down to the coffin. —*Ibid.*

Honor thy father and thy mother. —BIBLE, *Exodus* 20:12, and elsewhere

He that spareth his rod hateth his son. —BIBLE, *Proverbs* 13:24

Train up a child in the way he should go: and when he is old, he will not depart from it. —*Ibid.*, 22:6

Who doesn't desire his father's death? —FEODOR DOSTOEVSKI, *The Brothers Karamazov*

Happy that man whose children make his happiness in life and not his grief. —EURIPIDES, *Orestes*

A man who has been the indisputable favorite of his mother keeps for life the feeling of a conqueror, that confidence of success that often induces real success. —FREUD, quoted in Ernest Jones, *Life and Works* [For the opposite view, in the English tradition, see Maugham below.]

You are the bows from which your children are as living arrows sent forth. —KAHLIL GIBRAN, *The Prophet*

There are some extraordinary fathers who seem, during the whole course of their lives, to be giving their children reasons for being consoled at their death. —LA BRUYÈRE, *Les Caractères*

He that will have his son have respect for him and
his orders, must himself have a great reverence for his
son.   —JOHN LOCKE,
          Some Thoughts Concerning Education

wot in hell
have I done to deserve
all these kittens.
          —DON MARQUIS, *archy and mehitabel*

Few misfortunes can befall a boy which bring worse
consequence than to have a really affectionate mother.
     —W. SOMERSET MAUGHAM, *A Writer's Notebook*
[Cf. Freud, above.]

People are always rather bored with their parents.
That's human nature.
     —W. SOMERSET MAUGHAM, *The Bread-Winner*

How sharper than a serpent's tooth it is
To have a thankless child.
          —SHAKESPEARE, *King Lear*, I, iv

It is a wise father that knows his own child.
     —SHAKESPEARE, *The Merchant of Venice*, II, ii

If parents would only realize how they bore their own
children!   —GEORGE BERNARD SHAW, *Misalliance*

Trust yourself. You know more than you think you
do.   —DR. BENJAMIN SPOCK,
          opening line of *Baby and Child Care*,
          addressed to new parents

Most American children suffer too much mother and
too little father.   —GLORIA STEINEM, in
          The New York Times,
          Aug. 26, 1971

Happy he
With such a mother! faith in womankind
Beats with his blood.
     —ALFRED, LORD TENNYSON, *The Princess*

I have found the best way to give advice to your children is to find out what they want and then advise them to do it.   —HARRY S TRUMAN,
television interview, May 27, 1955

Children begin by loving their parents. After a time they judge them. Rarely, if ever, do they forgive them.
—OSCAR WILDE, *A Woman of No Importance*
[In *The Picture of Dorian Gray*, Wilde concludes the same thought more optimistically: "*Sometimes* they forgive them." (italics added)]

All women become like their mothers. That is their tragedy. No man does. That's his.
—OSCAR WILDE,
The Importance of Being Earnest

There are no illegitimate children—only illegitimate parents.   —JUDGE LÉON R. YANKWICH,
decision in *Zipkin* v. *Mozon*,
June 1928
[J. M. and M. J. Cohen, in *The Penguin Dictionary of Modern Quotations*, say that Yankwich was quoting the columnist O. O. McIntyre.]

PARIS   See CITIES

PARTIES   See CONVERSATION; HOSPITALITY

PASSION   See ENTHUSIASM, ENERGY, ZEAL;
LOVE; SEX

PAST, THE   See also HISTORY; MEMORY;
NOSTALGIA; REGRET

Of one power even God is deprived, and that is the power of making what is past never to have been.
—AGATHON, quoted in Aristotle,
The Nicomachean Ethics

In the carriages of the past you can't go anywhere.
—MAXIM GORKY, *The Lower Depths*

Yesterday
A night-gone thing
A sun-down name.
> —LANGSTON HUGHES, "Youth,"
> in *From My People*

The past lies like a nightmare upon the present.
> —KARL MARX,
> *The 18th Brumaire of Louis Bonaparte*

[A somewhat free translation. A more literal version
is: "The tradition of all the dead generations weighs
like a nightmare" (or "incubus") "upon the brain of
the living."]

The past is the present, isn't it? It's the future too.
> —EUGENE O'NEILL,
> *Long Day's Journey into Night*

Only the past when you were happy is real.
> —*Ibid.*

Don't look back. Something may be gaining on you.
> —SATCHEL PAIGE, *How to Keep Young*

[Not original with Paige, but now identified with him.]

I tell you the past is a bucket of ashes.
> —CARL SANDBURG, *Prairie*

Those who cannot remember the past are condemned
to repeat it.
> —GEORGE SANTAYANA, *The Life of Reason*

What's past is prologue.
> —SHAKESPEARE, *The Tempest*, II, i

The world is weary of the past,
Oh, might it die or rest at last.
> —PERCY BYSSHE SHELLEY, *Hellas*

All things are taken from us, and become
Portions and parcels of the dreadful past.
> —ALFRED, LORD TENNYSON, *The Lotus Eaters*

Mais où sont les neiges d'antan?
Where are the snows of yesteryear?
　　　　　—FRANÇOIS VILLON,
　　　　　　　Ballade des dames du temps jadis

We live in reference to past experience and not to future events, however inevitable.
　　　　　—H. G. WELLS, *Mind at the End of Its Tether*
[See also Auden, at HISTORY.]

PATIENCE　　　See also PERSEVERANCE & ENDURANCE

Patience is bitter but its fruit is sweet.
　　　　　—ANONYMOUS (FRENCH PROVERB)

Sit on the bank of a river and wait: your enemy's corpse will soon float by.
　　　　　—ANONYMOUS (INDIAN PROVERB)

Patience is the companion of wisdom.
　　　　　—ST. AUGUSTINE, *On Patience*

The end is not yet.　　　　—BIBLE, *Matthew* 24:6

Patience, n. A minor form of despair disguised as a virtue.　　—AMBROSE BIERCE, *The Devil's Dictionary*

Everything comes if a man will only wait.
　　　　　—BENJAMIN DISRAELI, *Tancred*

Beware the fury of a patient man.
　　　　　—JOHN DRYDEN, *Absalom and Achitophel*

Patience and delay achieve more than force and rage.
　　　　　—LA FONTAINE, *Fables*

They also serve who only stand and wait.
　　　　　—JOHN MILTON, *On His Blindness*

How poor are they that have not patience!
What wound did ever heal but by degrees?
　　　　　—SHAKESPEARE, *Othello*, II, iii

The strongest of all warriors are these two—Time and Patience.　　　—LEO TOLSTOY, *War and Peace*

PATRIOTISM See also AMERICA & AMERICANS;
AMERICAN HISTORY: MEMORABLE
MOMENTS; MILITARY BATTLES; HEROES

Patriotism is in political life what faith is in religion.
—LORD ACTON, *Nationality*, in
The Home and Foreign Review, July 1862

Plus je vis d'étrangers, plus j'aimai ma patrie.
The more I saw of foreigners, the more I loved my
country.   —P. L. DE BELLOY, *Le Siège de Calais*
[Madame de Staël later slightly rephrased the thought
in *Corinne*: "The more I see of other countries, the
more I love my own."]

"My country, right or wrong," is a thing no patriot
would think of saying except in a desperate case. It is
like saying, "My mother, drunk or sober."
—G. K. CHESTERTON, *Defense of Patriotism*,
in *The Defendant*
[He is referring to Decatur; see below.]

Our country: In her intercourse with foreign nations,
may she always be in the right; but our country right
or wrong.   —STEPHEN DECATUR, toast
at Norfolk, Va., April 1816
[Cf. Chesterton above. Carl Schurz also offered a cor-
rection, in a speech on Oct. 17, 1899: "Our country,
right or wrong. When right, to be kept right; when
wrong, to be put right."]

When a whole nation is roaring Patriotism at the top
of its voice, I am fain to explore the cleanness of its
hands and purity of its heart.
—RALPH WALDO EMERSON, *Journals*

Dulce et decorum est pro patria mori.
It is a sweet and seemly thing to die for one's country.
—HORACE, *Odes*

Patriotism is the last refuge of a scoundrel.
—SAMUEL JOHNSON, quoted in James Boswell,
Life of Johnson

Ask not what your country can do for you, ask what you can do for your country.
—JOHN F. KENNEDY, Inaugural Address, 1961
[*The Concise Oxford Dictionary of Quotations* notes that a similar exhortation was used in the funeral oration for John Greenleaf Whittier (died 1892). And *Bartlett's* cites several predecessors, not including Whittier but going back to an even earlier address by Oliver Wendell Holmes, Jr., on May 30, 1884: ". . . we pause . . . to recall what our country has done for each of us, and to ask ourselves what we can do for our country in return."]

You're not supposed to be so blind with patriotism that you can't face reality. Wrong is wrong no matter who does it or who says it.
—MALCOLM X, *Malcolm X Speaks Out*

Patriotism is a kind of religion; it is the egg from which wars are hatched.
—GUY DE MAUPASSANT, *My Uncle Sosthenes*

Breathes there the man, with soul so dead,
Who never to himself has said,
This is my own, my native land!
—SIR WALTER SCOTT,
The Lay of the Last Minstrel

No one loves his country for its size or eminence, but because it is his own.   —SENECA, *Letter to Lucilius*

"Shoot, if you must, this old gray head,
But spare your country's flag," she said.
—JOHN GREENLEAF WHITTIER, *Barbara Frietchie*

PATTERNS

Perfumes, colors, and sounds echo one another.
—CHARLES BAUDELAIRE, *Correspondances*

We all of us live too much in circles.
—BENJAMIN DISRAELI, *Sybil*

The life of man is a self-evolving circle.
—RALPH WALDO EMERSON, *Circles*

Network, n. Any thing reticulated or decussated at equal distances, with interstices between the intersections.   —SAMUEL JOHNSON, *Dictionary*

Christ! What are patterns for?
—AMY LOWELL, *Patterns*

The wheel is come full circle.
—SHAKESPEARE, *King Lear*, V, iii

PEACE   See also PACIFISM; WAR

They shall beat their swords into plowshares, and their spears into pruning hooks: nation shall not lift up sword against nation, neither shall they learn war any more.   —BIBLE, *Isaiah* 2:4;
also *Micah* 4:3

The wolf also shall dwell with the lamb, and the leopard shall lie down with the kid; and the calf and the young lion and the fatling together; and a little child shall lead them.   —*Ibid.*, 11:6

Saying, Peace, peace; when there is no peace.
—BIBLE, *Jeremiah* 6:14 and 8:11

Blessed are the peacemakers: for they shall be called the children of God.   —BIBLE, *Matthew* 5:9
[For other verses from the Sermon on the Mount, see VIRTUE.]

Give peace in our time, O Lord.
—BOOK OF COMMON PRAYER,
Morning Prayer
[See under APPEASEMENT VS. RESISTANCE for Neville Chamberlain's "peace for our time."]

Peace is liberty in tranquillity.

—CICERO, *Philippics*

Peace cannot be kept by force. It can only be achieved by understanding.
—ALBERT EINSTEIN, *Notes on Pacifism*

The most disadvantageous peace is better than the most just war. —ERASMUS, *Adagia*

You and me, we've made a separate peace.
—ERNEST HEMINGWAY, *A Very Short Story*

Better to live in peace than to begin a war and lie dead.
—CHIEF JOSEPH, quoted in Time-Life Books, *The Indians*

First keep peace within yourself, then you can also bring peace to others.
—THOMAS À KEMPIS, *Imitation of Christ*

Arms alone are not enough to keep the peace. It must be kept by men.
—JOHN F. KENNEDY, State of the Union message, 1963

Certain peace is better than anticipated victory.
—LIVY, *Ab urbe condita*

The inglorious arts of peace.
—ANDREW MARVELL, *Upon Cromwell's Return from Ireland*

Peace hath her victories
No less renowned than war.
—JOHN MILTON, *To Cromwell*

The only alternative to co-existence is co-destruction.
—JAWAHARLAL NEHRU, quoted in the *Observer*, Aug. 29, 1954

It isn't enough to talk about peace. One must believe in it. And it isn't enough to believe in it. One must work at it. —ELEANOR ROOSEVELT, Voice of America, Nov. 11, 1951

Peace, like charity, begins at home.
—FRANKLIN D. ROOSEVELT, speech,
Aug. 14, 1936

A peace is of the nature of a conquest;
For then both parties nobly are subdued,
And neither party loser.
—SHAKESPEARE, *Henry IV, Part II*, IV, ii

They make a desert and call it peace.
—TACITUS, *Agricola*

Ring out the thousand wars of old,
Ring in the thousand years of peace.
—ALFRED, LORD TENNYSON, *In Memoriam*

Peace hath higher tests of manhood
Than battle ever knew.
—JOHN GREENLEAF WHITTIER, *The Hero*

Only a peace between equals can last.
—WOODROW WILSON,
speech to U.S. Senate, 1917

PEOPLE   See DANGEROUS PEOPLE;
HUMANS & HUMAN NATURE;
PEOPLE, THE; RACES & PEOPLES;
REASONABLE & UNREASONABLE PEOPLE

PEOPLE, NOT LIKING   See MISANTHROPY

PEOPLE, THE   See also DEMOCRACY

Vox populi, vox Dei.
The voice of the people is the voice of God.
—ALCUIN, letter to Charlemagne, A.D. 800
[Alexander Pope was rather less sure of this—he wrote
as follows:
The people's voice is odd,
It is, and is not, the voice of God.
—*Imitations of Horace.*
William Tecumseh Sherman simply disagreed: "*Vox po-
puli, vox humbug,*" letter to his wife, June 2, 1863.]

Who builds upon the people, builds upon sand.
—ANONYMOUS (ITALIAN PROVERB)

The people want to be deceived.
—ANONYMOUS (ROMAN EPIGRAPH)

In the common people there is no wisdom, no penetration, no power of judgment.
—CICERO, *Pro planchio*

If it has to choose who is to be crucified, the crowd will always save Barabbas.
—JEAN COCTEAU, *Le rappel à l'ordre*

Nor is the people's judgment always true;
The most may err as grossly as the few.
—JOHN DRYDEN, *Absalom and Achitophel*

All the world over, I will back the masses against the classes.
—WILLIAM GLADSTONE, speech, June 6, 1886

There is not a more mean, stupid, dastardly, pitiful, selfish, spiteful, envious, ungrateful animal than the public. It is the greatest of cowards, for it is afraid of itself.   —WILLIAM HAZLITT, *Table Talk*

The wealth of a country is its working people.
—THEODOR HERZL, *Altneuland*

The great masses of the people will more easily fall victims to a big lie than to a small one.
—ADOLF HITLER, *Mein Kampf*

The people are a many-headed beast.
—HORACE, *Epistles*, first epistle

The people are the only sure reliance for the preservation of our liberty.
—THOMAS JEFFERSON,
letter to James Madison, 1787

About things on which the public thinks long it commonly thinks right.   —SAMUEL JOHNSON, *Addison*,
in *Lives of the English Poets*

Why should there not be a patient confidence in the ultimate justice of the people? Is there any better or equal hope in the world?
> —ABRAHAM LINCOLN,
> *First Inaugural Address*, 1861

[See under GOVERNMENT for "government of the people."]

You may fool all the people some of the time; you can even fool some of the people all the time; but you can't fool all of the people all the time.
> —ABRAHAM LINCOLN (possibly apocryphal)

[*Bartlett's* cites Alexander K. McClure, *Lincoln's Yarns and Stories*. Movie producer Joseph Levine had a different view of the issue. He quipped, "You can fool all the people if the advertising is right," quoted in *The New York Times*, obituary, Aug. 1, 1987.]

Every man a king!   —HUEY LONG, slogan

The people, and the people alone, are the motive force in the making of world history.
> —MAO ZEDUNG, *Quotations from Chairman Mao Zedung*

I am the people—the mob—the crowd—the mass.
Do you know that all the great work of the world is done through me?
> —CARL SANDBURG, *I Am the People, the Mob*

The pitifulest thing out is a mob.
> —MARK TWAIN,
> *The Adventures of Huckleberry Finn*

PEOPLES   See NATIONS; RACES & PEOPLES

**PERSEVERANCE   See also EFFORT; PATIENCE;
& ENDURANCE   SURVIVAL; WORK**

Slow and steady wins the race.
> —AESOP, *The Hare and the Tortoise*

He that can't endure the bad will not live to see the good.   —ANONYMOUS (JEWISH PROVERB)

He that endureth to the end shall be saved.
—BIBLE, *Matthew* 10:22

Be there a will, and wisdom finds a way.
—GEORGE CRABBE, *The Birth of Flattery*

To persevere, trusting in what hopes he has, is courage in a man. The coward despairs.
—EURIPIDES, *Heracles*

'Tis a lesson you should heed,
Try, try again.
If at first you don't succeed,
Try, try again.
—WILLIAM E. HICKSON,
Try and Try Again

Great works are performed not by strength, but by perseverance.
—SAMUEL JOHNSON, *Rasselas*

God helps those who persevere.
—KORAN

Sorrow and silence are strong, and patient endurance is godlike.
—HENRY WADSWORTH LONGFELLOW,
Evangeline

Endurance is the crowning quality,
And patience all the passion of great hearts.
—JAMES RUSSELL LOWELL, *Columbus*

Perseverance is more prevailing than violence; and many things which cannot be overcome when they are taken together, yield themselves up when taken little by little.
—PLUTARCH, "Life of Sertorius,"
in *Parallel Lives*

PHILOSOPHY   See also ETHICS & MORALITY

To be is to be perceived.
                    —GEORGE BERKELEY,
                    Philosophical Commentaries
[Popular form of Bishop Berkeley's fundamental philosophical statement, "Existence is *percipi* or *percipere*,
or *velle*, i.e., *agere*," which with the Latin translated
reads: "Existence is to be perceived or to perceive, or
to will, that is, to be active." Cf. Descartes below.]

A metaphysician is a man who goes into a dark cellar
at midnight without a light, looking for a black cat that
is not there.   —LORD BOWEN, attributed

There is but one truly serious philosophical problem,
and that is suicide. Judging whether life is or is not
worth living amounts to answering the fundamental
question of philosophy.
          —ALBERT CAMUS, *The Myth of Sisyphus*

There is nothing so ridiculous but some philosopher
has said it.   —CICERO, *De divinatione*
[Matters did not improve in the next seventeen hundred
years; see Descartes, below.]

There is nothing so strange and so unbelievable that
it has not been said by one philosopher or another.
          —RENÉ DESCARTES, *Discourse on Method*
[For Descartes' own fundamental dictum, the *cogito*
argument, see under MIND, THOUGHT, & UNDER-
STANDING.]

The test of a religion or philosophy is the number of
things it can explain.   —RALPH WALDO EMERSON,
                    Journals, 1836

What is it to be a philosopher? Is it not to be prepared
against events?   —EPICTETUS, *Discourses*

You can't do without philosophy, since everything
has its hidden meaning which we must know.
                    —MAXIM GORKY, *The Zykovs*

Philosophy will clip an angel's wing.
—JOHN KEATS, *Lamia*

Do not all charms fly
At the mere touch of cold philosophy? —*Ibid.*

Logic is the art of making truth prevail.
—LA BRUYÈRE, *Les Caractères*

Metaphysics is almost always an attempt to prove the incredible by an appeal to the unintelligible.
H. L. MENCKEN, *Minority Report*

Most philosophical treatises show the human cerebrum loaded far beyond its Plimsoll mark.
—H. L. MENCKEN, *Prejudices*

To philosophize is to doubt.
—MONTAIGNE, *Essays*

Wonder is the foundation of all philosophy, inquiry the process, ignorance the end. —*Ibid.*
[See also Plato and Whitehead below.]

True philosophers are lovers of the vision of truth.
—PLATO, *The Republic*

Wonder is the feeling of a philosopher, and philosophy begins in wonder. —PLATO, *Theaetetus*

To teach how to live without certainty and yet without being paralyzed by hesitation is perhaps the chief thing that philosophy, in our age, can do for those who study it. —BERTRAND RUSSELL,
History of Western Philosophy

Philosophy arises from an unusually obstinate attempt to arrive at real knowledge.
—BERTRAND RUSSELL. *An Outline of Philosophy*

There are more things in heaven and earth, Horatio,
Than are dreamt of in your philosophy.
—SHAKESPEARE, *Hamlet*, I, v

Adversity's sweet milk, philosophy.
                    —SHAKESPEARE, *Romeo and Juliet*, III, iii

The unexamined life is not worth living.
                    —SOCRATES, quoted in Plato, *Apology*

I am a citizen, not of Athens or Greece, but of the
world.   —SOCRATES, quoted in Plutarch, *De exilio*

Nero's mother turned him from the study of philosophy, warning that it was contrary to the needs of one
destined to rule.
                    —SUETONIUS, *Nero*, in *Lives of the Caesars*

The safest general characterization of the European
philosophical tradition is that it consists of a series of
footnotes to Plato.
                    —ALFRED NORTH WHITEHEAD,
                    Process and Reality

Philosophy begins in wonder, and at the end, when
philosophic thought has done its best, the wonder remains.
—ALFRED NORTH WHITEHEAD, *Modes of Thought*

Philosophy is not a body of doctrine but an activity.
                    —LUDWIG WITTGENSTEIN,
                    Tractatus logico-philosophicus

Most propositions and questions that have been written about philosophical matters are not false but
senseless.   —*Ibid.*
[One of Wittgenstein's own most celebrated propositions is: "The world is everything that is the case,"
Tractatus.]

PHYSICAL FITNESS   See also HEALTH; SPORTS

Strengthen the weak hands, and make firm the feeble
knees.
                    —BIBLE, *Isaiah* 35:3 (Revised Standard Version)

Whenever the urge to exercise comes upon me, I lie
down for a while and it passes.
　　　　—ROBERT MAYNARD HUTCHINS,
　　　　quoted in Harry S. Ashmore,
　　　　The Life of Robert Maynard Hutchins
[Hutchins, who headed the University of Chicago from
1929 to 1951, enjoyed good health throughout his life;
he died at age 78.]

PHYSICIANS　　　　　See DOCTORS & THE PRACTICE
　　　　　　　　　　　　　　　　　OF MEDICINE

PHYSICS　　　　See SCIENCE: PHYSICS & COSMOLOGY

PITY　See COMPASSION & PITY; FORGIVENESS & MERCY

PLANS

The best-laid schemes o' mice an' men
Gang aft a-gley.　　　—ROBERT BURNS, *To a Mouse*

It's a bad plan that can't be changed.
　　　　—PUBLILIUS SYRUS, *Moral Sayings*

PLANTS　See NATURE: GARDENS, FLOWERS, & TREES

PLEASURE　　　　　　　See HAPPINESS; HEDONISM;
　　　　　　　　　　　　　　　　SEX & SENSUALITY

POETRY & POETS　　　　See ARTS: POETRY & POETS

POLITICS　　　　See also CAPITALISM; COMMUNISM;
　　　DEMOCRACY; DIPLOMACY; FREEDOM; GOVERNMENT;
　　　　　　　　HIGH POSITION: RULERS & LEADERS;
　　　　　　　　POWER; REVOLUTION; SOCIALISM

Politics, as a practice, whatever its professions, has
always been the systematic organization of hatreds.
　　　　—HENRY BROOKS ADAMS,
　　　　The Education of Henry Adams

Knowledge of human nature is the beginning and end
of political education.　　　　　—*Ibid.*

Modern politics is, at bottom, a struggle not of men but of forces.   —*Ibid.*

My country has in its wisdom contrived for me the most insignificant office [the vice-presidency] that ever the invention of man contrived or his imagination conceived.   —JOHN ADAMS, letter to
Abigail Adams, Dec. 19, 1793

A liberal is a man who tells other people how to spend their money.   —ANONYMOUS
[Mencken traces this to Carter Glass, 1938; but it's not clear that it was original with him.]

You have all the characteristics of a popular politician: a horrible voice, bad breeding, and a vulgar manner.   —ARISTOPHANES, *Knights*

Man is by nature a political animal.
—ARISTOTLE, *Politics*

We know what happens to people who stay in the middle of the road. They get run over.
—ANEURIN BEVAN, *Observer*, Dec. 9, 1953,
Saying of the Week

Politics is a blood sport.
—ANEURIN BEVAN, quoted in Jennie Lee,
My Life with Nye

Politics is not an exact science.
—OTTO VON BISMARCK, speech, Dec. 1863

Politics is the art of the possible, the attainable . . . , the art of the next best.
—OTTO VON BISMARCK, conversation with
Meyer von Waldeck, Aug. 11, 1867
[The saying "politics is the art of compromise" derives in part from a speech by Edmund Burke on conciliation with America, made on March 22, 1775. The relevant passage is: "All government—indeed, every human

benefit and enjoyment, every virtue and every prudent act—is founded on compromise and barter."]

Politics ruins the character.
—OTTO VON BISMARCK, quoted by
    Bernhard Brige, *Berlin Tägliche Rundschau*, 1881

Politics are not the task of a Christian.
        —DIETRICH BONHOEFFER, *No Rusty Swords*
[An opinion of venerable age; see Tertullian, below.]

You scratch my back, I'll scratch yours.
            —SIMON CAMERON, attributed
[Cameron, a consummate and corrupt politician, was Lincoln's first Secretary of War, acquitting himself fairly scandalously. He created a powerful Republican party machine in Pennsylvania.]

Vain hope to make people happy by politics!
        —THOMAS CARLYLE, *Journal*, Oct. 10, 1831

Persistence in one opinion has never been considered a merit in political leaders.   —CICERO, *Ad familiares*

Politics are impossible without spoils. . . . You have to deal with men as they are . . . you must bribe the masses with spoils.
        —"BOSS" RICHARD CROKER, quoted in
            Richard Norton Smith, *Thomas E. Dewey*
[See also William Marcy under WINNING & LOSING.]

Since a politician never believes what he says, he is surprised when others believe him.
        —CHARLES DE GAULLE, quoted in *Newsweek*,
        Oct. 1, 1962

No government can long be secure without a formidable opposition.
            —BENJAMIN DISRAELI, *Coningsby*

Finality is not the language of politics.
        —BENJAMIN DISRAELI, speech, Feb. 28, 1859

A conservative government is an organized hypocrisy.   —BENJAMIN DISRAELI, speech, March 1845

A party is perpetually corrupted by personality.
> —RALPH WALDO EMERSON, *Politics*

Politics is not the art of the possible. It consists in choosing between the disastrous and the unpalatable.
> —JOHN KENNETH GALBRAITH,
> *Ambassador's Journal*

[This updates Bismarck; see above.]

Treason doth never prosper: what's the reason?
For if it prosper, none dare call it treason.
> —SIR JOHN HARINGTON, "Of Treason,"
> in *Epigrams*

You can't adopt politics as a profession and remain honest.
> —LOUIS MCHENRY HOWE, speech, Jan. 17, 1933

[Howe was Franklin D. Roosevelt's invaluable aide and adviser.]

When a man assumes a public trust, he should consider himself as public property.
> —THOMAS JEFFERSON, quoted in Rayner,
> *Life of Jefferson*

Political action is the highest responsibility of a citizen.
> —JOHN F. KENNEDY, speech, Oct. 20, 1960

[Plato is sometimes quoted on the importance of participation in politics: "The penalty that good men pay for indifference to politics is to be governed by evil men or, men worse than themselves." Unfortunately, a source for this comment is hard to find. The attribution to Plato is listed as "unverified" in the authoritative *Respectfully Quoted*, published by the Library of Congress.]

Politicians are the same all over. They promise to build bridges, even where there are no rivers.
> —NIKITA KHRUSHCHEV, to the press, Oct. 1960,
> in Glen Cove, L.I.

What is conservatism? Is it not adherence to the old and tried, against the new and untried?
—ABRAHAM LINCOLN, speech, Feb. 27, 1860

A politician must often talk and act before he has thought and read.
—THOMAS BABINGTON MACAULAY,
Gladstone on Church and State

In every age, the vilest specimens of human nature are to be found among demagogues.
—THOMAS BABINGTON MACAULAY,
History of England

Politics is war without bloodshed, while war is politics with bloodshed.
—MAO ZEDUNG,
Quotations from Chairman Mao Zedung
[For his observation on the source of political power, see under POWER.]

All reactionaries are paper tigers.
—MAO ZEDUNG, conversation with
Anna Louise Strong, 1946

Liberal institutions straightway cease from being liberal the moment they are soundly established.
—FRIEDRICH NIETZSCHE, *Twilight of the Idols*

All politics is local.
—THOMAS P. ("TIP") O'NEILL, saying.
[In his autobiography, *Man of the House*, Tip O'Neill credited his father with this insight.]

In our time, political speech and writing are largely the defense of the indefensible.
—GEORGE ORWELL,
Politics and the English Language

Never lose your temper with the press or the public is a major rule of political life.
—CHRISTABEL PANKHURST, *Unshackled Woman*

It is now known . . . that men enter local politics solely as a result of being unhappily married.
—C. NORTHCOTE PARKINSON, *Parkinson's Law*

Party-spirit . . . at best is but the madness of many for the gain of a few.
—ALEXANDER POPE, letter to E. Blount, Aug. 27, 1714

All politics are based on the indifference of the majority.   —JAMES RESTON, *The New York Times*, June 12, 1968

Politicians, after all, are not over a year behind public opinion.   —WILL ROGERS, *Autobiography*

I tell you folks, all politics is applesauce.
—WILL ROGERS, *The Illiterate Digest*

A radical is a man with both feet firmly planted in the air.
—FRANKLIN D. ROOSEVELT, radio speech, Oct. 26, 1939

A conservative is a man with two perfectly good legs who, however, has never learned how to walk forward.   —*Ibid.*

A reactionary is a somnambulist walking backward.
—*Ibid.*

A politician . . . one that would circumvent God.
—SHAKESPEARE, *Hamlet*, V, i

He knows nothing and thinks he knows everything. That points clearly to a political career.
—GEORGE BERNARD SHAW, *Major Barbara*

Politics is perhaps the only profession for which no preparation is thought necessary.
—ROBERT LOUIS STEVENSON, *Familiar Studies of Men and Books*

Nothing is more foreign to us Christians than politics.
—TERTULLIAN, *The Christian's Defense*

In politics, if you want anything said, ask a man; if you want anything done, ask a woman.
> —MARGARET THATCHER, quoted in Anthony Sampson, *The Changing Anatomy of Britain*

A statesman is a politician who's been dead ten or fifteen years. —HARRY S TRUMAN,
> *New York World-Telegram & Sun*, April 12, 1958

[Probably not original with Truman. The authors heard this from James F. Byrnes at least ten years earlier, and it seemed to have been around for a while even then.]

There is no distinctly native American criminal class except Congress.
—MARK TWAIN, "Pudd'nhead Wilson's New Calendar," in *Following the Equator*

Money is the mother's milk of politics.
> —JESSE UNRUH, saying, quoted in *The New York Times*, obituary, Aug. 6, 1987

Politics is the art of preventing people from taking part in affairs which properly concern them.
> —PAUL VALÉRY, *Tel quel*

Politics makes strange bedfellows.
> —CHARLES DUDLEY WARNER, *My Summer in a Garden*

[For misery and bedfellows, see Shakespeare *Tempest* quote under TROUBLE.]

Among politicians, the esteem of religion is profitable, the principles of it are troublesome.
> —BENJAMIN WHICHCOTE, *Moral and Religious Aphorisms*

Prosperity is necessarily the first theme of a political campaign.
> —WOODROW WILSON, speech, Sept. 4, 1912

POOR, THE   See HAVES & HAVE-NOTS; MONEY; POVERTY & HUNGER

POPULAR OPINION   See PEOPLE, THE;
                                       REPUTATION

POPULATION   See also ENVIRONMENT

Population, when unchecked, increases in a geometric ratio.
Subsistence increases only in an arithmetical ratio.
—THOMAS MALTHUS,
An Essay on the Principle of Population

In a foreseeable future we shall be smothered by our own numbers. . . . Preoccupation with survival has set the stage for extinction.
—JOHN STEINBECK, *Sweet Thursday*

POSSESSIONS   See THINGS & POSSESSIONS

POVERTY & HUNGER   See also HAVES &
                                       HAVE-NOTS; MONEY

Hunger knows no friend but its feeder.
—ARISTOPHANES, *The Wasps*

Poverty is the parent of revolution and crime.
—ARISTOTLE, *Politics*

The poor man's wisdom is despised, and his words are not heard.   —BIBLE, *Ecclesiastes* 9:16

For the poor always ye have with you.
—BIBLE, *John* 12:8

Poverty makes you sad as well as wise.
—BERTOLT BRECHT, *The Threepenny Opera*

Eats first, morals after.   —*Ibid.*

If the misery of our poor be caused not by laws of nature, but by our institutions, great is our sin.
—CHARLES DARWIN, *Voyage of the Beagle*

Poverty demoralizes.
—RALPH WALDO EMERSON, *Wealth*

There is no scandal like rags, nor any crime so shameful as poverty. —GEORGE FARQUHAR,
Beaux' Stratagem

The short and simple annals of the poor.
—THOMAS GRAY,
Elegy Written in a Country Churchyard

There is something about poverty that smells like death. Dead dreams dropping off the heart like leaves in a dry season and rotting around the feet.
—ZORA NEALE HURSTON, *Dust Tracks*

A decent provision for the poor is the true test of civilization.
—SAMUEL JOHNSON, quoted in James Boswell,
Life of Johnson, 1770

A man who has nothing can whistle in a robber's face. —JUVENAL, *Satires*

Love in a hut, with water and a crust,
Is—Love, forgive us—cinders, ashes, dust.
—JOHN KEATS, *Lamia*

If a free society cannot help the many who are poor, it cannot save the few who are rich.
—JOHN F. KENNEDY, Inaugural Address, 1961

Anticipate charity by preventing poverty.
—MAIMONIDES, *Charity's Eight Degrees*

The more humanity owes him [the poor man], the more society denies him. Every door is shut against him, even when he has a right to its being opened: and if he ever obtains justice, it is with much greater difficulty than others obtain favors.
—JEAN JACQUES ROUSSEAU,
A Discourse on Political Economy

The greatest of evils and the worst of crimes is poverty. —GEORGE BERNARD SHAW,
Major Barbara, Preface

I have been a common man and a poor man; and it has no romance for me.   —*Ibid.*

PICKERING: Have you no morals, man?
DOOLITTLE: Can't afford them, Governor. Neither could you if you was as poor as me.
                    —GEORGE BERNARD SHAW, *Pygmalion*

Poverty is no disgrace to a man, but it is profoundly inconvenient.   —REVEREND SYDNEY SMITH,
                    His Wit and Wisdom

A hungry man is not a free man.
                    —ADLAI STEVENSON, speech, Sept. 6, 1952

No one can worship God or love his neighbor on an empty stomach.
                    —WOODROW WILSON, speech, May 23, 1912

POWER   See also HIGH POSITION:
                    RULERS & LEADERS; STRENGTH;
                    TYRANNY & TOTALITARIANISM

Power tends to corrupt and absolute power corrupts absolutely. . . . Great men are almost always bad men.
                    —LORD ACTON, letter to
                    Bishop Mandell Creighton,
                    April 1887

I am more and more convinced that man is a dangerous creature and that power, whether vested in many or a few, is ever grasping, and like the grave, cries, "Give, give."
                    —ABIGAIL ADAMS, letter to John Adams,
                    Nov. 27, 1775

A friend in power is a friend lost.
                    —HENRY BROOKS ADAMS,
                    The Education of Henry Adams

Power always thinks it has a great soul and vast views beyond the comprehension of the weak; and that it is doing God's service, when it is violating all His laws.
                    —JOHN ADAMS, letter to Thomas Jefferson,
                    quoted by James Reston,
                    The New York Times, Nov. 21, 1984

I have seen the wicked in great power, and spreading himself like a green bay tree.
> —BIBLE, *Psalms* 37:35

There is no power but of God.
> —BIBLE, *Romans* 13:1

The greater the power, the more dangerous the abuse.   —EDMUND BURKE, speech on the Middlesex election, 1771

Power is the first good.
> —RALPH WALDO EMERSON, *Inspiration*

You shall have joy, or you shall have power, said God: you shall not have both.
> —RALPH WALDO EMERSON, *Journals*, 1842

Life is a search after power.
> —RALPH WALDO EMERSON, *Power*

Power is precarious.   —HERODOTUS, *Histories*

This is the bitterest pain among men, to have much knowledge but no power.   —*Ibid.*

Power is the supreme law.
> —ADOLF HITLER, *Mein Kampf*

An honest man can feel no pleasure in the exercise of power over his fellow citizens.
> —THOMAS JEFFERSON, letter to John Melish, Jan. 13, 1813

All power, of whatever sort, is of itself desirable.
> —SAMUEL JOHNSON, quoted in James Boswell, *Life of Johnson*, Apr. 14, 1775

Power is the great aphrodisiac.
> —HENRY KISSINGER, quoted in *The New York Times*, Jan. 19, 1971

Power never takes a back step—only in the face of more power.   —MALCOLM X, *Malcolm X Speaks*

Every Communist must grasp the truth: political power grows out of the barrel of a gun.
—MAO ZEDUNG, *Quotations from Chairman Mao Zedung*

Political power is merely the organized power of one class to oppress another.
—KARL MARX and FRIEDRICH ENGELS, *Communist Manifesto*

The object of power is power.
—GEORGE ORWELL, *1984*

We cannot all be masters.
—SHAKESPEARE, *Othello*, I, i

Power, like a desolating pestilence,
Pollutes whate'er it touches.
—PERCY BYSSHE SHELLEY, *Queen Mab*

Power takes as ingratitude the writhing of its victims.
—RABINDRANATH TAGORE, *Stray Birds*

In order to obtain and hold power, a man must love it.
—LEO TOLSTOY, *The Kingdom of God Is Within You*

We have, I fear, confused power with greatness.
—STEWART UDALL, Commencement speech, Dartmouth College, 1965

PRACTICAL WISDOM   See PRUDENCE & PRACTICAL WISDOM

PRAYER   See also PRAYERS; RELIGION

Ask the gods nothing excessive.
—AESCHYLUS, *The Suppliant Women*

It is in vain to expect our prayers to be heard, if we do not strive as well as pray.
—AESOP, *Hercules and the Waggoner*

Orare est laborare, laborare est orare.
To pray is to work, to work is to pray.
        —BENEDICTINE ORDER, motto

The wish to pray is a prayer in itself.
        —GEORGES BERNANOS,
        The Diary of a Country Priest

God is in heaven, and thou upon earth: therefore let thy words be few.   —BIBLE, *Ecclesiastes* 5:5

When thou prayest, thou shalt not be as the hypocrites are: for they love to pray standing in the synagogues and in the corners of the streets that they may be seen of men. Verily I say unto you, they have their reward.   —BIBLE, *Matthew* 6:6

Watch and pray.   —BIBLE, *Mark* 13:33

Pray, v. To ask that the rules of the universe be annulled in behalf of a single petitioner, confessedly unworthy.
        —AMBROSE BIERCE, *The Devil's Dictionary*

Prayer is conversation with God.
        —CLEMENT OF ALEXANDRIA, *Stromateis*

He prayeth well, who loveth well
Both man and bird and beast.
        —SAMUEL TAYLOR COLERIDGE,
        The Rime of the Ancient Mariner

He prayeth best, who loveth best
All things both great and small;
For the dear God who loveth us,
He made and loveth all.   —*Ibid.*

Prayer is the little implement
Through which men reach
Where presence—is denied them.
        —EMILY DICKINSON, poem no. 437

Prayer is the contemplation of the facts of life from the highest point of view.
—RALPH WALDO EMERSON, *Self-Reliance*

You pray in your distress and in your need: would that you might pray also in the fullness of your joy and in your days of abundance.
—KAHLIL GIBRAN, *The Prophet*

And fools, who came to scoff, remained to pray.
—OLIVER GOLDSMITH, *The Deserted Village*

Prayer indeed is good, but while calling on the gods, a man should himself lend a hand.
—HIPPOCRATES, *Regimen*

Pray, for all men need the aid of the gods.
—HOMER, *Odyssey*

Certain thoughts are prayers. There are moments when, whatever be the attitude of the body, the soul is on its knees.   —VICTOR HUGO,
Les Misérables

A single grateful thought raised to heaven is the most perfect prayer.   —GOTTHOLD EPHRAIM LESSING,
Minna von Barnhelm

There are few men who would dare publish to the world the prayers they make to almighty God.
—MONTAIGNE, *Essays*

My words fly up; my thoughts remain below.
Words without thoughts never to heaven go.
—SHAKESPEARE, *Hamlet*, III, iii

His worst fault is that he is given to prayer. He is something peevish that way.
—SHAKESPEARE, *The Merry Wives of Windsor*, I, iv

Complaint is the largest tribute Heaven receives, and the sincerest part of our devotion.
—JONATHAN SWIFT,
Thoughts on Various Subjects

Pray for my soul. More things are wrought by prayer
Than this world dreams of.
> —ALFRED, LORD TENNYSON,
> "The Passing of Arthur," in
> *Idylls of the King*

Whatever a man prays for, he prays for a miracle.
Every prayer reduces itself to this: "Great God, grant
that twice two be not four."
> —IVAN TURGENEV, *Prayer*

PRAYERS   See also PRAYER

Matthew, Mark, Luke, and John,
The bed be blest that I lie on.
Four angels to my bed,
Four angels round my head,
One to watch, and one to pray,
And two to bear my soul away.
> —THOMAS ADY, *A Candle in the Dark*

Now I lay me down to sleep;
I pray the Lord my soul to keep.
If I should die before I wake,
I pray the Lord my soul to take.   —ANONYMOUS

From ghoulies and ghosties and long-leggety beasties
And things that go bump in the night,
Good Lord deliver us!   —ANONYMOUS

May the road rise to meet you,
May the wind be always at your back,
May the sun shine warm upon your face,
May the rain fall soft upon your fields,
And, until we meet again,
May God hold you in the palm of his hand.
> —ANONYMOUS IRISH BLESSING

O Lord! thou knowest how busy I must be this day;
if I forget thee, do not thou forget me.
> —SIR JACOB ASTY, prior to the Battle of Edgehill,
> quoted in Sir Philip Warwick, *Memoirs*

Give me chastity and continency, but not yet.
                    —St. Augustine, *Confessions*

The Lord bless thee, and keep thee:
    The Lord make his face shine upon thee, and be
gracious unto thee:
    The Lord lift up his countenance upon thee, and
give thee peace.   —Bible, *Numbers* 6:24–26

Out of the depths have I cried unto thee, O Lord.
                    —Bible, *Psalms* 130:1

Glory to God in the highest, and on earth peace,
good will toward men.   —Bible, *Luke* 2:14

As it was in the beginning, is now, and ever shall be;
world without end. Amen.
                    —Book of Common Prayer

Teach me, my God and king,
In all things thee to see;
And what I do in anything,
To do it as for thee.
    —George Herbert, *The Elixir*, in *The Temple*

And help us, this and every day,
To live more nearly as we pray.
                    —John Keble, *The Christian Year*

Would to God that we might spend a single day really
well.   —Thomas à Kempis, *Imitation of Christ*

Lord God of Hosts, be with us yet,
Lest we forget—lest we forget.
                    —Rudyard Kipling, *Recessional*

Sabrina fair,
Listen where thou art sitting
Under the glassy, cool, translucent wave,
In twisted braids of lilies knitting
The loose train of thy amber-dropping hair;
Listen for dear honor's sake,
Goddess of the silver lake,
Listen and save.   —John Milton, *Comus*

What in me is dark
Illumine, what is low raise and support;
That to the height of this great argument
I may assert eternal Providence,
And justify the ways of God to men.
　　　　　　　—JOHN MILTON, *Paradise Lost*

God, give us grace to accept with serenity the things that cannot be changed, courage to change the things which should be changed, and the wisdom to distinguish the one from the other.
　　　　　　　—REINHOLD NIEBUHR, *The Serenity Prayer*

Angels and ministers of grace defend us.
　　　　　　　—SHAKESPEARE, *Hamlet*, I, iv

Good night, sweet prince,
And flights of angels sing thee to thy rest.
　　　　　　　—*Ibid.*, V, ii

Mount, mount my soul! thy seat is up on high,
Whilst my gross flesh sinks downward, here to die.
　　　　　　　—SHAKESPEARE, *King Richard II*, V, v

Wild Spirit, which art moving everywhere;
Destroyer and preserver;
Hear, oh, hear!
　　—PERCY BYSSHE SHELLEY, *Ode to the West Wind*

PREJUDICE　　　　　　　See RACES & PEOPLES

PRESENT, THE　　　　See also MODERN TIMES; TIME

Take therefore no thought for the morrow: for the morrow shall take thought for the things of itself. Sufficient unto the day is the evil thereof.
　　　　　　　—BIBLE, *Matthew* 6:34

Happy the man, and happy he alone,
He, who can call today his own:

He who, secure within, can say,
Tomorrow do thy worst, for I have lived today.
                              —JOHN DRYDEN, *Imitation of Horace*

We want to live in the present, and the only history
that is worth a tinker's damn is the history we make
today.
          —HENRY FORD, *Chicago Tribune*, May 25, 1916

Every situation—no, every moment—is of infinite
worth; for it is the representative of a whole eternity.
          —GOETHE, quoted in Johann Peter Eckermann,
                Conversations with Goethe

Carpe diem, quam minimum credula a postero.
Seize the day, and put the least possible trust in tomorrow.   —HORACE, *Odes*

No mind is much employed upon the present; recollection and anticipation fill up almost all our moments.   —SAMUEL JOHNSON, *Rasselas*

Each day the world is born anew
For him who takes it rightly.
                              —JAMES RUSSELL LOWELL,
                                  Gold Egg: A Dream-Fantasy

Tomorrow's life is too late. Live today.
                              —MARTIAL, *Epigrams*

Each day provides its own gifts.   —*Ibid.*

The only living life is in the past and future—the
present is an interlude—strange interlude in which we
call on past and future to bear witness we are living.
                    —EUGENE O'NEILL, *Strange Interlude*

Let others praise ancient times. I am glad that I was
born in these.   —OVID, *Ars amatoria*

Past, and to come, seems best; things present, worst.
                    —SHAKESPEARE, *Henry IV, Part II*, I, iii

Do not say, "It is morning," and dismiss it with a name of yesterday. See it for the first time as a newborn child that has no name.
—RABINDRANATH TAGORE, *Stray Birds*

Life is all memory except for the one present moment that goes by so quick you can hardly catch it going.
—TENNESSEE WILLIAMS, *The Milk Train Doesn't Stop Here Anymore*

He who lives in the present lives in eternity.
—LUDWIG WITTGENSTEIN, *Tractatus logico-philosophicus*

PRESS, THE   See also CENSORSHIP; FREE SPEECH; MEDIA; NEWS

What the proprietorship of these newspapers is aiming at is power, and power without responsibility—the prerogative of the harlot through the ages.
—PRIME MINISTER STANLEY BALDWIN [referring to press barons Beaverbrook and Rothermere], quoted in D. Butler and A. Sloman, *British Political Facts*
[J. M. and M. J. Cohen in *The Penguin Dictionary of Modern Quotations* note that Lord Birkenhead, Kipling's biographer, credits Kipling with originating the key phrase here. Baldwin was Kipling's cousin.]

Publish, and conceal not.   —BIBLE, *Jeremiah* 50:2

When a dog bites a man, that is not news. But when a man bites a dog, that is news.
—JOHN B. BOGART, quoted in Frank M. O'Brien, *The Story of the Sun*
[Bogart was the city editor of *The New York Sun*. This quote may have originated with his boss, Charles Henry Dana.]

The pen is mightier than the sword.
—EDWARD GEORGE BULWER-LYTTON, *Richelieu*

A free press can, of course, be good or bad, but, most certainly without freedom, the press will never be anything but bad.
> —ALBERT CAMUS,
> *Resistance, Rebellion, and Death*

The duty of a newspaper is to comfort the afflicted and afflict the comfortable.
> —FINLEY PETER DUNNE, 1902

[The correct attribution of this often-quoted remark was discovered by Justin Kaplan, editor of the 1992 edition of *Bartlett's Familiar Quotations*.]

The press must be free; it has always been so and much evil has been corrected by it. If Government finds itself annoyed by it, let it examine its own conduct and it will find the cause.
> —LORD CHANCELLOR THOMAS ERSKINE,
> *Rex* v. *Paine*, 1792

Madame, we are the press. You know our power. We fix all values. We set all standards. Your entire future depends on us.
> —JEAN GIRAUDOUX, *The Madwoman of Chaillot*

You furnish the pictures and I'll furnish the war.
> —WILLIAM RANDOLPH HEARST,
> telegram allegedly sent to Frederic Remington on the eve of the Spanish-American War

[The story of this famous, but perhaps apocryphal telegram was told by reporter James Creelman. Hearst denied it.]

[Editor:] A person employed on a newspaper, whose business it is to separate the wheat from the chaff, and to see that the chaff is printed.
> —ELBERT HUBBARD,
> *Roycroft Dictionary and Book of Epigrams*

Our liberty depends on the freedom of the press, and that cannot be limited without being lost.
> —THOMAS JEFFERSON,
> letter to James Currie, 1786

Were it left to me to decide whether we should have a government without newspapers, or newspapers without a government, I should not hesitate a moment to prefer the latter.   —THOMAS JEFFERSON, letter to
                        Colonel Edward Carrington,
                        June 16, 1787

If the myth gets bigger than the man, print the myth.
                —DOROTHY JOHNSON,
                        The Man Who Shot Liberty Valance
[Johnson's story was adapted for the movie by James Warner Bellan and Willis Goldbeck.]

Why should any man be allowed to buy a printing press and disseminate pernicious opinions calculated to embarrass the government?
                —V. I. LENIN, speech, Moscow, 1920

Freedom of the press is guaranted only to those who own one.
—A. J. LIEBLING, "Do You Belong in Journalism?"
   The New Yorker, May 14, 1960

The gallery in which the reporters sit has become a fourth estate of the realm.
                —THOMAS BABINGTON MACAULAY, "Hallam's
                        Constitutional History," in *Historical Essays*
[Often attributed to Edmund Burke, because of this passage from Thomas Carlyle's *Heroes and Hero-Worship*: "Burke said that there were three estates in Parliament; but in the reporters' gallery yonder, there sat a fourth estate more important far than them all." But the phrase has not been found in Burke, and Carlyle actually may have had Macaulay in mind. William Safire notes that the phrase was used earlier to refer to "the mob" and credits its application to the press to an 1821 essay by William Hazlitt.]

All I know is just what I read in the papers.
                —WILL ROGERS, saying used as a lead-in
                        to his routines

There aren't any embarrassing questions—only embarrassing answers.   —CARL ROWAN, saying

The difference between burlesque and the newspapers is that the former never pretended to be performing a public service by exposure.
—I. F. STONE, *I. F. Stone's Weekly*, Sept. 7, 1952

I don't care what the papers say about me as long as they spell my name right.
—"BIG TIM" SULLIVAN, attributed

The report of my death has been grossly exaggerated.
—MARK TWAIN, cable from London to the Associated Press, 1897

Possible? Is anything impossible? Read the newspapers.   —DUKE OF WELLINGTON,
quoted in *Words of Wellington*

Publish and be damned.
—DUKE OF WELLINGTON, attributed
[The woman threatening to publish Wellington's letters to her, and her own memoirs, was Harriette Wilson.]

In old days, men had the rack. Now they have the press.
—OSCAR WILDE,
The Soul of Man Under Socialism
[For a final negative view of journalism, see George Bernard Shaw at INSULTS & PUT-DOWNS.]

PRIDE & VANITY   See also AMBITION;
SELF-CONFIDENCE

It's a fine thing to rise above pride, but you must have pride in order to do so.
—GEORGES BERNANOS,
The Diary of a Country Priest

The Lord will destroy the house of the proud.
—BIBLE, *Proverbs* 15:25

Pride goeth before destruction, and an haughty spirit before a fall.   —BIBLE, *Proverbs* 16:18

Vanity of vanities, saith the Preacher, vanity of vanities; all is vanity.   —BIBLE, *Ecclesiastes* 1:2

Half of the harm that is done in this world
Is due to people who want to feel important.
—T. S. ELIOT, *The Cocktail Party*

Pride ruined the angels.
—RALPH WALDO EMERSON, *The Sphinx*

Who does not detest a haughty man?
—EURIPIDES, *Hippolytus*

Pride is said to be the last vice the good man gets clear of.
—BENJAMIN FRANKLIN, *Poor Richard's Almanac*

I'm the straw that stirs the drink.
—REGGIE JACKSON, saying

Vanity is the greatest of all flatterers.
—LA ROCHEFOUCAULD, *Maxims*

The most violent passions sometimes leave us at rest, but vanity agitates us constantly.   —*Ibid.*

I never wanted to be a crumb. If I had to be a crumb, I'd rather be dead.
—SALVATORE "LUCKY" LUCIANO,
quoted in Richard Norton Smith,
Thomas E. Dewey

Better to reign in hell than serve in heaven.
—JOHN MILTON, *Paradise Lost*

For he will never follow anything
That other men begin.
—SHAKESPEARE, *Julius Caesar*, II, i

He that is proud eats up himself.
                    —SHAKESPEARE, *Troilus and Cressida*

Nobody holds a good opinion of a man who has a low opinion of himself.
                    —ANTHONY TROLLOPE, *Orley Farm*

Vanity is only being sensitive to what other people probably think of us.
                    —PAUL VALÉRY, *Mauvaises pensées*

I have nothing to declare except my genius.
                    —OSCAR WILDE, remark at the
                    New York Customs House,
                    quoted in F. Harris, *Oscar Wilde*

PRINCES   See HIGH POSITION:
                    RULERS & LEADERS

PRINCIPLES   See ETHICS & MORALITY;
                    IDEAS & IDEALS

PRISONS   See PUNISHMENT

PRIVACY   See also SOLITUDE

The right to be let alone—The most comprehensive of rights and the most valued by civilized men.
                    —JUSTICE LOUIS D. BRANDEIS,
                    Olmstead v. *the U.S.*
[For another observation on civilization and privacy, see Ayn Rand at CIVILIZATION.

"If everybody minded their own business," said the Duchess in a hoarse growl, "the world would go round a deal faster than it does."
                    —LEWIS CARROLL,
                    Alice's Adventures in Wonderland

A man's house is his castle.
                    —SIR EDWARD COKE, *Institutes*
[Americans may be more familiar with the statement by James Otis; see below.]

The saint and poet seek privacy.
>—RALPH WALDO EMERSON, *Culture*

One of the most essential branches of English liberty is the freedom of one's house. A man's house is his castle; and whilst he is quiet, he is as well guarded as a prince in his castle.
>—JAMES OTIS, argument on the
>Writs of Assistance, Boston, 1761

[See also Coke, above.]

PROBLEMS   See TROUBLE

PROCRASTINATION   See also TIME

Never do today what you can do as well tomorrow.
>—AARON BURR, quoted in James Parton,
>*Life and Times of Aaron Burr*

[See Rands, below, for a British variant.]

Delay always breeds anger, and to protract a great design is often to ruin it.
>—CERVANTES, *Don Quixote*

No idleness, no laziness, no procrastination; never put off till tomorrow what you can do today.
>—EARL OF CHESTERFIELD, letter to his son,
>Dec. 26, 1749

[This intolerable piece of advice is at least as old as Hesiod; see below. For the relationship between murder and procrastination, see De Quincey under CRIME.]

Don't put things off till tomorrow or the day after!
>—HESIOD, *Works and Days*

Delay is preferable to error.
>—THOMAS JEFFERSON, letter to
>George Washington,
>May 16, 1792

The time to repair the roof is when the sun is shining.
>—JOHN F. KENNEDY,
>State of the Union address, 1962

Never do today what you can
Put off till tomorrow.
                —WILLIAM BRIGHTY RANDS, *Lilliput Levee*
[The witticism has occurred to many. We also cite
Aaron Burr, above.]

Delays have dangerous ends.
                —SHAKESPEARE, *Henry VI, Part I*, III, ii

He who hesitates is sometimes saved.
                —JAMES THURBER, "The Glass in the Field," in
                The Thurber Carnival

Procrastination is the thief of time.
                —EDWARD YOUNG, *Night Thoughts*

PROGRESS   See also CHANGE; CIVILIZATION;
        FUTURE, THE; MODERN TIMES; TECHNOLOGY

Quo vadis?
Whither goest thou?
[The Latin is in the Vulgate version.]
                —BIBLE, *John* 16:5

Progress, man's distinctive mark alone,
Not God's and not the beasts'.
                —ROBERT BROWNING, *A Death in the Desert*

Progress is
The law of life, man is not man as yet.
                —ROBERT BROWNING, *Paracelsus*

The march of the human mind is slow.
                —EDMUND BURKE, speech, March 22, 1775

All progress is based upon a universal innate desire
of every organism to live beyond its means.
                —SAMUEL BUTLER, *Notebooks*

Change is certain. Progress is not.
                —E. H. CARR, *From Napoleon to Stalin,
                and Other Essays*

As natural selection works solely by and for the good of each being, all corporeal and mental endowments will tend to progress toward perfection.
—CHARLES DARWIN, *The Origin of Species*

All that is human must retrograde if it does not advance.   —EDWARD GIBBON,
Decline and Fall of the Roman Empire

We still dream what Adam dreamt.
—VICTOR HUGO, *Horror*

All progress is precarious, and the solution of one problem brings us face to face with another problem.
—MARTIN LUTHER KING, JR., *Strength to Love*

Is it progress if a cannibal uses a fork?
—STANISLAW J. LEC, *Unkempt Thoughts*

Human progress is furthered, not by conformity, but by aberration.
—H. L. MENCKEN, *Prejudices: Third Series*

The desire to understand the world and the desire to reform it are the two great engines of progress.
—BERTRAND RUSSELL, *Marriage and Morals*

All progress means war with society.
—GEORGE BERNARD SHAW, *Getting Married*

Progress, therefore, is not an accident, but a necessity. . . . It is a part of nature.
—HERBERT SPENCER, *Social Statics*

Yet I doubt not through the ages one increasing purpose runs,
And the thoughts of men are widened,
With the process of the suns.
—ALFRED, LORD TENNYSON, *Locksley Hall*

Progress imposes not only new possibilities for the future but new restrictions.
—NORBERT WIENER,
The Human Use of Human Beings

PROPERTY   See CAPITALISM;
                        THINGS & POSSESSIONS

PROPHETS   See VISION & VISIONARIES

PROVERBS   See QUOTATIONS,
                        MAXIMS, & PROVERBS

PROVIDENCE, DIVINE

The Lord is my shepherd; I shall not want.

He maketh me to lie down in green pastures; he leadeth me beside the still waters.

He restoreth my soul: he leadeth me in the paths of righteousness for his name's sake,

Yea, though I walk through the valley of the shadow of death, I will fear no evil: for thou art with me; thy rod and thy staff they comfort me.

Thou preparest a table before me in the presence of mine enemies: thou anointest my head with oil; my cup runneth over.

Surely goodness and mercy shall follow me all the days of my life: and I will dwell in the house of the Lord forever.   —BIBLE, *Psalms* 23

For he shall give his angels charge over thee, to keep thee in all thy ways.

They shall bear thee up in their hands, lest thou dash thy foot against a stone.   —*Ibid.*, 91:11–12

The Lord shall preserve thy going out and thy coming in.   —*Ibid.*, 121:8

We degrade Providence too much by attributing our ideas to it out of annoyance at being unable to understand it.   —FEODOR DOSTOEVSKI, *The Idiot*

Know from the bounteous heaven all riches flow.
                        —HOMER, *Odyssey*

**PRUDENCE &
PRACTICAL WISDOM**

Don't count your chickens before they are hatched.
—AESOP, *The Milkmaid and Her Pail*

Slow and steady wins the race.
—AESOP, *The Hare and the Tortoise*

Never eat at a place called Mom's. Never play cards
with a man named Doc. And never lie down with a
woman who's got more troubles than you.
—NELSON ALGREN,
What Every Young Man Should Know
[Algren credited "a Negro lady" with formulating these
words of wisdom.]

One swallow does not make a spring.
—ARISTOTLE, *Nicomachean Ethics*

Prudence is a rich, ugly old maid courted by
Incapacity. —WILLIAM BLAKE,
The Marriage of Heaven and Hell

A wise man does not trust all his eggs to one basket.
—CERVANTES, *Don Quixote*
[But see Mark Twain, below.]

The cautious seldom err. —CONFUCIUS,
Analects

Trust everybody, but cut the cards.
—FINLEY PETER DUNNE,
Mr. Dooley's Philosophy

You have the world before you. Stoop as you go
through it, and you will miss many hard thumps.
—COTTON MATHER,
advice given to Benjamin Franklin
[Franklin, writing to his son on May 12, 1784, revealed
that Mather had given him this valuable advice in a
farewell visit 60 years earlier.]

You will go most safely in the middle.
>—OVID, *Metamorphoses*

Be not the first by whom the new are tried,
Nor yet the last to lay the old aside.
>—ALEXANDER POPE, *An Essay on Criticism*

Be wisely worldly, be not worldly wise.
>—FRANCIS QUARLES, *Emblems*

If you want to get along, go along.
>—[Speaker of the House] SAM RAYBURN, saying

The better part of valor is discretion.
>—SHAKESPEARE, *Henry IV, Part I*, V, iv

Moderation in all things.   —TERENCE, *Andria*

Put all your eggs in one basket—and watch that basket.
>—MARK TWAIN, "Pudd'nhead Wilson's Calendar"
>in *Pudd'nhead Wilson*
[Cf. Cervantes, above.]

Common sense is not so common.
>—VOLTAIRE, *Dictionnaire philosophique*,
>"Self-Love"

PUBLIC, THE   See PEOPLE, THE

PUBLIC OFFICE   See GOVERNMENT; HIGH POSITION:
>RULERS & LEADERS; POLITICS

PUBLICITY &   See also ADVERTISING
PUBLIC RELATIONS

You must stir it and stump it,
And blow your own trumpet,
Or trust me, you haven't a chance.
>—W. S. GILBERT, *Ruddigore*

The art of publicity is a black art; but has come to stay, and every year adds to its potency.
>—LEARNED HAND, address at the
>Elizabethan Club, May 1951

[For another, more lighthearted comment on the power of publicity and advertising, see Joseph Levine's update of Abraham Lincoln's assessment of the possibility of fooling all of the people—given at PEOPLE under Lincoln.]

It is most expedient for the wise . . . to be the trumpet of his own virtues.
—SHAKESPEARE,
Much Ado About Nothing, V, ii

PUBLISHING   See BOOKS & READING;
MEDIA; PRESS, THE

PUNISHMENT   See also JUSTICE;
REVENGE

Eye for eye, tooth for tooth, hand for hand, foot for foot. Burning for burning, wound for wound, stripe for stripe.   —BIBLE, *Exodus* 21:24–25

Let the punishment match the offense.
—CICERO, *De legibus*

To punish and not prevent is to labor at the pump and leave open the leak.
—THOMAS FULLER, *Gnomologia*

If a man destroy the eye of another man, they shall destroy his eye.   —CODE OF HAMMURABI

Distrust all in whom the impulse to punish is powerful.
—FRIEDRICH NIETZSCHE, *Thus Spake Zarathustra*

Punishment brings wisdom. It is the healing art of wickedness.   —PLATO, *Gorgias*

Frequent punishments are always a sign of weakness or laziness on the part of the government.
—JEAN JACQUES ROUSSEAU,
The Social Contract

The reformative effect of punishment is a belief that dies hard, chiefly I think, because it is so satisfying to our sadistic impulses.

—BERTRAND RUSSELL,
Ideas That Have Harmed Mankind

While we have prisons, it matters little which of us occupy the cells.

—GEORGE BERNARD SHAW, *Man and Superman*,
"Maxims for Revolutionists"

I am all for bringing back the birch but only between consenting adults.

—GORE VIDAL, television interview
with David Frost

The vilest deeds like poison weeds
Bloom well in prison air:
It is only what is good in man
That wastes and withers there.

—OSCAR WILDE, *The Ballad of Reading Gaol*

Q

QUESTIONS & ANSWERS

A sudden, bold, and unexpected question doth many times surprise a man and lay him open.
—FRANCIS BACON, *Of Cunning*

The answer, my friend, is blowin' in the wind.
—BOB DYLAN, *Blowin' in the Wind*

More trouble is caused in this world by indiscreet answers than by indiscreet questions.
—SYDNEY J. HARRIS, *Chicago Daily News*, Mar. 27, 1958
[A saying sometimes used by the press in defense of probing questions. See the similar Carl Rowan quote at PRESS, THE.]

All clues, no solutions. That's the way things are.
—DENNIS POTTER, *The Singing Detective*

Be patient toward all that is unsolved in your heart. Try to love the questions themselves.
—RAINER MARIA RILKE, letter to Franz Xaver Kappus, July 16, 1903.
[The full final sentence is: "Try to love the questions themselves like locked rooms and like books in a very foreign language."]

QUOTATIONS, MAXIMS, & PROVERBS

A proverb is the child of experience.
—ANONYMOUS (ENGLISH PROVERB)

The maxims of men disclose their hearts.
—ANONYMOUS (FRENCH PROVERB)

Despise not the discoveries of the wise, but acquaint
thyself with their proverbs.
—BIBLE, *Ecclesiasticus* 8:8

It is a good thing for an uneducated man to read
books of quotations.
—WINSTON CHURCHILL, "Roving Commission,"
in *My Early Life*

Proverbs are the sanctuary of the intuitions.
—RALPH WALDO EMERSON, *Compensation*

Next to the originator of a good sentence is the first
quoter of it.   —RALPH WALDO EMERSON,
Quotation and Originality

I hate quotations, tell me what you know.
—RALPH WALDO EMERSON,
Journal, Dec. 20, 1822

A book that furnishes no quotations is, *me judice*, no
book—it is a plaything.
—THOMAS LOVE PEACOCK, *Crochet Castle*

Some, for renown, on scraps of learning dote,
And think they grow immortal as they quote.
—EDWARD YOUNG, *Love of Fame*

R

The most certain test by which we judge whether a country is really free is the amount of security enjoyed by minorities.
> —LORD ACTON,
> *The History of Freedom in Antiquity*

The Pilgrim Fathers landed on the shores of America and fell upon their knees. Then they fell upon the aborigines.
> —ANONYMOUS, cited in H. L. Mencken,
> *A New Dictionary of Quotations*

Am I not a man and a brother?
> —ANONYMOUS, inscription on the seal of the
> Antislavery Society of London, c. 1770

We shall overcome, we shall overcome,
We shall overcome some day.
Oh, deep in my heart, I do believe
We shall overcome some day.
> —ANONYMOUS, song associated with
> the Civil Rights movement of the 1960s,
> adapted from a Baptist hymm

Black is beautiful.
> —ANONYMOUS, slogan, ca. 1967

[Cf. *The Song of Solomon*, Douay version 1:5, "I am black but beautiful."]

If we do not now dare everything, the fulfillment of that prophecy, recreated from the Bible in song by a slave, is upon us:

God gave Noah the rainbow sign,
No more water, the fire next time!
—JAMES BALDWIN, *The Fire Next Time*

It is not healthy when a nation lives within a nation, as colored Americans are living inside America. A nation cannot live confident of its tomorrow if its refugees are among its own citizens.
—PEARL S. BUCK, *What America Means to Me*

Yes, I am a Jew, and when the ancestors of the right honorable gentleman were brutal savages in an unknown island, mine were priests in the temple of Solomon. —BENJAMIN DISRAELI, reply to
Daniel O'Connell, in the
House of Commons

The destiny of the colored American . . . is the destiny of America.
—FREDERICK DOUGLASS, speech, Feb. 12, 1862

To be a poor man is hard, but to be a poor race in a land of dollars is the very bottom of hardships.
—W. E. B. DU BOIS, *The Souls of Black Folk*

However painful it may be for me to accept this conclusion, I am obliged to state it: for the black man there is only one destiny. And it is white.
—FRANTZ FANON, *Black Skin, White Masks*

Death is a slave's freedom.
—NIKKI GIOVANNI, speech at the funeral of
Martin Luther King, Jr.

The American economy, the American society, the American unconscious are all racist.
—MICHAEL HARRINGTON, *The Other America*

I swear to the Lord
I still can't see

Why democracy means
Everybody but me.
>—LANGSTON HUGHES, *The Black Man Speaks*

Among the thousand white persons, I am a dark rock
surged upon, and overswept.
>—ZORA NEALE HURSTON, *Mules and Men*

We will not be satisfied until justice rolls down like
waters and righteousness like a mighty stream.
>—MARTIN LUTHER KING, JR., speech,
>June 15, 1963

[Based on *Amos* 5:24, See under JUSTICE.]

You're a better man than I am, Gunga Din!
>—RUDYARD KIPLING, *Gunga Din*

All I ask for the Negro is that if you do not like him,
let him alone. If God gave him but little, that little let
him enjoy.
>—ABRAHAM LINCOLN, speech, July 17, 1858

We didn't land on Plymouth Rock. Plymouth Rock
landed on us.
>—MALCOLM X, saying,
>quoted in the 1992 movie *Malcolm X.*

A foreigner scarcely counts as a human being for
someone of another race.
>—PLINY, *Natural History*

No democracy can long survive which does not accept
as fundamental to its very existence the recognition of
the rights of minorities.
>—FRANKLIN D. ROOSEVELT,
>letter to the NAACP,
>June 25, 1938

We don't have to be what you want us to be.
>—BILL RUSSELL, quoted by George Vecsey,
>*The New York Times*, 1985

When the last red man shall have become a myth
among the white man ... when your children's children
think themselves alone in the fields or the pathless

woods, they will not be alone . . . your lands will throng
with the returning hosts that once filled them and still
love this beautiful land. The white man will never be
alone.   —SEATTLE, quoted in Joseph Epes Brown,
                    The Spiritual Legacy of the
                    American Indian

[This is from a speech by Seattle, probably given in the
Salish dialect in 1854. A translation by Dr. Henry Smith
was published in 1887. Since then, Seattle's comments
have been richly embroidered. The 1971 film *Home*
transformed the speech into an ecological manifesto.]

Hath not a Jew eyes? Hath not a Jew hands, organs,
dimensions, senses, affections, passions? Fed with the
same food, hurt with the same weapons, subject to the
same diseases, healed by the same means, warmed and
cooled by the same winter and summer as a Christian
is? If you prick us, do we not bleed? If you tickle us,
do we not laugh? If you poison us, do we not die? And
if you wrong us, shall we not revenge?
        —SHAKESPEARE, *The Merchant of Venice*, III, i

"Do you know who made you?" "Nobody, as I knows
on," said the child, with a short laugh. . . . "I 'spect I
grow'd. Don't think nobody never made me."
        —HARRIET BEECHER STOWE, *Uncle Tom's Cabin*

The danger of a conflict between the white and the
black inhabitants perpetually haunts the imagination of
the Americans like a bad dream.
                    —ALEXIS DE TOCQUEVILLE,
                        Democracy in America

We have ground the manhood out of them, and the
shame is ours not theirs, and we should pay for it.
        —MARK TWAIN, letter to Francis Wayland,
            Dean of the Yale Law School,
            offering to pay the tuition and board
            of a black student

Segregation now . . . Segregation tomorrow . . . Segregation forever.
                —GEORGE WALLACE, inaugural speech
                    on becoming governor of Alabama, 1963

[The lines were apparently written by Asa Earl Carter, a right-wing extremist, who under the pseudonym Forrest Carter was responsible for the well-received, politically correct memoirs of an Indian named Little Tree.]

The slave system on our place, in large measure, took the spirit of self-reliance and self-help out of the white people.
> —BOOKER T. WASHINGTON, *Up from Slavery*

J'accuse.
I accuse you.
> —ÉMILE ZOLA, title of a letter to the
> president of the French Republic, accusing the
> government of wrongdoing in the
> Dreyfus case, published Jan. 13, 1898

RAIN   See NATURE: SEASONS;
                              NATURE: WIND & WEATHER

RAINBOW   See NATURE: THE HEAVENS,
                                          THE SKY

REALITY & ILLUSIONS

Every age is fed on illusions, lest men should renounce life early and the human race come to an end.
> —JOSEPH CONRAD, *Victory*

Between the idea and the reality
Between the motion and the act
Falls the Shadow.
> —T. S. ELIOT, *The Hollow Men*

[William Safire, in his column on language, May 12, 1991, pointed out that Eliot here drew on Ernest Dowson's "There fell thy shadow, Cynara!" See also Dowson and Cynara under WOMEN & MEN.]

Humankind
Cannot bear very much reality.
> —T. S. ELIOT, *Murder in the Cathedral*

We live in a fantasy world, a world of illusion. The great task in life is to find reality.
—IRIS MURDOCH, quoted by Rachel Billington, interview in *The Times*, London, April 15, 1983

Reality is a staircase going neither up nor down; we don't move, today is today, always is today.
—OCTAVIO PAZ, *The Endless Instant*

All that we see or seem
Is but a dream within a dream.
—EDGAR ALLAN POE, *A Dream Within a Dream*

In the American metaphysic, reality is always material reality, hard, resistant, unformed, impenetrable, unpleasant.
—LIONEL TRILLING, "Reality," in *The Liberal Imagination*

REASON & REASONS   See also MIND, THOUGHT, & UNDERSTANDING; PHILOSOPHY; REASONABLE & UNREASONABLE PEOPLE

Come now, and let us reason together.
—BIBLE, *Isaiah* 1:18
[A favorite saying of President Lyndon B. Johnson.]

Let reason go before every enterprise, and counsel before every action.   —BIBLE, *Ecclesiasticus* 37:16

Reason is the ruler and queen of all things.
—CICERO, *Tusulanae disputationes*

If everything on earth were rational, nothing would happen.
—FEODOR DOSTOEVSKI, *The Brothers Karamazov*

Reason can wrestle and overthrow terror.
—EURIPIDES, *Iphigenia in Aulis*

The sleep of reason begets monsters.
—GOYA, motto for the intended frontispiece of his 1799 graphic series, the *Caprichos*

In this world there is one terrible thing, and that is that everyone has his reasons.
　　　　—JEAN RENOIR, *The Rules of the Game*

Tout par raison.
Everything according to reason.
　　　　—CARDINAL RICHELIEU, *Mirame*

There is occasions and causes why and wherefore in all things.　　　—SHAKESPEARE, *Henry V*, V, i
[Also, "Every why hath a wherefore," *The Comedy of Errors*, II, ii.]

Reason is God's crowning gift to man.
　　　　—SOPHOCLES, *Antigone*

Passion and prejudice govern the world; only under the name of reason.
　　　　—JOHN WESLEY, letter to Joseph Benson, Oct. 5, 1770

REASONABLE &　　　See also MIND, THOUGHT, &
UNREASONABLE PEOPLE　　　UNDERSTANDING;
　　　　　　　　　　　　REASON & REASONS

When a man begins to reason, he ceases to feel.
　　　　—ANONYMOUS (FRENCH PROVERB)

Falling in love is one of the activities forbidden that tiresome person, the consistently reasonable man.
　　　　—SIR ARTHUR EDDINGTON, *News Chronicle*, London, March 2, 1932

Who reasons wisely is not therefore wise;
His pride in reasoning, not in acting, lies.
　　　　—ALEXANDER POPE, *Moral Essays*

Pure logic is the ruin of the spirit.
　　　　—ANTOINE DE SAINT-EXUPÉRY, *Flight to Arras*

The reasonable man adapts himself to the world; the unreasonable one persists in trying to adapt the world to himself. Therefore all progress depends on the unreasonable man.
　　　　—GEORGE BERNARD SHAW, *Man and Superman*, "Maxims for Revolutionists"

A mind all logic is like a knife all blade. It makes the hand bleed that uses it.

—RABINDRANATH TAGORE, *Stray Birds*

REGRET   See also PAST, THE

If you board the wrong train, it is no use running along the corridor in the other direction.

—DIETRICH BONHOEFFER, *The Way to Freedom*

We have left undone those things which we ought to have done; and we have done those things which we ought not to have done; and there is no health in us.

—BOOK OF COMMON PRAYER

Of all the horrid, hideous notes of woe,
Sadder than owl songs or the midnight blast,
Is that portentous phrase, "I told you so."

—LORD BYRON, *Don Juan*

Footfalls echo in the memory
Down the passage which we did not take
Towards the door we never opened
Into the rosegarden.

—T. S. ELIOT, "Burnt Norton," in *Four Quartets*

I shall be telling this with a sigh
Somewhere ages and ages hence:
Two roads diverged in a wood, and I—
I took the one less traveled by,
And that has made all the difference.

—ROBERT FROST, *The Road Not Taken*

God has little patience with remorse.

—MALCOLM LOWRY, *Under the Volcano*

When I am dead and opened, you shall find "Calais" written on my heart.

—MARY I, quoted in Holinshed's *Chronicles*
[In some versions, it is "Philip and Calais" that is written.]

Why should I mourn at the untimely fate of my people? Tribe follows tribe, and nation follows nation, and regret is useless.
>—SEATTLE, quoted in Joseph Epes Brown,
>*The Spiritual Legacy of the
>American Indian*

What's done is done.
>—SHAKESPEARE, *Macbeth*, III, ii

Oh, call back yesterday, bid time return.
>—SHAKESPEARE, *Richard II*, III, ii

What's gone and what's past help
Should be past grief.
>—SHAKESPEARE, *The Winter's Tale*, III, ii

To regret deeply is to live afresh.
>—HENRY DAVID THOREAU,
>*Journal*, Nov. 13, 1839

For of all sad words of tongue or pen,
The saddest are these: "It might have been!"
>—JOHN GREENLEAF WHITTIER, *Maud Muller*

RELIGION See also ATHEISM; FAITH; GOD; MYSTICISM; PRAYER; SELF-RIGHTEOUSNESS

Man doth not live by bread only, but by every word that proceedeth out of the mouth of the Lord doth man live. —BIBLE, *Deuteronomy* 8:3 [Also *Matthew* 4:4: "Man shall not live by bread alone . . ."—and *Luke* 4:4.]

I am holier than thou. —BIBLE, *Isaiah* 65:5 [More, with a note, at SELF-RIGHTEOUSNESS.]

No man can serve two masters.
>—BIBLE, *Matthew* 6:24

Ye cannot serve God and mammon. —*Ibid.*

Thou art Peter, and upon this rock I will build my church; and the gates of hell shall not prevail against it.   —*Ibid.*, 16:18

Heathen, n. A benighted creature who has the folly to worship something that he can see and feel.
                              —AMBROSE BIERCE,
                                   The Devil's Dictionary

To die for a religion is easier than to live it absolutely.
                              —JORGE LUIS BORGES,
                                   "Deutsches Requiem," in *Labyrinths*

How very hard it is
To be a Christian!
                              —ROBERT BROWNING, *Easter-Day*

Every day, people are straying away from the church and going back to God.
                              —LENNY BRUCE, *The Essential Lenny Bruce*

This Ariyan Eightfold Path, that is to say: Right view, right aim, right speech, right action, right living, right effort, right mindfulness, right contemplation.
                              —BUDDHA, from F. L. Woodward,
                                   Some Sayings of the Buddha

One religion is as true as another.
                              —ROBERT BURTON,
                                   The Anatomy of Melancholy

Wonder is the basis of worship.
                              —THOMAS CARLYLE, *Sartor Resartus*

Religion is by no means a proper subject of conversation in mixed company.
                              —EARL OF CHESTERFIELD, letter to his godson,
                              #112, undated

The Christian ideal has not been tried and found wanting. It has been found difficult; and left untried.
                              —G. K. CHESTERTON,
                                   What's Wrong with the World

The all-male religions have produced no religious imagery. . . . The great religious art of the world is deeply involved with the female principle.
—SIR KENNETH CLARK, *Civilization*

In my religion, there would be no exclusive doctrine; all would be love, poetry, and doubt.
—CYRIL CONNOLLY, *The Unquiet Grave*

Science without religion is lame; religion without science is blind.   —ALBERT EINSTEIN, quoted in
The Reader's Digest, Nov. 1973

I like the silent church before the service begins, better than any preaching.
—RALPH WALDO EMERSON, *Self-Reliance*

God builds his temple in the heart on the ruins of churches and religions.
—RALPH WALDO EMERSON, *Worship*

Religion is an illusion and it derives its strength from the fact that it falls in with our instinctual desires.
—FREUD, "A Philosophy of Life," in
Lectures in Psychoanalysis

The Bible shows the way to go to heaven, not the way the heavens go.   —GALILEO, fragment

All religions are ancient monuments to superstitions, ignorance, ferocity; and modern religions are only ancient follies rejuvenated.
—BARON D' HOLBACH, *Le Bon Sens* . . .

Writing for a penny a word is ridiculous. If a man really wants to make a million dollars, the best way would be to start his own religion.
—L. RONALD HUBBARD, founder
of Scientology, 1949 lecture, quoted in
The New York Times, July 11, 1984

I am for religion, against religions.
—VICTOR HUGO, *Les Misérables*

Religion is a monumental chapter in the history of human egotism.
—WILLIAM JAMES,
The Varieties of Religious Experience

It does me no injury for my neighbor to say there are twenty Gods, or no God.   —THOMAS JEFFERSON,
*Notes on the State
of Virginia*

The church must be reminded that it is not the master or the servant of the state, but rather the conscience of the state.
—MARTIN LUTHER KING, JR., *Strength to Love*

Here I stand, I cannot do otherwise.
—MARTIN LUTHER, speech, Diet of Worms, 1521

Religion is the sign of the oppressed creature, the sentiment of a heartless world, and the soul of soulless conditions. It is the opium of the people.
—KARL MARX, *Criticism of Hegel's Philosophy
of Right*

What mean and cruel things men do for the love of God.
—W. SOMERSET MAUGHAM, *A Writer's Notebook*

We must respect the other fellow's religion, but only in the sense and to the extent that we respect his theory that his wife is beautiful and his children smart.
—H. L. MENCKEN, *Minority Report*

Fear of death and fear of life both become piety.
—*Ibid.*

A nation must have a religion, and that religion must be under the control of the government.
—NAPOLEON BONAPARTE, to Count Thibaudeau,
June 6, 1801

I want nothing to do with any religion concerned with keeping the masses satisfied to live in hunger, filth, and ignorance.
—JAWAHARLAL NEHRU, quoted in Edgar Snow,
Journey to the Beginning

Dogma has been the fundamental principle of my religion.... Religion, as mere sentiment, is to me a mockery,
> —CARDINAL NEWMAN, *Apologia pro Vita Sua*

Any system of religion that has anything in it that shocks the mind of a child, cannot be a true system.
> —THOMAS PAINE, *The Age of Reason*

Men despise religion; they hate it, and they fear it is true.
> —PASCAL, *Pensées*

Religion is so great a thing that it is right that those who will not take the trouble to seek it if it be obscure, should be deprived of it.
> —*Ibid.*

To be like Christ is to be a Christian.
> —WILLIAM PENN, last words

The world would be poorer without the antics of clergymen.
> —V. S. PRITCHETT, "The Dean," in *My Good Books*

Religion is something infinitely simple, ingenuous.... In the infinite extent of the universe, it is a direction of the heart.
> —RAINER MARIA RILKE, letter to Ilse Blumenthal-Weiss, Dec. 28, 1921

The Bible is literature, not dogman.
> —GEORGE SANTAYANA, *The Ethics of Spinoza*

Religion is the love of life in the consciousness of impotence.
> —GEORGE SANTAYANA, *Winds of Doctrine*

He worships God who knows him.
> —SENECA, *Letters to Lucilius*

The devil can cite Scripture for his purpose.
> —SHAKESPEARE, *The Merchant of Venice*, I, iii

There is only one religion though there are a hundred versions of it,
  —GEORGE BERNARD SHAW, *Arms and the Man*

How many divisions has the Pope?
      —STALIN, attributed

I never saw, heard, nor read that the clergy were beloved in any nation where Christianity was the religion of the country. Nothing can render them popular but some degree of persecution.
  —JONATHAN SWIFT, *Thoughts on Religion*

We have just enough religion to make us hate, but not enough to make us love one another.
  —JONATHAN SWIFT, *Thoughts on Various Subjects*

There is perhaps no greater hardship at present inflicted on mankind in civilized and free countries than the necessity of listening to sermons.
  —ANTHONY TROLLOPE, *Barchester Towers*

Quoi que vous fassiez, écrasez l'infâme, et aimez qui vous aime.
Whatever you do, crush this infamy, and love those who love you.
  —VOLTAIRE, letter to d'Alembert, Nov. 28, 1762
[The "infamy," or "infamous thing," is usually interpreted as referring to superstition.]

Orthodoxy is my doxy; heterodoxy is another man's doxy.   —WILLIAM WARBURTON, quoted in
      Joseph Priestley, *Memoirs*

Religion is love; in no case is it logic.
  —BEATRICE POTTER WEBB, *My Apprenticeship*

As society is now constituted, a literal adherence to the moral precepts scattered throughout the Gospels would mean sudden death.
  —ALFRED NORTH WHITEHEAD,
  Adventures of Ideas

And I could wish my days to be
Bound each to each by natural piety.
   —WILLIAM WORDSWORTH, *My Heart Leaps Up*

REMEDIES   See ILLNESS & REMEDIES;
QUESTIONS & ANSWERS; TROUBLE

REMORSE   See REGRET

REPENTANCE   See FORGIVENESS &
MERCY; REGRET

REPUTATION

A good name is rather to be chosen than great riches.
   —BIBLE, *Proverbs* 22:1

A good name endureth forever.
   —BIBLE, *Ecclesiasticus* 41:13

One who has a reputation for rising early can sleep
until noon.
   —ALPHONSE DAUDET, *Tartarin sur les Alpes*
[Probably proverbial. *Yiddish Proverbs*, edited by
Hanan J. Ayalti, includes the same observation.]

Reputation, like a face, is the symbol of its possessor
and creator, and another can use it only as a mask.
   —LEARNED HAND,
      Yale Electric Company v. *Robertson*
[A key case in trademark law, dating from 1928.]

The worst of me is known, and I can say that I am
better than my reputation.
   —J. C. F. VON SCHILLER, *Maria Stuart*

Good name in man and woman, dear my lord,
Is the immediate jewel of their souls.
   —SHAKESPEARE, *Othello*, III, iii

The purest treasure mortal times afford
Is spotless reputation.
—SHAKESPEARE, *Richard II*, I, i

If we disregard what the world says of someone, we
live to repent it.
—LOGAN PEARSALL SMITH, *All Trivia*

RESIGNATION   See also OBEDIENCE

Naked came I out of my mother's womb, and naked
shall I return thither: the Lord gave, and the Lord hath
taken away; blessed be the name of the Lord.
—BIBLE, *Job* 1:21

Teach us to care and not to care.
Teach us to sit still.
—T. S. ELIOT, *Ash Wednesday*

Better to accept whatever happens.
—HORACE, *Odes*

Hear me, my chiefs, I am tired; my heart is sick and
sad. From where the sun now stands, I will fight no
more forever.
—CHIEF JOSEPH, speech at the conclusion
of the Nez Percé War

A calm despair, without angry convulsion or re-
proaches directed to heaven, is the essence of wisdom.
—ALFRED DE VIGNY, *Journal d'un poète*

RESISTANCE   See APPEASEMENT VS. RESISTANCE;
COURAGE; REVOLUTION

RESPONSIBILITY   See also FATE; SELF;
SELF-RELIANCE

Everybody's business is nobody's business.
—ANONYMOUS
[Sometimes attributed to Lord Macaulay or Izaak
Walton, but evidently an ancient byword; see Aris-
totle, for example, on everybody's property, under
COMMUNISM.]

Every man is the architect of his own fortune.
>—APPIUS CLAUDIUS CAECUS,
>quoted in Sallust, *De civitate*

Am I my brother's keeper?
>—BIBLE, *Genesis* 4:9

Unto whomsoever much is given, of him shall be much required. —BIBLE, *Luke* 12:48

You're either part of the solution or part of the problem.
>—ELDRIDGE CLEAVER

[A common saying of the time. *Bartlett's* attributes it to Cleaver from 1968.]

When your neighbor's wall is on fire, it becomes your business. —HORACE, *Epistles*

Our privileges can be no greater than our obligations. The protection of our rights can endure no longer than the performance of our responsibilities.
>—JOHN F. KENNEDY, speech, May 18, 1963

I believe that every right implies a responsibility; every opportunity, an obligation; every possession, a duty.
>—JOHN D. ROCKEFELLER, speech, July 8, 1941

To be a man is, precisely, to be responsible.
>—ANTOINE DE SAINT-EXUPÉRY,
>*Wind, Sand, and Stars*

The fault, dear Brutus, is not in our stars,
But in ourselves, that we are underlings.
>—SHAKESPEARE, *Julius Caesar*, I, ii

The buck stops here.
>—HARRY S TRUMAN, handwritten sign
>on his White House desk

REST See LEISURE; SLEEP & DREAMS

REVENGE   See also JUSTICE; PUNISHMENT

Revenge is a dish that should be eaten cold.
                    —ANONYMOUS (ENGLISH PROVERB)

Men regard it as their right to return evil for evil—
and if they cannot, feel they have lost their liberty.
                    —ARISTOTLE, *Nicomachean Ethics*

In taking revenge, a man is but even with his enemy;
but in passing it over, he is superior.
                    —FRANCIS BACON, *Of Revenge*

A man that studieth revenge keeps his own wounds
green, which otherwise would heal and do well.
                                        —*Ibid.*

Thou shalt not avenge.   —BIBLE, *Leviticus* 19:18

Vengeance is mine; I will repay, saith the Lord.
                    —BIBLE, *Romans* 12:19

Living well is the best revenge.
                    —GEORGE HERBERT, *Jacula Prudentum*

Revenge is the poor delight of little minds.
                    —JUVENAL, *Satires*

REVOLUTION   See also APPEASEMENT VS.
                    RESISTANCE; TURBULENT TIMES;
                            VIOLENCE & FORCE

I came not to send peace, but a sword.
                    —BIBLE, *Matthew* 10:34

Revolutions are not made with rosewater.
                    —EDWARD GEORGE BULWER-LYTTON,
                    The Parisians

In the groves of *their* academy, at the end of every
walk, you see nothing but the gallows.
                    —EDMUND BURKE,
                    Reflections on the French Revolution

Lay the proud usurpers low!
Tyrants fall in every foe!
Liberty's in every blow!
Let us do or die!
                    —ROBERT BURNS, *Scots Wha Hae*

What is a rebel? A man who says no.
                    —ALBERT CAMUS, *The Rebel*

All modern revolutions have ended in a reinforcement of the power of the state.   —*Ibid.*

The revolutionary spirit is mighty convenient in this, that it frees one from all scruples as regards ideas.
                    —JOSEPH CONRAD, *A Personal Record*

The blow by which kings fall causes a long bleeding.
                    —PIERRE CORNEILLE, *Cinna*

Plots true or false are necessary things,
To raise up commonwealths and ruin kings.
                    —JOHN DRYDEN, *Absalom and Achitophel*

When you strike at a king, you must kill him.
                    —RALPH WALDO EMERSON, attributed
[*Bartlett's* traces this to a recollection of Oliver Wendell Holmes, Jr., quoted in Max Lerner, *The Mind and Faith of Justice Holmes*.]

Desperate diseases require desperate remedies.
                    —GUY FAWKES, attributed in connection with the Gunpowder Plot
[Cf. Shakespeare, below.]

A great revolution is never the fault of the people, but of the government.
                    —GOETHE, quoted in Johann Peter Eckermann, *Conversations with Goethe*

What happens to a dream deferred?
Does it dry up
Like a raisin in the sun? . . .
Or does it explode?
                    —LANGSTON HUGHES, *Harlem*

Fire in the lake: the image of revolution.
—I CHING,
Book I

The tree of liberty must be refreshed from time to time with the blood of patriots and tyrants. It is its natural manure.
—THOMAS JEFFERSON, letter to
Col. William S. Smith, Nov. 13, 1787

If you feed the people just with revolutionary slogans, they will listen today, they will listen tomorrow, they will listen the day after tomorrow, but on the fourth day, they will say "To hell with you."
—NIKITA KHRUSHCHEV, quoted in
The New York Times,
Oct. 4, 1964

When smashing monuments, save the pedestals— they always come in handy.   —STANISLAW J. LEC,
Unkempt Thoughts

Inciting to revolution is treason, not only against man, but also against God.
—POPE LEO XIII, *Immortale Dei*

Revolution is the proper occupation of the masses.
—MAO ZEDUNG, quoted in Dennis Bloodworth,
The Messiah and the Mandarins

The workers have nothing to lose in this but their chains. They have a world to gain. Workers of the world, unite!
—KARL MARX and FRIEDRICH ENGELS,
The Communist Manifesto

In revolutions everything is forgotten. . . . Gratitude, friendship, parentage; every tie vanishes, and all that is sought is self-interest.
—NAPOLEON BONAPARTE, quoted in
Barry E. O'Meara, *Napoleon at St. Helena*

A share in two revolutions is living to some purpose.
—THOMAS PAINE, quoted in Eric Foner,
Tom Paine and Revolutionary America

Après nous le déluge.
After us, the flood.
> —MADAME DE POMPADOUR, quoted in
> Mme. de Hausset, *Mémoires*

I will have no laws. I will acknowledge none. I protest against every law which an authority calling itself necessary imposes upon my free will.
> —PIERRE-JOSEPH PROUDHON,
> *Idée générale de la révolution*

Revolutions never go backward.
> —WILLIAM HENRY SEWARD,
> *Speech at Rochester on the Irrepressible Conflict*
[Seward's speech was given in 1858. Wendell Phillips made the same remark in a speech on Feb. 17, 1861.]

Diseases desperate grown
By desperate appliance are relieved,
Or not at all.   —SHAKESPEARE, *Hamlet*, IV, iii
[Cf. Guy Fawkes, above.]

Revolutions have never lightened the burden of tyranny. They have only shifted it to another shoulder.
> —GEORGE BERNARD SHAW, *Man and Superman*,
> "The Revolutionist's Handbook"

All changed, changed utterly:
A terrible beauty is born.
> —WILLIAM BUTLER YEATS, *Easter 1916*

RICH, THE   See HAVES & HAVE-NOTS; MONEY

RIGHTEOUSNESS   See SELF-RIGHTEOUSNESS;
VIRTUE

RIGHTS   See also DEMOCRACY; EQUALITY;
FREEDOM; FREE SPEECH;
LAW, LAWYERS; PRESS, THE; PRIVACY

A right sometimes sleeps but it never dies.
> —ANONYMOUS (Legal Maxim)

Rights are lost by disuse.
                    —ANONYMOUS (Legal Maxim)
[These contradictory maxims cover both sides of the
issue, as is necessary in law.]

The public good is in nothing more essentially inter-
ested than in the protection of every individual's private
rights.   —WILLIAM BLACKSTONE, *Commentaries*

There is no such thing as rights anyhow. It is a question of whether you can put it over. In any legal sense
or practical sense, whatever is, is "a right."
        —CLARENCE DARROW, debate on Prohibition,
            quoted in Kevin Tierney, *Darrow*

[All men] are endowed by their Creator with certain
inalienable rights.
            —THOMAS JEFFERSON,
                The Declaration of Independence
[A full citation is given under AMERICAN HISTORY:
MEMORABLE MOMENTS.]

A bill of rights is what the people are entitled to
against every government on earth.
        —THOMAS JEFFERSON, letter to James Madison,
            Dec. 1787

Nobody talks more passionately of his rights than he
who, in the depths of his soul, is doubtful about them.
    —FRIEDRICH NIETZSCHE, *Human, All-Too-Human*

ROME   See CITIES

RUDENESS   See MANNERS;
                        INSULTS & PUT-DOWNS

RUIN   See also POVERTY & HUNGER;
                    TROUBLE; WINNING & LOSING,
                        VICTORY & DEFEAT

The road to ruin is always kept in good repair.
                            —ANONYMOUS

He bears the seed of ruin in himself.
> —MATTHEW ARNOLD,
> *Merope*

How are the mighty fallen in the midst of the battle!
> —BIBLE, *II Samuel* 1:25

MENE, MENE, TEKEL, UPHARSIN.
> —BIBLE, *Daniel* 5:25

[The writing on the wall announcing the destruction of Babylon.]

But the children of the kingdom shall be cast out into outer darkness: there shall be weeping and gnashing of teeth.
> —BIBLE, *Matthew* 8:12

All men that are ruined are ruined on the side of their natural propensities.
> —EDMUND BURKE, *Letters on a Regicide Peace*

Let everyone witness how many different cards fortune has up her sleeve when she wants to ruin a man.
> —BENVENUTO CELLINI, *Autobiography*

There is no loneliness greater than the loneliness of failure. The failure is a stranger in his own house.
> —ERIC HOFFER, *The Passionate State of Mind*

There is not a fiercer hell than the failure in a great object.
> —JOHN KEATS, *Endymion*, Preface

Men fall from great fortune because of the same shortcomings that led to their rise.
> —LA BRUYÈRE, *Les Caractères*

From the sublime to the ridiculous there is only one step.
> —NAPOLEON BONAPARTE, remark to the
> Polish ambassador De Pradt
> after the retreat from Moscow, 1812

Men shut their doors against a setting sun.
> —SHAKESPEARE, *Timon of Athens*, I, ii

RULERS See HIGH POSITION:
RULERS & LEADERS

RUMOR

There is a demon who puts wings on certain stories and who launches them like eagles in the air.
—ALEXANDRE DUMAS, *La Dame du Monsoreau*

I know nothing swifter in life than the voice of rumor.
—PLAUTUS, fragment

Rumor travels faster, but it don't stay put as long as truth. —WILL ROGERS, *The Illiterate Digest*

Rumor is not always wrong.
—TACITUS, *Life of Agricola*

RUSSIA See COMMUNISM; NATIONS

S

Enough research will tend to support your theory.
—ANONYMOUS, quoted in A. Bloch, *Murphy's
Law*, and titled "Murphy's Law of Research"

Theory like mist on eyeglasses. Obscure facts.
—EARL DERR BIGGERS, *Charlie Chan in Egypt*
[We credit the author of the Chan series of books
with this comment, described by biologist Stephen Jay
Gould as one of Chan's "most delightfully anachronistic
pseudo-Confucian sayings." The movie dates from
1935.]

What is now proved was once only imagined.
—WILLIAM BLAKE, *The Marriage of
Heaven and Hell*

It is a capital mistake to theorize before one has data.
—A. CONAN DOYLE, *Scandal in Bohemia*

Most of the fundamental ideas of science are essentially simple, and may, as a rule, be expressed in a
language comprehensible to everyone.
—ALBERT EINSTEIN, *The Evolution of Physics*

The whole of science is nothing more than a refinement of everyday thinking.
—ALBERT EINSTEIN, *Out of My Later Years*

Men love to wonder, and that is the seed of science.
—RALPH WALDO EMERSON, *Society and Solitude*

Science is the knowledge of consequences and the dependence of one fact upon another.
—THOMAS HOBBES, *Leviathan*

Science says the first word on everything, and the last word on nothing.
—VICTOR HUGO, *Things of the Infinite*

The result, therefore, of our present enquiry is that we find no vestige of a beginning—no prospect of an end. —JAMES HUTTON, *Theory of the Earth*
[The last sentence in the original, 1788, version of this work, a sentence called by Stephen Jay Gould "the most famous words ever written by a geologist."]

The great tragedy of science—the slaying of a beautiful hypothesis by an ugly fact.
—T. H. HUXLEY, *Biogenesis and Abiogenesis*

It is the first duty of a hypothesis to be intelligible.
—T. H. HUXLEY, *Evidence as to Man's Place in Nature*

I am sorry to say that there is too much point to the wisecrack that life is extinct on other planets because their scientists were more advanced than ours.
—JOHN F. KENNEDY, speech, Dec. 11, 1959

Science without conscience is but the death of the soul. —MONTAIGNE, *Essays*
[Or Rabelais: "Science without conscience is but the ruin of the soul," Gargantua's Letter to Pantagruel.]

If I have seen further, . . . it is by standing upon the shoulders of giants.
—ISAAC NEWTON, letter to Robert Hooke, Feb. 5, 1675/76

[Robert K. Merton has written a little book on this quotation, in which, among other things, he demonstrates that it was a commonplace of the period. He traces it back to Bernard of Chartres; see under VISION.]

Hypotheses non fingo.
I feign no hypotheses.
　　　　　—ISAAC NEWTON, *Principia mathematica*,
　　　　　scholium

I know not what I may appear to the world, but to myself I seem to have been only like a boy playing on the sea-shore, and diverting myself in now and then finding a smoother pebble or a prettier shell than ordinary, whilst the great ocean of truth lay all undiscovered before me.
　　　　　—ISAAC NEWTON, quoted in David Brewster,
　　　　　Memoirs of Newton

Entia non sunt multiplicanda praeter necessitatem.
Entities should not be multiplied unnecessarily.
　　　　　—WILLIAM OF OCKHAM, *Quodlibeta*
[This is known as "Ockham's razor." A modern version is the KISS Principle: Keep It Simple, Stupid.]

I am become Death, the shatterer of worlds.
　　　—J. ROBERT OPPENHEIMER, quoting a line from
　　　　　the Bhagavad Gita that came to his mind
　　　　　at the test of the first atom bomb,
　　　　　July 16, 1945, cited in N. P. Davis,
　　　　　Lawrence and Oppenheimer

Science is built of facts the way a house is built of bricks; but an accumulation of facts is no more a science than a pile of bricks is a house.
　　　　　—HENRI POINCARÉ, *La Science et l'hypothèse*

Nature and nature's laws lay hid in night:
God said, "Let Newton be!" and all was light.
　　　　　—ALEXANDER POPE, epitaph written for
　　　　　Sir Isaac Newton

The simplest schoolboy is now familiar with facts for which Archimedes would have sacrificed his life.
>—ERNEST RENAN, *Souvenirs d'enfance et de jeunesse*

The work of science is to substitute facts for appearances, and demonstration for impressions.
>—JOHN RUSKIN, *The Stones of Venice*

Even if the open windows of science at first make us shiver . . . in the end, the fresh air brings vigor, and the great spaces have a splendor of their own.
>—BERTRAND RUSSELL, *What I Believe*

Science is always simple and profound. It is only the half truths that are dangerous.
>—GEORGE BERNARD SHAW, *The Doctor's Dilemma*

Science is the great antidote to the poison of enthusiasm and superstition.
>—ADAM SMITH, *Wealth of Nations*

The religions disperse, kingdoms fall apart, but works of science remain for all ages. —ULUGH-BEG
[Words carved on stone astronomical observatory erected by Ulugh-Beg, Tamerlane's grandson, in Samarkand in 1528–29.]

Science is a cemetery of dead ideas.
>—MIGUEL DE UNAMUNO, *The Tragic Sense of Life*

Happy is he who has been able to learn the causes of things. —VIRGIL, *Georgics*

Familiar things happen, and mankind does not bother about them. It requires a very unusual mind to undertake the analysis of the obvious.
>—ALFRED NORTH WHITEHEAD *Science and the Modern World*

SCIENCE: BIOLOGY

Is man an ape or an angel? Now I am on the side of the angels.
> —BENJAMIN DISRAELI, speech, Nov. 25, 1864

Anatomy is destiny.   —FREUD, attributed

Ex ovo omnia.
Everything from an egg.
> —WILLIAM HARVEY, *De generatione animalium*, frontispiece.

Species do not evolve to perfection, but quite the contrary. The weak, in fact, always prevail over the strong, not only because they are in the majority, but also because they are the more crafty.
> —FRIEDRICH NIETZSCHE, *The Twilight of the Idols*

[For the opposing view, see Darwin at PROGRESS.]

This survival of the fittest . . . I have here sought to express in mechanical terms.
> —HERBERT SPENCER, *Principles of Biology*

[This phrase, "survival of the fittest," became identified with Darwinism, but was not used by Darwin himself.]

SCIENCE: DISCOVERY & EXPLORATION

Eureka!
I have found it!
> —ARCHIMEDES, quoted in Vitruvius Polla, *De architectura*

[What he had found is what is now called Archimedes' principle, which relates the density of a body to the quantity of fluid it will displace. This enabled him to solve a problem posed, according to tradition, by King Hiero II: was the king's crown pure gold or a gold and silver alloy?]

That's one small step for [a] man, one giant leap for mankind.　　　—NEIL A. ARMSTRONG, disembarking from the Eagle moon lander, July 20, 1969, mission of Apollo II
["A man" is the official version; but he said "for man," according to recordings of the landing.]

Then I felt like some watcher of the skies
When a new planet swims into his ken;
Or like stout Cortez, when with eagle eyes
He stared at the Pacific—and all his men
Looked at each other with a wild surmise—
Silent, upon a peak in Darien.
　　　—JOHN KEATS, *On First Looking into Chapman's Homer*

What hath God wrought!
　　　—SAMUEL F. B. MORSE, first electric telegraph message, May 24, 1844
[Morse was quoting the Bible, *Numbers* 23:23; he had asked Annie Ellsworth, daughter of the U.S. Commissioner of Patents, to provide a suitable message for him, and the Biblical text was her suggestion.]

Doctor Livingstone, I presume?
　　　—SIR HENRY MORTON STANLEY, on finding David Livingstone at Lake Tanganyika, Nov. 10, 1871; cited in Stanley's book *How I Found Livingstone*

It was wonderful to find America, but it would have been still more wonderful to miss it.
　　—MARK TWAIN, "Pudd'nhead Wilson's Calendar," in *Pudd'nhead Wilson*

SCIENCE: MATHEMATICS & STATISTICS

Mathematics is the door and the key to the sciences.
　　　—ROGER BACON, *Opus Majus*

Numbers are intellectual witnesses that belong only to mankind.
—HONORÉ DE BALZAC, *Louis Lambert*

A witty statesman said, you might prove anything by figures. —THOMAS CARLYLE, *Chartism*

There are three kinds of lies—lies, damned lies, and statistics.
—BENJAMIN DISRAELI, quoted in Mark Twain, *Autobiography*

I don't believe in mathematics.
—ALBERT EINSTEIN, quoted in Carl Seelig, *Albert Einstein*

It is here [in mathematics] that the artist has the fullest scope of his imagination.
—HAVELOCK ELLIS, *The Dance of Life*

The mathematician has reached the highest rung on the ladder of human thought. —*Ibid.*

There is no royal road to geometry.
—EUCLID, quoted in Proclus' *Commentaries*

It has been said that figures rule the world. Maybe. But I am sure that figures show us whether it is being ruled well or badly.
—GOETHE, quoted in Johann Peter Eckermann, *Conversations with Goethe*

I tell them that if they will occupy themselves with the study of mathematics, they will find in it the best remedy against the lusts of the flesh.
—THOMAS MANN, *The Magic Mountain*

To understand God's thoughts, we must study statistics, for these are the measure of his purpose.
—FLORENCE NIGHTINGALE, quoted in K. Pearson, *Life . . . of Francis Galton*

Let no one ignorant of geometry enter my door.
> —PLATO, *The Republic*

[Plato's interest, however, had its limits; see below.]

The ludicrous state of solid geometry made me pass over this branch. —*Ibid.*

Order is heaven's first law.
> —ALEXANDER POPE, *An Essay on Man*

Mathematics possesses not only truth, but supreme beauty—a beauty cold and austere, like that of sculpture.
> —BERTRAND RUSSELL, "The Study of Mathematics," in *Mysticism and Logic*

Prayers for the condemned man will be offered on an adding machine. Numbers constitute the only universal language.
> —NATHANAEL WEST, *Miss Lonelyhearts*

The science of pure mathematics . . . may claim to be the most original creation of the human spirit.
> —ALFRED NORTH WHITEHEAD, *Science and the Modern World*

SCIENCE: See also CREATION, DIVINE;
PHYSICS NATURE: THE HEAVENS,
& COSMOLOGY THE SKY; UNIVERSE

Give me a firm spot on which to stand, and I will move the earth.
> —ARCHIMEDES, commenting on the principle of the lever, quoted in Pappus of Alexandria, *Collectio*

If you aren't confused by quantum physics, then you haven't really understood it.
> —NIELS BOHR, saying

[Bohr, who created the quantum theory, was not troubled by its paradoxes; see the note below under Einstein. This saying of Bohr's was picked up by one of his most famous students, the American physicist John A. Wheeler of Princeton.]

Nothing exists except atoms and empty space; everything else is opinion.   —DEMOCRITUS, fragment

Everything existing in the universe is the fruit of chance and necessity.   —DEMOCRITUS, fragment

God does not play dice with the universe.
                            —ALBERT EINSTEIN, saying
[Einstein objected to the random element at the heart of modern quantum physics, expressed especially in Werner Heisenberg's uncertainty principle: the energy and position of a subatomic particle cannot both be known simultaneously. Niels Bohr, the father of quantum physics, responded to Einstein's complaint: "Nor is it our business to prescribe to God how He should run the world." See also Stephen Hawking's reaction below, and the Einstein quote at GOD.]

Physical concepts are free creations of the human mind, and are not, however it may seem, uniquely determined by the external world.
                —ALBERT EINSTEIN, *Evolution of Physics*

God not only plays dice, he also sometimes throws the dice where they cannot be seen.
            —STEPHEN HAWKING, in *Nature* 257, 1975
[A comment on Einstein's famous saying, see above.]

Space isn't remote at all. It's only an hour's drive away if your car could go straight upwards.
        —FRED HOYLE, in the *Observer*, Sept. 9, 1979

Nothing puzzles me more than time and space; and yet nothing troubles me less as I never think about them.
            —CHARLES LAMB, letter to Thomas Manning,
                Jan. 2, 1806

Every body continues in its state of rest, or of uniform motion in a right [straight] line, unless it is compelled to change that state by forces impressed upon it.
                —ISAAC NEWTON, the first law of motion,
                Principia mathematica, A. Motte, transl.

To every action there is always opposed an equal reaction.
>—ISAAC NEWTON, third law of motion, *Ibid.*

We have no right to assume that any physical laws exist, or if they have existed up to now, that they will continue to exist in a similar manner in the future.
>—MAX PLANCK, *The Universe in the Light of Modern Physics*

Astronomy compels the soul to look upwards and leads us from this world to another.
>—PLATO, *The Republic*

Natura vacuum abhorret.
Nature abhors a vacuum.
>—RABELAIS, *Gargantua*

[He is quoting a Latin proverb. Another citation often given is Spinoza, *Ethics.*]

Water is the principle, or the element, of all things. All things are water.
>—THALES OF MILETUS, quoted in Plutarch, *Placita philosophorum*

SCIENCE: PSYCHOLOGY & PSYCHOANALYSIS   See also MADNESS; SELF-KNOWLEDGE

Of course "behaviorism" works. So does torture.
>—W. H. AUDEN, "Behaviorism," in *A Certain World*

The true science and study of man is man.
>—PIERRE CHARRON, *De la sagesse*, Preface

It might be said of psychoanalysis that if you give it your little finger, it will soon have your whole hand.
>—FREUD, *Introductory Lectures on Psychoanalysis*

Freud is the father of psychoanalysis. It has no mother.
>—GERMAINE GREER, *The Female Eunuch*

I am still more frightened by the fearless power in the eyes of my fellow psychiatrists than by the powerless fear in the eyes of their patients.
—R. D. LAING, *Wisdom, Madness, and Folly*

Dreams are the true interpreters of our inclinations; but there is art required to sort and understand them.
—MONTAIGNE, *Essays*

Psychology which explains everything
explains nothing,
and we are still in doubt.   —MARIANNE MOORE,
Marriage

MACBETH: Canst thou not minister to a mind diseased,
Pluck from memory a rooted sorrow,
Raze out the written troubles of the brain . . . ?
. . .
DOCTOR: Therein the patient
Must minister to himself.   —SHAKESPEARE,
Macbeth V, iii

If you talk to God, you are praying; if God talks to you, you have schizophrenia.
—THOMAS SZASZ, "Schizophrenia,"
in *The Second Sin*

SEAS & SHIPS,   See also NATURE:
SAILING & BOATING   THE OCEAN

They that go down to the sea in ships, that do business in great waters;
These see the works of the Lord, and his wonders in the deep.   —BIBLE, *Psalms* 107:23–24

What is a ship but a prison?
—ROBERT BURTON,
The Anatomy of Melancholy
[The thought was elaborated by Samuel Johnson; see below.]

Water, water, every where,
And all the boards did shrink;
Water, water, every where,
Nor any drop to drink.
—SAMUEL TAYLOR COLERIDGE,
The Rime of the Ancient Mariner

There is nothing more enticing, disenchanting, and
enslaving than the life at sea.
—JOSEPH CONRAD, *Lord Jim*

The life of a sailor is very unhealthy.
—FRANCIS GALTON,
Inquiries into Human Faculty

There is *nothing*—absolutely nothing—half so much
worth doing as simply messing about in boats.
—KENNETH GRAHAME, *The Wind in the Willows*

He that will learn to pray, let him go to sea.
—GEORGE HERBERT, *Jacula Prudentum*

His heart was mailed with oak and triple brass who
first committed a frail ship to the wild seas.
—HORACE, *Odes*

Being in a ship is being in jail, with the chance of
being drowned.
—SAMUEL JOHNSON, quoted in James Boswell,
Life of Johnson, 1759

The Owl and the Pussycat went to sea
In a beautiful pea-green boat,
They took some honey, and plenty of money,
Wrapped up in a five-pound note.
—EDWARD LEAR, *The Owl and the Pussycat*

I must down to the seas again, to the lonely sea and
the sky,
And all I ask is a tall ship and a star to steer her by,
And the wheel's kick and the wind's song and the
white sail's shaking,
And a grey mist on the sea's face and a grey dawn
breaking.   —JOHN MASEFIELD, *Sea Fever*

Call me Ishmael.

—HERMAN MELVILLE, *Moby-Dick*, opening line
[In the Bible, Ishmael is the son of Abraham and the
bondservant Hagar, and the older half-brother of Isaac.
He was disinherited and sent away, and the name came
to stand for an outcast.]

A man who is not afraid of the sea will soon be
drowned.   —J. M. SYNGE, *The Aran Islands*

SEASONS IN LIFE   See GENERATIONS; LIFE

SEASONS OF THE YEAR   See NATURE: SEASONS

SECURITY   See also TALK

It is good to keep close the secret of a king.
—BIBLE, *Tobit* 12:7

Let not thy left hand know what thy right hand doeth.
—BIBLE, *Matthew* 6:3
[More at CHARITY: PHILANTHROPY.]

In time of war, when truth is so precious, it must be
attended by a bodyguard of lies.
—WINSTON CHURCHILL, remark at
Teheran, 1943.
["Bodyguard of Lies" was used as the title of Anthony
Cave-Brown's book on deception in World War II.]

What one man can invent another can discover.
—A. CONAN DOYLE,
The Adventure of the Dancing Men
[The speaker is Sherlock Holmes.]

Quis custodiet ipsos custodes?
Who will guard the guardians themselves?

—JUVENAL, *Satires*
[In this passage from the poet's sixth satire on the failings of women, the reference is to guards hired by jealous husbands to keep their wives faithful. It is usually
applied to government officials—for example, it is the
opening line of the 1987 Tower Commission Report on
the so-called Iran-Contra scandal in the administration
of President Ronald Reagan.]

Thou wilt not utter what thou dost not know.
—SHAKESPEARE, *Henry IV, Part I*, II, iii
[Hotspur is explaining to his wife why he will not tell
her his plans for an armed rebellion.]

ALBANY: . . . You may fear too far.
GONERIL: Safer than trust too far.
—SHAKESPEARE, *King Lear*, I, iv

SELF   See also HONESTY & SINCERITY;
                        PRIDE & VANITY; SELF entries below

Resolve to be thyself: and know that he
Who finds himself, loses his misery.
—MATTHEW ARNOLD, *Self-Dependence*

The kingdom of God is within you.
—BIBLE, *Luke* 17:21

Angels can fly because they take themselves lightly.
—G. K. CHESTERTON, *Orthodoxy*

The man who masters himself is delivered from the
force that binds all creatures.
—GOETHE, *Die Geheimnisse*

What other dungeon is so dark as one's own heart!
What jailer so inexorable as one's self!
—NATHANIEL HAWTHORNE,
The House of the Seven Gables

The least pain in our little finger gives more concern
and uneasiness than the destruction of millions of our
fellow beings.
—WILLIAM HAZLITT, "Dr. Channing," in
American Literature

There is only one corner of the universe you can be
certain of improving, and that's your own self.
—ALDOUS HUXLEY, *Time Must Have a Stop*

Self-love is the greatest of all flatterers.
—LA ROCHEFOUCAULD, *Maxims*

He that would govern others first should be
The master of himself.
　　　　　　　—PHILIP MASSINGER, *The Bondman*

The greatest thing in the world is to know how to belong to oneself.
　　　　　　　—MONTAIGNE, *Essays*, "To the Reader"

The worst of all deceptions is self-deception.
　　　　　　　—PLATO, *Cratylus*

To understand oneself is the classic form of consolation; to elude oneself is the romantic.
　　　　　　　—GEORGE SANTAYANA, "Genteel Tradition in
　　　　　　　American Philosophy," in *Winds of Doctrine*

Our remedies oft in ourselves do lie.
　　　　　　　—SHAKESPEARE, *All's Well That Ends Well*, I, i

This above all: To thine own self be true,
And it must follow, as the night the day,
Thou canst not then be false to any man.
　　　　　　　—SHAKESPEARE, *Hamlet*, I, iii

My closest relation is myself.　　—TERENCE, *Andria*

I celebrate myself, and sing myself.
　　　　　　　—WALT WHITMAN, *Song of Myself*
[For Whitman on self-contradiction, see under CONSISTENCY.]

To love oneself is the beginning of a life-long romance.　　　—OSCAR WILDE, *An Ideal Husband*

Men can starve from a lack of self-realization as much as they can from a lack of bread.
　　　　　　　—RICHARD WRIGHT, *Native Son*

SELF-CONFIDENCE　　　　　See also AMBITION;
　　　　　　　　　　　BOLDNESS & INITIATIVE;
　　　　　　　　　　　PRIDE & VANITY

Who has self-confidence will lead the rest.
—HORACE, *Epistles*

The bullet that will kill me is not yet cast.
—NAPOLEON BONAPARTE, attributed remark
from 1814

I bear a charmed life.   —SHAKESPEARE, *Macbeth*,
V, viii

They can do all because they think they can.
—VIRGIL, *Aeneid*

SELF-INTEREST   See also CAPITALISM;
EXPEDIENCY

Greed is healthy.
—IVAN BOESKY, speech at the University of
California Business School in Berkeley, 1986
[Financier Boesky was later indicted for fraud and
jailed. He was the model for the Gordon Gekko character in the movie *Wall Street*, directed and co-authored
by Oliver Stone. Gekko tells stockholders: "Greed, for
lack of a better word, is good. Greed is right. Greed
works."]

Everyone believes that what suits him is the right
thing to do.   —GOETHE, *Tasso*

If I am not for myself, who is for me?
—HILLEL "THE ELDER," quoted in C. Taylor,
ed., *Sayings of the Jewish Fathers*

It makes a difference whose ox is gored.
—MARTIN LUTHER, *Works*

SELF-KNOWLEDGE   See also SCIENCE:
PSYCHOLOGY &
PSYCHOANALYSIS

Gnóthi seautón.
Know thyself.
> —ANONYMOUS, inscription at the temple of
> Apollo at Delphi

[An axiom of ancient wisdom, repeated often.]

The questions which one asks oneself begin, at last, to illuminate the world, and become one's key to the experience of others.   —JAMES BALDWIN,
> *Nobody Knows My Name*

To know oneself, one should assert oneself.
> —ALBERT CAMUS, *Notebooks*

The humble knowledge of thyself is a surer way to God than the deepest search after science.
> —THOMAS À KEMPIS, *Imitation of Christ*

Know then thyself, presume not God to scan;
The proper study of mankind is man.
> —ALEXANDER POPE, *An Essay on Man*

We know what we are, but know not what we may be.   —SHAKESPEARE, *Hamlet*, IV, v

To know oneself is not necessarily to improve oneself.
> —PAUL VALÉRY, *Choses tués*

To enter one's own self, it is necessary to go armed to the teeth.   —PAUL VALÉRY, *Quelques Pensées de Monsieur Teste*

SELF-PROMOTION   See PUBLICITY & PUBLIC
RELATIONS

SELF-RELIANCE   See also BOLDNESS &
INITIATIVE; FATE;
RESPONSIBILITY; WORK & WORKERS

The gods help them that help themselves.
> —AESOP, *Hercules and the Waggoner*

[Appears in other works, including Benjamin Franklin's *Poor Richard's Almanac*.]

If the hill will not come to Mahomet, Mahomet will come to the hill.   —FRANCIS BACON, *Of Boldness*

Put your trust in God, my boys, and keep your powder dry!   —VALENTINE BLACKER, *Oliver Cromwell's Advice*

He was a self-made man who owed his lack of success to nobody.   —JOSEPH HELLER, *Catch-22*

I am the master of my fate;
I am the captain of my soul.
    —W. E. HENLEY, "Invictus,"
    in *In Memoriam*
    R. T. Hamilton Bruce

Never depend on anyone except yourself.
    —LA FONTAINE, *Fables*

Help yourself and heaven will help you.   —*Ibid.*

If you want a thing done well, do it yourself.
    —NAPOLEON BONAPARTE, *Maxims*

SELF-RIGHTEOUSNESS   See also VIRTUE

Righteous people terrify me. . . . Virtue is its own punishment.   —ANEURIN BEVAN, quoted in
    Michael Foot, *Aneurin Bevan*

Stand by thyself, come not near me: for I am holier than thou.   —BIBLE, *Isaiah* 65:5
[Here God himself describes the smug self-satisfaction of his people, with whom He is not pleased.]

God, I thank thee, that I am not as other men are.
    —BIBLE, *Luke* 18:11

God hates those who praise themselves.
    —ST. CLEMENT, *First Epistle to the Corinthians*

Moral indignation is in most cases two percent moral, forty-eight percent indignation, and fifty percent envy.
    —VITTORIO DE SICA, quoted in the
    Observer, 1961

The louder he talked of his honor, the faster we counted our spoons.
> —RALPH WALDO EMERSON, "Worship," in
> *The Conduct of Life*

SEX & SENSUALITY   See also HEDONISM; LOVE;
SIN, VICE, & NAUGHTINESS

I made love and was happy.
> —JOSEPH ADDISON, *The Spectator*, Aug. 27, 1711

Post coitum omne animal triste.
After coition every animal is sad.
> —ANONYMOUS, Latin saying

Bed is the poor man's opera.
> —ANONYMOUS (ITALIAN PROVERB), quoted in
> Aldous Huxley, *Heaven and Hell*

[See also BAUDELAIRE, below.]

To many, total abstinence is easier than perfect moderation.
> —ST. AUGUSTINE, *On the Good of Marriage*

[On the other hand, see Augustine under PRAYERS.]

Sexuality is the lyricism of the masses.
> —CHARLES BAUDELAIRE, *Mon Coeur mis à nu*

Men make love more intensely at twenty, but make love better, however, at thirty.
> —CATHERINE THE GREAT, letter to Voltaire, in
> *The Complete Works of Catherine II*,
> Evdokimov ed.

Those pleasures so lightly called physical.
> —COLETTE, *Mélanges*

For goodness' sake, if the English hear that Palmerston still has a mistress at eighty, they will make him a dictator!
> —BENJAMIN DISRAELI, response when advised
> that his rival, Lord Palmerston, might
> be ruined as a result of a sex scandal

License my roving hands, and let them go,
Before, behind, between, above, below.
>—JOHN DONNE, *To His Mistress Going to Bed*

I am the Love that dare not speak its name.
>—LORD ALFRED DOUGLAS, *Two Loves*

Sex lies at the root of life, and we can never learn to reverence life until we know how to understand sex.
>—HAVELOCK ELLIS, *Studies in the Psychology of Sex*

If your life at night is good, you think you have everything.   —EURIPIDES, *Medea*

While a person does not give up on sex, sex does not give up on the person.
>—GABRIEL GARCÍA MÁRQUEZ, on sex and growing old, *The New York Times*, April 7, 1985

That nameless charm, with a strong magnetism, which can only be called "It."   —ELINOR GLYN, *It*
[More at CHARM.]

People will insist . . . on treating the *mons Veneris* as though it were Mount Everest.
>—ALDOUS HUXLEY, *Eyeless in Gaza*

and his heart was going like mad and yes I said yes I will Yes.   —JAMES JOYCE, *Ulysses*, the ending

A man who has not passed through the inferno of his passions has never overcome them.
>—CARL JUNG, *Memories, Dreams, Reflections*

Most mothers think that to keep young people away from lovemaking it is enough never to speak of it in their presence.
>—MARIE MADELEINE DE LA FAYETTE, *La Princesse de Clèves*

If we resist our passions, it is due more to their weakness than our own strength.

—LA ROCHEFOUCAULD, *Maxims*

Sex and beauty are inseparable, like life and consciousness.

—D. H. Lawrence, *Sex Versus Loneliness*

You mustn't force sex to do the work of love or love to do the work of sex.

—MARY MCCARTHY, *The Group*

Contraceptives should be used on all conceivable occasions.

—SPIKE MILLIGAN, *The Last Goon Show of All*

The daughter-in-law of Pythagoras said that a woman who goes to bed with a man ought to lay aside her modesty with her skirt, and put it on again with her petticoat.   —MONTAIGNE, *Essays*

Whether a pretty woman grants or withholds her favors, she always likes to be asked for them.

—OVID, *Ars amatoria*

Men seldom make passes
At girls who wear glasses.

—DOROTHY PARKER, *News Item*

Sex Is Never an Emergency.

—DR. ELAINE PIERSON, title of guide
for college students

Civilized people cannot fully satisfy their sexual instinct without love.

—BERTRAND RUSSELL, *Marriage and Morals*

As I grow older and older
And totter towards the tomb,
I find I care less and less
Who goes to bed with whom.

—DOROTHY SAYERS, *That's Why I Never
Read Modern Novels*

Is it not strange that desire should so many years outlive performance.
>—SHAKESPEARE, *Henry IV, Part II*, Il, iv

She is a woman, therefore may be wooed;
She is a woman, therefore may be won.
>—SHAKESPEARE, *Titus Andronicus*, II, i

There are worse occupations in this world than feeling a woman's pulse.
>—LAURENCE STERNE,
>*A Sentimental Journey*

A laugh at sex is a laugh at destiny.
>—THORNTON WILDER, *The Journals of Thornton Wilder*

SHIPS   See SEAS & SHIPS, SAILING & BOATING

SICKNESS   See ILLNESS & REMEDIES

SILENCE   See also SECURITY; TALK

The silent dog is the first to bite.
>—ANONYMOUS (GERMAN PROVERB)

Drawing on my fine command of language, I said nothing.
>—ROBERT BENCHLEY, *Chips off the Old Benchley*

Try as we may to make a silence, we cannot.
>—JOHN CAGE, *Silence*

Speech is of time, silence is of eternity.
>—THOMAS CARLYLE, *Sartor Resartus*

Years of close familiarity rendered silence congenial.
>—COLETTE, *Cheri*

Blessed is the man who, having nothing to say, abstains from giving in words evidence of the fact.
>—GEORGE ELIOT, *Impressions of Theophrastus Such*

Silence gives consent.
　　　—OLIVER GOLDSMITH, *The Good-Natured Man*

The silence of the mind is the true religious mind, and the silence of the gods is the silence of the earth.
　　　—KRISHNAMURTI, quoted in *The Second Penguin Krishnamurti Reader*

Do you wish people to believe good of you? Don't speak.　　　—PASCAL, *Pensées*

A sage thing is timely silence, and better than any speech.　　　—PLUTARCH, *The Education of Children*

An absolute silence leads to sadness: it is the image of death.　　　—JEAN JACQUES ROUSSEAU, *Reveries of a Solitary Walker*

Wise men say nothing in dangerous times.
　　　—JOHN SELDEN, *Table Talk*

The silence often of pure innocence
Persuades when speaking fails.
　　　—SHAKESPEARE, *The Winter's Tale*, II, ii

God is the friend of silence. Trees, flowers, grass grow in silence. See the stars, moon, and sun, how they move in silence.
　　　—MOTHER TERESA, *For the Brotherhood of Man*

Only silence is great; all else is weakness.
　　　—ALFRED DE VIGNY, *La Mort du loup*

Whereof one cannot speak, thereof one must be silent.　　　—LUDWIG WITTGENSTEIN, *Tractatus logico-philosophicus*

SIMPLICITY　　　　　　See also INNOCENCE; THINGS & POSSESSIONS

Less is more.　　　—ROBERT BROWNING, *Andrea del Sarto*
[Also a saying of the architect Mies Van Der Rohe.]

Everything should be made as simple as possible, but not simpler.
> —ALBERT EINSTEIN, *Reader's Digest*, Oct. 1977

[This is similar to "Ockham's razor"; see under SCIENCE.]

O sancta simplicitas!
O holy simplicity!
> —JOHN HUSS, last words before burning at the stake

Manifest plainness,
Embrace simplicity,
Reduce selfishness,
Have few desires.
> —LAO-TZU, *Tao Te Ching*

Simplicity, most rare in our age.
> —OVID, *Ars amatoria*

Beauty of style and harmony and grace and good rhythm depend on simplicity.
> —PLATO, *The Republic*

Simplify, simplify.
> —HENRY DAVID THOREAU, *Walden*

The art of art, the glory of expression, and the sunshine of the light of letters, is simplicity.
> —WALT WHITMAN, *Leaves of Grass*, Preface

SIN
See EVIL; SIN, VICE, & NAUGHTINESS

SIN, VICE, & NAUGHTINESS
See also ALCOHOL & DRINKING; EVIL; EXCESS; HEDONISM; SEX & SENSUALITY; TEMPTATION

The vice is not in entering, but in not coming out again.
> —ARISTIPPUS, remark to pupils who saw him entering the house of a prostitute, cited in Montaigne, *Essays*

Never practice two vices at once.
—TALLULAH BANKHEAD, *Tallulah*

I'm as pure as the driven slush.
—TALLULAH BANKHEAD, attributed

I once was a maid, tho' I cannot tell when,
And still my delight is in proper young men:
Some one of a troop of dragoons was my daddie,
No wonder I'm fond of a sodger laddie.
—ROBERT BURNS, *The Jolly Beggars*

It is the function of vice to keep virtue within reasonable bounds. —SAMUEL BUTLER, *Notebooks*

What men call gallantry, and gods adultery,
Is much more common where the climate's sultry.
—LORD BYRON, *Don Juan*

Pleasure's a sin, and sometimes sin's a pleasure.
—*Ibid.*

Vice is its own reward.
—QUENTIN CRISP, *The Naked Civil Servant*

Do you think your mother and I should have lived comfortably so long together if ever we had been married? —JOHN GAY, *The Beggar's Opera*

The probable fact is that we are descended not only from monkeys but from monks.
—ELBERT HUBBARD, *Roycroft Dictionary and Book of Epigrams*

Really to sin you have to be serious about it.
—HENRIK IBSEN, *Peer Gynt*

We're poor little lambs who've lost our way,
Baa! Baa! Baa!
We're little black sheep who have gone astray,
Baa - aa - aa!
Gentlemen rankers out on the spree,
Damned from here to Eternity,

God ha' mercy on such as we,
Baa! Yah! Baa!
>—RUDYARD KIPLING, *Gentlemen Rankers*
[Known to most Americans as "the Whiffenpoof song,"
after the famous Yale University singing group.]

You know, of course, that the Tasmanians, who
never committed adultery, are now extinct.
>—W. SOMERSET MAUGHAM,
>*The Bread-Winner*

All fashionable vices pass for virtues.
>—MOLIÈRE, *Don Juan*

Of course heaven forbids certain pleasures, but one
finds means of compromise.   —MOLIÈRE, *Tartuffe*

Men are more easily governed through their vices
than through their virtues.
>—NAPOLEON BONAPARTE, *Maxims*

If all the girls attending it [the Yale prom] were laid
end to end—I wouldn't be at all surprised.
>—DOROTHY PARKER, quoted in
>Alexander Woollcott, *While
>Rome Burns*

Enjoyed it! One more drink and I'd have been under
the host.
>—DOROTHY PARKER, on being asked if
>she enjoyed a cocktail party; quoted
>in Howard Teichmann, *George S. Kaufman*
[See also Parker at ALCOHOL & DRINKING.]

When the passions become masters, they are vices.
>—PASCAL, *Pensées*

For lawless joys a bitter ending waits.   —PINDAR,
>*Odes*

Every vice has its excuse ready.
>—PUBLILIUS SYRUS, *Moral Sayings*

Vices can be learnt even without a teacher.
>—SENECA, *Natural Questions*

Commit
The oldest sins the newest kind of ways.
>—SHAKESPEARE, *Henry IV, Part II*, IV, v

It's a bawdy planet.   —SHAKESPEARE,
>*The Winter's Tale*, I, ii

Certainly nothing is unnatural that is not physically impossible.   —RICHARD SHERIDAN, *The Critic*

[On baseball players who break curfew:] It ain't getting it that hurts them, it's staying up all night looking for it. They got to learn that if you don't get it by midnight, you ain't gonna get it, and if you do, it ain't worth it.
>—CHARLES DILLON "CASEY" STENGEL,
>quoted in Robert Creamer, *Stengel*

There is a charm about the forbidden that makes it unspeakably desirable.   —MARK TWAIN, *Notebooks*

When I'm good I'm very, very good, but when I'm bad I'm better.   —MAE WEST, *I'm No Angel*

Goodness, what beautiful diamonds!
Goodness had nothing to do with it dearie.
>—MAE WEST, *Diamond Lil*,
>also in the movie *Night After Night*, 1932
[The line was one of Mae West's favorites, and she titled her autobiography *Goodness Had Nothing to Do with It*, 1959.]

There is nothing in the world like the devotion of a married woman. It's a thing no married man knows anything about.
>—OSCAR WILDE, *Lady Windermere's Fan*

All the things I really like to do are either immoral, illegal, or fattening.
>—ALEXANDER WOOLLCOTT, quoted in
>Howard Teichmann, *George S. Kaufman*

SINCERITY   See HONESTY & SINCERITY

SKEPTICISM   See also ATHEISM; FAITH

Except I shall see in his hands the print of the nails, and put my finger into the print of the nails, and thrust my hand into his side, I will not believe.

—BIBLE, *John* 20:25

["Doubting Thomas" is speaking.]

He that doubteth is damned.

—BIBLE, *Romans* 14:23

Mock on, mock on Voltaire, Rousseau;
Mock on, mock on; 'tis all in vain!
You throw the sand against the wind,
And the wind blows it back again.

—WILLIAM BLAKE, *Mock on, Mock on*

If you would be a real seeker after truth, you must at least once in your life doubt, as far as possible, all things.   —DESCARTES, *Discourse on Method*

Skepticism is the first step toward truth.

—DENIS DIDEROT, *Pensées philosophiques*

Do we, holding that the gods exist, deceive ourselves with unsubstantial dreams and lies, while random careless chance and change alone control the world?

—EURIPIDES, *Hecuba*

Ignorance is preferable to error; and he is less remote from the truth who believes nothing, than he who believes what is wrong.

—THOMAS JEFFERSON,
Notes on the State of Virginia

Que sais-je?
What do I know?   —MONTAIGNE, motto

Great intellects are skeptical.

—FRIEDRICH NIETZSCHE, *The Antichrist*

The pragmatist knows that doubt is an art which has to be acquired with difficulty.

—C. S. PEIRCE, *Collected Papers*

Of the gods I know nothing, whether they exist or
do not exist, nor what they are like in form. Many things
stand in the way of knowledge—the obscurity of the
subject, the brevity of human life.
> —PROTAGORAS, quoted in Diogenes Laërtius,
> *Lives of Eminent Philosophers*

Modest doubt is called
The beacon of the wise.
> —SHAKESPEARE, *Troilus and Cressida*, II, ii

Life is doubt, and faith without doubt is nothing but
death.   —MIGUEL DE UNAMUNO, *Poesías*

One never knows, do one?
> —THOMAS "FATS" WALLER, saying, quoted by
> Roger Angell, *The New Yorker*, Aug. 5, 1985

SKY   See NATURE: THE HEAVENS,
                                    THE SKY

SLEEP & DREAMS   See also SCIENCE:
                    PSYCHOLOGY & PSYCHOANALYSIS

The beginning of health is sleep.
> —ANONYMOUS (IRISH PROVERB)

Dreaming men are haunted men.
> —STEPHEN VINCENT BENÉT, *John Brown's Body*

He giveth his beloved sleep.
> —BIBLE, *Psalms* 127:2

Sleep hath its own world,
And a wide realm of wild reality.
> —LORD BYRON, *The Dream*

Now blessings light on him that first invented this
same sleep! It covers a man all over, thoughts and all,
like a cloak. . . . 'Tis the current coin that purchases
all the pleasures of the world cheap; and the balance
that sets the king and the shepherd, the fool and the
wise man even.   —CERVANTES, *Don Quixote*

Men have conceived a twofold use of sleep: that it is a refreshing of the body in this life; that it is a preparing of the soul for the next.
> —JOHN DONNE, *Meditation xv*

Wynken, Blynken, and Nod one night
Sailed off in a wooden shoe—
Sailed on a river of crystal light
Into a sea of dew.
> —EUGENE FIELD, *Wynken, Blynken, and Nod*

We are not hypocrites in our sleep.
> —WILLIAM HAZLITT, *On Dreams*

Sleep is the twin of death.   —HOMER, *Iliad*

Preserve me from unseasonable and immoderate sleep.   —SAMUEL JOHNSON, *Prayers and Meditations*

Methought I heard a voice cry "Sleep no more!
Macbeth does murder sleep"—the innocent sleep,
Sleep that knits up the ravelled sleeve of care,
The death of each day's life, sore labor's bath,
Balm of hurt minds, great nature's second course,
Chief nourisher in life's feast.
> —SHAKESPEARE, *Macbeth*, II, ii

Sleep my little one, sleep my pretty one, sleep.
> —ALFRED, LORD TENNYSON, *The Princess*

SMALL THINGS   See DETAILS & OTHER SMALL THINGS; THINGS & POSSESSIONS

SNOW   See NATURE: SEASONS; NATURE: WIND & WEATHER

SOCIALISM   See also CAPITALISM; COMMUNISM

I am for socialism because I am for humanity.
> —EUGENE V. DEBS, speech, Jan. 1, 1897

We are all socialists nowadays.
> —EDWARD VII, speech, 1895, when he was Prince of Wales

Socialism is . . . not only a way of life, but a certain scientific approach to social and economic problems.
—JAWAHARLAL NEHRU, *Credo*

All socialism involves slavery.
—HERBERT SPENCER, *The Coming Slavery*

Any man who is not something of a socialist before he is forty has no heart. Any man who is still a socialist after he is forty has no head.
—WENDELL L. WILLKIE, quoted in
Richard Norton Smith,
Thomas E. Dewey

SOLITUDE

He who is unable to live in society, or who has no need because he is sufficient for himself, must be either a beast or a god.
—ARISTOTLE, *Politics*

Woe to him that is alone when he falleth; for he hath not another to help him up.
—BIBLE, *Ecclesiastes* 4:10

'Tis solitude should teach us how to die;
. . . alone—man with his God must strive.
—LORD BYRON, *Childe Harold's Pilgrimage*

We live, as we dream—alone.
—JOSEPH CONRAD, *Heart of Darkness*

I want to be alone.
—GRETA GARBO, saying, and also one of
her lines in *Grand Hotel*
[Her *New York Times* obituary in 1990 stated that she actually said, "I want to be let alone."]

Full many a flower is born to blush unseen,
And waste its sweetness on the desert air.
—THOMAS GRAY, *Elegy Written in a
Country Churchyard*

Pray that your loneliness may spur you into finding
something to live for, great enough to die for.
—DAG HAMMARSKJÖLD, *Diaries*

The strongest man in the world is he who stands most
alone.   —HENRIK IBSEN, *An Enemy of the People*

In solitude pride quickly creeps in.
—ST. JEROME, letter to Rusticus

Then on the shore
Of the wide world I stand alone, and think
Till love and fame to nothingness do sink.
—JOHN KEATS, *When I Have Fears*

This delicious Solitude.   —ANDREW MARVELL,
The Garden

Solitude is the playfield of Satan.
—VLADIMIR NABOKOV, *Pale Fire*

If you would live innocently, seek solitude.
—PUBLILIUS SYRUS, *Moral Sayings*

To be adult is to be alone.
—JEAN ROSTAND, *Thoughts of a Biologist*

I love all waste
And solitary places; where we taste the pleasure of
    believing what we see
Is boundless, as we wish our souls to be.
—PERCY BYSSHE SHELLEY, *Julian and Maddalo*

I never found the companion that was so compan-
ionable as solitude.
—HENRY DAVID THOREAU, *Walden*

The happiest of all lives is a busy solitude.
—VOLTAIRE, letter to Frederick the Great,
    Aug. 1751

She dwelt among the untrodden ways
Beside the springs of Dove,
A maid whom there were none to praise
And very few to love.
—WILLIAM WORDSWORTH, *Ruth*

Avoid the reeking herd,
Shun the polluted flock,
Live like that stoic bird
The eagle of the rock.
          —ELINOR WYLIE, *The Eagle and the Mole*

The wind blows out of the gates of the day,
The wind blows over the lonely of heart,
And the lonely of heart is withered away.
          —WILLIAM BUTLER YEATS,
          The Land of Heart's Desire

SORROW, SADNESS,   See also DESPAIR,
& SUFFERING   DEPRESSION, MISERY;
          EMOTIONS; RESIGNATION; TROUBLE

What do I care if you are good?
Be beautiful! and be sad!
          —CHARLES BAUDELAIRE, "Madrigal triste,"
          in *Nouvelles Fleurs du mal*

Suffering is the sole origin of consciousness.
          —FEODOR DOSTOEVSKI, *Notes from Underground*

Know how sublime a thing it is
To suffer and be strong.
          —HENRY WADSWORTH LONGFELLOW,
          The Light of the Stars

La chair est triste, hélas! et j'ai lu tous les livres.
The flesh is sad, alas, and I've read all the books.
          —STÉPHANE MALLARMÉ, *Brise marine*

It is not true that suffering ennobles the character;
happiness does that sometimes, but suffering, for the
most part, makes men petty and vindictive.
          —W. SOMERSET MAUGHAM,
          The Moon and Sixpence

Happiness is beneficial for the body, but it is grief
that develops the powers of the mind.
          —MARCEL PROUST, *Remembrance of Things Past:
          The Past Recaptured*

When sorrows come, they come not single spies,
But in battalions!   —SHAKESPEARE, *Hamlet*, IV, v

One woe doth tread upon another's heel,
So fast they follow.   —*Ibid.*, IV, vii

SOUL   See also MIND, THOUGHT, &
                            UNDERSTANDING

What shall it profit a man, if he shall gain the whole
world, and lose his own soul?   —BIBLE, *Mark* 8:36

The human soul develops up to the time of death.
                            —HIPPOCRATES, *Aphorisms*

The soul is the mirror of an indestructible universe.
                —G. W. LEIBNIZ, *The Monadology*

The wealth of the soul is the only true wealth.
                            —LUCIAN, *Dialogues*

Every soul is a melody which needs renewing.
                —STÉPHANE MALLARMÉ, *Crise de vers*

Those things that nature denied to human sight, she
revealed to the eyes of the soul.
                            —OVID, *Metamorphoses*

A beautiful soul has no other merit than its own
existence.   —J. F. C. VON SCHILLER,
                            Über Anmut und Würde

The soul alone raises us to nobility.   —SENECA,
                            Epistles

Throughout this varied and eternal world
Soul is the only element.
                —PERCY BYSSHE SHELLEY, *Queen Mab*

Teach me, like you, to drink creation whole
And casting out my self, become a soul.
                —RICHARD WILBUR, "The Aspen and the
                Stream," in *Advice to a Prophet*

SPACE   See NATURE: THE HEAVENS, THE SKY;
SCIENCE: PHYSICS & COSMOLOGY

SPEAKING & SPEECH   See LANGUAGE &
WORDS; TALK

SPEECH, FREE   See FREE SPEECH

SPEED   See HASTE

SPIRIT   See ARTS entries; COURAGE;
CULTURE; SOUL

SPIRITS, OTHER-   See OCCULT, THE
WORLDLY

SPORTS   See also GAMES; PHYSICAL
FITNESS; WINNING & LOSING,
VICTORY & DEFEAT

Float like a butterfly,
Sting like a bee!
Rumble young man! Rumble!
Waaa!

> —MUHAMMAD ALI and DREW
> "BUNDINI" BROWN, their "war cry,"
> *The Greatest: My Own Story*

Ave Caesar, morituri te salutant.
Hail Caesar, we who are about to die salute you.

> —ANONYMOUS, gladiators' salute,
> quoted in Suetonius, *Life
> of Claudius*

In America, it is sport that is the opiate of the masses.

> —RUSSELL BAKER, *The New York Times*,
> Oct. 3, 1967

Whoever wants to know the heart and mind of America had better learn baseball.
>—JACQUES BARZUN, *God's Country and Mine*

The game isn't over till it's over.
>—LAWRENCE PETER "YOGI" BERRA,
>remark in 1973

[Also given as "It ain't over till it's over" and in several other slightly different wordings. This is a variant of the traditional saying, "The ball game isn't over until the last man is out." See also ENDINGS.]

Tennis, anyone? —HUMPHREY BOGART, attributed
[A line that is a proverbial device for getting unwanted actors off the stage for a scene transition. Bogart is said to have spoken the line in a play from the 1920s, but the attribution has not been pinned down. Bogart, himself, denied ever having posed this question.]

The bigger they come, the harder they fall.
>—BOB FITZSIMMONS, remark before losing
>his fight with Jim Jeffries, 1899

[Also attributed to John L. Sullivan, and probably of ancient origin.]

[Baseball:] It breaks your heart. It is designed to break your heart.   —A. BARTLETT GIAMATTI, *The Green
>Fields of the Mind*

Because it's there.
>—G. H. L. MALLORY, explaining why he
>wanted to climb Mt. Everest, quoted in
>John Hunt, *The Ascent of Everest*

Serious sport has nothing to do with fair play. It is bound up with hatred, jealousy, boastfulness, disregard of all rules, and sadistic pleasure in witnessing violence: in other words, it is war minus the shooting.
>—GEORGE ORWELL, *Shooting an Elephant*

Win this one for the Gipper.
>—KNUTE ROCKNE, exhortation to the
>Notre Dame football team

[Rockne seems to have used this line more than once to urge on the team. According to *The Fireside Book of Football*, the first occasion was prior to the Indiana game in 1921, a year after Notre Dame player George Gipp died from a streptococcus infection. In the movie *Knute Rockne—All American*, a thoroughly sanitized Gipp was played by Ronald Reagan.]

The race is not always to the swift nor the battle to the strong—but that's the way to bet it.
—DAMON RUNYON,
More Than Somewhat

A hit, a very palpable hit.   —SHAKESPEARE,
Hamlet, V, ii

There be some sports are painful.
—SHAKESPEARE, *The Tempest*, III, i

Oh! somewhere in this favored land the sun is shining bright;
The band is playing somewhere; and somewhere hearts are light;
And somewhere men are laughing and somewhere children shout,
But there is no joy in Mudville—mighty Casey has struck out.   —ERNEST LAWRENCE THAYER,
Casey at the Bat

I love any discourse of rivers, and fish and fishing.
—IZAAK WALTON, *Compleat Angler*

The English country gentleman galloping after a fox—the unspeakable in full pursuit of the uneatable.
—OSCAR WILDE, *A Woman of No Importance*

SPRING   See NATURE: SEASONS

STARS   See NATURE: THE HEAVENS,
THE SKY; OCCULT, THE; SCIENCE:
PHYSICS & COSMOLOGY

STATISTICS   See SCIENCE:
                          MATHEMATICS & STATISTICS

STOICISM   See PATIENCE; RESIGNATION

STORIES   See also ARTS; WRITING;
                             BOOKS & READING

This is the saddest story I ever heard.
  —FORD MADOX FORD, *The Good Soldier*,
  opening sentence

And thereby hangs a tale.
  —SHAKESPEARE, *As You Like It*, II, vii
[Shakespeare used the phrase in four other plays, as
well.]

A sad tale's best for winter.
  —SHAKESPEARE, *The Winter's Tale*, II, i

STRENGTH   See also POWER;
                             VIOLENCE & FORCE

When the going gets tough, the tough get going.
 —ANONYMOUS, popularized by John N. Mitchell,
 Attorney General under Richard M. Nixon

Kraft durch Freude.
Strength through joy.
  —ROBERT LEY, slogan for the German
  Labor Front, 1933

If we must choose between them, it is far better to
be feared than loved. —MACHIAVELLI, *The Prince*

A nation does not have to be cruel to be tough.
  —FRANKLIN D. ROOSEVELT, radio speech,
  Oct. 13, 1940

Physical strength can never permanently withstand
the impact of spiritual force.
  —FRANKLIN D. ROOSEVELT,
  speech, May 4, 1941

There is a homely adage which runs: "Speak softly and carry a big stick; you will go far."
——THEODORE ROOSEVELT, speech, Sept. 2, 1901
[Stephen Jay Gould in his column in *Natural History* magazine, May 1985, traced this adage back to an African proverb.]

The strongest is never strong enough always to be master, unless he transforms strength into right, and obedience into duty.
——JEAN JACQUES ROUSSEAU, *The Social Contract*

O! it is excellent
To have a giant's strength, but it is tyrannous
To use it like a giant.
——SHAKESPEARE, *Measure for Measure*, II, ii

The Gods are on the side of the stronger.
——TACITUS, *Histories*

If you can't stand the heat, get out of the kitchen.
——HARRY S TRUMAN, *Mr. Citizen*
[David McCullough reports in *Truman* that this is an old Missouri saying that Truman first heard in the 1930s.]

There is no need to fear the strong. All one needs to know is the method of overcoming them. There is a special jujitsu for every strong man.
——YEVGENY YEVTUSHENKO,
A Precocious Autobiography

STUPIDITY   See FOOLS & STUPIDITY

STYLE   See also APPEARANCES; ARTS:
STYLE IN WRITING & EXPRESSION;
FASHION & CLOTHES; GRACE

Our style betrays us.
——ANONYMOUS (LATIN PROVERB)

Le style est l'homme même.
The style is the man himself.
——GEORGES LOUIS DE BUFFON,
Discours sur le style

To achieve harmony in bad taste is the height of elegance.   —JEAN GENET, *The Thief's Journal*

In matters of great importance, style, not sincerity, is the vital thing.   —OSCAR WILDE,
The Importance of Being Earnest

SUCCESS & FAME   See also ACCOMPLISHMENT;
GREATNESS; HIGH POSITION:
RULERS & LEADERS; MONEY; POWER

Sic transit gloria mundi.
So passes away the glory of this world.
—ANONYMOUS
[Used in papal coronations since the 15th century but probably of earlier origin. Essentially the same phrase is found in *The Imitation of Christ*; see Thomas à Kempis, below.]

The desire for fame tempts even noble minds.
—ST. AUGUSTINE, *The City of God*

Fame is like a river, that beareth up things light and swollen, and drowns things weighty and solid.
—FRANCIS BACON,
Of Ceremonies and Respects

Fame always brings loneliness. Success is as ice cold and lonely as the North Pole.
—VICKI BAUM, *Grand Hotel*

Let us now praise famous men.
—BIBLE, *Ecclesiasticus* 44:1
[More at GENERATIONS.]

The celebrity is a person who is known for his well-knownness.   —DANIEL BOORSTIN,
The Image

A sign of a celebrity is often that his name is worth more than his services.   —*Ibid.*

Success produces success, just as money produces money.   —SÉBASTIEN R. N. CHAMFORT,
Maximes et pensées

That's what fame is: solitude.
                    —COCO CHANEL, quoted in Marcel Haedrich,
Coco Chanel: Her Life, Her Secrets

We are all motivated by a keen desire for praise, and the better a man is, the more he is inspired by glory.
                              —CICERO, *Pro archia*

Fame is a bee.
It has a song—
It has a sting—
Ah, too, it has a wing.
                    —EMILY DICKINSON, poem no. 1763

Nothing succeeds like success.
                    —ALEXANDRE DUMAS, *Ange pitou*
[For Oscar Wilde's variation, see EXCESS.]

Along with success comes a reputation for wisdom.
                              —EURIPIDES, *Hippolytus*

Success has ruined many a man.
    —BENJAMIN FRANKLIN, *Poor Richard's Almanac*

Fame hath sometimes created something of nothing.
                    —THOMAS FULLER, *Of Fame*, in
Holy and Profane State

The paths of glory lead but to the grave.
                    —THOMAS GRAY, *Elegy
Written in a Country Churchyard*

Success has killed more men than bullets.
    —TEXAS GUINAN, saying used in nightclub act

It is better to be envied than pitied.

—HERODOTUS, *Histories*

The moral flabbiness born of the bitch goddess Success. That—with the squalid cash interpretation put on the word success—is our national disease.

—WILLIAM JAMES, letter to H. G. Wells, Sept. 11, 1906

Oh how quickly the world's glory passes away.

—THOMAS À KEMPIS, *The Imitation of Christ*
[A variation of the anonymous *sic transit gloria mundi*; see above.]

There is no business in the world so troublesome as the pursuit of fame: life is over before you have hardly begun your work.   —LA BRUYÈRE, *Les Caractères*

Be nice to people on your way up because you'll need them on your way down.

—WILSON MIZNER, quoted in A. Johnson,
The Incredible Mizners
[Also attributed to Jimmy Durante.]

Success is like a liberation or the first phase of a love affair.   —JEANNE MOREAU, quoted in
Oriana Fallaci, *The Egoists*

There is only one success—to be able to spend your life in your own way.   —CHRISTOPHER MORLEY,
Where the Blue Begins

Fame can never make us lie down contentedly on a deathbed.

—ALEXANDER POPE, letter to William Trumbell, March 12, 1713

The highest form of vanity is love of fame.

—GEORGE SANTAYANA, *Reason in Society*

There's hope a great man's memory may outlive his life half a year. —SHAKESPEARE, *Hamlet*, III, ii

There are two tragedies in life. One is to lose your heart's desire. The other is to gain it.
—GEORGE BERNARD SHAW,
Man and Superman

All you need in this life is ignorance and confidence, and then success is sure.
—MARK TWAIN, letter to Mrs. Foote,
Dec. 2, 1887

In the future, everyone will be famous for fifteen minutes.
—ANDY WARHOL, *Andy Warhol's Exposures*

There is always room at the top.
—DANIEL WEBSTER, attributed

What rage for fame attends both great and small!
Better be damned than mentioned not at all.
—JOHN WOLCOT ("Peter Pindar"),
To the Royal Academicians

SUFFERING   See SORROW, SADNESS, &
                                           SUFFERING; TROUBLE

SUICIDE

As soon as one does not kill oneself, one must keep silent about life. —ALBERT CAMUS, *Notebooks* [For his view of suicide and philosophy, see PHILOSOPHY.]

When all the blandishments of life are gone,
The coward sneaks to death, the brave live on.
—MARTIAL, *Epigrams*

A suicide kills two people . . . that's what it's for.
—ARTHUR MILLER, *After the Fall*

It is always consoling to think of suicide: in that way one gets through many a bad night.
—FRIEDRICH NIETZSCHE, *Beyond Good and Evil*

Razors pain you;
Rivers are damp;
Acids stain you;
And drugs cause cramp;
Guns aren't lawful;
Nooses give;
Gas smells awful;
You might as well live.
—DOROTHY PARKER, "Résumé," in
Enough Rope

Amid the sufferings of life on earth, suicide is God's best gift to man.   —PLINY, *Natural History*

There is nothing in the world to which every man has a more unassailable title than to his own life and person.
—SCHOPENHAUER, *On Suicide*

To be, or not to be—that is the question:
Whether 'tis nobler in the mind to suffer
The slings and arrows of outrageous fortune,
Or to take arms against a sea of troubles,
And by opposing end them.
—SHAKESPEARE, *Hamlet*, III, i

It is silliness to live when to live is torment.
—SHAKESPEARE, *Othello*, I, iii

The man who, in a fit of melancholy, kills himself today, would have wished to live had he waited a week.
—VOLTAIRE, *Philosophical Dictionary*, "Cato"

SUMMER   See NATURE: SEASONS

SURVIVAL   See also APPEASEMENT VS.
                                RESISTANCE; CRAFTINESS;
                                PERSEVERANCE & ENDURANCE

He that fights and runs away
May live to fight another day.
                    —ANONYMOUS, in *Musarium deliciae*,
                        17th century

To all the living there is hope; for a living dog is
better than a dead lion.   —BIBLE, *Ecclesiastes* 9:4

It isn't important to come out on top. What matters
is to be the one who comes out alive.
                    —BERTOLT BRECHT, *In the Jungle of Cities*

Happiness in the ordinary sense is not what one needs
in life, though one is right to aim at it. The true satis-
faction is to come through and see those whom one
loves come through.
                    —E. M. FORSTER, letter, 1922, in
                        Selected Letters, Vol. II (1921–1970)

In the clutch of circumstance,
I have not winced or cried aloud;
Under the bludgeoning of chance
My head is bloody but unbowed.
                    —WILLIAM E. HENLEY, "Invictus," in
                        In Memoriam R. T. Hamilton Bruce

I bend but do not break.
                    —LA FONTAINE, "The Oak and the Reed,"
                        in *Fables*

We shall live to fight again and to strike another blow.
                    —ALFRED, LORD TENNYSON, *The Revenge*

Endure, and preserve yourselves for better things.
                    —VIRGIL, *Aeneid*

SWITZERLAND   See NATIONS

T

TALK   See also CONVERSATION;
                     LANGUAGE & WORDS; SILENCE

Loose lips sink ships.
            —ANONYMOUS (World War II poster)
[See also SECURITY.]

A fool uttereth all his mind.
                          —BIBLE, *Proverbs* 29:11

Refrain not to speak, when there is occasion to do
good.   —BIBLE, *Ecclesiasticus* 4:23

Every idle word that men shall speak, they shall give
account thereof in the day of judgment.
For by thy words thou shalt be justified, and by thy
words thou shalt be condemned.
                          —BIBLE, *Matthew* 12:36–37

When you're leading, don't talk.
      —THOMAS E. DEWEY, remark during the 1948
      presidential campaign

But far more numerous was the herd of such
Who think too little and who talk too much.
                          —JOHN DRYDEN,
                          Absalom and Achitophel

Then words came like a fall of winter snow.
                          —HOMER, *Iliad*

Speech is a mirror of the soul; as a man speaks so he
is.   —PUBLILIUS SYRUS, *Moral Sayings*

Men of few words are the best men.
—SHAKESPEARE, *Henry V*, III, ii
[Not necessarily Shakespeare's own view, for he also observed that there are those who are "reputed wise for saying nothing," *Merchant of Venice*, I. i. And in the quote below, it is a murderer who speaks.]

Talkers are no good doers.
—SHAKESPEARE, *Richard III*, I, iii

Talkativeness is one thing, speaking well another.
—SOPHOCLES, *Oedipus at Colonus*

TAXES

Render therefore unto Caesar the things which are Caesar's; and unto God the things that are God's.
—BIBLE, *Matthew* 22:21

To tax and to please, no more than to love and be wise, is not given to man.
—EDMUND BURKE, speech, Apr. 9, 1774

The art of taxation consists in so plucking the goose as to obtain the largest possible amount of feathers with the least possible amount of hissing.
—JEAN BAPTISTE COLBERT, attributed

In this world, nothing can be said to be certain except death and taxes.
—BENJAMIN FRANKLIN, letter to J.-B. LeRoy, Nov. 13, 1789

Taxes are what we pay for civilized society.
—OLIVER WENDELL HOLMES, JR.,
Compania de Tabacos v. *Collector*

The wisdom of man never yet contrived a system of taxation that operates with perfect equality.
—ANDREW JACKSON, *Proclamation to the People of South Carolina*

Excise, n. A hateful tax levied upon commodities, and adjudged not by the common judges of property, but by wretches hired by those to whom the excise is paid.   —SAMUEL JOHNSON, *Dictionary*

The power to tax involves the power to destroy.
            —JOHN MARSHALL, *McCulloch* v. *Maryland*

Taxation without representation is tyranny.
                    —JAMES OTIS, attributed

Where there is an income tax, the just man will pay more and the unjust less on the same income.
                    —PLATO, *The Republic*

The income tax has made more liars out of the American people than golf has.
            —WILL ROGERS, *The Illiterate Digest*

Taxes, after all, are dues that we pay for the privileges of membership in an organized society.
            —FRANKLIN D. ROOSEVELT, speech,
            Oct. 21, 1936

To be a good shepherd is to shear the flock, not skin it!   —TIBERIUS, favorite proverbial saying,
            quoted in Suetonius, *Lives of the Caesars*

TECHNOLOGY   See also MEDIA; SCIENCE

Garbage in, garbage out.
            —ANONYMOUS, on why computer findings
            may be unsatisfactory

To err is human, but to really foul things up requires a computer.   —ANONYMOUS

And was Jerusalem builded here
Among those dark Satanic Mills?
            —WILLIAM BLAKE, *Milton*, prefatory poem

The "control of nature" is a phrase conceived in arrogance, born of the Neanderthal age of biology and the convenience of man.

—RACHEL CARSON, *Silent Spring*

Machines, from the Maxim gun to the computer, are for the most part means by which a minority can keep free men in subjection.

—SIR KENNETH CLARK, *Civilization*

Any sufficiently advanced technology is indistinguishable from magic. —ARTHUR C. CLARKE, *The Lost Worlds of 2001*

If true computer music were ever written, it would only be listened to by other computers.

—MICHAEL CRICHTON, *Electronic Life*

For a successful technology, reality must take precedence over public relations, for Nature cannot be fooled.

—RICHARD P. FEYNMAN, *What Do You Care What Other People Think?*

[Professor Feynman's most famous demonstration of the relative value of reality vs. public relations came in 1986, in the hearings on the cause of the explosion of the space shuttle Challenger after a cold-weather launch. He dropped a sample of the rubber used for the O-ring seals in the booster rockets into a glass of ice water, then clamped the sample and released it— the rubber had lost its resilience.]

Technology . . . the knack of so arranging the world that we don't have to experience it.

—MAX FRISCH, quoted in Daniel J. Boorstin, *The Image*

Is it a fact, or have I dreamt it—that, by means of electricity, the world of matter has become a great nerve, vibrating thousands of miles in a breathless point of time? —NATHANIEL HAWTHORNE, *The House of the Seven Gables*

Have you heard of the wonderful one-hoss shay,
That was built in such a logical way
It ran a hundred years to a day?
>   —OLIVER WENDELL HOLMES, SR.,
>   *The Deacon's Masterpiece*

The automobile changed our dress, manners, social customs, vacation habits, the shape of our cities, consumer purchasing patterns, common tastes, and positions in intercourse.
>   —JOHN KEATS, *The Insolent Chariots*

Our scientific power has outrun our spiritual power. We have guided missiles and misguided men.
>   —MARTIN LUTHER KING, JR., *Strength to Love*

To George F. Babbitt . . . his motor-car was poetry and tragedy, love and heroism.
>   —SINCLAIR LEWIS, *Babbitt*

It is critical vision alone which can mitigate the unimpeded operation of the automatic.
>   —MARSHALL MCLUHAN, *The Mechanical Bride*

The electric age . . . establishes a global network that has much the character of our central nervous system.
>   —MARSHALL MCLUHAN, *Understanding Media*

The car has become the carapace, the protective and aggressive shell, of urban and suburban man.
>   —*Ibid.*

Machines are worshipped because they are beautiful and valued because they confer power; they are hated because they are hideous and loathed because they impose slavery.
>   —BERTRAND RUSSELL, *Sceptical Essays*

The machine does not isolate man from the great problems of nature but plunges him more deeply into them.   —ANTOINE DE SAINT-EXUPÉRY,
>   *Wind, Sand, and Stars*

The machine yes the machine
never wastes anybody's time
never watches the foreman
never talks back.
                              —CARL SANDBURG,
                                The People, Yes

The real problem is not whether machines think, but
whether men do.
    —B. F. SKINNER, *Contingencies of Reinforcement*

Men have become the tools of their tools.
                        —HENRY DAVID THOREAU, *Walden*

Everything in life is somewhere else, and you get
there in a car.   —E. B. WHITE, *One Man's Meat*
[For E. B. White on television, see under MEDIA.]

In the past, human life was lived in a bullock cart; in
the future, it will be lived in an aeroplane; and the
change of speed amounts to a difference in quality.
                        —ALFRED NORTH WHITEHEAD,
                          Science and the Modern World

TELEVISION   See MEDIA

TEMPTATION   See also SIN, VICE, &
                                      NAUGHTINESS

Opportunity can often sway even an honest man.
                        —ANONYMOUS (LATIN PROVERB)

Saintliness is also a temptation.   —JEAN ANOUILH,
                                        Becket

Lead us not into temptation.
[Also *Luke* 11:4]   —BIBLE, *Matthew* 6:13

Get thee behind me, Satan.   —*Ibid.*, 16:23

Watch and pray, that ye enter not into temptation: the spirit indeed is willing, but the flesh is weak.
—*Ibid.*, 26:41

Blessed is the man that endureth temptation.
—BIBLE, *James* 1:12

For to tempt and to be tempted are things very nearly allied, and in spite of the finest maxims of morality impressed upon the mind, whenever feeling has anything to do in the matter, no sooner is it excited than we have already gone vastly farther than we are aware of.   —CATHERINE THE GREAT, *Memoirs*

Tempt not a desperate man.
—SHAKESPEARE, *Romeo and Juliet*, V, iii

I generally avoid temptation unless I can't resist it.
—MAE WEST, *My Little Chickadee*, movie

I can resist everything except temptation.
—OSCAR WILDE, *Lady Windermere's Fan*

THEATER   See ARTS: DRAMA & ACTING

THEORY   See SCIENCE

THINGS   See DETAILS & OTHER SMALL THINGS;
                     NEW THINGS; OLD THINGS, OLD
                     FRIENDS; SIMPLICITY; THINGS &
                                         POSSESSIONS

THINGS &   See also NEW THINGS; OLD
POSSESSIONS   THINGS; OLD FRIENDS;
                                      SIMPLICITY

The goal of all inanimate objects is to resist man and ultimately to defeat him.
—RUSSELL BAKER, *The New York Times*, June 18, 1968

Inanimate objects are classified scientifically into three major categories—those that don't work, those that break down, and those that get lost.   —*Ibid.*

Things have their laws as well as men; things refuse to be trifled with.
—RALPH WALDO EMERSON, *Politics*

We are the slaves of objects around us.
—GOETHE, quoted in Johann Peter Eckermann, *Conversations with Goethe*

The generality of mankind are contented to be estimated by what they possess instead of what they are.
—WILLIAM HAZLITT, *On Personal Identity*

Every increased possession loads us with a new weariness.   —JOHN RUSKIN, *The Eagle's Nest*

An ill-favored thing, sir, but mine own.
—SHAKESPEARE, *As You Like It*, V, iv

A place for everything and everything in its place.
—SAMUEL SMILES, *Thrift*

How many things I can do without!
—SOCRATES, in a marketplace, quoted in Diogenes Laërtius, *Lives of Eminent Philosophers*

A coin, sleeve button, or a collar button dropped in a bedroom will hide itself and be hard to find. A handkerchief in bed *can't* be found.
—MARK TWAIN, *Notebook*

THINKING & THOUGHT   See MIND, THOUGHT, & UNDERSTANDING

TIME   See also PRESENT, THE; PROCRASTINATION

Time brings all things to pass.
—AESCHYLUS, *The Libation Bearers*

Time and tide wait for no man.
　　　　　　　　　—ANONYMOUS (ENGLISH PROVERB)

Vulnerat omnes, ultima necat.
Each hour injures, the last one slays.
　　　　　　　　　—ANONYMOUS (LATIN PROVERB)

What then is time? If no one asks me, I know what
it is. If I wish to explain it to him who asks, I do not
know.　　　　　　—ST. AUGUSTINE, *Confessions*

Time is a great teacher, but unfortunately it kills all
its pupils.　　　　　—HECTOR BERLIOZ, quoted in
　　　　　　　　　Almanach des lettres françaises

Men talk of killing time, while time quietly kills them.
　　　　　—DION BOUCICAULT, *London Assurance*
[Herbert Spencer in *Definitions* wrote "*Time:* That
which man is always trying to kill, but which ends in
killing him."]

Time ripens all things. No man's born wise.
　　　　　　　　　—CERVANTES, *Don Quixote*

Time is the great physician.
　　　　—BENJAMIN DISRAELI, *Henrietta Temple*

Time present and time past
Are both perhaps present in time future,
And time future contained in time past.
　　—T. S. ELIOT, "Burnt Norton," in *Four Quartets*

The Moving Finger writes; and having writ
Moves on: nor all your Piety nor Wit
Shall lure it back to cancel half a Line,
Nor all your Tears wash out a Word of it.
　　　　　　　—EDWARD FITZGERALD, *The Rubáiyát*
　　　　　　　of Omar Khayyám

Time is money.
　　　　　　　—BENJAMIN FRANKLIN, *Advice to*
　　　　　　　a Young Tradesman

Dost thou love life? Then do not squander time, for that's the stuff life is made of.
>—BENJAMIN FRANKLIN, *The Way to Wealth*

Time flies over us, but leaves its shadow behind.
>—NATHANIEL HAWTHORNE, *The Marble Faun*

But at my back I always hear
Time's wingèd chariot hurrying near.
>—ANDREW MARVELL, *To His Coy Mistress*

[For more, see under HEDONISM.]

I must govern the clock, not be governed by it.
>—GOLDA MEIR, quoted in Oriana Fallaci,
>*L'Europeo*

Time is the best medicine.   —OVID, *Remedia amoris*

In theory, one is aware that the earth revolves, but in practice one does not perceive it; the ground upon which one treads seems not to move, and one can live undisturbed. So it is with time in one's life.
>—MARCEL PROUST, *Remembrance of Things Past: Within a Budding Grove*

Everything is a matter of chronology.
>—MARCEL PROUST, *Remembrance of Things Past: The Past Recaptured*

Time, which changes people, does not alter the image we have retained of them.   —*Ibid.*

To realize the unimportance of time is the gate of wisdom.
>—BERTRAND RUSSELL, *Mysticism and Logic*,
>title essay

Nothing is ours except time.   —SENECA, *Epistles*

Ah! the clock is always slow;
It is later than you think.
>—ROBERT W. SERVICE, *Songs of a Sourdough*

Come what come may,
Time and the hour runs through the roughest day.
—SHAKESPEARE, *Macbeth*, I, iii

I wasted time, and now doth time waste me.
—SHAKESPEARE, *Richard II*, V, v

Time eases all things.   —SOPHOCLES, *Oedipus Rex*
[Or, from his *Electra*, "Gentle time will heal our sorrows."]

The butterfly counts not months but moments, and
has time enough.
—RABINDRANATH TAGORE, *Stray Birds*

Oh as I was young and easy in the mercy of his means,
Time held me green and dying
Though I sang in my chains like the sea.
—DYLAN THOMAS, *Fern Hill*

As if you could kill time without injuring eternity.
—HENRY DAVID THOREAU, *Walden*

Time is but the stream I go a-fishing in.   —*Ibid.*

Time bears away all things, even the mind.
—VIRGIL, *Eclogues*

The years like great black oxen tread the world,
And God the herdsman goads them on behind,
And I am broken by their passing feet.
—WILLIAM BUTLER YEATS,
The Countess Cathleen

TIMES   See FUTURE, THE; GENERATIONS;
                         MODERN TIMES;
                         PAST, THE; PRESENT,
                         THE; TURBULENT TIMES

TIMES OF DAY   See NATURE: TIMES OF DAY

TOBACCO

Tobacco, divine, rare, superexcellent tobacco . . . a sovereign remedy to all diseases. . . . But, as it is commonly abused by most men, which take it as tinkers do ale, 'tis a plague, a mischief, a violent purger of goods, lands, health, hellish, devilish, and damned tobacco, the ruin and overthrow of body and soul.
—ROBERT BURTON, *The Anatomy of Melancholy*

The believing we do something when we do nothing is the first illusion of tobacco.
—RALPH WALDO EMERSON, *Journals*, 1859

A custom [smoking] loathsome to the eye, harmful to the brain, dangerous to the lungs, and in the black stinking fume thereof, nearest resembling the horrible Stygian smoke of the pit that is bottomless.
—JAMES I OF ENGLAND,
Counterblaste to Tobacco

A woman is only a woman, but a good cigar is a smoke.   —RUDYARD KIPLING, "The Betrothed,"
in *Departmental Ditties*

What this country needs is a really good five-cent cigar.
—THOMAS R. MARSHALL, remark ca. 1920 to
John Crockett, chief clerk of the Senate

There's nothing like tobacco; it is the passion of all decent men; a man who lives without tobacco does not deserve to live.   —MOLIÈRE, *Don Juan*

I have never smoked in my life and look forward to a time when the world will look back in amazement and disgust to a practice so unnatural and offensive.
—GEORGE BERNARD SHAW, *The New York
Herald Tribune*, April 14, 1946

TODAY   See MODERN TIMES;
                              PRESENT, THE

TOLERANCE   See also FORGIVENESS
& UNDERSTANDING   & MERCY

Live and let live.   —ANONYMOUS (SCOTTISH
                              PROVERB)

Judge not, that ye be not judged.
                              —BIBLE, *Matthew* 7:1
[See also *Luke*, below.]

Why beholdest thou the mote that is in thy brother's
eye, but considerest not the beam that is in thine own
eye?   —*Ibid.*, 7:3

Judge not, and ye shall not be judged: condemn not,
and ye shall not be condemned: forgive, and ye shall
be forgiven.   —BIBLE, *Luke* 6:37

He that is without sin among you, let him first cast
a stone at her.   —BIBLE, *John* 8:7

It is right to hate sin, but not to hate the sinner.
                    —GIOVANNI GUARESCHI, *The Little World
                        of Don Camillo*

There is so much good in the worst of us.
And so much bad in the best of us,
That it hardly becomes any of us
To talk about the rest of us.
              —EDWARD WALLIS HOCH, *Good and Bad*

The highest result of education is tolerance.
                        —HELEN KELLER, *Optimism*

No law or ordinance is mightier than understanding.
                              —PLATO, *Laws*

Tout comprendre rend très indulgent.
To understand everything makes one very tolerant.
                        —MADAME DE STAËL, *Corinne*
[Commonly quoted as, *Tout comprendre, c'est tout par-*

donner, "To understand everything is to forgive everything."]

TOMORROW	See FUTURE
TOO MUCH	See EXCESS
TOTALITARIANISM	See TYRANNY & TOTALITARIANISM
TRAGEDY	See ARTS entries
TRAVEL	See also CITIES; ESCAPE; NATIONS

When I am here [Milan], I do not fast on the Sabbath; when I am at Rome, I do fast on the Sabbath.
—ST. AMBROSE, *Letters to Augustine*
[Often rephrased as, "When in Rome do as the Romans do, when elsewhere live as they live elsewhere." In *Don Quixote*, Cervantes phrased it, "When thou art at Rome, do as they do at Rome."]

Travelling is the ruin of all happiness. There's no looking at a building here after seeing Italy.
FANNY BURNEY, *Cecilia*

Travellers, like poets, are mostly an angry race.
—SIR RICHARD BURTON, *Narrative of a Trip to Harar*

All places are distant from heaven alike.
—ROBERT BURTON, *The Anatomy of Melancholy*

Why do people so love to wander? I think the civilized parts of the world will suffice for me in the future.
—MARY CASSATT, letter to Louisine Havemeyer, Feb. 11, 1911

Men travel faster now, but I do not know if they go to better things.
—WILLA CATHER, *Death Comes for the Archbishop*

Travelling is almost like talking with men of other centuries.
—RENÉ DESCARTES, *Discourse on Method*

I want to travel in Europe . . . I know that I am only going to a graveyard, but it's a most precious graveyard.
—FEODOR DOSTOEVSKI, *The Brothers Karamazov*

No man should travel until he has learned the language of the country he visits. Otherwise he voluntarily makes himself a great baby,—so helpless and ridiculous.   —RALPH WALDO EMERSON, *Journals*

Travelling is a fool's paradise.
—RALPH WALDO EMERSON, *Self-Reliance*

The woods are lovely, dark and deep,
But I have promises to keep,
And miles to go before I sleep,
And miles to go before I sleep.
—ROBERT FROST, *Stopping by Woods
on a Snowy Evening*

He that travels much knows much.
—THOMAS FULLER, *Gnomologia*

One of the pleasantest things in the world is going a journey; but I like to go by myself.
—WILLIAM HAZLITT, *On Going a Journey*

There is nothing worse for mortals than a wandering life.   —HOMER, *Odyssey*

Those who go overseas find a change of climate, not a change of soul.   —HORACE, *Epistles*

He travels fastest who travels alone.
—RUDYARD KIPLING, *The Winners*

Ship me somewheres east of Suez, where the best is like the worst,

Where there aren't no Ten Commandments, an' a
man can raise a thirst.
> —RUDYARD KIPLING, *Mandalay*

I love to sail forbidden seas, and land on barbarous
coasts.   —HERMAN MELVILLE, *Moby-Dick*

Travel is the most private of pleasures. There is no
greater bore than the travel bore. We do not in the least
want to hear what he has seen in Hong Kong.
> —VITA SACKVILLE-WEST, *Passenger to Teheran*

He who would travel happily must travel light.
> —ANTOINE DE SAINT-EXUPÉRY,
> *Wind, Sand, and Stars*

When I was at home, I was in a better place.
> —SHAKESPEARE, *As You Like It*, II, iv

Foreigners can always tempt one to abandon any sen-
sible habit.   —C. P. SNOW, *Strangers and Brothers*,
television broadcast, 1985

A man should know something of his own country,
too, before he goes abroad.   —LAURENCE STERNE,
Tristram Shandy

I travel not to go anywhere but to go. I travel for
travel's sake. The great affair is to move.
> —ROBERT LOUIS STEVENSON,
> *Travels with a Donkey*

To travel hopefully is better than to arrive.
> —ROBERT LOUIS STEVENSON,
> *Virginibus Puerisque*

[More of this is given at WORK.]

Three things are weakening: fear, sin, and travel.
> —TALMUD

I never travel without my diary. One should always
have something sensational to read in the train.
> —OSCAR WILDE, *The Importance of Being Earnest*

TROUBLE   See also CONFLICT; DESPAIR,
                                       DEPRESSION, & MISERY; RUIN;
                                   SORROW, SADNESS, & SUFFERING;
                                            TURBULENT TIMES

Who except the gods can live time through forever
without any pain?
                              —AESCHYLUS, *Prometheus Bound*

Many are the troubles of mankind.
                              —AESCHYLUS, *The Suppliant Maidens*

If anything can go wrong, it will.
                                    —ANONYMOUS, Murphy's Law
[This appears in many versions, and has apparently a
military origin.]

In the river, there is the crocodile. On the riverbank,
there is the tiger. If you go to the forest, there are the
thorns. If you go to the market, there is the policeman.
                              —ANONYMOUS (CAMBODIAN PROVERB)

If fortune turns against you, even jelly breaks your
tooth.   —ANONYMOUS (PERSIAN PROVERB)

You can't have more bedbugs than a blanket-full.
                              —ANONYMOUS (SPANISH PROVERB)

Man is born unto trouble, as the sparks fly upward.
                                          —BIBLE, *Job* 5:7

Weeping may endure for a night, but joy cometh in
the morning.   —BIBLE, *Psalms* 30:5

Take us the foxes, the little foxes, that spoil the vines:
for our vines have tender grapes.
                              —BIBLE, *Song of Solomon* 2:15
[In her book *Little Foxes*, Harriet Beecher Stowe explained that by "little foxes" she meant "those unsus-
pected, unwatched, insignificant *little* causes that nibble
away domestic happiness." Lillian Hellman later used
this title for a play about a family quite eaten away by
little foxes.]

If it be possible, let this cup pass from me.
—BIBLE, *Matthew* 26:39

Whom the Lord loveth he chasteneth.
—BIBLE, *Hebrews* 12:6

I am convinced that we have a degree of delight, and that no small one, in the real misfortunes and pains of others.
—EDMUND BURKE, *On the Sublime and Beautiful*
[The thought, horrid as it may be, has occurred to many, including La Rochefoucauld, quoted below. The Germans call it *Schadenfreude*.]

Adversity is the first path to truth.
—LORD BYRON, *Don Juan*

If there were no tribulation, there would be no rest; if there were no winter, there would be no summer.
—ST. JOHN CHRYSOSTOM, *Homilies*

A *wounded* deer—leaps highest.
—EMILY DICKINSON, poem no. 165

Every calamity is a spur and valuable hint.
—RALPH WALDO EMERSON, *Fate*

Everything has two handles: one by which it may be borne, another by which it cannot.
—EPICTETUS, *Enchiridion*

There is no wind that always blows a storm.
—EURIPIDES, *Alcestis*
[The classical version of the proverbial, "It's an ill wind that blows no good."]

Problems are only opportunities in work clothes.
—HENRY J. KAISER, saying

When written in Chinese, the word *crisis* is composed of two characters. One represents danger and the other represents opportunity.
—JOHN F. KENNEDY, speech, April 12, 1959

Our problems are man-made; therefore they may be solved by man.
—JOHN F. KENNEDY, speech, June 10, 1963

If we can really understand the problem, the answer will come out of it, because the answer is not separate from the problem.
—KRISHNAMURTI, *The Penguin Krishnamurti Reader*

In the misfortunes of our best friends, we find something that is not unpleasing.
—LA ROCHEFOUCAULD, *Maxims*
[Cf. Edmund Burke, above.]

The cares that infest the day
Shall fold their tents, like the Arabs,
And as silently steal away.
—HENRY WADSWORTH LONGFELLOW,
The Day Is Done

Into each life some rain must fall,
Some days must be dark and dreary.
—HENRY WADSWORTH LONGFELLOW,
The Rainy Day

Fasten your seat belts. It's going to be a bumpy night.
—JOSEPH L. MANKIEWICZ, *All About Eve*

If you are distressed by anything external, the pain is not due to the thing itself, but to your own estimate of it; and this you have the power to revoke at any moment.   —MARCUS AURELIUS, *Meditations*

The world is quickly bored by the recital of misfortune, and willingly avoids the sight of distress.
—W. SOMERSET MAUGHAM,
The Moon and Sixpence

Care
Sat on his faded cheek.   —JOHN MILTON,
Paradise Lost

That which does not kill me makes me stronger.
　　—FRIEDRICH NIETZSCHE, *Twilight of the Idols*

I never knew any man in my life who could not bear
another's misfortunes perfectly like a Christian.
　　—ALEXANDER POPE, *Thoughts on Various Subjects*

Fire is the test of gold, adversity of strong men.
　　　　　　—SENECA, *On Providence*

Sweet are the uses of adversity.
　　　　　—SHAKESPEARE, *As You Like It*, II, i

The worst is not
So long as we can say, "This is the worst."
　　　　　—SHAKESPEARE, *King Lear*, IV, i

There's small choice in rotten apples.
　　—SHAKESPEARE, *The Taming of the Shrew*, I, i

Misery acquaints a man with strange bedfellows.
　　　　　—SHAKESPEARE, *The Tempest*, II, ii
[For politics and bedfellows, see Warner at POLITICS.]

We have seen better days.
　　　　—SHAKESPEARE, *Timon of Athens*, IV, ii

Grief teaches the steadiest minds to waver.
　　　　　　—SOPHOCLES, *Antigone*

The greatest griefs are those we cause ourselves.
　　　　　　—SOPHOCLES, *Oedipus Rex*

The worst is yet to come.
　　　　—ALFRED, LORD TENNYSON, *Sea Dreams*

Pure and complete sorrow is as impossible as pure
and complete joy.　　—LEO TOLSTOY, *War and Peace*

Suffering is permanent, obscure, and dark,
And shares the nature of infinity.
　　　　—WILLIAM WORDSWORTH, *The Borderers*

Too long a sacrifice
Can make a stone of the heart.
—WILLIAM BUTLER YEATS, *Easter 1916*

TRUST

Poor Trust is dead; Bad Pay killed him.
—ANONYMOUS (ENGLISH PROVERB)

Trust men and they will be true to you.
—RALPH WALDO EMERSON,
Prudence
[But don't forget to cut the cards—see the Dunne quote
under PRUDENCE & PRACTICAL WISDOM.]

Trust, like the soul, never returns once it is gone.
—PUBLILIUS SYRUS, *Sentences*

Love all, trust a few.
—SHAKESPEARE,
All's Well That Ends Well, I, i.

I have always depended on the kindness of strangers.
—TENNESSEE WILLIAMS,
A Streetcar Named Desire
[Final words of Blanche DuBois.]

TRUTH   See also HONESTY & SINCERITY

All truth is good, but not all truth is good to say.
—ANONYMOUS (AFRICAN PROVERB)

Truth brings forth hatred.   —ANONYMOUS
(LATIN PROVERB)

The truth shall make you free.   —BIBLE, *John* 8:32

Pilate saith unto him, What is truth?
—*Ibid.*, 18:38

Great is truth and mighty above all things.
—BIBLE, *I Esdras* 4:41

Truth crushed to earth shall rise again.
—WILLIAM CULLEN BRYANT, *The Battle-Field*

'Tis strange—but true; for truth is always strange;
Stranger than fiction.   —LORD BYRON, *Don Juan*

Truth ever lovely—since the world began,
The foe of tyrants and the friend of man.
—THOMAS CAMPBELL, *The Pleasures of Hope*

The aim of the superior man is truth.
—CONFUCIUS, *Analects*

The truth is always modern, and there never comes
a time when it is safe to give it voice.
—CLARENCE DARROW, writing on Voltaire, cited
in George Seldes, *The Great Quotations*

Nature has buried truth at the bottom of the sea.
—DEMOCRITUS, attributed

We swallow greedily any lie that flatters us, but we
sip only little by little at a truth we find bitter.
—DENIS DIDEROT, *Le Neveu de Rameau*

I can be expected to look for truth, but not to find
it.   —DENIS DIDEROT, *Pensées philosophiques*

When you have eliminated the impossible, whatever
remains, *however improbable*, must be the truth.
—A. CONAN DOYLE, *The Sign of Four*,
"A Demonstration"

Hell is truth seen too late.
—TRYON EDWARDS, *A Dictionary of Thoughts*
[Probably not original with Edwards. The full line is:
"Hell is truth seen too late—duty neglected in its
season."]

God offers to every mind its choice between truth
and repose.   —RALPH WALDO EMERSON, *Intellect*

To love the truth is to refuse to let oneself be saddened by it.　　　　　—ANDRÉ GIDE, *Journals*

There are truths which can kill a nation.
　　　　　—JEAN GIRAUDOUX, *Electra*

Political truth is a libel—religious truth, blasphemy.
　　　　　—WILLIAM HAZLITT, "Commonplaces," in
　　　　　The Round Table

Truth is tough.
　　　　　—OLIVER WENDELL HOLMES, SR.,
　　　　　The Professor at the Breakfast Table

It is the customary fate of new truths to begin as heresies and to end as superstitions.
　　　　　—T. H. HUXLEY, *The Coming of Age of*
　　　　　"The Origin of Species"

There is not a truth existing which I fear, or would wish unknown to the whole world.
　　　　　—THOMAS JEFFERSON, letter to
　　　　　Henry Lee, 1826

What the imagination seizes as beauty must be truth.
　　　　　—JOHN KEATS, letter to Benjamin Bailey,
　　　　　Nov. 22, 1817
[See Keats also under BEAUTY.]

The exact opposite of what is generally believed is often the truth.　　　　　—LA BRUYÈRE, *Les Caractères*

Truth is often eclipsed but never extinguished.
　　　　　—LIVY, *History of Rome*

Truth, like gold, is not less so for being newly brought out of the mine.
　　　　　—JOHN LOCKE, *An Essay Concerning*
　　　　　Human Understanding

To love truth is the principal part of human perfection in this world, and the seed-plot of all other virtues.
　　　　　—JOHN LOCKE, letter to Anthony Collins,
　　　　　Oct. 29, 1703

A great truth is a truth whose opposite is also a truth.
—THOMAS MANN, *Essay on Freud*

The love of truth has its reward in heaven and even on earth.
—FRIEDRICH NIETZSCHE, *Beyond Good and Evil*

We arrive at truth, not by reason only, but also by the heart.
—PASCAL, *Pensées*

Truth is the beginning of every good thing, both in heaven and on earth; and he who would be blessed and happy should be from the first a partaker of truth, for then he can be trusted.
—PLATO, *Laws*
[See also Plato at PHILOSOPHY.]

Truth is no road to fortune.
—JEAN JACQUES ROUSSEAU, *The Social Contract*

Life is short, but truth works far and lives long; let us speak the truth.
—ARTHUR SCHOPENHAUER,
The World as Will and Idea

How dreadful knowledge of the truth can be when there's no help in truth.
—SOPHOCLES, *Oedipus Rex*

Truth is the only safe ground to stand upon.
—ELIZABETH CADY STANTON,
The Woman's Bible

Rather than love, than money, than fame, give me truth.
—HENRY DAVID THOREAU, *Walden*

I never give them hell. I just tell the truth, and they think it's hell.
—HARRY S TRUMAN, cited in William Safire,
Safire's Political Dictionary

Truth is mighty and will prevail. There is nothing the matter with this, except that it ain't so.
—MARK TWAIN, *Notebook*

Truth confronts us, and we can no longer understand anything.   —PAUL VALÉRY, *Eupalinos*

Truth is rarely pure and never simple.
                    —OSCAR WILDE, *The Importance of
                        Being Earnest*

Truth is on the march; nothing can stop it now.
                    —ÉMILE ZOLA, *J'accuse*

TURBULENT TIMES   See also CONFLICT;
                    MODERN TIMES; REVOLUTION;
                                    TROUBLE

Chaos often breeds life, when order breeds habit.
    —HENRY BROOKS ADAMS, *The Education of
        Henry Adams*

Dictators ride to and fro on tigers from which they dare not dismount. And the tigers are getting hungry.
    —WINSTON CHURCHILL, *While England Slept*
[Churchill wrote that the observation, "Dictators ride tigers from which they are afraid to dismount," is a Hindustani proverb. There is a similar proverb among the Chinese: "He who rides a tiger is afraid to dismount."]

It was the best of times, it was the worst of times, it was the age of wisdom, it was the age of foolishness, it was the epoch of belief, it was the epoch of incredulity, it was the season of Light, it was the season of Darkness, it was the spring of hope, it was the winter of despair, we had everything before us, we had nothing before us, we were all going direct to Heaven, we were all going direct the other way.
    —CHARLES DICKENS, *A Tale of Two Cities*

The time is out of joint; O cursèd spite,
That ever I was born to set it right!
                    —SHAKESPEARE, *Hamlet*, I, v

So foul and fair a day I have not seen.
—SHAKESPEARE, *Macbeth*, III, iii

Lechery, lechery; still wars and lechery; nothing else holds fashion.
—SHAKESPEARE, *Troilus and Cressida*, V, ii

TWENTIETH CENTURY   See MODERN TIMES

TYRANNY & TOTALITARIANISM

Death is preferable—it is a milder fate than tyranny.
—AESCHYLUS, *Agamemnon*

Any excuse will serve a tyrant.
—AESOP, *The Wolf and the Lamb*

Dictators ride to and fro on tigers from which they dare not dismount.
—ANONYMOUS (HINDUSTANI PROVERB)
[More is given at TURBULENT TIMES, under Churchill.]

Government by a tyrant is the worst form of rule.
—ST. THOMAS AQUINAS, *On Princely Government*

Under conditions of tyranny, it is far easier to act than to think.
—HANNAH ARENDT, quoted in W. H. Auden, *A Certain World*

When a nation has allowed itself to fall under a tyrannical regime, it cannot be absolved from the faults due to the guilt of that regime.
—WINSTON CHURCHILL, speech, July 28, 1944

All men would be tyrants if they could.
—DANIEL DEFOE, *The History of the Kentish Petition*, addenda

The history of most countries has been that of majorities—mounted majorities, clad in iron, armed with death, treading down the ten-fold more numerous minorities.
> —OLIVER WENDELL HOLMES, SR., address,
> Massachusetts Medical Society, May 30, 1860

Resistance to tyrants is obedience to God.
> —THOMAS JEFFERSON, motto on his seal,
> original author not known

Truth forever on the scaffold, Wrong forever on the throne.   —JAMES RUSSELL LOWELL,
> *The Present Crisis*

I am the state—I alone am here the representative of the people.
> —NAPOLEON BONAPARTE, in the French Senate,
> 1814 [See also Louis XIV at HIGH POSITION:
> RULERS & LEADERS.]

Big Brother is watching you.   —GEORGE ORWELL,
> *1984*

Who controls the past controls the future. Who controls the present controls the past.   —*Ibid.*

Tyranny is always better organized than freedom.
> —CHARLES PÉGUY, "War and Peace," in
> *Basic Virtues*

Necessity is the plea for every infringement of human freedom. It is the argument of tyrants; it is the creed of slaves.   —WILLIAM PITT, speech, Nov. 18, 1783 [See also John Milton at NECESSITY.]

The people always have some champion whom they set over them and nurse into greatness. . . . This and no other is the root from which a tyranny springs.
> —PLATO, *The Republic*

The face of tyranny is always mild at first.
> —RACINE, *Britannicus*

Man was born free, and everywhere he is in chains.
—JEAN JACQUES ROUSSEAU, *The Social Contract*

Why, man, he doth bestride the narrow world like a Colossus. —SHAKESPEARE, *Julius Caesar*, I, ii

They squeeze the orange and throw away the peel.
—VOLTAIRE, describing his experience
in the court of Frederick the Great,
letter to Mme. Denis, Sept. 9, 1751

The despot, be assured, lives night and day like one condemned to death by the whole of mankind for his wickedness. —XENOPHON, *Hiero*

U

UNDERSTANDING

See MIND, THOUGHT, & UNDERSTANDING; TOLERANCE & UNDERSTANDING; VISION & VISIONARIES; WISDOM

UNHAPPINESS

See DESPAIR, DEPRESSION, MISERY; HAPPINESS; SORROW, SADNESS, & SUFFERING; TROUBLE

UNITED STATES

See AMERICA & AMERICANS; AMERICAN HISTORY: MEMORABLE MOMENTS

UNITY & LOYALTY

See also CONFLICT

United we stand, divided we fall.
—AESOP, *The Four Oxen and the Lion*
[For Benjamin Franklin's similar observation on hanging together, see AMERICAN HISTORY: MEMORABLE MOMENTS.]

Union gives strength.   —AESOP,
The Bundle of Sticks

Whose bread I eat, his song I sing.
—ANONYMOUS, German saying

No man can serve two masters.   —BIBLE,
Matthew 6:24

He that is not with me is against me.
—*Ibid.* [also *Luke* 11:23]

I have kept the faith. —BIBLE, *II Timothy* 4:7
[The full verse is given at ACCOMPLISHMENT.]

When bad men combine, the good must associate;
else they will fall, one by one, an unpitied sacrifice in
a contemptible struggle.
> —EDMUND BURKE, *Thoughts on the Cause of
> the Present Discontents*

All for one, one for all.
> —ALEXANDRE DUMAS, *The Three Musketeers*

Something there is that doesn't love a wall.
> —ROBERT FROST, *Mending Wall*

There are only two forces that unite men—fear and
interest. —NAPOLEON BONAPARTE, *Maxims*

He may be a son of a bitch, but he's our son of a
bitch. —FRANKLIN D. ROOSEVELT, referring to
> Anastasio Somoza of Nicaragua,
> cited by William Pfaff in
> *The New Yorker*, May 27, 1985

UNIVERSE See also CREATION, DIVINE; NATURE;
> SCIENCE: PHYSICS & COSMOLOGY;
> WORLD, END OF

The universe . . . is a machine for making deities.
> —HENRI BERGSON, *Les deux sources de la
> morale et de la religion*

I don't pretend to understand the universe—it's a
great deal bigger than I am. . . . People ought to be
modester.
> —THOMAS CARLYLE, quoted in D. A. Wilson and
> D. Wilson McArthur, *Carlyle in Old Age*

[The universe:] The most exquisite masterpiece ever
composed by nobody.
> —G. K. CHESTERTON, quoted by Martin Gardner
> in *New York Review of Books*,
> June 13, 1985

Law rules throughout existence, a Law which is not intelligent, but Intelligence.
> —RALPH WALDO EMERSON, *Fate*

Ah Love! Could thou and I with Fate conspire
To grasp this sorry Scheme of Things entire,
Would we not shatter it to bits—and then remold it
   nearer to the Heart's Desire!
> —EDWARD FITZGERALD, *The Rubáiyát of*
> *Omar Khayyám*

The cosmic process has no sort of relation to moral ends.
> —T. H. HUXLEY,
> *Evolution and Ethics*

The universe begins to look more like a great thought than like a great machine.
> —SIR JAMES JEANS, *The Mysterious Universe*

All are but parts of one stupendous whole,
Whose body nature is, and God the soul.
> —ALEXANDER POPE,
> *An Essay on Man*

The universe is a spiraling Big Band in a polka-dotted speakeasy, effusively generating new light every one-night stand.
> —ISHMAEL REED, cited in Jim Haskins,
> *The Cotton Club*

Don't let me catch anyone talking about the Universe in my department.
> —LORD ERNEST RUTHERFORD,
> quoted by John Kendrew,
> BBC broadcast, July 3, 1968

Let the great world spin forever down the ringing grooves of change.
> —ALFRED, LORD TENNYSON, *Locksley Hall*

Thou canst not stir a flower
Without the troubling of a star.
  —FRANCIS THOMPSON, *The Mistress of Vision*

O amazement of things—even the least particle!
  —WALT WHITMAN, *Song at Sunset*

UNREASONABLE PEOPLE See REASONABLE &
           UNREASONABLE PEOPLE

V

VALUE

Neither cast ye your pearls before swine, lest they trample them under their feet, and turn again and rend you.　　　　　　　　　—BIBLE, *Matthew* 7:6

[T. H. White, in *The Bestiary*, notes that "pearls," written in Latin *margarites*, may be a mistranslation of the Latin *marguerites*, which means "daisies."]

Things are only worth what you make them worth.
　　　　　　　—MOLIÈRE, *Les Précieuses ridicules*

Good merchandise, even when hidden, soon finds buyers.　　　　　　　　—PLAUTUS, *Poenulus*

[A cynic:] a man who knows the price of everything and the value of nothing.
　　　　　—OSCAR WILDE, *Lady Windermere's Fan*

VANITY　　　　　　　　See PRIDE & VANITY

VARIETY　　　　　　　　See also CHANGE;
　　　　　　　　　　　　　　　　NEW THINGS

Every fool is different.　　—ANONYMOUS
　　　　　　　　　　　　　(GERMAN PROVERB)

Variety's the very spice of life,
That gives it all its flavor.　　—WILLIAM COWPER,
　　　　　　　　　　　　　　The Task

What is food to one is to another bitter poison.
　　　　　　　—LUCRETIUS, *De rerum natura*

[This is an early version of the English proverb "One man's meat is another man's poison."]

Letting a hundred flowers blossom and a hundred schools of thought contend is the policy.
　　　　　　—MAO ZEDUNG, speech, May 2, 1956
[Usually shortened to, "Let a hundred flowers blossom."]

No pleasure lasts long unless there is variety in it.
　　　　　　—PUBLILIUS SYRUS, *Moral Sayings*

It were not best that we should all think alike; it is difference of opinion that makes horse races.
　　　　　—MARK TWAIN, "Pudd'nhead Wilson's Calendar,"
　　　　　in *Pudd'nhead Wilson*

VENGEANCE　　　　　　　　　　　See REVENGE

VICE　　　See EVIL; EXCESS; SIN, VICE, & NAUGHTINESS

VICTORY　　　　　　　　See MILITARY BATTLES; WAR;
　　　　　　　WINNING & LOSING, VICTORY & DEFEAT

VIOLENCE & FORCE　　　　　　　See also ANGER;
　　　　　　　REVOLUTION; TYRANNY &
　　　　　　　TOTALITARIANISM; WAR

They have sown the wind, and they shall reap the whirlwind.　　　　　　　—BIBLE, *Hosea* 8:7

All they that take the sword shall perish with the sword.　　　　　　—BIBLE, *Matthew* 26:52
[But see also *Matthew* at REVOLUTION.]

A whiff of grapeshot.
　　　　　　—THOMAS CARLYLE,
　　　　　　History of the French Revolution

God hates violence. He has ordained that all men fairly possess their property, not seize it.
　　　　　　—EURIPIDES, *Helen*

It is better to be violent, if there is violence in our hearts, than to put on the cloak of non-violence to cover impotence.
> —MOHANDAS K. GANDHI, "Non-Violence," in *Peace and War*

Where wisdom is called for, force is of little use.
> —HERODOTUS, *Histories*

Force without wisdom falls of its own weight.
> —HORACE, *Odes*

A man may build himself a throne of bayonets, but he cannot sit on it.
> —WILLIAM RALPH INGE, *Wit and Wisdom of Dean Inge*

Force cannot give right.
> —THOMAS JEFFERSON, *The Rights of British America*

It is far more convenient to commit an act of violence, and afterwards excuse it, than laboriously to consider convincing arguments, and lose time listening to objections. This very boldness itself indicates a sort of conviction of the legitimacy of the action, and the God of success is afterwards the best advocate.
> —IMMANUEL KANT, *Perpetual Peace*, appendix

Be peaceful, be courteous, obey the law, respect everyone; but if someone puts his hand on you, send him to the cemetery.
> —MALCOLM X, *Malcolm X Speaks*

In violence, we forget who we are.
> —MARY McCARTHY, *On the Contrary*

Who overcomes
By force, hath overcome but half his foe.
> —JOHN MILTON, *Paradise Lost*

If aggressors are wrong above, they are right here
below.   —NAPOLEON BONAPARTE, *Maxims*

Violence is good for those who have nothing to lose.
        —JEAN-PAUL SARTRE, *Le Diable et le bon Dieu*

Uncontrolled violence is a fault of youth.
        —SENECA, *Troades*

Lay on, Macduff,
And damn'd be him that first cries "Hold, enough!"
        —SHAKESPEARE, *Macbeth*, V, viii

Not believing in force is the same as not believing in
gravity.   —LEON TROTSKY, *What Next?*

VIRGIN MARY   See JESUS CHRIST

VIRTUE   See also COMPASSION & PITY; COURAGE;
        FORGIVENESS & MERCY; GRACE;
        HONESTY & SINCERITY; INNOCENCE;
        SELF-RIGHTEOUSNESS; STRENGTH; WISDOM

Virtue is not always amiable.
        —JOHN ADAMS, *Diary*, Feb. 9, 1779

The happiness of man, as well as his dignity, consists
in virtue.
        —JOHN ADAMS, *Thoughts on Government*

No act of kindness, no matter how small, is ever
wasted.   —AESOP, *The Lion and the Mouse*

Kindness effects more than severity.
        —AESOP, *The Wind and the Sun*

Righteousness exalteth a nation.
        —BIBLE, *Proverbs* 14:34

What doth the Lord require of thee, but to do justly, and to love mercy, and to walk humbly with thy God?
BIBLE, *Micah* 6:8

Blessed are the poor in spirit: for theirs is the kingdom of heaven.

Blessed are they that mourn: for they shall be comforted.

Blessed are the meek: for they shall inherit the earth.

Blessed are they which do hunger and thirst after righteousness: for they shall be filled.

Blessed are the merciful: for they shall obtain mercy.

Blessed are the pure in heart: for they shall see God.

Blessed are the peacemakers: for they shall be called the children of God.

Blessed are they which are persecuted for righteousness sake:

for theirs is the kingdom of heaven.

—BIBLE, *Matthew* 5:3–10,
The Sermon on
the Mount

Strait is the gate, and narrow is the way, which leadeth unto life, and few there be that find it.
—*Ibid.*, 7:14

If thine eye offend thee, pluck it out, and cast it from thee: it is better for thee to enter into life with one eye, rather than having two eyes to be cast into hell fire.
—*Ibid.*, 18:9

Unto the pure all things are pure.   —BIBLE,
Titus 1:15

The souls of the righteous are in the hand of God, and there shall no torment touch them.
—BIBLE, *Wisdom of Solomon* 3:1

My will was to live worthily as long as I lived, and after my life to leave them that should come after, my memory in good works.
—BOETHIUS, *Consolation of Philosophy*,
translated by Alfred the Great

There is no road or ready way to virtue.
> —THOMAS BROWNE, *Religio medici*

The humblest citizen of all the land, when clad in the armor of a righteous cause, is stronger than all the hosts of error.
> —WILLIAM JENNINGS BRYAN, speech at the
> Democratic National Convention, 1896

The upright, honest-hearted man
Who strives to do the best he can,
Need never fear the church's ban
Or hell's damnation.
> —ROBERT BURNS, *Epistle to the Rev. John McMath*

Absolute virtue is as sure to kill a man as absolute vice is, let alone the dullness of it and the pomposities of it.   —SAMUEL BUTLER, *Notebooks*

In my experience, good deeds usually do not go unpunished.
> —WILLIAM SLOANE COFFIN, speech, Oct. 1984,
> in behalf of the Sanctuary Program
> for protecting refugees

[This bit of sharp cynicism seems to have been around a while in various forms. Clare Boothe Luce was credited by H. Farber, in *The Book of Laws*, with the even harsher, "No good deed goes unpunished."]

It is a far, far better thing that I do, than I have ever done; it is a far, far better rest that I go to, than I have ever known.
> —CHARLES DICKENS, *A Tale of Two Cities*

The essence of greatness is the perception that virtue is enough.   —RALPH WALDO EMERSON, *Heroism*
[But for Emerson's view of people who *talk* about their virtue, see SELF-RIGHTEOUSNESS.]

Life is mostly froth and bubble,
Two things stand like stone,
Kindness in another's trouble,
Courage in your own.
> —ADAM LINDSAY GORDON,
> *Ye Wearie Wayfarer*

I shall pass through this world but once. If therefore there be any kindness I can show, or any good thing I can do, let me do it now; let me not defer it or neglect it.   —ÉTIENNE DE GRELLET, attributed
[Also attributed to others.]

Be good, sweet maid, and let who will be clever;
Do noble things, not dream them, all day long.
                    —CHARLES KINGSLEY, *A Farewell*

If you can keep your head when all about you
Are losing theirs and blaming it on you.
If you can trust yourself when all men doubt you
And make allowance for their doubting, too.
                    —RUDYARD KIPLING, *If*
[In *Please Don't Eat the Daisies*, Jean Kerr observed, "If you can keep your head when all about you are losing theirs, it is just possible that you haven't grasped the situation."]

If you can meet with Triumph and Disaster, and treat those two impostors just the same.   —*Ibid.*

If you can talk with crowds and keep your virtue
Or walk with Kings—nor lose the common touch.
                    —*Ibid.*

If you can fill the unforgiving minute
With sixty seconds' worth of distance run,
Yours is the earth and everything that's in it,
And—which is more—you'll be a Man, my son!
                    —*Ibid.*

Very often our virtues are only vices in disguise.
                    —LA ROCHEFOUCAULD, *Maxims*

Virtue would not go to such lengths if vanity did not keep her company.   —*Ibid.*

Virtue is harder to be got than knowledge of the world; and, if lost in a young man, is seldom recovered.
                    —JOHN LOCKE, *Some Thoughts Concerning Education*

I could not love thee, dear, so much,
Loved I not honor more.
—RICHARD LOVELACE, *To
Lucasta, Going to the Wars*

I cannot praise a fugitive and cloistered virtue, unexercised and unbreathed, that never sallies out and sees her adversary, but slinks out of the race, where that immortal garland is to be run for, not without dust and heat. —JOHN MILTON, *Areopagitica*

Virtue may be assailed, but never hurt,
Surprised by unjust force, but not enthralled.
—JOHN MILTON, *Comus*

I prefer an accommodating vice to an obstinate virtue. —MOLIÈRE, *Amphitryon*

Virtue in this world should be malleable.
—MOLIÈRE, *Le Misanthrope*

There may be guilt when there is too much virtue.
—PASCAL, *Pensées*

Do good by stealth, and blush to find it fame.
—ALEXANDER POPE, *Epilogue to the Satires*

Charms strike the sight, but merit wins the soul.
—ALEXANDER POPE, *The Rape of the Lock*

When men grow virtuous in their old age, they only make a sacrifice to God of the devil's leavings.
—ALEXANDER POPE, *Thoughts on Various Subjects*

Nature does not bestow virtue, it is an art.
—SENECA, *Letters to Lucilius*

Assume a virtue, if you have it not.
—SHAKESPEARE, *Hamlet*, III, iv

Virtue is bold, and goodness never fearful.
　　　—SHAKESPEARE, *Measure for Measure*, III, i

How far that little candle throws his beams!
So shines a good deed in a naughty world.
　　　—SHAKESPEARE, *The Merchant of Venice*, V, i

Mine honor is my life.　　　　　　—SHAKESPEARE,
　　　　　　　　　　　　　　　　Richard II, I, i

He lives in fame that died in virtue's cause.
　　　—SHAKESPEARE, *Titus Andronicus*, I, i

He profits most who serves best.
　—A. F. SHELDON, motto for International Rotary

Nothing can harm a good man, either in life or after
death.　　　　—SOCRATES, quoted in Plato, *Apology*

True virtue is life under the direction of reason.
　　　　　　　　　　　—SPINOZA, *Ethics*

She would rather light candles than curse the darkness, and her glow has warmed the world.
　　—ADLAI STEVENSON, said of Eleanor Roosevelt
　　　　after her death, 1962
[Cf. the Christopher Society motto, under DOING.]

My strength is as the strength of ten,
Because my heart is pure.
　　　—ALFRED, LORD TENNYSON, *Sir Galahad*

'Tis only noble to be good.
Kind hearts are more than coronets.
　　　　　—ALFRED, LORD TENNYSON,
　　　　　　Lady Clara Vere de Vere

Be good and you will be lonesome.
　　　　—MARK TWAIN, *Following the Equator*,
　　　　　　caption for frontispiece photo of Twain

Few things are harder to put up with than the annoyance of a good example.
　—MARK TWAIN, "Pudd'nhead Wilson's Calendar"

Always do right. This will gratify some people and astonish the rest.
　—MARK TWAIN, speech, Greenpoint Presbyterian
　　Church, Brooklyn, N.Y., 1901

Virtue, study, and gaiety are three sisters who should not be separated.
　—VOLTAIRE, letter to Frederick the Great, 1737

That best portion of a good man's life,
His little, nameless, unremembered acts
Of kindness and of love.
　—WILLIAM WORDSWORTH, *Tintern Abbey*

VISION & VISIONARIES　　　See also IDEAS &
　　　　　　　　　　　　　IDEALS; MYSTICISM; WISDOM

We are like dwarves upon the shoulders of giants, and so able to see more and farther than the ancients.
　—BERNARD OF CHARTRES, quoted in
　　John of Salisbury, *Metalogicon*
[For Newton's version, see SCIENCE. Robert K. Merton, in his entertaining book on this aphorism, offered many examples of variations. A late one is from Coleridge: "The dwarf sees farther than the giant, when he has the giant's shoulder to mount on" (*The Friend*).]

Behold, this dreamer cometh.　　　—BIBLE,
　　　　　　　　　　　　　　　Genesis 37:19

Where there is no vision, the people perish.
　　　　　　　　　　　—BIBLE, *Proverbs* 29:18

Your sons and your daughters shall prophesy, your old men shall dream dreams, your young men shall see visions.　　　　　　　　—BIBLE, *Joel* 2:28

A prophet is not without honor, save in his own country.　　　　　—BIBLE, *Matthew* 13:57
[For Matthew on false prophets, see under HYPOCRISY.]

If the blind lead the blind, both shall fall into the ditch.   —*Ibid.*, 15:14

For now we see through a glass, darkly; but then face to face: now I know in part; but then I shall know even as I am known.   —BIBLE, *I Corinthians* 13:11–12

A fool sees not the same tree that a wise man sees.
                        —WILLIAM BLAKE,
                            The Marriage of Heaven and Hell

It isn't that they can't see the solution. It is that they can't see the problem.
                        —G. K. CHESTERTON, "The Point of
                            a Pin," in *The Scandal of
                            Father Brown*

People see only what they are prepared to see.
                        —RALPH WALDO EMERSON, *Journals*, 1863

A danger foreseen is half avoided.
                        —THOMAS FULLER, *Gnomologia*

Only he who keeps his eye fixed on the far horizon will find his right road.
                        —DAG HAMMARSKJÖLD, *Markings*

A moment's insight is sometimes worth a life's experience.   —OLIVER WENDELL HOLMES, SR.,
                            The Professor at the Breakfast Table

You can only predict things after they've happened.
                        —EUGÈNE IONESCO, *Rhinoceros*

I have a dream.
                        —MARTIN LUTHER KING, JR.,
                            theme of his speech in the March
                            on Washington, August 28, 1963

Two men look out through the same bars:
One sees the mud, and one the stars.
                        —FREDERICK LANGBRIDGE,
                            Cluster of Quiet Thoughts

All armed prophets have been victorious, and all unarmed prophets have been destroyed.
—MACHIAVELLI, *The Prince*

The fellow that can only see a week ahead is always the popular fellow, for he is looking with the crowd. But the one that can see years ahead, he has a telescope but he can't make anybody believe that he has it.
—WILL ROGERS,
The Autobiography of Will Rogers

Vision is the art of seeing things invisible.
—JONATHAN SWIFT,
Thoughts on Various Subjects

A dreamer is one who can only find his way by moonlight, and his punishment is that he sees the dawn before the rest of the world.
—OSCAR WILDE, *The Critic as Artist*

W

WAR   See also CONFLICT; MILITARY, THE; MILITARY
BATTLES; PEACE; VIOLENCE & FORCE;
WINNING & LOSING, VICTORY & DEFEAT

What Price Glory?
> —MAXWELL ANDERSON, title of his
> play about World War I

To win a war quickly takes long preparation.
> —ANONYMOUS (LATIN PROVERB)

The price of pride is high, and paid by the young.
> —ANONYMOUS, inscription on the
> German memorial at El Alamein

A bayonet is a weapon with a worker at both ends.
> —ANONYMOUS, British pacifist slogan

It takes twenty years or more of peace to make a
man; it takes only twenty seconds of war to destroy
him.
> —KING BAUDOUIN I, of Belgium, speech in the
> U.S. Congress, May 12, 1959

It is not merely cruelty that leads men to love war,
it is excitement.
> —HENRY WARD BEECHER, *Proverbs from
> Plymouth Pulpit*

This strategy would involve us in the wrong war, at
the wrong place, at the wrong time, and with the wrong
enemy.   —GEN. OMAR BRADLEY, testimony in the
> U.S. Senate, May 15, 1951

[The general was referring to confrontation with Communist China.]

War is like love, it always finds a way.
> —BERTOLT BRECHT, *Mother Courage*

God is ordinarily for the big battalions against the little ones. —COUNT BUSSY-RABUTIN, letter to the Count of Limoges, Oct. 18, 1677
[A thought also voiced by Voltaire, Napoleon, and others.]

In war, whichever side may call itself the victor, there are no winners but all are losers.
> —NEVILLE CHAMBERLAIN, speech, July 3, 1938

The sinews of war, unlimited money.
> —CICERO, *Philippic*, V

Laws are silent in time of war. —CICERO, *Pro milone*

All great civilizations, in their early stages, are based on success in war.
> —SIR KENNETH CLARK, *Civilization*

War is nothing more than the continuation of politics by other means. —KARL VON CLAUSEWITZ, *On War*
[This is the traditional translation. In the original German the quote is less succinct and slightly different: "*Der Krieg ist nichts als eine Fortsetzung des politischen Verkehrs mit Einmischung anderer Mittel.*" ("War is nothing but a continuation of political intercourse with the intermixing of other means.")]

There is nothing that war has ever achieved that we could not better achieve without it.
> —HAVELOCK ELLIS, *The Philosophy of Conflict*

War educates the senses, calls into action the will, perfects the physical constitution, brings men into such swift and close collision in critical moments that man measures man. —RALPH WALDO EMERSON, *War*

Men love war because it allows them to look serious. Because it is the one thing that stops women laughing at them. —JOHN FOWLES, *The Magus*

There never was a good war or a bad peace.
—BENJAMIN FRANKLIN, letter to Josiah Quincy,
Sept. 11, 1783

Either man is obsolete or war is.
—R. BUCKMINSTER FULLER, *I Seem to Be a Verb*

Guns will make us powerful; butter will only make us fat.   —HERMANN GOERING, radio speech, 1936

It has been a splendid little war.
—JOHN HAY, letter to Theodore Roosevelt,
July 27, 1898
[The Secretary of State was referring to the war with Spain. He goes on: " . . . begun with the highest motives, carried on with magnificent intelligence and spirit, favored by the Fortune which loves the brave."]

War is death's feast.   —GEORGE HERBERT,
Outlandish Proverbs

In starting and waging a war, it is not right that matters but victory.
—ADOLF HITLER, quoted in William L. Shirer,
The Rise and Fall of the Third Reich
[See also the first MacArthur quote below.]

Older men declare war. But it is the youth that must fight and die.   —HERBERT HOOVER, speech,
Republican National Convention

The first casualty when war comes is truth.
—SEN. HIRAM JOHNSON, attributed

The slaying of multitudes should be mourned with sorrow.
A victory should be celebrated with the funeral rite.
—LAO-TZU, *Tao Te Ching*

It is well that war is so terrible, or we should grow too fond of it.   —GEN. ROBERT E. LEE,
at Fredericksburg, Dec. 1862

War is the greatest plague that can afflict humanity; it destroys religion, it destroys states, it destroys families. Any scourge is preferable to it.
—MARTIN LUTHER, *Table-Talk*

In war there is no substitute for victory.
>—GEN. DOUGLAS MACARTHUR,
>address to Congress, April 19, 1951

It is fatal to enter any war without the will to win it.
>—GEN. DOUGLAS MACARTHUR, speech,
>Republican National Convention, 1952

War is just when it is necessary; arms are permissible when there is no hope except in arms.
>—MACHIAVELLI, *The Prince*

To the ashes of the dead, glory comes too late.
>—MARTIAL, *Epigrams*

War will never cease until babies begin to come into the world with larger cerebrums and smaller adrenal glands.
>—H. L. MENCKEN, "Minority Report," in *Notebooks*

For what can war, but endless war still breed?
>—JOHN MILTON, *To Fairfax*

There will be no veterans of World War III.
>—WALTER MONDALE, speech, Sept. 5, 1984

An empire founded by war has to maintain itself by war.
>—MONTESQUIEU, *Considérations sur les causes de la grandeur des Romains et de leur décadence*

Against war it may be said that it makes the victor stupid and the vanquished revengeful.
>—FRIEDRICH NIETZSCHE, *Human, All-Too-Human*

He who is the author of a war lets loose the whole contagion of hell and opens a vein that bleeds a nation to death.
>—THOMAS PAINE, *The American Crisis*

No one won the last war, and no one will win the next.   —ELEANOR ROOSEVELT,
          letter to Harry S Truman,
          Nov. 5, 1948

War is not an adventure. It is a disease.
    —ANTOINE DE SAINT-EXUPÉRY, *Flight to Arras*

Sometime they'll give a war and nobody will come.
    —CARL SANDBURG, *The People, Yes*

When the rich wage war, it is the poor who die.
    —JEAN-PAUL SARTRE, *Le Diable et le bon Dieu*

We ask the outcome of a war, not the cause.
          —SENECA, *Hercules furens*

O war, thou son of hell!
    —SHAKESPEARE, *Henry VI, Part II*, V, ii

Cry "Havoc!" and let slip the dogs of war.
          —SHAKESPEARE, *Julius Caesar*, III, i

War is hell.
  —WILLIAM TECUMSEH SHERMAN,
    attributed, graduation
speech at the Michigan Military Academy, 1879
[Better known but less well documented than the statement at Columbus, below.]

There is many a boy here today who looks on war as all glory, but, boys, it is all hell.
          —WILLIAM TECUMSEH SHERMAN, speech,
          Columbus, Ohio, 1880

War is cruelty, and you cannot refine it.
          —WILLIAM TECUMSEH SHERMAN, letter to
          James M. Calhoun, Sept. 12, 1864

War is much too serious a thing to be left to military men.
    —CHARLES-MAURICE DE TALLEYRAND, attributed
[Also attributed to Clemenceau.]

War is a matter not so much of arms as of expenditure, through which arms may be made of service.
—THUCYDIDES, *Historia*

War is the unfolding of miscalculations.
—BARBARA TUCHMAN, *The Guns of August*

He, therefore, who desires peace should prepare for war. He who aspires to victory should spare no pains to form his soldiers. And he who hopes for success should fight on principle, not chance.
—VEGETIUS, *Re Militari*
[A favorite quote of George Washington. Used also by President George Bush in 1990 during preparations for the Gulf War.]

WASHINGTON, D.C. See CITIES

WEALTH See HAVES & HAVE-NOTS; MONEY

WEATHER See NATURE: WIND & WEATHER

WICKEDNESS See EVIL; SIN, VICE, & NAUGHTINESS

WILL

The good or ill of man lies within his own will.
—EPICTETUS, *Discourses*

If you will it, it is no dream.
—THEODOR HERZL, saying
[Herzl was the founder of political Zionism.]

The will to do, the soul to dare.
—SIR WALTER SCOTT,
The Lady of the Lake

Our wills and fates do so contrary run
That our devices still are overthrown;
Our thoughts are ours, their ends none of our own.
—SHAKESPEARE, *Hamlet*, III, ii

WIND　　　　　　　　See NATURE: WIND & WEATHER

WINE　　　　　　　　See ALCOHOL & DRINKING;
　　　　　　　　　　　　FOOD, WINE, & EATING

WINNING & LOSING,　See also GAMES; MILITARY
VICTORY & DEFEAT　　BATTLES; RUIN; SPORTS;
　　　　　　　　　　　　SUCCESS & FAME; WAR

The laugh is always on the loser.
　　　　　　　—ANONYMOUS (GERMAN PROVERB)

'Tis better to have loved and lost than never to have
lost at all.
　　　　　　　—SAMUEL BUTLER, *The Way of All Flesh*

Victory at all costs, victory in spite of all terror, victory however long and hard the road may be; for without victory, there is no survival.
　　　　　　　—WINSTON CHURCHILL, speech, May 13, 1940

The problems of victory are more agreeable than
those of defeat, but they are no less difficult.
　　　　　　　—WINSTON CHURCHILL, speech, Nov. 11, 1942

As always, victory finds a hundred fathers, but defeat
is an orphan.　　　　　—COUNT GALEAZZO CIANO,
　　　　　　　　　　　The Ciano Diaries: 1939–1943
[A favorite observation of John F. Kennedy and others,
and used in the 1951 film *The Desert Fox*. The wording
often varies.]

Victory is by nature insolent and haughty.
　　　　　　　—CICERO, *Pro Marcello*

The race is to the swift;
The battle to the strong.　　　—JOHN DAVIDSON,
　　　　　　　　　　　　　　War Song
[For a concurring opinion, see Damon Runyon, under
SPORTS; for the opposing Biblical view, see LUCK.]

Nice guys finish last.　—LEO DUROCHER, attributed
[According to Paul F. Boller, Jr., and John George,

authors of *They Never Said It*, baseball manager Leo Durocher claimed to have actually said, of the New York Giants football team, "All nice guys. They'll finish last. Nice guys. Finish last." Sportswriter Jimmy Cannon used the version we know to summarize Durocher's view of life.]

All is lost save honor.
> —FRANCIS I, letter referring to his
> defeat at Pavia, 1525

All victories breed hate.
—BALTASAR GRACIÁN, *The Art of Worldly Wisdom*

If you think you can win, you can win. Faith is necessary to victory.
—WILLIAM HAZLITT, *On Great and Little Things*

Lose as if you like it; win as if you were used to it.
> —TOMMY HITCHCOCK, saying, passed on by
> his father, Jonas Hitchcock

[Tommy Hitchcock's sport was polo.]

Victory often changes her side.   —HOMER, *Iliad*

[I feel] somewhat like the boy in Kentucky who stubbed his toe while running to see his sweetheart. The boy said he was too big to cry, and far too badly hurt to laugh.
> —ABRAHAM LINCOLN, reply when asked
> how he felt about the Democrats winning
> the N.Y. State elections, quoted in
> *Leslie's Illustrated Weekly*, Nov. 22, 1862

[Adlai Stevenson, crediting Lincoln, used this same anecdote to illustrate his feelings after his loss in the presidential election of 1952.]

Winning isn't everything, it's the only thing.
> —VINCENT LOMBARDI, attributed

[Widely attributed to Lombardi, the legendary football coach of the Green Bay Packers (1959–1969), but not original with him. In *Respectfully Quoted*, published by the Library of Congress, the saying is traced to Red Sanders, football coach of Vanderbilt University, and dated ca. 1948. In a letter to *The New York Times*, Sept. 17, 1986, Jerry James notes that the line was used in a 1953 John Wayne movie, written by Michael Shavelson. Lombardi claimed that what he actually said was something on the lines of: winning isn't everything, but wanting to win (or, making the effort to win) is. But others recollect him taking the harder line.]

Victory puts us on a level with heaven.
　　　　　　　　　—LUCRETIUS, *De rerum natura*

To the victor belongs the spoils of the enemy.
　　　　　　　　　—WILLIAM LEARNED MARCY,
　　　　　　　　　　　speech, U.S. Senate, Jan. 1832
[See also "Boss" Croker under POLITICS.]

There are defeats more triumphant than victories.
　　　　　　　　　—MONTAIGNE, *Essays*
[On this subject, see King Pyrrhus at MILITARY BATTLES.]

The loser is always suspicious.
　　　　　　　　　—PUBLILIUS SYRUS, *Moral Sayings*

For when the One Great Scorer comes
To mark against your name,
He writes—not that you won or lost—
But how you played the game.
　　　　　　　　　—GRANTLAND RICE, *Alumnus Football*

Show me a good and gracious loser, and I'll show you a failure.　　　—KNUTE ROCKNE, attributed
[According to *Bartlett's*, he made this remark to Wisconsin basketball coach Walter Meanwell.]

Once you hear the details of a victory, it is hard to distinguish it from a defeat.
　　　　　　　　　—JEAN-PAUL SARTRE, *Le Diable et le bon Dieu*

It is best to win without fighting.
　　　　　　　　　—SUN TZE, *Sun Tze Ping Fa*

WINTER See NATURE: SEASONS

WISDOM See also MIND, THOUGHT &
UNDERSTANDING; PHILOSOPHY; PRUDENCE &
PRACTICAL WISDOM; VISION & VISIONARIES

The hours of a wise man are lengthened by his ideas.
—JOSEPH ADDISON, *The Spectator*,
June 18, 1711

Wisdom comes only through suffering.
—AESCHYLUS, *Agamemnon*

Wonder is the beginning of wisdom.
—ANONYMOUS (GREEK PROVERB)

The fox knows many things, but the hedgehog knows
one great thing. —ARCHILOCHUS, fragment
[For a slightly different version of this saying see Pigres
at CRAFTINESS. Isaiah Berlin titled his classic study of
Tolstoy, *The Hedgehog and the Fox* (1953), with reference to this quote. Writers and thinkers can be cate-
gorized as foxes or hedgehogs, he said. The latter are
inspired by a single organizing principle or world view,
and include Dante, Plato, Dostoevski, and Nietzsche.
The foxes seize upon a variety of experiences without
trying to impose a unitary vision; foxes include Aristotle, Shakespeare, Montaigne, and Balzac. Tolstoy is
both fox and hedgehog, according to Berlin.]

The great good is wisdom. —ST. AUGUSTINE,
Soliloquies

The price of wisdom is above rubies. —BIBLE,
Job 28:18

The fear of the Lord is the beginning of wisdom.
—BIBLE, *Psalms* 11:10
[Slightly different is *Proverbs* 1:7, "The fear of the Lord
is the beginning of knowledge."]

Happy is the man that findeth wisdom, and the man that getteth understanding.
—BIBLE, *Proverbs* 3:13

In much wisdom is much grief: and he that increaseth knowledge increaseth sorrow.
—BIBLE, *Ecclesiastes* 1:18

The children of this world are in their generation wiser than the children of light.
—BIBLE, *Luke* 16:8

Be wiser than other people if you can, but do not tell them so.   —EARL OF CHESTERFIELD,
letter to his son, Nov. 19, 1745

The function of wisdom is discriminating between good and evil.   —CICERO, *De officiis*

A sadder and a wiser man
He rose the morrow morn.
—SAMUEL TAYLOR COLERIDGE,
The Ancient Mariner

Errors, like straws, upon the surface flow;
He who would search for pearls must dive below.
—JOHN DRYDEN, *All for Love*, prologue

Those who are held wise among men, and who search for the reason of things, are those who bring the most sorrow on themselves.   —EURIPIDES, *Medea*

How prone to doubt, how cautious are the wise!
—HOMER, *Odyssey*

Wisdom denotes the pursuing of the best ends by the best means.
—FRANCIS HUTCHESON, *Inquiry into the
Original of Our Ideas of Beauty and Virtue*

The world is full of people who are not wise enough.
—LA FONTAINE, *Fables*

The Way of the sage is to act but not to compete.
—LAO-TZU, *Tao Te Ching*

To know
That which lies before us in daily life,
Is the prime wisdom.
—JOHN MILTON, *Paradise Lost*

Pure reason avoids extremes, and requires one to be wise in moderation.   —MOLIÈRE, *Le Misanthrope*

The growth of wisdom may be gauged exactly by the diminution of ill-temper.
—FRIEDRICH NIETZSCHE,
*The Wanderer and
His Shadow*

Wisdom sends us back to our childhood.
PASCAL, *Pensées*

No one is wise at all times.
—PLINY, *Natural History*
[Emerson said it too: "Wise men are not wise at all times."—*Wealth*]

Nine-tenths of wisdom consists in being wise in time.
—THEODORE ROOSEVELT, speech, June 14, 1917

Wisdom comes by disillusionment.
—GEORGE SANTAYANA, *Reason in Common Sense*

The wise want love; and those who love want wisdom.
—PERCY BYSSHE SHELLEY, *Prometheus Unbound*

Wisdom outweighs any wealth.   —SOPHOCLES,
Antigone

Knowledge comes, but wisdom lingers.
> —ALFRED, LORD TENNYSON, *Locksley Hall*

It is a characteristic of wisdom not to do desperate things.   —HENRY DAVID THOREAU, *Walden*

The highest wisdom has but one science—the science of the whole—the science explaining the whole creation and man's place in it.
> —LEO TOLSTOY, *War and Peace*

He who is only wise lives a sad life.
> —VOLTAIRE, letter to Frederick the Great, 1740

Wisdom is ofttimes nearer when we stoop
Than when we soar   —WILLIAM WORDSWORTH, *The Excursion*

Be wise with speed;
A fool at forty is a fool indeed.
> —EDWARD YOUNG, *Love of Fame*

WIT   See ARTS: STYLE IN WRITING & EXPRESSION; HUMOR

WITCHES   See OCCULT, THE

WOMEN   See also HOME; LOVE; MARRIAGE; WOMEN, BEAUTIFUL & HOMELY; WOMEN & MEN

A whistling girl and a crowing hen never came to a good end.   —ANONYMOUS (IRISH PROVERB)
[Courtesy of the Irish-American great-grandmother of one of the authors. Muriel Spark, in a *New Yorker* article, Sept. 11, 1989, quoted her grandmother's version: A whistling woman, a crowing hen / Is neither fit for God nor man.]

Join the union, girls, and together say, "Equal Pay for Equal Work!"
> —SUSAN B. ANTHONY, in *The Revolution*, March 18, 1869

Woman must not depend upon the protection of man, but must be taught to protect herself.
  —SUSAN B. ANTHONY, speech, July 1871

With women, the heart argues, not the mind.
  —MATTHEW ARNOLD, *Merope*

One is not born a woman, one becomes one.
  —SIMONE DE BEAUVOIR, *The Second Sex*

Alas! the love of women! it is known
To be a lovely and a fearful thing.
    —LORD BYRON, *Don Juan*
[See Congreve at HATE for the reaction of "a woman scorned."]

Women never have young minds. They are born three thousand years old.
  —SHELAGH DELANEY, *A Taste of Honey*

If I were asked . . . to what the singular prosperity and growing strength of that people [Americans] ought mainly to be attributed, I should reply: to the superiority of their women.
  —ALEXIS DE TOCQUEVILLE,
  Democracy in America

A woman's hopes are woven of sunbeams; a shadow annihilates them. —GEORGE ELIOT, *Felix Holt*

The happiest women, like the happiest nations, have no history.
  —GEORGE ELIOT, *The Mill on the Floss*

A sufficient measure of civilization is the influence of good women.
  —RALPH WALDO EMERSON, *Civilization*

A woman should always challenge our respect, and never move our compassion.
  —RALPH WALDO EMERSON, *Journals*, 1836

Woman is woman's natural ally.
—EURIPIDES, *Alope*

Love's all in all to women.
—EURIPIDES, *Andromache*

Women are but women—tears are their portion.
—EURIPIDES, *Medea*

I have not yet been able to answer . . . the great question that has never been answered: What does a woman want?
—FREUD, quoted in Ernest Jones,
The Life and Works of Sigmund Freud, Vol. 2.

As men become aware that few have had a fair chance, they are inclined to say that no women have had a fair chance.
—MARGARET FULLER,
Woman in the Nineteenth Century

I have been a woman for fifty years, and I've never been able to discover precisely what it is I am.
—JEAN GIRAUDOUX, *Tiger at the Gates*

The eternal female draws us onward.
—GOETHE, *Faust*

So few grown women like their lives.
—KATHARINE GRAHAM, quoted by
Jane Howard, *Ms.*, Oct. 1974

Women never reason, and therefore they are (comparatively) seldom wrong.
—WILLIAM HAZLITT, *Characteristics*

HELMER: First and foremost, you are a wife and mother.
NORA: That I don't believe any more. I believe that first and foremost, I am an individual, just as much as you are.   —HENRIK IBSEN, *A Doll's House*

There is in every true woman's heart, a spark of heavenly fire, which lies dormant in the broad daylight of

prosperity, but which kindles up and beams and blazes in the dark hour of adversity.
> —WASHINGTON IRVING, *The Wife*, in
> *The Sketch Book of*
> *Geoffrey Crayon, Gent.*

The female of the species is more deadly than the male.
> —RUDYARD KIPLING, *The Female of the Species*

For the Colonel's lady an' Judy O'Grady
Are sisters under their skins!
> —RUDYARD KIPLING, *The Ladies*

Women run to extremes; they are either better or worse than men.   —LA BRUYÈRE, *Les Caractères*

A woman's best protection is a little money of her own.   —CLARE BOOTHE LUCE, attributed

Can we today measure devotion to husband and children by our indifference to everything else?
> —GOLDA MEIR, *The Plough Woman*

There is nothing worse than a woman—even a good woman!   —MENANDER, fragment
[This pretty well sums up the great majority of established quotes on women, most of which we did not feel compelled to include. For an observation on this hostility, see Germaine Greer in WOMEN & MEN.]

Women have simple tastes. They can get pleasure out of the conversation of children in arms and men in love.
> —H. L. MENCKEN, "Sententiae," in
> *A Book of Burlesques*

When women kiss, it always reminds me of prize-fighters shaking hands.   —*Ibid.*

Many women do not recognize themselves as discriminated against; no better proof could be found of the totality of their conditioning.
> —KATE MILLETT, *Sexual Politics*

O fairest of creation! last and best
Of all God's works.
> —JOHN MILTON, *Paradise Lost*

Women would rather be right than reasonable.
> —OGDEN NASH,
> *Frailty, Thy Name
> Is a Misnomer*

What one beholds of a woman is the least part of
her. —OVID, *Love's Cure*

If women are expected to do the same work as men,
we must teach them the same things.
> —PLATO,
> *The Republic*

Most women have no characters at all.
> —ALEXANDER POPE,
> *Moral Essays*

A free race cannot be born of slave mothers.
> —MARGARET SANGER,
> *Women and the New Race*

Frailty thy name is woman! —SHAKESPEARE,
> *Hamlet*, I, ii

Her voice was ever soft,
Gentle and low, an excellent thing in woman.
> —SHAKESPEARE,
> *King Lear*, V, iii

By now you will have discovered that women, too,
can be militant. —SOPHOCLES, *Electra*

Women are always eagerly on the lookout for any
emotion. —STENDHAL, *On Love*

The woman is so hard
Upon the woman.
> —ALFRED, LORD TENNYSON,
> *The Princess*

[That little man in black says] woman can't have as much rights as man because Christ wasn't a woman. Where did your Christ come from? . . . From God and a woman. Man has nothing to do with him.
                              —SOJOURNER TRUTH,
                                   Women's Rights Convention,
                                   Akron, Ohio, 1851
[She was referring to a clergyman in the audience.]

If the first woman God ever made was strong enough to turn the world upside down all alone, these women together ought to be able to turn it back, and get it right side up again!   —*Ibid.*

The hand that rocks the cradle
Is the hand that rules the world.
                              —W. R. WALLACE,
                                   The Hand That Rules the World

Whatever women do, they must do it twice as well as men to be thought half as good. Luckily, this is not difficult.   —CHARLOTTE WHITTON, quoted in
                                   Canada Month, June 1963
[She was mayor of Ottawa.]

A woman's work is seldom done.
                              —THORNTON WILDER, *The Skin of Our Teeth*

WOMEN, BEAUTIFUL   See also BEAUTY
& HOMELY

She walks in beauty, like the night
Of cloudless climes and starry skies;
And all that's best of dark and bright
Meet in her aspect and her eyes.
                              —LORD BYRON, *She Walks in Beauty*

It was a blonde. A blonde to make a bishop kick a hole in a stained glass window.
                              —RAYMOND CHANDLER, *Farewell, My Lovely*

Women who are either indisputably beautiful, or indisputably ugly, are best flattered upon the score of their understandings. —EARL OF CHESTERFIELD,
letter to his son, Sept. 5, 1748

She strode like a grenadier, was strong and upright like an obelisk, had a beautiful face, a candid brow, and not a thought of her own in her head.
—JOSEPH CONRAD, "The Return,"
in *Tales of Unrest*

A beautiful woman is a practical poet.
—RALPH WALDO EMERSON, *Beauty*

Was this the face that launched a thousand ships?
And burnt the topless towers of Ilium?
Sweet Helen, make me immortal with a kiss!
—CHRISTOPHER MARLOWE, *Dr. Faustus*

Oh, thou art fairer than the evening air
Clad in the beauty of a thousand stars. —*Ibid.*

If the nose of Cleopatra had been a little shorter, the whole face of the world would have been changed.
—PASCAL, *Pensées*

If to her share some female errors fall,
Look on her face, and you'll forget 'em all.
—ALEXANDER POPE, *The Rape of the Lock*

Age cannot wither her, nor custom stale
Her infinite variety; other women cloy
The appetites they feed.
—SHAKESPEARE, *Antony and Cleopatra*, II, ii

She never yet was foolish that was fair.
—SHAKESPEARE, *Othello*, II, i

A thoroughly beautiful woman and a thoroughly homely woman are creations which I love to gaze upon, and which I cannot tire of gazing upon, for each is perfect in her own line.
—MARK TWAIN, *Autobiography*

WOMEN & MEN See also LOVE; MARRIAGE; MEN; WOMEN

Do not put such unlimited power into the hands of husbands. Remember all men would be tyrants if they could. [We ladies] will not hold ourselves bound by any laws in which we have no voice, or representation.
—ABIGAIL ADAMS, letter to John Adams, March 31, 1776
[See also Defoe at TYRANNY & TOTALITARIANISM.]

A lady's imagination is very rapid; it jumps from admiration to love, from love to matrimony in a moment. —JANE AUSTEN, *Pride and Prejudice*

Women are very pleased when you call them cruel.
—PIERRE-AUGUSTIN DE BEAUMARCHAIS, *The Barber of Seville*

It is not good that the man should be alone; I will make him a help meet for him. —BIBLE, *Genesis* 2:18

That's the nature of women, not to love when we love them, and to love when we love them not.
—CERVANTES, *Don Quixote*

There's no fury like an ex-wife searching for a new lover. —CYRIL CONNOLLY, *The Unquiet Grave*
[For the original comment on woman's fury, see Congreve at HATE.]

I have been faithful to thee, Cynara! in my fashion.
I have forgot much, Cynara, gone with the wind,
Flung vases, roses, riotously, with the throng.
—ERNEST DOWSON, *Non Sum Qualis Eram*
[Cynara, the daughter of a French café owner in London, was twelve years old when Dowson wrote this poem to her in 1891.]

Women fail to understand how much men hate them.
—GERMAINE GREER, *The Female Eunuch*

The masculine tone is passing out of the world. It's a feminine, a nervous, hysterical, chattering, canting age. —HENRY JAMES, *The Bostonians*

Oh what can ail thee, wretched wight,
Alone and palely loitering;
The sedge is withered from the lake,
And no birds sing.   —JOHN KEATS, *La Belle*
                                          Dame sans Merci

The silliest woman can manage a clever man; but it
needs a very clever woman to manage a fool.
                              —RUDYARD KIPLING,
                                   "Three and—an Extra,"
                              in *Plain Tales from the Hills*

Women want mediocre men, and men are working
hard to be as mediocre as possible.
                         —MARGARET MEAD, in *Quote Magazine*,
                    May 15, 1958

Maleness in America is not absolutely defined; it has
to be kept and reearned every day, and one essential
element in the definition is beating women in every
game that both sexes play.

                                 —MARGARET MEAD,
                                  Male and Female

For contemplation he and valor formed;
For softness she and sweet attractive grace,
He for God only, she for God in him.
                         —JOHN MILTON, *Paradise Lost*

Disguise our bondage as we will,
'Tis woman, woman, rules us still.
                    —THOMAS MOORE, *Sovereign Woman*

Woman was God's *second* mistake.
                 —FRIEDRICH NIETZSCHE, *The Antichrist*

I can't live either without you or with you.
                                   —OVID, *Amores*

Kindness in women, not their beauteous looks,
Shall win my love.
               —SHAKESPEARE,
                   The Taming of the Shrew, IV, ii

The queens in history compare favorably with the kings.
—ELIZABETH CADY STANTON and SUSAN
B. ANTHONY, *History of Woman Suffrage*

We hold these truths to be self-evident, that all men and women are created equal. . . .
—ELIZABETH CADY STANTON, *Declaration of
Sentiment*, First Woman's Rights Convention, 1848

Man for the field and woman for the hearth:
Man for the sword and for the needle she:
Man with the head and woman with the heart:
Man to command and woman to obey;
All else confusion.   —ALFRED, LORD TENNYSON,
The Princess

The woman's cause is man's: they rise or sink
Together.   —*Ibid.*

'Tis strange what a man may do, and a woman yet think him an angel.
—WILLIAM THACKERAY, *Henry Esmond*

Why are women . . . so much more interesting to men than men are to women?
—VIRGINIA WOOLF, *A Room of One's Own*

Women have served all these centuries as looking-glasses possessing the magic and delicious power of reflecting the figure of man at twice its natural size.
—*Ibid.*

WORDS   See ARTS: STYLE IN WRITING
& EXPRESSION; LANGUAGE & WORDS

WORK & WORKERS   See also ACCOMPLISHMENT;
DOING; LEISURE; METHOD; PERSEVERANCE & ENDURANCE

Work is the curse of the drinking classes.
—ANONYMOUS

Work is not the curse, but drudgery is.
—HENRY WARD BEECHER,
Proverbs from Plymouth Pulpit

What is work? And what is not work? These are
questions that perplex the wisest of men.

—Bhagavad Gita

Go to the ant, thou sluggard; consider her ways, and
    be wise:
Which having no guide, overseer, or ruler,
    Provideth her meat in the summer, and gathereth
    her food in the harvest.

—Bible, *Proverbs* 6:6–8

The laborer is worthy of his hire.

—Bible, *Luke* 10:7

All composite things decay. Strive diligently.

—Buddha, reputed last words

Be not solitary, be not idle.

—Robert Burton, *The Anatomy of Melancholy*,
    the closing words

Blessed is he who has found his work. Let him ask
no other blessedness.

—Thomas Carlyle, *Past and Present*

"A fair day's wages for a fair day's work": it is as
just a demand as governed men ever made of governing.
It is the everlasting right of man.   —*Ibid.*

Work is the grand cure of all the maladies and miseries that ever beset mankind.

—Thomas Carlyle, speech, April 2, 1886

It is better to wear out than to rust out.

—Richard Cumberland, quoted in
    George Horne, *Sermon on the Duty of
    Contending for the Truth*

Working people have a lot of bad habits, but the worst
of them is work.   —Clarence Darrow, quoted in
    Kevin Tierney, *Darrow*

A lot of fellows nowadays have a B.A., M.D., or Ph.D. Unfortunately, they don't have a J.O.B.
—"Fats" Domino, attributed

Originality and a feeling of one's own dignity are achieved only through work and struggle.
—Feodor Dostoevski, *A Diary of a Writer*

There is no substitute for hard work.
—Thomas Alva Edison, *Life*

The bitter and the sweet come from the outside, the hard from within, from one's own efforts.
—Albert Einstein, *Out of My Later Years*

Farming looks mighty easy when your plow is a pencil and you're a thousand miles from a cornfield.
—Dwight D. Eisenhower, speech, Sept. 25, 1956

To the worker, God himself lends aid.
—Euripides, *Hippolytus*

Men for the sake of getting a living forget to live.
—Margaret Fuller, *Summer on the Lakes*

All work is empty save when there is love.
—Kahlil Gibran, *The Prophet*

When work is a pleasure, life is a joy! When work is duty, life is slavery.
—Maxim Gorky, *The Lower Depths*

It is weariness to keep toiling at the same things so that one becomes ruled by them.
—Heraclitus, fragment

More men are killed by overwork than the importance of the world justifies.
—Rudyard Kipling, *The Phantom 'Rickshaw*

I am glad to know that there is a system of labor where the laborer can strike if he wants to! I wish to God that such a system prevailed all over the world.
—Abraham Lincoln, speech, March 5, 1860

[On the subject of strikes, another American president, Calvin Coolidge, was less enthusiastic: "There is no right to strike against the public safety by anybody, anywhere, any time," telegram to Samuel Gompers re the Boston police strike, Sept. 14, 1919.]

Labor is prior to, and independent of, capital. Capital is only the fruit of labor. . . . Labor is the superior of capital, and deserves much the higher consideration.
—ABRAHAM LINCOLN, first annual
message to Congress, Dec. 3, 1862
[But see also the continuation of this quote under CAPITALISM.]

Under the spreading chestnut tree
The village smithy stands;
The smith a mighty man is he
With large and sinewy hands.
And the muscles of his brawny arms
Are strong as iron bands.
His brow is wet with honest sweat,
He earns whate'er he can,
And looks the whole world in the face,
For he owes not any man.
—HENRY WADSWORTH LONGFELLOW,
The Village Blacksmith

Constant labor of one uniform kind destroys the intensity and flow of a man's animal spirits, which find recreation and delight in mere change of activity.
—KARL MARX, *Capital*

The average male gets his living by such depressing devices that boredom becomes a sort of natural state to him. —H. L. MENCKEN, *In Defence of Women*

No one hates his job so heartily as a farmer.
—H. L. MENCKEN, "What Is Going On
in the World Now?" in
American Mercury, Nov. 1933

Figure it out. Work a lifetime to pay off a house. You finally own it, and there's no one to live in it.
—ARTHUR MILLER, *Death of a Salesman*

Work expands so as to fill the time available for its completion. —C. NORTHCOTE PARKINSON, *Parkinson's Law*

In a hierarchy, every employee tends to rise to his level of incompetence.
—LAURENCE J. PETER, *The Peter Principle*

When you cease to make a contribution, you begin to die. —ELEANOR ROOSEVELT, letter to Mr. Horne, Feb. 19, 1960

Far and away the best prize that life offers is the chance to work hard at work worth doing.
—THEODORE ROOSEVELT, Labor Day speech, 1903

Which of us . . . is to do the dirty work for the rest —and for what pay? Who is to do the pleasant and clean work, and for what pay?
—JOHN RUSKIN, "Of King's Treasuries," in *Sesame and Lilies*

If I were a medical man, I should prescribe a holiday to any patient who considered his work important.
—BERTRAND RUSSELL, *Autobiography*

I will have an eternity to rest.
—ANDRÉS SEGOVIA, quoted in *The New York Times*, obituary, 1987
[The great guitarist was explaining why he continued a heavy work schedule into old age.]

Nothing will come of nothing. —SHAKESPEARE, *King Lear*, I, i

My nature is subdued
To what it works in, like the dyer's hand.
> —SHAKESPEARE, sonnet 3

You may tempt the upper classes
With your villainous demitasses,
But Heaven will protect the working girl.
> —EDGAR SMITH,
> *Heaven Will Protect the Working Girl*

To travel hopefully is a better thing than to arrive,
and true success is to labor.
> —ROBERT LOUIS STEVENSON,
> *Virginibus Puerisque*

Death is the end of life; ah, why
Should life all labor be?
> —ALFRED, LORD TENNYSON, *The Lotus-Eaters*

Where our work is, there let our joy be.
> —TERTULLIAN, *Women's Dress*

A small daily task if it be really daily, will beat the
labors of a spasmodic Hercules.
> —ANTHONY TROLLOPE, *An Autobiography*

Thou, O God, dost sell us all good things at the price
of labor.   —LEONARDO DA VINCI, *Notebooks*

Work spares us from three evils: boredom, vice, and
need.   —VOLTAIRE, *Candide*

There is as much dignity in tilling a field as in writing
a poem.
> —BOOKER T. WASHINGTON,
> speech, Sept. 9, 1895

How doth the little busy bee
Improve each shining hour,
And gather honey all the day
From every opening flower.
> —ISAAC WATTS, *Against Idleness and Mischief*

WORKING PEOPLE   See PEOPLE, THE; WORK &
                                              WORKERS

WORLD   See CREATION, DIVINE; LIFE; NATURE;
                              REALITY & ILLUSION; UNIVERSE;
                                            WORLD, END OF

WORLD, END OF   See also LAST JUDGMENT &
                                            THE HEREAFTER

Overhead without any fuss the stars were going out.
                              —ARTHUR C. CLARKE,
                                    The Nine Billion Names of God,
                                    final sentence

This is the way the world ends
Not with a bang but a whimper.
                              —T. S. ELIOT, *The Hollow Men*

Some say the world will end in fire,
Some say in ice.
From what I've tasted of desire
I hold with those who favor fire.
But if it had to perish twice
I think I know enough of hate
To say that for destruction ice
Is also great
And would suffice.   —ROBERT FROST, *Fire and Ice*

And what rough beast, its hour come round at last,
Slouches towards Bethlehem to be born?
                              —WILLIAM BUTLER YEATS,
                                    The Second Coming

When shall the stars be blown about the sky,
Like the sparks blown out of a smithy, and die?
                              —WILLIAM BUTLER YEATS, *The Secret Rose*

WRATH   See ANGER

WRITING   See ARTS: WRITING

XYZ

The young are permanently in a state resembling intoxication; for youth is sweet and they are growing.
—ARISTOTLE, *Nicomachean Ethics*
[See also La Rochefoucauld, below. Aristotle believed that the young are too distractible to benefit from lectures on serious subjects. Shakespeare alluded to this in his reference to "young men, whom Aristotle thought unfit to hear moral philosophy," *Troilus and Cressida*, II, ii.]

Youth is easily deceived because it is quick to hope.
—ARISTOTLE, *Rhetoric*

Young men are fitter to invent than to judge, fitter for execution than for counsel, fitter for new projects than settled business.
—FRANCIS BACON, *Of Youth and Age*

Youth is the pollen
That blows through the sky
And does not ask why.
—STEPHEN VINCENT BENÉT,
John Brown's Body

Rejoice, O young man in thy youth.
—BIBLE, *Ecclesiastes* 11:9

Youth will be served, every dog has his day, and mine
has been a fine one.
>—GEORGE BORROW, *Lavengro*

Youth means love.
>—ROBERT BROWNING, *The Ring and the Book*

Youth is like spring, an overpraised season.
>—SAMUEL BUTLER, *The Way of All Flesh*

Youth is something very new: twenty years ago, no
one mentioned it.
>—COCO CHANEL, quoted in Marcel Haedrich,
>*Coco Chanel, Her Life, Her Secrets*

A youth is to be regarded with respect. How do you
know that his future will not be equal to our present?
>—CONFUCIUS, *Analects*

Youth is a period of missed opportunities.
>—CYRIL CONNOLLY, *Journal and Memoir*

They are not long, the days of wine and roses.
>—ERNEST DOWSON, *Vitae Summa Brevis Spem
>Nos Vetat Incohare Longham*

[The author died at age 33.]

Youth is the best time to be rich and the best time
to be poor.
>—EURIPIDES, *Heracles*

Alas, that Spring should vanish with the Rose!
That Youth's sweet-scented Manuscript should close.
>—EDWARD FITZGERALD, *The Rubáiyát of
>Omar Khayyám*

One could do worse than be a swinger of birches.
>—ROBERT FROST, *Birches*

Youth's the season made for joys,
Love is then our duty.
>—JOHN GAY, *The Beggar's Opera*

Give me back my youth!
>—GOETHE, *Faust*

No young man believes he shall ever die.
> —WILLIAM HAZLITT, *On the Feeling of Immortality in Youth*

Youth is quick in feeling but weak in judgment.
> —HOMER, *Iliad*

Fugit juventus.
Youth flies.   —HORACE, *Epodes*

Youth, even in its sorrows, has a brilliance of its own.
> —VICTOR HUGO, *Les Misérables*

Be gentle with the young.   —JUVENAL, *Satires*

When all the world is young, lad,
And all the trees are green;
And every goose a swan, lad,
And every lass a queen;
Then hey for boot and horse, lad,
And round the world away:
Young blood must have its course, lad,
And every dog its day.
> —CHARLES KINGSLEY, *Water Babies*

Youth is unending intoxication; it is a fever of the mind.   —LA ROCHEFOUCAULD, *Maxims*
[He knew his Aristotle; see above.]

A boy's will is the wind's will,
And the thoughts of youth are long, long thoughts.
> —HENRY WADSWORTH LONGFELLOW, *My Lost Youth*

It is only an illusion that youth is happy, an illusion of those who have lost it.
> —W. SOMERSET MAUGHAM, *Of Human Bondage*

We were very young, we were very merry—
We went back and forth all night on the ferry.
> —EDNA ST. VINCENT MILLAY, *Recuerdo*

The American ideal is youth—handsome, empty
youth.   —HENRY MILLER,
                                    The Wisdom of the Heart

No time to marry, no time to settle down;
I'm a young woman, and I ain't done runnin' around.
                    —BESSIE SMITH, *Young Woman's Blues*

Pay attention to the young, and make them just as
good as possible.
                    —SOCRATES, quoted in Plato, *Euthyphro*

Bright youth passes swiftly as a thought.
                                    —THEOGNIS, *Elegies*

Don't trust anyone over thirty.
                    JACK WEINBERG, attributed
[The saying was associated with the free speech movement at the University of California at Berkeley in the
early 1960s.]

Bliss it was that dawn to be alive,
But to be young was very heaven!
                                    —WILLIAM WORDSWORTH,
                                    The French Revolution

ZEAL   See ENTHUSIASM, ENERGY, ZEAL

INDEX